BEHIND THE SCENES

IN TWO WORLDS

BEHIND THE SCENES
IN TWO WORLDS

ELAINE MENSH & HARRY MENSH

INTERNATIONAL PUBLISHERS
New York

COPYRIGHT ACKNOWLEDGMENTS

REVOLUTION AS THEATRE, Notes on the New Radical Style, by Robert Brustein, with the permission of Liveright Publishing Corporation. Copyright © 1971 by Robert Brustein. Excerpts from *BRECHT: THE MAN AND HIS WORK* by Martin Esslin. Copyright © 1959, 1960 by Martin Esslin. Used by permission of Doubleday & Company, Inc. *DOES SOCIALISM LIBERATE WOMEN?* by Hilda Scott, © 1974 Beacon Press. "Black" Shows For White Viewers by E. Collier and "The Black Film –'Supernigger' As Folk Hero" by L. Hairston. Reprinted by permission of *FREEDOMWAYS* magazine published at 799 Broadway, New York City. Vol. 14, #3, 1974. *THE SEASON* by William Goldman. Copyright © 1970 Harcourt Brace Jovanovich, Inc. *TOMS, COONS, MULATTOES, MAMMIES & BUCKS* by Donald Bogle. Copyright © 1973 by Donald Bogle; Published by The Viking Press, Inc., and Bantam Books, Inc. "Media Image of Black Women" by Jean Carey Bond. Reprinted by permission of *FREEDOMWAYS* magazine. Vol. 15, #1, 1975. *THE SECOND SEX* by Simone de Beauvoir, translated by H.M. Parshley, © 1974, Alfred A. Knopf, Inc. *THE FEMININE MYSTIQUE* by Betty Friedan. Copyright © 1974, 1963 by Betty Friedan. W.W. Norton & Co., Inc. Reprinted with permission of Macmillan Publishing Co., Inc. from *THE IMPOSSIBLE THEATRE* by Herbert Blau. Copyright © Herbert Blau, 1964. From *BERTOLT BRECHT POEMS—1913-1956,* John Willett & Ralph Manheim, eds., "Hollywood" translated by Michael Hamburger, 'Gedichte im Exil': Copyright by Stefan S. Brecht, 1964, translation copyright © 1976 by Eyre Methuen; "Not What Was Meant": translated by Frank Jellinek, Volumes 5, 6 and 7 of 'Gedichte': Copyright © Suhrkamp Verlag Frankfurt am Main, 1964, translation copyright © 1976 by Eyre Methuen and "General Your Tank Is A Powerful Machine" translated by Lee Baxendall, 'Svendborger Gedichte': Copyright © 1939 by Malik-Verlag, London, translation copyright © 1976 by Eyre Methuen. *TRAVESTIES* by Tom Stoppard. Reprinted by permission of Grove Press, Inc. Copyright © 1975 by Tom Stoppard. From *THE FERVENT YEARS: THE STORY OF THE GROUP THEATRE AND THE THIRTIES,* by Harold Clurman. Copyright © 1945 and renewed 1973 by Harold Clurman. Copyright © 1957 by Harold Clurman. Reprinted by permission of Alfred A. Knopf, Inc.

Library of Congress Cataloging in Publication Data

Mensh, Elaine
    Behind the scenes in two worlds.

    Includes index.
    1. Performing arts Germany, East. 2. Performing arts United States. 3. Germany, East—Civilization. I. Mensh, Harry, joint author. II. Title.
PN2654.M45   790.2   77-19314
ISBN 0-7178-0497-6
ISBN 0-7178-0489-5 (pbk.)

Contents

Acknowledgments

We are grateful to those women and men who spent hour after hour with us, talking things over, answering our endless questions. The reader will meet them on the pages of this book.

So many people helped us in our work—including many whose names do not appear on these pages—that to single out any one is difficult. Yet we must mention Stefanie Liedtke, who helped us in far more ways than we have space to tell—whose perception and commitment were invaluable in all we strove to do.

Our special appreciation also to Wolfgang Pintzka for his assistance and warm encouragement.

Our thanks for the cooperation of the Brecht Archives.

BEHIND THE SCENES
IN TWO WORLDS

Some ask that human affairs
with names, surnames and elegies
not be the themes of the pages in my books.
They assert that poetry dies in such writing.
Others ask that I no longer proceed.
The plain truth is, I do not want to please them.

Pablo Neruda, Do Not Ask (excerpt)

My obligations move together with my song:
I exist; I do not exist: that is my responsibility.
I cannot be said to be alive if I pay no heed
To the agony of those who are in pain; their pains are mine;
For I cannot live without living for all,
For those who are silent, yet oppressed.
I come from the people, and I sing for them.

Pablo Neruda, So Is My Life (excerpt)

1. Double Image

This is a record of exploration and discovery. Like all explorers past and present, we discovered only what was already well known to the people of the country we visited: the German Democratic Republic. Despite, or perhaps because of, mass communications, most of the people of the United States have no more information about the German Democratic Republic than Columbus had about this continent before he "discovered" it. In fact, so little is known about the German Democratic Republic by most people of the United States that they recognize it only under a fictitious name, East Germany, which denies its existence as a sovereign state—implying instead that it is merely a temporarily divided part of the German state existing before the end of World War II.

For most U.S. citizens there have been few avenues to information about the German Democratic Republic (GDR). The sparse media coverage of "East Germany" portrays a people leading dull, gray, regimented lives behind an ominous "wall." Only one aspect of this coverage has been modified in recent years: As it became known that the tiny German Democratic Republic had emerged as the world's ninth industrial power, there have been occasional admissions about substantial improvements in the material standard of living. Although this rise occurred as our own living standards were plummeting— gnawed away by lethal unemployment and inflation—the impact of this information has been blunted: The media continue to tell us that "East Germans" lead regimented lives—that their prosperity has been purchased at the cost of freedom, of human rights. Of course, these reports come to us from the same sources that supply all our information: the government and media channels charged in the 1960s with creating the "credibility gap."

At the same time a strange parallel to this information is to be found in certain publications designating themselves as "radical." In agreement with the mass media, they too say that rising living standards in the GDR have come at the expense of human rights and, they add, at the expense of revolutionary spirit.

U.S. citizens able to go and see for themselves what's happening in the German Democratic Republic add up to a less-than-minute fraction of a percent. Until 1974 when diplomatic relations were established between the two countries, the U.S. government officially did not recognize the existence of the GDR. Although it was technically possible for U.S. citizens to travel in "East Germany," the intimidation in the U.S. against going there was so great that for many years few U.S. citizens would even have considered it. Now not only have U.S. diplomatic relations been established with the GDR, there is also a growing resistance by U.S. citizens to government intimidation—as well as a growing interest in the countries of the socialist community. Certainly large numbers of people from our country would like to go and see what life under socialism is like—and they are presumably free to do so. But like most of our freedoms, this one exists in theory rather than fact.

Only a tiny minority of people here are planning trips abroad or anywhere else. Instead they're debating with themselves whether to pay another exorbitant bus or subway fare, put in another gallon of gas with a champagne price tag—or just stay home. In reality, most people of the U.S. have as much chance of traveling abroad as the rest of the Europeans had of accompanying Columbus on the voyage that brought him to this continent.

OUR OWN journey to the German Democratic Republic was unusual not only because we are among the relative handful of U.S. citizens who have been able to go there, but also because of the nature of our travels—which consisted of three very different trips that were in reality three parts of one whole.

On the first trip, we walked through the cities and drove through the countryside and along the seashore, and we saw what can be seen by any tourist.

We visited Berlin, Rostock, Dresden, Neubrandenburg, and Herringsdorf. We saw people walking down clean streets. They looked healthy and were well dressed—many, young people in particular, stylishly so. On weekends the people strolled, but on weekdays everyone appeared to have a destination. We saw cranes, hard hats and all the other elements of construction everywhere—most of it for housing developments. These are not housing projects as we know them, dividing people according to income and/or color. In the GDR people in every field—workers, artists, professionals—live in the same developments, irrespective of income. Since enough housing is still a problem, building according to plan continues constantly. All livable older housing is still in use, much of it remodeled. And there are no slums. None.

In the restaurants we ate good—and frequently excellent—food. Even on the road we were served real, not plastic meals. We attended the theaters: full houses and large numbers of young people in the audience. Tickets are so inexpensive, we discovered, anyone can easily afford to go. We stopped for coffee and cake in the little cafés that surround the city plazas and watched the people. We spent a few days on the Baltic and learned that the mansions along the road were once for the Kaiser and his entourage. Now working people holiday there.

But everywhere in the German Democratic Republic we were as aware of what we did not see as of what we saw—for our minds registered a double image. As we surveyed Berlin, Dresden, and Rostock, we saw New York, Chicago, and Los Angeles as well.

In Berlin, Dresden, and Rostock we saw no lines of people waiting for unemployment or welfare checks, as we see in New York, Chicago, and Los Angeles. In the GDR there is no unemployment. On the contrary, there's a labor shortage. (Can this be because the GDR is so small, only 17 million people? Hardly. Puerto Rico, a U.S. "possession," has only 3.3 million people on the island, yet 40 percent are unemployed.)

As we walked down the GDR's clean streets, we saw the double image: New York with its overflowing garbage cans and black plastic bags filled with refuse, heaped up and waiting for burial like victims of the plague. In Berlin, Dresden and Rostock we saw only clean and well dressed people, but we saw no one entering a limousine or wearing clothes by St. Laurent. And we saw no beggars, no drug addicts, no prostitutes, no deranged individuals alone and raving—we saw none of those who, abandoned by society, are our constant companions on the streets of every city in our own country. The double image answers many questions. But not all.

THE U.S. is a multi-racial, multi-national country. You can tell just by looking how it treats dark-skinned people: Anyone can see that Blacks are forced into ghettos, Puerto Ricans and Chicanos into barrios, Asian-Americans into "Chinatowns," and Native American Indians exiled to reservations.

In the GDR, the society's attitude toward dark-skinned people is not so immediately visible. When this territory was part of the old German state, the population was taught that Germans were "supermen," and all "non-aryans" their inferiors. Today one sees dark-skinned people in the GDR—mainly Africans studying there—and one may well wonder: What is the attitude of GDR citizens toward them and all the Black, brown, yellow and red peoples of the world? And, aware of the terrible history of the old Germany, one may certainly wonder: What is their attitude toward Jews?

And in an area where women's place was once *Kinder, Kirche und Küche* (children, church and kitchen), one will want to know: What is the status of women?

The GDR occupies part of a territory where not so long ago people as well as books were burned. And it is only a little over thirty years since the survivors of the concentration camps were liberated—clad in black and white striped uniforms, a red triangle on those worn by political prisoners, a yellow star on those worn by Jews. What is the status of human rights in the GDR, on the same territory where death camps once operated?

Is the GDR a place where, as we in this country are constantly told, one form of "totalitarianism" has been substituted for another? What is the relationship between the rising standard of living and personal, social, and artistic freedom? Has the one been achieved at the expense of the other?

It's quite logical that many people in the U.S. would wonder about these particular questions. After all, in the U.S. even relative security comes only through conformity. The McCarthy era gave ample evidence of this when those who refused to conform lost their jobs, went to jail, were deported and suffered in many other ways. And many of them, including many artists, have never again worked in their own fields.

While in the U.S. there is no security without conformity, even conformity today rarely brings security. Certainly millions of those out of work didn't lose their jobs because they expressed radical opinions—although the bitter crisis of their daily existence has begun to make millions aware of the need for fundamental change.

In the U.S., a relative handful can still buy security at the price of conformity, their standard of living rising while that of the great majority goes down, down. But is there a relationship between security and conformity in the GDR—where living standards are going up not for just a few, but for the whole society?

What, in short, is the quality of life in the GDR—materially, culturally, spiritually, humanly?

There are many ways in which these questions about a nation can be answered. We chose as our starting point the performing arts, in particular, the theater. Why? Because a nation's performance can be seen in its relationship to the performing arts. We learned that in our own country.

MANY REMEMBER the 1930s depression as a time when the banks closed. Many will remember the 1970s depression as a time when the symphony halls, the operas, the libraries and the museums closed.

"Why are we so loath to change our priorities?" asked opera star Beverly Sills at a 1975 arts symposium (held in, of all places, the Lyndon Baines Johnson Library in Austin, Texas). "Why are wars never underfinanced, although museums are closing the doors? Why does a war never go out of business for lack of funds, when the Metropolitan Opera may have to do that in a very little while?"[1]

Interestingly, Beverly Sills might have found at least part of the answer in a story appearing in *Variety* not long before the symposium. Under the headline, "Vietnam: Major Market Fades," the show business publication wrote: "The takeover by Communists in Vietnam was the final closing of a mart that had meant countless thousands of dollars in record sales for U.S. labels. . . "[2]

Despite the fact that Vietnam has been taken over by the Vietnamese, it's been a great period for those who control the performing arts. Unfortunately, the same can't be said for the performing artists. Writing from Hollywood, *The New York Times'* Murray Schumach reported:

Booming prosperity and vast unemployment are playing a strange double feature in this collection of movie and television studios that still is the world's major factory of mass entertainment.

The "vast unemployment," Schumach went on to say,

is widely attributed here to the avarice of the television networks in greatly increasing the number of reruns of video series.

The chairman of the board of the Music Corporation of America (MCA), which owns Universal Pictures, confirmed this view. He told Shumach:

Television profits are going straight up. Their profits are mind-boggling. There is no question that there is a connection between the size of network profits and the increase in reruns. I think the increase in reruns has eliminated 40 per cent of the employment in Hollywood.[3]

Although the MCA chairman somehow neglected to mention it, Universal's profits are also "mind-boggling." Universal, Schumach stated,

. . . is now in its third record-breaking year of profits—it netted $40.7 million in its first nine months of [1974], compared with $17.6 million for the same period in 1973. . .[4]

But equally as "mind-boggling" as the profits of the corporations are the problems of the actors: The Screen Actors Guild reports 85 percent of its 30,000 members out of work (and this overall figure doesn't reveal the vastly greater unemployment among Black, Latin and other actors belonging to oppressed minorities). Citing a 114 percent profit increase for NBC, 67 percent for CBS, and 62 percent for ABC, the Screen Actors Guild points out that the networks' rerun policy costs actors and other workers in the entertainment industry $320 million a year in paychecks.

You can see for yourself what reruns have done to actors and others in this industry if you pass by the Hollywood office where they come to collect unemployment insurance (if they're lucky enough to have had sufficient work to qualify for it). Describing this scene, Schumach writes,

[This office] is packed from counter to doors with long lines waiting to apply for insurance. For the first time the building has all 34 windows working and the personnel there has risen from 90 to 150 to cope with the needs of the unemployed.

"None of us has ever seen anything like this," says James Heaney, who is in charge of the office.[5]

Reruns not only make a special contribution to the networks' profits but to the film studios' too: They rent their old movies to TV without having to pay residuals to actors. One of the biggest rental fees ($5 million) went for that epic of racism, *Gone With The Wind*, promoted as TV's most spectacular—and its climactic—Bicentennial Year presentation.

Still, *Gone With The Wind* was merely a special dish on the networks' steady menu of racism, whose offerings include such staples as *All In the Family. All In the Family,* it seems, sometimes runs into censorship problems, but the blue pencil is never applied to its racism:

What disagreements arise almost never concern the over-all subject matter of [producer Norman Lear's] shows but rather the "taste" of individual lines, generally those with sexual or religious innuendos. The script for the first "All in the Family" show was not approved by the network censor until the very last moment; the stock point—one that Lear eventually won—was never the dozen racial and ethnic slurs Archie Bunker avails himself of, but an incredulous remark he makes when he comes home from church to find an amorous Mike and Gloria ready to repair to their bedroom: "Eleven o'clock on a Sunday morning!"[6]

Since the struggles of the civil rights era, TV has added a few shows featuring Black characters. But this addition "has not heralded social progress," asserts Eugenia Collier, a Black professor of English, in a 1974 article in *Freedomways*. Instead it has meant old stereotypes in new (or not-so-new) forms. "For the most part," says Professor Collier, these shows are "conceived, written and directed by whites— and in this time and place it is a rare white person who has the knowledge and compassion to recreate in art a believable Black world." Instead these white writers provide what they are paid for: shows "profitable to big money interests," featuring "slickly disguised versions of those white-created agents of Black destruction, Rastus and Mandy."

Even that TV rarity, an apparent attempt to deal seriously with Black life, may not be precisely what it seems to be. "Rarely has there been a serious portrayal of Blacks," notes Collier. "The most serious attempt was probably *The Autobiography of Miss Jane Pittman*—but even here the suffering of Blacks, their strength in withstanding it, and the significance of their struggle were muted in comparison with Ernest J. Gaines' fine novel and with reality." She cites an example:

An important distortion occurs at the climax of the film. The novel ends with Miss Jane leading a civil rights march, surrounded by the people. Her triumph, then, belongs to the community. On TV she leaves the people and walks *alone* to the white drinking fountain, and faces the white sheriff who has known her for years and who *permits* her to drink.[7]

In one scene, corporate TV wipes out years of Black struggle and replaces it with a benign proffering of favors by a representative of this society's most racist forces!

TV's CLIMAX to the Bicentennial Year, *Gone With The Wind,* won an immense share of the viewing audience. The new year began with *Roots.* With its share of the audience smashing all previous records, *Roots* provoked a massive nationwide discussion of Black people's lives under slavery.

To portray slave-system brutalities on TV was certainly a media concession to the insistent struggles of Black people. Welcome as this concession is, it would be more than premature to consider it as representing a new direction for the media or even intentions to "liberalize" the present one. The thrust of day-to-day programming is intensifyingly racist, corporate media's counterpart to what corporate interests are doing in all phases of this society. Bringing about basic changes in the media, as well as in society as a whole, will require very great battles of the people, white people together with Black people.

Media and government officials bask in the aura of *Roots*—as if they were the champions of human rights they claim to be. But should they be permitted to congratulate themselves for allowing it to be known that slavery was brutal more than 100 years after it was ended? Further, *Roots* itself is a complex mixture, an admission of certain facts combined with the continued withholding or distortion of others. On one hand *Roots* gave us a picture of the horrors of slavery and a revealing glimpse of the strength of the Black family, so maligned by the racist Daniel Moynihan. On the other hand there was no recognition of the slaves' role in abolishing slavery—including many heroic uprisings. And while there was the creation of a "good" white captain of a slave ship (!), there was no portrayal of the Abolitionists—Black and white—from whose struggles we could learn much (too much, so far as the corporate media are concerned). And in its final episode, *Roots* left the impression that the troubles of the Kinte family—and by implication those of Black people as a whole—ended with slavery. With the showing of *Roots,* powerful forces made certain admissions about the past in order to deny the present. When the mayors of Birmingham and twenty other Southern cities, as well as the mayor of New York, proclaimed "Roots Week" while *Roots* was being televised, it became clear that a "human rights" facade was being painted over the economic and social aggression in progress against all the people, particularly the oppressed minorities. And the facade was also intended to extend internationally, especially over U.S. actions in relation to the *Roots* continent of Africa. South Africa—the notorious apartheid-fascist state—"has a legally constituted Government and is a stabilizing influence in the southern part of that continent," declared President Carter,[8] (thus indicating his intentions of "stabilizing" racism, reaction and poverty at home as well). Only weeks earlier a photo had appeared of Carter and daughter Amy, in which she was carrying a copy of *Roots.*

IT's TYPICAL of the mass media to maintain as lengthy a "cooling-off" period as possible before dealing with what they consider a controversial topic. But the major networks' treatment in the seventies of blacklisting in the McCarthyite fifties has not only been belated and sparse. Worse, they have continued the McCarthyism of the past in a new form: In their two films on the subject, they permitted no objection to blacklisting as such, only to the blacklisting of people accused of being Communists who really weren't Communists at all.

One honorable exception to this approach came not in TV but with the film, *The Front,* which opposes denial of work to Communists as well as non-Communists because of political views. Still, as portrayed in *The Front*—which is not satire, but, for the most part, broad comedy—this terrible chapter from the past hardly seems real. From this film, as from the TV films on this subject, one gets the impression that McCarthyism died with the man whose name describes the era.

Yet any admissions whatsoever about this period have been engulfed by an altogether different view of that time. Through music revivals, films and such a TV series as *Happy Days,* the media have tried to create a wave of nostalgia for "The Fabulous Fifties."

WHAT'S HAPPENING in films in general closely parallels TV: There have been a few concessions to social demands (although always with contradictory aspects), but the direction has been anti-social. There are more movies where the vigilante hero takes things into his own gun-bearing hands. There are more predominantly white or all-white films with racist scenes. And then there are the "blaxploitation" movies. Loyle Hairston, a Black writer and critic, states in *Freedomways:*

. . . the mind boggled at the amount of mindless brutality and murder portrayed in these films; a wanton violence executed by Black stereotypes who would make *Ol Rastus* appealing by comparison. . . From *Superfly* to *Foxy Brown,* the public has been treated to a spate of lewd little minstrel shows whose content mocks the lives of Black people in reels of crude, cynical buffoonery.[9]

Thus a performer, Black or white, fortunate enough to find work is all too likely to find this good luck cancelled out by the nature of the work: It's increasingly difficult to escape being cast in a film or TV show that's not racist, violent, degrading to women, police-glorifying and/or pornographic. The same influences exist in the theater, with plays mostly ranging from the presumably innocuous to outright anti-social. Not only does the theater compete with TV and films, but the same material is more and more frequently used in all three media.

In the theater, too, things have been looking good for the producers and bad for the actors. "Suddenly everything has changed on Broadway—it's booming, that's what's changed. . . ," exulted critic Walter Kerr in an article, "Broadway's Coming Up Roses!"[10] published in the midst of the 1974-75 season. "Money?" exclaimed Kerr. "It's coming in"—with grosses for producers double the previous year's. Only it wasn't and isn't coming in for actors: Actors Equity Association reports 80 percent unemployment among its members (again, there are no figures indicating the far greater unemployment among actors of the oppressed minorities).

While Kerr saw everything "coming up roses" on Broadway, to Actors Equity "the theater district in New York looked like a disaster area" which actors are being forced to evacuate: Actors "must go where the work is, and it is only too clear that there has been less and less of it in New York City," reported Equity. The 1972-73 season "may have been the last time for some time in which Broadway was the leading area of employment," and performers are now "roaming farther from Times Square to find work on a stage." The lack of work is so acute that it casts a shadow far into the actors' future. "With the considerable reduction in employment under production contracts for Broadway and the Road, where the highest salaries are paid, it seems inevitable that gross wages paid to members should be less. This is bound to be reflected in employer payments into Equity's Pension and Welfare Fund."[11]

As the Equity report suggests, there are different kinds of contracts for actors. Because producers have been able to impose their profits-before-people principle on the theater, there are all types of special contracts (for stock, children's and dinner theaters, etc.) with even lower minimums than the Broadway—or standard production—contract. And when Joseph Papp was at Lincoln Center, he arranged a special "Mitzi E. Newhouse" contract for the theater of that name. "Papp," commented an actor at that time, "was given a special deal so the country's biggest producer of plays wouldn't have to meet the standard production contract."

When actors, like other workers, try to improve their conditions, they run into the steely opposition of their employers. This is what happened in 1975 when Equity tried to institute a "Showcase Code" for off-off Broadway productions, where actors had been performing for nothing under the illusion that their talents were being "show-cased" (how effective these "showcases" are in opening up jobs is attested to by the actors' staggering unemployment rate).

"Why in hell are they penalizing the Showcases which have done more for actors in this city than unions...," demanded Joseph Papp.[12] Insisting that it was up to producers to decide whether actors should be paid, Papp declared, "If a group is capable of affording $100, they should pay it. But most can't afford it."[13] To make sure that actors would continue to work for nothing, Papp and other producers suspended all off-off Broadway shows. Papp then became the central figure in a producer-organized chain of intimidation against the actors, culminating in the threat of a blacklist of Equity members if the Showcase Code went into effect.

In the midst of this producer-instigated hysteria, Equity called a membership meeting for a vote on the code. Papp was permitted to come, and given speaking rights. This was as if Henry Ford had been allowed to participate in a meeting where auto workers were voting on their contract. Only Papp was an even more intimidating presence because Ford doesn't do his hiring personally, and Papp does. Any actor speaking for the code had to know that she or he would never again be hired by the man who was then the nation's most powerful theater producer. Despite this, some actors fought for acceptance of the Showcase Code. After a fierce meeting, Papp rose to congratulate the Equity members for what he called an "extraordinary, historic event." The actors had voted down the Showcase Code.

Commenting on this "extraordinary, historic event," Walter Kerr wrote that the Equity membership had "voted down its right to carfare to and from the theater, regular pay for its performances, a closed shop, and a permanent stake in any tryout venture that went on to eventual commerical success. Actors, born broke, are perfectly willing to stay that way." Actors, he added approvingly, "thrive on insecurity."[14]

Far from thriving on insecurity, the actors voted down the Showcase Code because—under threat of producer reprisals—they feared the code would add to their insecurity. So intense was the actors' insecurity, they were not yet ready to give up the illusion that showcases paying them nothing could nonetheless be their avenue to security and recognition.

Insecurity, the constant companion of U.S. actors, is inevitably joined by humiliation and desperation. When novelist, playwright and film writer William Goldman was doing research for his book on Broadway, *The Season,* he visited a class for professional actors, entitled "How To Audition." The teacher, casting director Michael Shurtleff, was engaged in telling an incident to his students:

I remember an actor who had auditioned half a dozen times for a lead opposite a star; it would have been the best part of his life. The seventh time they brought him back, he came out on stage, and the director saw him and said, "Not yet. I don't want you yet." The actor got off and waited, and then the stage manager brought him back out again, and this time when the director saw him, he said, "Get off, I don't want to see you now!" And the actor left again and waited again, and later the stage manager brought him out a third time, and the director said the same thing to him again, "What's the matter with you? I told you to get off, now get off!" The actor didn't say anything; he just left again and he waited in the wings for a long long time and finally, when he came back out on stage and the director saw him, the director couldn't believe it, and he said, "I don't want you. Get off! *Off!*" And the actor exploded... He started shouting and screaming at the director... And when he was done, he stormed out, and the director turned to me, bewildered, and said, "I don't know what got into him, but he'll never work in the theater again and—"[15]

Shurtleff's anecdote had been cut off by an actor's voice shouting, "WHO WAS THE DIRECTOR?!!!" Ignoring Shurtleff's admonitions to "Take it easy," the actor continued to scream, "WHO WAS IT? THAT DIRECTOR? TELL ME HIS NAME!" Shurtleff retorted, "That's going to get you a lot of jobs isn't it? Look at you. I wouldn't hire you." But the actor refused to subside. Instead he said, "What right does any man have to say who's going to work and who isn't?"

ACCORDING to one of our national myths, performing artists live in a world apart. In reality, like all working people, they face a battle for existence. In fact, they were among the first to suffer the shocks of the present crisis.

In certain ways actors' lives in the U.S. are like those of itinerant workers. Like them, actors "must go where the work is," and when they get there "shape up" for the hiring boss. Like casual workers, actors must pick up odd jobs to eke out a living: 50 percent of Equity's members hold non-acting jobs, taking unskilled blue- or white-collar work—if they can get it.

But unlike itinerant workers, actors are in their field by choice, and trying desperately to stay there. It keeps getting harder and harder.

While media references to the "crisis in the arts" are now commonplace, few established members of the arts publicly question the source of the crisis, connect it to the very nature of this system, or suggest ways out. By contrast, certain figures in the arts accept what is happening here while denouncing what is allegedly happening in countries with a different social system. Among those who've been doing this for a long time is Joseph Papp. Speaking in 1966 to a national conference of state art agencies, Papp said,

In totalitarian societies which do not draw the line between art and politics, the artist is pressured into fulfilling the aims and objectives of the state.[16]

Papp, speaking in the language of his audience of corporate executives and government officials, used "totalitarian societies" as a synonym for socialist societies. Although professing familiarity with the "aims and objectives" of those states, Papp made no mention of the "aims and objectives" of *this* state. But U.S. artists are constantly confronted with *this* state's "aims and objectives": Few can escape acting in or writing material whose subject matter has been imposed or delimited by the corporate interests for whom this state exists.

At the moment Papp spoke, this state was attempting to "pressure" the Vietnamese into conformity with its "aims and objectives" through escalating bombings. "Pressure" from this state against a state with different "aims and objectives" led, not long after, to the overthrow of Chile's popularly elected Allende government—and its replacement by a fascist junta whose "aims and objectives" do not conflict with those of this government.

When actors tried to better their lives, they ran into the "pressure" instigated by Papp, who was certainly acting in accordance with this state's "aims and objectives." And when people in any trade or profession, as well as those who've been denied the right to one, initiate struggles against unemployment, inflation, racism or any form of reaction, they too find themselves "pressured" to cease and desist by this state or those who back its "aims and objectives."

This is a government of, by and for a white corporate minority— whose "aims and objectives" conflict with those of the overwhelming majority. And millions now know this. And those millions who've lost all confidence in this state's "aims and objectives" should no longer rely on its anti-socialist officials, media and educational institutions for information about the socialist countries.

During our travels through the German Democratic Republic, we learned firsthand about the "aims and objectives" of this country—a member of the socialist community that ranges from the Soviet Union to Cuba.

Most of our first trip was devoted to seeing things. On our second and third trips we went into theaters, plants, schools and homes to ask questions of people, to discuss the many dimensions of their lives in a socialist country. This is the record of our exploration and discovery. It begins in a theater.

2. Theater: Microcosm of a Society

There is not one single unemployed actor in the German Democratic Republic," said Erhard Schmidt as we talked with him at the Volkstheater Rostock. A tall man who appeared to be in his late thirties, Schmidt was wearing the undeniable mark of the working actor: a costume.

"I can only say that's very sad," responded Schmidt soberly when we told him of the unemployment among U.S. actors. "But we know first hand from our visits to the Federal Republic of Germany that there are thousands of jobless actors there."

Schmidt had just come from taping a play for television. Midway in our talk, we were interrupted by the arrival of an invitation from the theater's *Intendant*,* Hanns Anselm Perten, to watch editing of the tape. Joining Perten and his associates, we found them seated in front of a TV monitor scanning takes from the play. Actors, still in costume and makeup, entered the room and watched the screen intently.

The play was about the Spanish Inquisition, the playwright a

*Overall director of a theater, masculine form.

Spanish anti-fascist. As the cast credits flashed on, we noted many Spanish as well as German surnames. The former, we learned, belonged to Chilean artists. Refugees from the fascist junta, they are now working with the Volkstheater. The Volkstheater's internationalist spirit, as we were to see, is characteristic of life in the GDR in and out of the theater.

"Far from having unemployed actors," pointed out Schmidt when we resumed our talk, "we need more actors."

The GDR has a remarkably active and varied theater life: There are 113 permanent repertory theaters—drama, opera, dance. (New York, which bills itself as the theater capital of the world, has in itself almost half the population of the entire GDR, but not one permanent dramatic theater company). The dramatic theaters give about 9,000 performances each year to audiences of about three and a half million. Another 7,000 performances are attended by about three million children and young people. Opera attracts two million spectators and ballet 400,000.

In addition to a dramatic ensemble, the Volkstheater Rostock includes an opera, musical theater, symphony and ballet—permanent companies comprising some 600 artists, technicians, etc. These groups perform for an annual audience of 370,000 to 400,000, "which is very big for a city of 200,000 people," pointed out Heinz Buchholz, the Volkstheater's director of economy and planning. (Founded in early times as a seaport, Rostock in the old Germany had no theater. Still a seaport, Rostock is now also a shipbuilding and university city.)

FEW U.S. actors would disagree with their fellow actor who shouted, "What right does any man have to say who's going to work and who isn't?" But in the U.S. one man *does* have the "right" to decide who will or will not be hired for any production. As a result, actors are worried about their relationship with the man who does the hiring, and they feel beholden to whoever gives them a job.

And most U.S. actors think the same holds true for actors in a socialist country. In fact, we said—as we talked one morning with members of the Dresden State Theater—most U.S. actors have the impression it's much worse in a socialist country, where they believe actors are beholden not just to one producer but to an entire state— that is, to an alien, forbidding presence.

"Where to start answering that?" laughed Dr. Gerhard Piens, the theater's *Chefdramaturg.** "With *State and Revolution?*** It would be good for American actors to know that this is a workers and farmers state—which guarantees everyone the right to work." Putting aside for the moment the larger question of the entire social system, Piens said, "Let's start with the actors: They're actors because they want to be actors!"

Like many of their U.S. counterparts, would-be actors in the GDR start their hoped-for theater careers by applying to drama school. In the U.S., however, they will be accepted only if they can pay the ever-steeper tuition. In the GDR, drama schools—which are not separate little enterprises but a part of a total, unified educational system—are subsidized. The students, who pay no fees of any sort during the three to four years they study acting, receive a stipend for their living expenses.

Talent is, of course, evaluated and everyone who applies to drama school is not accepted. If an applicant is turned down, does this mean he or she has to give up hopes of a dramatic career? No, responded Piens. If you're not accepted the first time, you can try again. "Some actors who were rejected or even chucked out by the drama schools have gone on to become good actors, or even stars. But these are the exceptions, not the rule," he said.

Besides drama schools, the GDR also offers opportunities to aspiring actors via the workers' theaters established by many plants. Through these theaters, young actors have a chance to learn their craft, generally under the guidance of a director from the professional theater. And the workers' theaters are a genuine showcase for new talent. (Some of Brecht's Berliner Ensemble actors came from workers' theaters.)

Every actor who finishes drama school is guaranteed a place with a theater and given a *permanent* contract. "In a factory you don't employ people for two months, you just employ them. Why shouldn't it apply to the theater too?" declared Dr. Klaus Pfützner, first secretary of the Association of Theater Workers. (This organization, with headquarters in Berlin, is not a trade union. It deals with plays and their production from a social and artistic standpoint.)

Pfützner was, of course, talking about conditions in a GDR factory. In a U.S. factory, a worker can be laid off in two months or two

*Chief literary adviser, masculine form
***State and Revolution,* by V.I. Lenin.

weeks—or two hours for that matter. And the same conditions extend to actors: even those under Equity's best contract get no more than one week's notice when a show is closing.

In the GDR, too, conditions for all working people are an extension of those in the factories—but not because the total society is "like a factory" in the sense that that expression is used in the U.S. The workers and farmers state has ended the conditions prevailing in the corporate U.S.A., and established one Labor Code guaranteeing the conditions for all working people, whether in a plant or a theater.

"In the theater everyone—actors, musicians, singers—has a contract without end. To the end of their lives, if they want it," Gerhard Piens told us. Although the performers have permanent contracts, they aren't bound tó stay in one place. To leave, an actor simply gives one year's notice with no explanation required.

"The permanent contracts mean we can plan with our actors far in advance," continued Piens. "On the other hand, if we find we need such and such an actor, it can be very difficult. There are no jobless and we have to win the actor away from another theater."

If a theater is interested in a certain actor, the *Intendant* may go to see that actor perform. "But," pointed out Klaus Pfützner, "an *Intendant* cannot do any direct hiring. He must first consult with the trade union representatives elected by the actors." Further, before offering a contract to a prospective member of the ensemble, the *Intendant* is "expected to listen to the opinions of the actors."

But, we asked, what happens if an *Intendant* no longer wants an actor in the company?

"The *Intendant* can't dismiss anyone," replied Pfützner. "If the *Intendant* feels someone doesn't fit in, he or she can talk to the person. If the person agrees, okay. It's mutual. The contract is cancelled.

"But if the actor doesn't want to go, if he or she has no chance for another theater—socialist democracy goes into action: The *Intendant* cannot let anyone go unless the Cultural Workers' Union agrees. This is true for the whole GDR. A manager can do nothing without the trade union."

But what if an impasse develops between the *Intendant* and the trade union?

"If the *Intendant* continues to believe the artist isn't up to the standards of this theater, if he believes it's not possible to work with this actor—and if the trade union continues to disagree with him—the

Intendant can contact a special labor court which defends the interests of the state and the individual. Or the individual can also go there and complain."

However, while there can be conflicts between manager and theater workers, they are not of the same nature as those between producers and actors in the U.S. In the U.S., the producer has no interest in the theater or an actor—unless it's profitable for him. But there are no private profit-makers in the GDR theater, and both *Intendant* and theater workers have the same goal: a creative theater playing its unique role in helping to develop socialist society.

At the Volksbühne Theater in Berlin, which has a company of 400, we gained further insight into the new relationships that emerge between management and actors when the exploitation of actors by management has been ended. "Everyone who works here has the same social status. No one can be sent away," explained Dieter Klein, deputy to the Volksbühne's *Intendant*. "This is not always easy for the *Intendant*—I must add that—but it's done deliberately.

"Even if one of our colleagues doesn't work properly, it's difficult to send him away. The conflict committee, which is elected by the trade union members—or the labor court—would tell the *Intendant*, 'You're of the opinion that the person isn't doing a good job. But in asking that he be dismissed, you're also asking that he be sent somewhere else. We're asking that you keep him here and transform him.'"

At the Berliner Ensemble we learned more about the new role of management in a socialist enterprise from Pilka Häntzsche. She is the theater's cadre director, whose counterpart in a U.S. enterprise would be the personnel director who hires and fires and in general acts on behalf of management against workers.

"A director in a theater sometimes needs a very long time to decide if an artist is up to all that's demanded of him," pointed out Häntzsche. "An artist might be very good for one task but not another. One must really judge the entire person, from all sides." If there is a negative opinion of an artist's work, "a large circle of people—including the trade union—will have to hear him. With socialist democracy, which is the principle in all our enterprises, leading people can't decide things willfully. That's a very great thing if you think about it. Socialist democracy is organized in such a way that things are really discussed collectively. Seldom is a decision made against an artist. The suits that come up in the labor courts are almost always decided for the worker. The security of artists in their work is assured."

In a socialist country the trade union's role as well as that of management is transformed. Just as management shares the union's concern with working conditions, the union shares management's concern with the quality of work. This is because the product— whether in theater or plant—benefits the entire population.

"The trade union wants its members' work to be on a high level, and it keeps encouraging actors to improve their quality," Klaus Pfützner told us. In one theater, he said, there was an incident where "not the *Intendant* but the trade union wanted an actor's contract ended. His acting was just not good enough. The theater worked with him for two years but he didn't improve. He was convinced of this by his colleagues who themselves asked for his contract to be terminated.

"But," emphasized Pfützner, "such a way of doing things is possible only if the whole society is pro-human. Those who leave the theater must know society will help them find something else."

□ □ □

ON OUR second trip to the GDR we brought with us a story from *The New York Times* titled "How 'All Over Town' Got On Boards." It began:

"If you do a play on Broadway without a half a million dollar advance, you've got a 100-to-1 shot," said Dustin Hoffman, director of Murray Schisgal's new comedy, "All Over Town."

Hoffman made these remarks while working on an "under-financed" show which opened "after seven months of work filled with such possible calamities as lost backers, cast changes . . . and emergency repairs." The "calamities" began, at least for actors, with auditions that ran through multitudes of performers in order to select a cast of eighteen.

Mr. Schisgal and Mr. Hoffman auditioned 1,500 actors, not all of them professionals, including several cab drivers, a cleaning woman and the man who shines shoes in their office building. They considered hiring the shoeshine man, but he decided against giving up his security of shoes for the insecurity of the stage.[1]

Six days before rehearsals were to begin, the show's backers pulled out. Hoffman began making phone calls to find new ones.

"It was like being at a crap table," he said. Discouraged, he decided to make one more call. The next name on the list was Adela Holzer.[2]

Holzer, who "has made a fortune through investments in sugar and spice and everything nice including real estate, butter and cement," agreed to back the play. As it turned out, she didn't restrict herself to being an angel. She also played God with the cast: During the out-of-town tryout she had one of the featured actresses fired.

The actress' departure had an immediate, jarring effect on the rest of the cast. As Mr. Hoffman acknowledged, "Any time you fire someone, it disturbs actors. They always think they're next."

Hoffman's own methods may have been almost equally disturbing to the actors and technicians:

From the first day of rehearsal, [Hoffman] complained that he did not have enough time for rehearsal (three weeks). To gain more, he stopped eating lunch and juggled his actors.
"If you work during lunch, you save an hour a day," he said. "That's an extra week of rehearsal." Technical slowdown and excess costs annoyed him. "It's money that stops work from being quality."[3]

In the GDR this story was read (either in the original or in translation) by a number of theater people, including Maik Hamburger, a director and *Dramaturg* at the Deutsches Theater in Berlin, and Johannes Wieke, an actor at the Dresden State Theater.

"I'm not surprised. It's nothing new to me," responded Wieke. He was about sixty and his acting career dates from prewar Germany.

"No one in the GDR could grasp that people work under those conditions," exclaimed Hamburger, who laughed almost continuously as he read the story—not with amusement but incredulity. He was forty-three and his theater experience began after the founding of the GDR.

"All of those conditions are just diametrically opposite to conditions GDR actors know and have come to accept as normality," Hamburger said as we talked at the Deutsches Theater. (In 1922 the Deutsches was the scene of the first performance of Brecht's *Drums In The Night* and in 1949 of the first performance on a German stage of *Mother Courage.)*

"As you know," he continued, "the theater people here are all employed at a specific theater—which of course they can leave at their own discretion. They are absolutely protected from dismissal by the trade union and the Labor Code." As for casting, the brutal audition system doesn't exist. "Each theater has its own ensemble and the cast is decided upon by the director after consulting the theater's artistic/economic council." Although directors make the final decisions, they can't work on their own. The artistic/economic council, an advisory body elected by the union members, discusses such questions as plays, the work of directors and actors, and whether an actor is getting enough parts.

Although in the U.S. a play may be staged because an actor who's big at the box office wants to be in it and the producer feels sure of a hit, stars aren't needed to fill houses in the GDR. There an actor's wishes may be taken into consideration for entirely different reasons.

"The actors are people who have a professional interest in the plays being done" and the "particular wishes of an actor to do a certain part" will be taken into account if possible, Hamburger pointed out. "You can't always do this but if you feel the actor has a right and the maturity, you'll endeavor to satisfy him."

For example, "we were doing many plays with a working-class setting, not so many conversation plays." As a result, "there was a very fine actress who plays Shaw—socially upper-class ladies—who wasn't getting any parts." In such an instance "the artistic/economic council discusses whether this particular actor should be cast in a different type of play so as to broaden his or her spectrum, or whether a particular play should be put on which could supply a part for the actor according to type. I wouldn't say a play is chosen for this reason often, but it is done if we feel it's necessary for development."

As for rehearsal time, Hamburger went on, "no director—even in the smallest provincial theater—would consider doing a play in three weeks." The minimum is six weeks "but this is the minimum for very small theaters." GDR theater workers themselves determine in advance the time required for each production (ten weeks is not at all unusual), but more rehearsal time will be added if director and cast consider it necessary. (However, the difference between GDR and U.S. rehearsals, which usually run four weeks, can't be gauged by the time differential alone: Almost all U.S. casts are composed of actors who never worked together before, while GDR actors are part of an ensemble.)

What happens in the GDR, we asked Hamburger, if a director wants to make cast changes during rehearsal? "If any controversies develop about whether an actor can master a part or if he feels unjustly dealt with in any way, he can appeal to the trade union commission. If the problem isn't solved in the theater—which it almost always is—the actor can go to a labor court."

Although Maik Hamburger's entire career has been in the GDR theater, almost all of the first half of his life was spent in other lands. "My family emigrated from Germany before 1933 for political and racial reasons. I spent my youth going from one country to another." When Hamburger was ten, his family settled in England. "I came back here in 1951 partially out of curiosity. I was at a far-off university in the north of Scotland and I was quite happy there. But I was out of things, away from the important developments in Berlin which interested me very much.

"I came to the democratic German state where a new future was being constructed, where the crimes and catastrophes the German nation had repeatedly pulled down upon itself would be made impossible by the construction of a socialist society." Hamburger paused. "Of course, one of those crimes was anti-Semitism. Our family managed to escape but many friends and acquaintances did not." Noting that "Hamburger is a Jewish name," he said, "I've never come across any vestige of anti-Semitism here."

At the time we talked with Maik Hamburger all we knew about *All Over Town* as a play came from the author's own description of it in the *Times*'s story as a "contemporary comedy about city life with eighteen characters of diverse and multifarious ethnic and social backgrounds." After we returned to New York we saw the play, whose claim to "contemporary comedy" lies in a supposed switch on a Black stereotype. In reality the racist essence of the stereotype is left intact, and the caricaturing of Blacks opens the way to "diverse and multifarious" caricaturing of Jews, Greeks, Swedes and the French as well.

The role of GDR theater is in striking contrast to the increasingly anti-humanist direction of U.S. theater. Right after World War II the theater in what was then the Eastern part of Germany began to play a special part in the total society's struggle to eradicate racism, anti-Semitism and national chauvinism.

"The Deutsches Theater," said Maik Hamburger, "was the first to start playing. And the first play put on was *Nathan The Wise*"— whose protagonist is a Jew—"with its message of peace and understanding amongst the people." He added: "When we started to build a new society the ruins, as Brecht put it, were not only in the street but in the heads of people. We had to start off by propagating the normal humanities amongst the people."

Only by establishing the "normal humanities amongst the people"—so increasingly abnormal, one might say, in our own country—was it possible to build the new society, whose conditions are reflected in the theater.

It has become customary in the U.S. to speak of the arts in the terms of mortal catastrophe—featuring both laments for the dead and exhortations to prevent further fatalities.

"We must not let the opera house die," exclaimed the Metropolitan Opera's Executive Director Anthony A. Bliss, in a typical pronouncement, at the start of 1975.

Bliss said "we" but as it turned out he meant "they"—that is, the Met's employees—because he simultaneously announced a shorter season and a cut in pay for the remaining weeks.

A reaction to this announcement came from Max Arons, president of the Musicians Union, Local 802:

Considering the reduction of the season, the pay cuts and the rise of the cost of living, these proposals amount to a 40 percent reduction in our members' income. This is maybe my 23rd contract with the Met. For years we struggled to bring up the standard of living of skilled musicians. We thought the idea that working people should subsidize the arts was discredited a long time ago.[4]

Although Arons was trying to counter the bourgeoisie's old but frequently resurrected demand that workers "save the arts" by accepting cuts in pay, he did not express this in accurate terms. The "idea that working people should subsidize the arts" is *not* "discredited." Whether in a capitalist or socialist society it is the workers who subsidize the arts through the wealth they create. What is discredited is the idea that the wealth should be appropriated by private corporate interests, who then decide what to do with it. The Rockefellers are a perfect example of how this system works.

The Rockefellers control a web of transnational corporations, and they also control the Rockefeller Foundation. Through the latter, a tax-free fund, they can see to it that even allegedly public art conforms to private "aims and objectives." By giving or witholding money, the Rockefeller and other mammoth corporate interests set the limits for those who manage such a "public" organization as Lincoln Center.

When Joseph Papp took charge of the Lincoln Center theaters one of his first moves was to arrange a luncheon engagement with John D. Rockefeller III. "In this town the name of Rockefeller meant money. That man was money. On his say-so the money could be found. He had an enormous personal stake in the success of Lincoln Center ... ," points out Papp's biographer Stuart Little.[5] Papp wanted Rockefeller to become chairman of Lincoln Center's board, but a Rockefeller doesn't like his control to be that obvious ("He had a sure way of forestalling such overtures," notes Little.[6]) Still the lunch "had accomplished [its] purpose. Now, when he had to," Papp could "go back to Rockefeller."[7]

A few days later Papp had another luncheon engagement, this time with a Mrs. Samuel I. Newhouse whose husband had "amassed a Rockefeller-size fortune." Papp came quickly to the point:

"This is a very nice luncheon and I'm enjoying it. But you know we're really here to discuss money." Papp suggested that she accept a place on the board.
"What would I do?" she asked.
"Well, I don't know. What would you be interested in doing?"
"I like to do rather personal things, things that I can get involved in myself."[8]

But what Papp offered her was hardly "personal":

He proposed that she buy the [Forum] theater and put her name on it. Then she could become involved in the program of that theater.
"But who would run it?" she wanted to know.
"I would help," Papp volunteered. "I would help you."[9]

Papp suggested a "total benefaction" of $1.5 million. When the deal was consummated, the Forum Theater became the Mitzi E. Newhouse Theater, complete with a special cut-rate contract for actors.

IN THE GDR as in the USA, the working people subsidize the arts. But in the GDR this subsidization is decided upon by the people, and thus is used for and not against the people's "aims and objectives." Since cultural affluence is among the "aims and objectives" of socialist society, both theaters and theater workers are assured of financial security.

"It's a fact that we get very generous help from the state. We know a long time ahead what our budget will be and we can work without financial worries," said Dieter Klein at the Volksbühne.

"We get large subsidies from the state. And our ticket prices are more than popular. They were fixed in 1945 and we have a law prohibiting price increases," related Heinz Buchholz at the Volkstheater Rostock.

The amount of a theater's annual subsidy is the result of collective discussion between the theater workers and the state (of which theater workers are a part, as elected people's representatives). "We argue with the state each year for a few hundred thousand more marks and finally we agree," said Gerhard Piens in Dresden.

Because GDR theaters don't have to rely on box-office receipts, they are freed from the instant-hit syndrome. "It's possible for us to do plays of great value that aren't known to the public," pointed out Dresden actor Johannes Wieke. "We can continue a worthwhile play even if only half the seats are sold. By and by people will learn of it."

This doesn't mean that the theater is unconcerned with the box office, even from a financial standpoint. "I don't want the impression to arise that financial aspects play no part in our repertory," commented Maik Hamburger. "If things go badly, the financial manager of a theater could say, 'We need a bit of light comedy or something to get more people into the theater.' But," he stressed, "financial managers don't have much influence on the repertories. Generally the theater says we must do a play because it's experimental or has artistic and social merit—and that's what is done."

IN THE U.S. there's a grim correlation between rising profits and living standards: As profits rise (witness the TV industry), so do unemployment and inflation. But in a society where working people are in power, it's only natural that working people would live as well as production of material wealth permits. In the early days of the GDR, with much of the country still in ruins from World War II, life was hard. But along with the increase in productivity has come a remarkable rise in living standards for the people, including, naturally, theater people.

"Our actors are paid from well to very well," declared Dr. Fritz Rödel, *Chefdramaturg* and deputy to the *Intendant* at Berlin's Maxim Gorki Theater.

Because the value of money to a working person is represented by its buying power, one can't compare material conditions of GDR and U.S. actors by converting marks to dollars (although one can say that with an 80 percent unemployment rate most U.S. actors have very few dollars). Such a comparison would not reveal that prices for GDR consumer goods were set in the fifties and sixties, and that rent averages only 5 to 7 percent of a person's income. Nor would the GDR's virtually free medical care, paid maternity leaves, subsidized vacations and low-cost hot meals at the workplace (including the theaters) be reflected in such a comparison. Nor would this comparison show that special coaching and voice training, a great personal expense to U.S. actors, are provided free in the GDR. And a GDR actor has no need for an agent. But in the U.S., as one actor—who refers to his agent as a "barracuda"—puts it, "You're always trying to market yourself to get more under the prevailing conditions."

Since the GDR is a society with no rich and no poor, there are no "star" and no "walk-on" salaries. And the GDR has wiped out the wage differentials that existed between actors and actresses in the old Germany—which still exist in the Federal Republic of Germany (FRG), not to mention the U.S. But every GDR artist doesn't get the same pay: there's a minimum and maximum.

"Every theater worker earns according to what he or she can do," pointed out Klaus Pfützner. "There's a permanent discussion about everyone's work and the *Intendant* must estimate the workers' value twice a year. In this way, salary—which can go up, or also down—is determined."

But the *Intendant* cannot make such estimations alone: They can be made only through collective discussions involving the trade union. And unlike U.S. producers who make more if actors make less, a GDR *Intendant* has no incentive to lower salaries. On the contrary, it's in the *Intendant's* interest to encourage creativity—and material recognition, the means to live better, is welcomed by actors along with all other working people.

IF IN the U.S. we are skeptical of the idea that relationships become more human when people improve their material conditions, it's because the evidence in our own country appears to be to the contrary. Here most individuals who better their own situation do so at the expense of others. (Even those individuals who aren't rich but just comparatively well off frequently become callous toward the growing impoverishment of others.)

The standard for human relationships in the U.S. is set by the profit motive, and the way those who profit treat those they profit from infects the entire society—as the theater attests.

The casting director who taught classes in "How To Audition" dispensed the following advice to actors arriving for a tryout:

> . . . when they say, "How are you?," don't tell them. You're always saying, "Well, I've got this terrible cough, and I can't for the life of me shake it and. . . . " The state of your health interests absolutely no one.[10]

That the state of an actor's health interests "absolutely no one" who does the hiring is absolutely accurate information in the U.S. (Of course, if a star becomes ill during the run of a show the producers certainly will be interested, since a star's illness would almost surely close the show.)

In a society where *everyone's* standard of living rises—when one person's efforts don't hurt others but assist a collective advance—there's an entirely different relationship between material conditions and human relations. There the "state of your health" *is* of interest.

"We have a doctor here about twenty hours a week and a nurse here permanently," said Dieter Klein at the Volksbühne. "And naturally we have a sauna."

Nothing is more revealing of a society's humanity than the way it treats people as they grow older. In the U.S. even very young performers begin to dread what will happen to them later on.

A twenty-seven-year-old actress, Priscilla Lopez, who was appearing in the musical, *A Chorus Line,* said in an interview:

> . . . after so many years, you just don't want to be in the chorus anymore, especially if you've had a speaking role. About the oldest you can be is 35. How long can you keep smiling and looking-cutesy? It's when you look old that you've got to go.[11]

If a U.S. performer's marketability goes into decline when she's thirty-five, it's not difficult to imagine what happens when she really gets old. How many actors have anything to live on then except a Social Security pittance?

In the GDR actors not only receive a comfortable pension, they will get that pension even if they continue working in the theater, which is their option.

THOSE IN the U.S. who have financial security are fond of telling artists that insecurity is a spur to creativity. Artists who have to take acting or writing jobs that degrade their talents just in order to stay in their field know otherwise. As do artists who have to leave the field—and those who couldn't even make a break into it—because they must find other ways to pay the rent. Almost all U.S. artists are harassed by financial insecurity, and this is doubly true for artists of the Black and other oppressed minorities.

To solve material problems is to create the basis for consistent creative work for artists as a whole. But solving the old problems doesn't mean solving *all* problems. New ones will arise. Yet the new ones are of an entirely different nature from those in the U.S., where antagonistic contradictions exist between a small exploiting class and those they exploit. In a socialist country where the corporate forces responsible for racism, poverty and unemployment are gone, the contradictions are between what has been achieved and what is yet to be achieved. And these contradictions are a spur to further development.

In the theater, as in all areas of GDR society, these new conflicts take many forms. "Permanent contracts are against all traditions of the theater," noted Klaus Pfützner. "But there wasn't just a bad side to these traditions—such as managers who employed people not only to manipulate them for money but also to control their entire being as artists. There was also a positive side: Managers could engage special actors for certain roles. But now our ensembles are permanent and the necessary renewal by young actors becomes more difficult."

Pfützner laughed. "I sound like a capitalist! But I'm making a different point. We have no intention of going backward. We want to apply the Labor Code better and guarantee the necessary regeneration of theater groups.

"We also," he continued, "have to assure the unity of director and cast. With the new Labor Code, the *Intendant* can't let anyone go and this can cement conflicts. It's very hard for some people to work together—and art should be pleasant. This means people must discuss things, must become more qualified so they can work together as a collective." There are, he said, "remnants of the past" that must be overcome to achieve this.

"The director is very important, he puts the stamp of his personality on a production. But there are little czars, artistic directors who won't discuss things with others. If a director's very gifted it might be all right for him to do things by himself. But in the end he won't have a collective of quality."

However, for work to proceed "in a quality way," a director "must be a strong personality. I'm not speaking of a certain terrorism that directors could exert in the past"—and still do in the U.S. and other Western countries. "Our actors wouldn't accept that," declared Pfützner. But given certain conditions, "some actors will try to direct. Then chaos starts. You cannot direct yourself in a play and the work of the whole cast is disrupted."

A basic reason why a GDR director must be a strong but not authoritarian personality is the changes occurring in actors "during the process of our thirty years of development," pointed out Pfützner. "The emancipation of actors is a social phenomenon with many different facets. We now have artists who think, who are active in our political and cultural life, in the artistic councils, the Party, in the mass organizations. They are very strong personalities."

In the GDR, Pfützner stressed, conflicts between management and actors are qualitatively different from those in a capitalist country. "We have individual conflicts—egoism, opportunism, people who still misuse their positions. But the *Intendant* cannot act against the interests of his colleagues. And these conflicts aren't rooted in antagonistic contradictions between management and cast"—as they are in the U.S where producers try to extract the greatest profits possible by paying actors as little as they can get away with (nothing, if they can get away with that). In the GDR, "the principles of both management and theater workers are pro-human, pro-society."

In the GDR film industry as well as in the theater, the problems "contrast very greatly with those in the U.S.," Konrad Wolf, a GDR film director told us. Because of the increasing need of films for TV, "there's a shortage of actors and"—although it would be difficult for U.S. actors to view it as such—"this is a real problem." He went on to tell us of another problem, one that arose from the new need for more actors and the survivals of old ways.

Wolf's wife, Christel Bodenstein, had been under contract to DEFA, the film organization, where for a considerable time she was cast only as a young girl. "She was afraid she'd become a cliché and was eager to get character parts," said Wolf. The studio didn't agree and for a time she got no parts at all. But she got her regular salary.

For a period of two years she took singing and guitar lessons and went on to become a professional performer. During this time, noted Wolf, "she was socially secure." She herself took the initiative to cancel her film contract.

The problem affecting Christel Bodenstein, said Wolf, also affects other actors. "We don't have a star cult but if an actor is successful in one role, directors sometimes continue to cast him or her in similar ones." Although "type-casting" is a survival from the past, a new problem—the shortage of actors because of the greater demand—has prolonged the day of its departure.

Our talk with Wolf, who is president of the GDR's Academy of Arts, took place not in the GDR but in New York. The director, whose films have won prizes in Cannes, Vienna, Moscow and Edinburgh, had just completed a tour of the U.S. There had been non-commercial showings of his films in several cities, followed by discussions. "I was always confronted," he said, "by one opinion": disbelief that films on a high artistic level were made in the GDR. "They had expected 'propaganda' movies." (Wolf was told by one viewer of his films, "I can't believe they weren't made especially for export.")

One of the films, *Goya,* was screened in a private home in Los Angeles for an audience that included many people from the film industry. Wolf was showered with congratulations. A top executive in the film industry was so enthusiastic about the picture that Wolf said, "You praise it so highly—why don't you give the American public a chance to see it?" The man's expression "changed by 180 degrees. He said, 'Impossible. It wouldn't make money.' I said, 'If you like it, show it. We don't want to make a penny from it.' 'Americans wouldn't want to see it,' the executive insisted. 'There's not enough action.'"

"Not enough action" was interpreted by Wolf to mean "not enough sex, horror and violence." "Politicians from the capitalist countries," said Wolf, "always claim that socialist countries set up barriers for free exchange of culture. Of course, we do have one barrier. Our constitution prohibits producing or importing racist films or films glorifying war."

3. "We Are the State"

Dan Sullivan, drama reviewer for the *Los Angeles Times,* did something almost unheard of for a mass media critic. He criticized a theater for dealing with an issue crucial to the United States "metaphorically" rather than "directly."

In his review of the South African play, *Sizwe Bansi Is Dead,* presented in Los Angeles during the 1974-75 season by the Mark Taper Forum (part of the city's performing arts center), Sullivan stated, "there was the nagging suspicion that it's time the Taper directly, rather than metaphorically, addressed itself to the racial situation in our community—developed its own 'Sizwe Bansi' in workshop."[1] *Sizwe Bansi* deals with the passbooks Black South Africans are forced to carry, and Sullivan noted that Black Americans also "have to carry identity cards (albeit invisible ones) that keep them from living here or working there."

Yet in offering *Sizwe Bansi* as a model for the way in which the Taper might directly treat the "racial situation" in the U.S., Sullivan was observing the "establishment"'s boundaries for plays dealing with racism—as he himself implied: *Sizwe Bansi* is, he said, "if anything an

34

overingratiating play," a play that a "good white liberal audience" finds "right up its street." (In fact, *Sizwe Bansi* toured this country with the tacit approval of the apartheid fascist rulers of South Africa, who were trying at that time to "liberalize" their image in the U.S.—an effort that was having a certain effect before the Soweto massacres.)

But the Mark Taper Forum had no plans for dealing "directly" with racism or any other issue vital to the U.S. Even "good white liberal" limits for plays on social questions went out of bounds for the 1975-76 season when the Taper announced both a "return to the classics" and cancellation of New Theater for Now, its new play series.

Why was the Taper turning its back on new plays? The reply came in an interview with the theater's artistic director, Gordon Davidson, who said:

> If anyone thinks I'm not doing more new plays because I'm afraid to—that's ridiculous. There just isn't a lot of good new material around. That will infuriate a lot of people whose scripts are on my desk but it's true. The quantity is there; people are still writing. But there's something about this time in our history. We're having a little trouble focusing on where we are in viable dramatic terms. It's hard to come to grips with the values of a society that's spinning around as ours has been. It's hard for today's theater to make a commentary except in a small way, as in the TV sitcoms.[2]

When the artistic director of a prominent theater offers a rationale for keeping social commentary on the TV sit-com level, one begins to get an idea of the enormous barriers to production faced by a play dealing seriously with social issues. To allege it's too hard for a playwright to "come to grips" with a "society that's spinning around" is to ignore the fact that times of great social change have been the challenge to playwrights from Shakespeare to Brecht! There are U.S. playwrights only too anxious to "come to grips with the values" of this society, as Black playwrights in particular have demonstrated. All they need is a theater.

But they won't find it at the Mark Taper Forum, whose financial backers aren't interested in plays that "come to grips with the values" of this society, or even plays that give those "values" a slight rap on the knuckles. The "extinction" of New Theater for Now, said Davidson, was "an extremely painful step," but the program was "getting too expensive."

To make up its $2.3 million annual budget, the Taper relies heavily on corporate and government sources. One of these sources, the Mellon Foundation, came up with a special grant to subsidize the "return to the classics" (some of which were not classics but merely old plays). Cancellation of the new plays resulted in enough protest from Taper subscribers to force modification of the program: A few new plays were finally added—but nothing to disturb the Mellon Foundation. ("Essentially a collection of blackout sketches that might be performed on the Carol Burnett TV show" is the way a mass media writer described one of the plays.)

DURING THE 1975–76 season, Lincoln Center also announced a "return to the classics." And for the same reasons.

Joseph Papp's new play program, on which he raised "nearly $5 million in new money" when he took charge of Lincoln Center in 1973, was "now virtually bankrupt," reported his biographer, Stuart Little, in a *Times* story. In order to get money to continue, Papp had "to scrap his cherished scheme to make the Beaumont the national platform for the new American playwright." Soon Papp announced that he would "present only classics, with name performers wherever possible."

The erosion of Papp's corporate financial backing was tied in with a plunge in subscriptions to his theaters. The reason for the attendance drop, according to Little, was:

> In two seasons the Beaumont's theatrically conservative subscribers had been aroused to the point of rebellion by Papp's new-play choices—works whose toughness, profanity, and frank scenes of sexual behavior offended audiences . . . [3]

One may well wonder whether even this "theatrically conservative" audience was "offended" by profanity and "frank scenes of sexual behavior," or merely bored by them. What may have seemed daring in the sixties, well before "hard-core" pornography had reached its present saturation level, was apt to be met with yawns in the seventies.

The corporations that were cutting back on support to Lincoln Center had no objection as such to the plays with "frank scenes of sexual behavior." On the contrary, they subsidized them. Their objection was that these plays had not drawn audiences. And the plays that would draw an audience—the huge potential audience for plays telling the truth about life in the U.S.—are the very plays that would contradict corporate "aims and objectives." Funds from the Rockefeller and Ford foundations are doled out in a way to keep such plays from emerging.

During the sixties into the early seventies, the gains made by the civil rights and peace forces were to an extent reflected in the theater, particularly in the formation of Black theater groups. However, the plays of this period dealing with social issues usually presented them in distorted form (for instance, the anti-militarist aspects of *The Basic Training of Pavlo Hummel,* produced at the Public Theater, were contradicted by the racist treatment of Black and Vietnamese characters).

But for some time now the corporate forces who resisted the peace and civil rights demands have been trying to reverse the advances these movements made. And this too is reflected in the theater—in the substitution of classics for new plays when both should be done, in the staging of new plays that substitute sensation for substance, as well as the current staging of plays of a more openly racist and/or generally reactionary nature.

During that same 1975–76 season Papp further revealed how he conformed to his backers' "aims and objectives." Papp, reported Little in his *Times'* article, "conceived of a two-company plan for the Beaumont. One black. One white. A combined or integrated company would not encompass the great ethnic divisions in the city." Clearly, a theater representing the people's true "aims and objectives" would not "encompass the great ethnic divisions"—which are caused by racism. A real theater would be part of the movement to overcome these divisions!

By way of further explanation for the "two-company plan," Papp said, "When you integrate, you make color a factor. I want to erase color entirely." While asserting that he wanted to "erase color entirely," Papp was making color *the* condition for admission to a particular theater company. Moreover, the idea of "erasing color" is not only impossible, but a racist insult to people of color! The issue is not to "erase color" but to erase the color *line* drawn by racism.

It is one thing for Black people, whose culture has been both suppressed and exploited, to form a theater and take charge of decision making. But it is the continuation of an old old pattern when a white man makes decisions for Black people. "My opinion is the most important opinion," says Papp. "The selection of plays is unilateral."[4]

In a literal sense Papp's plan for segregated companies was never carried out. It never could have been in a theater that had no companies but did its casting on a single-production basis. Yet in essence this plan was in effect at Lincoln Center and still is at Papp's other theaters: Most Papp productions have been all- or almost all-white, while a few have been all- or almost all-Black. And what has guaranteed preservation of the "great ethnic divisions" is the content of these plays. For example, in one all-white Papp production an actor put on blackface to emerge as a racist caricature; another production, predominantly white, featured a psychopathic, murderous Black caricature whose lines are a stream of obscene graffiti.

Papp assists his corporate backers in carrying out their "aims and objectives" when he perpetuates through the theater the racist divisions they impose on the industries and housing they own, and the educational institutions whose policies they control.

IF A REALLY large number of new plays were staged in times of crisis such as these, plays of real social and artistic value—particularly from new playwrights—would emerge among them. But almost every area of the theater functions in a way to block this development.

While the "elite" performing arts centers refer to plays they stage from other times as "classics" (whether they are or not), other areas of the theater bluntly call such productions "revivals." Of the 1975–76 season *The New York Times'* theater writer Mel Gussow states:

When one goes to the theater these days, it is often a step into a time machine. Thus far, half of [the Broadway] shows . . . have been revivals . . . In addition, Off Broadway and even Off Off Broadway were struck by the antiquary fever, trying to revive plays as distant as "Our American Cousin."[5]

To justify their resistance to new plays, producers and artistic directors all around the country assert that good new plays simply aren't available. "I hear over and over that good plays are not being written. It just isn't true. It's just that no one has the facilities to produce them," declared David Ball, script reader at the Tyrone Guthrie Theater in Minneapolis, adding: "Really, what producer in his right mind can afford to take a chance?"[6]

Pointing out the specifics of why producers don't care to "take a chance" on new plays, Mel Gussow writes:

. . . revivals are cheaper, easier to produce, and more likely to succeed than new plays. Presumably they once were hits, so there is no need for an out-of-town tryout. When revivals tour, it is usually to gather profits before facing New York . . . [7]

All of this results in what Gussow describes as "limited" options for contemporary playwrights: "If you want to work in live theater in New York"—the so-called theater capital of the world—"your options are limited." One of these "options," he says, is Papp:

> He keeps stashing young playwrights in cubicles at the Public . . . Does he forget any of them? Everybody waits, breathlessly, for word from Papp. Does he like me? Will he hire me? Will he do my next play . . . How do you get to Papp?[8]

□ □ □

"I CAN only say this is another world. It's very difficult for us to understand," responded Fritz Rödel soberly when we told him of the enormous barriers facing new playwrights in the U.S.

"All our theaters are just searching for new authors," said the Gorki's *Chefdramaturg.* "This is not a question of profit or loss, but the artistic intentions of the theater. Every theater here feels bound to produce contemporary playwrights."

Although a substantial part of a GDR theater's repertory is made up of new plays, "that doesn't mean we have a richer number of plays than you have in the U.S.," noted Rödel. "Real dramatic talent is rare in literature. But we think only by being very attentive to all the new plays can we discover where the real talent is."

In GDR theaters there's no basis for conflict between staging classics and contemporary plays. The first post-war production in the Eastern part of Germany—the classic, *Nathan The Wise*—played an important part in helping to overcome the "ethnic divisions" left by twelve years of Hitler fascism. But the theater's role in the struggle to end the "ethnic divisions" caused by anti-Semitism, racism and superior attitudes toward all the "non-aryan" peoples of the world could not be carried out only through classics. The work of contemporary playwrights, especially Brecht, was vital in this respect.

Today GDR theater—sharing the "aims and objectives" of the total society—plays a special role in helping to develop a new consciousness among people, that is, new attitudes toward social and personal relations, including between men and women, and an internationalist identification with all the peoples of the world. This kind of theater demands new plays. Many many new plays.

"GDR audiences," continued Rödel, "are interested in all contemporary lives, but especially their own—not only in the GDR but the other socialist countries too. They particularly want to see plays about people living together in a new way—with new conflicts, serious and comic." However, he emphasized, "this is not an exclusive interest." In addition to German and world classics, the GDR theater stages contemporary plays from the "third world" and the West. "In the GDR we've produced the works of a number of American playwrights. The world is divided into two camps but it's one world after all, and its fate depends on the entire world."

At the Deutsches Theater Maik Hamburger also emphasized the "enormous demand in the GDR for contemporary plays. Anyone who writes a play with even a few good points in it—even if there are weaknesses—will immediately get a theater interested." In fact, the theater will assist the playwright in overcoming the play's weaknesses.

"Playwrights are given a great deal of help by the theaters," related Hamburger. "As a *Dramaturg,* part of my job is to advise young authors on their plays. It often happens that a team from a theater—a *Dramaturg* and a director—will work for many months with a young author in order to develop a workmanlike play from the promising beginnings the writer brings in.

"We've had several instances where workers—quite inexperienced in the literary area—brought us plays, which were then very carefully and very sensitively developed until they were ready for production. In fact, several workers have become playwrights in this way."

Some of the theaters, said Hamburger, have workshops where aspiring playwrights meet regularly with theater professionals. "We call these playwrights 'working writers.' If they show any promise, they have every opportunity of working professionally with the theaters. But most of the larger plants have their own theatrical groups—the workers' theaters—and some of these playwrights prefer to work with them."

Commenting on the complementary relationship between new plays and classics in a GDR theater's repertory, Dieter Klein said, "At the Volksbühne our aim is to develop a popular socialist theater—classics and contemporary plays, but not on a percentage basis. We think it's just as much our job to treat our cultural inheritance properly as to do contemporary plays."

The night before talking with Klein we saw the Volksbühne's production of *The Robbers* by Schiller. The staging captured the spirit of the band of young rebels and all the revolutionary implications of this classic in a way that made it seem amazingly contemporary. At the end there was an ovation from the audience.

Because of the production's freshness, we assumed it was an early performance in the play's run. "You saw one of the last performances," Klein informed us. "We played it seventy-seven times." Far from being on its way out of the repertory for lack of an audience, *The Robbers* was playing to full houses.

"We organize our repertory in a very intensive way," Klein explained. "If we want to stage a large number of plays of very high quality, we can't keep a play running indefinitely." To keep a hit on the boards until the audience for it has been exhausted—as is customary in the U.S.—"would cut off the liveliness of our repertory. We wouldn't be able to produce enough new things." One of the successful new plays in the Volksbühne's repertory was *The Award,* by a worker/ playwright, Regina Weicker. In addition to staging *The Award* in one of its own theaters, the Volksbühne had also put on special performances of the play in plants.

In the early days of the GDR one of those most active in encouraging the development of new playwrights was Brecht. "Brecht didn't produce only his own plays. He was always looking for new plays," Wolfgang Pintzka, a Berliner Ensemble director, told us. In the early fifties Brecht directed *Katzgraben,* by a new playwright, Erwin Strittmatter. "It was about the agrarian reform, the changes in people when they suddenly become owners," said Pintzka. (During the post-war agrarian reform the property of the Junkers, the traditionally militarist group from which the majority of Nazi officers came, and that of the other big landowners was expropriated. The property of *all* war criminals, including those with small holdings, was expropriated. The redistribution of this property to agricultural workers and small farmers was a preliminary step toward socialist production in agriculture.)

A tremendous success, *Katzgraben* was "in the repertory for five or six years, and we staged it again recently," related Pintzka, adding: "The play also had a great effect on theater theories—in writing about it Brecht made fundamental comments on contemporary theater." (*Katzgraben,* stated Brecht, "is a historical comedy. The author puts his period on show and favors the progressive, productive, revolutionary forces.") Today the Berliner Ensemble continues Brecht's policy of working with new playwrights.

A theater's relationship with playwrights must, of course, include financial aspects. A GDR theater can arrange a state subsidy lasting from six months to two years for writers with works in progress. Authors also receive a stipulated percentage each time a play is performed. But even with what would be called a smash hit in the U.S., a playwright can expect no six-figure film and TV offers.

"That couldn't possibly happen here," declared Erhard Schmidt, who is a playwright as well as an actor, at the Volkstheater Rostock. "There are no privately owned film companies here that would make such offers to a writer. There are no private film companies at all. Besides, no author would need the excess money."

True enough. Every writer needs security but no writer needs "excess money." When material rewards become gigantic and an end in themselves, they mark the end of creativity.

GDR authors are well compensated for their work but there are greater rewards. Erwin Strittmatter recalls one of them: After submitting *Katzgraben* to the Berliner Ensemble, he tried to convince himself—as insulation against the possibility of rejection—that he would get a letter from the theater opening with, "We regret." Instead he got a telegram from Brecht himself: "Play accepted. Please come for discussion." The young playwright read the wire and "ran into the wood, because you can't shout in the streets of a small town without being taken for a lunatic."[9]

How plays are chosen for production reflects not only the way the theater but the social system itself works.

When a U.S. producer—that is, theater businessman—selects a play, his overriding consideration is its profit potential. If a play has social value, the producer will consider this reason enough to drop it. On those rare occasions when a producer decides the times are ripe for a play with a social theme, he'll make sure to select one that won't disturb a "good white liberal audience."

The procedure followed by a "public" theater is simply a variation of this same formula. Joseph Papp's selection of plays, according to his own description, is "unilateral." But Papp's "unilateral" action is of an extremely limited nature.

One year Papp dropped new plays and announced the substitution of classics. Later he dropped most of the classics, cutting his program in half because of mammoth financial problems. Whatever specific form they may take, Papp's "unilateral" actions occur in a territory defined for him by the "aims and objectives" of those from whom he must constantly try to get money. In relationship to his staff and actors, however, his actions certainly are "unilateral": Since he does the hiring and firing, there's no opinion he's bound to listen to, no collective to which he's responsible. His sole responsibility at Lincoln Center was to a board of big corporate names, and this is his sole responsibility at his remaining theater.

IN THE GDR the method of play selection is equally intrinsic to the social system. "Almost all plays put on originate from proposals within the theater itself," said Maik Hamburger. "The ones who propose the repertory are the *Dramaturgen.** The final decision is the *Intendant's* but in most cases he listens to the *Dramaturg*. He knows these proposals have been arrived at after careful consideration and consultation with other members of the theater. And one of the primary considerations is the wishes of the directors, who are members of the theater."

At the same time, all the proposed plays are discussed by the theater's artistic/economic council—an elected body of actors, directors, set designers, etc. Any member of the theater may participate in these discussions, but only council members may vote on final proposals to be made to the *Intendant*. "The *Intendant*," explained Hamburger, "is responsible to the theater on one hand, and he's legally responsible to the state on the other." Although "all final decisions are made by the *Intendant*," this does not diminish the importance of the theater workers' role in the decision-making process. "The *Intendant* has the possibility of acting on his own—but it doesn't work that way in practice," stated Hamburger. "Our labor regulations include collective discussions. The *Intendant* would be taking a great responsibility if he made a decision contrary to his artistic advisors. He'd have a great responsibility if things went wrong. Everyone would say, 'Well, I told you so!'"

At the Gorki, Fritz Rödel concurred. "The law says the *Intendant* can choose a play against the advice of his council—but he certainly won't do it! If he did, plenty of problems would crop up!"

To illustrate the decision-making process, Rödel told us how one very successful production, *Weather For Tomorrow*, was added to the Gorki's repertory. "One group was very much for it, another group

*Literary adviser, plural form.

very much against it, and a third group was unsure. The decision to do it was made against a minority. If we hadn't applied a simple democratic rule"—majority vote—"we wouldn't have produced it."

What about the allegation—made by Papp and many others—that artists in a socialist country are "pressured" by the state into carrying out a program? "If that were true," responded Klaus Pfützner of the Association of Theater Workers, "our actors wouldn't care to do contemporary plays and audiences wouldn't want to see them."

"It's especially important," commented Fritz Rödel, "for our theater to take into account the personal views of our actors. There has to be the necessary interest for a play to be effective—and if anyone plays against his will, it can't be effective."

IN THE U.S. a producer has no motivation for discussing a play with the cast after it's been staged. If it's a hit, that's all that matters. If it's not, it soon closes. Even in those few theaters where there's some form of a company, open discussion is very difficult. Since management can hire and fire unilaterally—and because of the intense competition engendered by the system—criticism can hardly be exchanged in an objective (let alone friendly) spirit.

But in the GDR's permanent ensembles there are ongoing discussions of plays and productions, of collective work and the work of individuals by such groups as the artistic/economic council, trade union collectives, various committees, etc. In addition, "once every season a meeting is held with the entire ensemble in which the coming repertory is discussed," related Maik Hamburger. "Another meeting is held with all the members of the theater to evaluate the results of the previous season's work. At these meetings anyone—from the *Intendant* to a small-part actor, an assistant director or a prompter—can say what they think of the work that's been done and the proposals for the coming period."

But *do* the theater workers say what they think? Because of what they've been told about socialist countries, most people in the U.S., we remarked, would think the theater workers say only what the *Intendant* wants to hear.

Hamburger smiled. "There is no insecurity so people can be very critical. I've been at meetings where the *Intendant* really had to duck."

THE SAME principles that operate in play selection apply to decision making in all phases of a GDR theater's activities. "We apply the principle of democratic centralism: collective discussion and then a decision by the *Intendant*," related Fritz Rödel.

"Democratic centralism"? These appear as scare words in the Western media and would, we said, be interpreted by most U.S. theater workers to mean that the state through its representative imposes a decision on the theater against the wishes of the ensemble.

On the contrary, replied Joachim Tenschert, a director and deputy to the *Intendant* at the Deutsches. The theater, he said, is composed of a "collective—and the collective is a group of experts, people who know their business. Take Brecht, Helene Weigel, Hanns Eisler, Paul Dessau and Caspar Neher*—all experts. When they worked in one theater they were a collective and a collective includes different opinions." (Tenschert, at one time *Chefdramaturg* at the Berliner Ensemble, has directed plays abroad for several years, including *Coriolanus* at the National Theater in London.)

Because of the new relations in socialist society, Tenschert continued, "it's quite evident that there are also new possibilities in the theater. Several social groups—elected committees—function as advisers and participate very broadly in decisions. The centralism principle—surrounded by all these democratic controls—applies because the *Intendant* makes the final decisions.

"The actor, the composer, the designer—they all must contribute. But one *Intendant* must organize, otherwise it would be like an orchestra without a conductor. You can choose the word—ensemble or collective—but in the theater or socialist society as a whole, it's a process, not a fixed fact. All this is alive."

And at the Dresden State Theater, Gerhard Piens remarked, "Of course we have a central leadership in the GDR—I don't want to misrepresent democratic centralism. There is a clear cut leadership and a central plan that is discussed and corrected locally.

"In our case our plan is our theater program," which originates in the theater. "We discuss it with the theater workers, the trade union, our spectators council, with the Party leadership, with the elected city council, with the Ministry of Culture—everyone must be convinced."

"But it's our experience that no basic changes are made during these discussions," pointed out Horst Seeger, who heads the Dresden State Opera.

*Helene Weigel, the actress and wife of Brecht; Hanns Eisler and Paul Dessau, composers; Caspar Neher, set designer.

"They all realize we know our area," agreed Dresden actor Johannes Wieke.

"It's the policy of our state that decisions are made where there's the greatest knowhow," emphasized Piens. "Decisions concerning the theater can be best made by the theater. But we must convince others. This is sometimes tiring. We want to act according to mood—but that's not scientific. We need reasons for what we do."

Such a relationship between the theater and other social groups comes into conflict with the views of those U.S. cultural workers who assert that art should be independent from society. It's understandable that many U.S. artists would feel this way, since they base their ideas on what they *know* about the treatment of art in this country and what they *hear* about its treatment in socialist countries.

But art has never existed apart from society, and it never will. Whatever the social system, art has a relationship to the total society. What is important is the *nature* of that relationship, and the basis for that is determined by the nature of the social system.

In the U.S., a "public" theater must have its program endorsed by a corporate board of directors, whose interests clash with those of artists and all working people. In the GDR the social groups that must endorse a theater's program not only represent the interests of theater workers, but theater workers themselves play a prominent role in these bodies.

"An actor is a worker whose work is art—but life is not limited to creating art. In the GDR almost every artist has some function aside from art," pointed out Gerhard Piens. Each of the theater workers we met in Dresden told us of his own social function.

Johannes Wieke is a part of the leadership of the Dresden State Theater, and an elected member of the regional council, a state body, in the area. Horst Seeger is a member of the regional committee of the Socialist Unity Party (SUP), and president of the regional committee of the Association of Theater Workers. Before his recent arrival in Dresden, Gerhard Piens had been president of the trade union in a Berlin drama school, "and I'll soon have a function here. Our aim is for everyone to take part. We have parents committees, buyers committees, spectators councils in the theaters. People are elected from plants and delegated to discuss everything." Many theater people are elected members of state bodies. Ruth Berghaus, a director at the Deutsche

State Opera, and formerly *Intendantin** of the Berliner Ensemble, is a people's representative in the Berlin City Council. Thus through elected bodies and social groups, as well as in many other forms, socialist society encourages close ties between artists and the people.

The plan for each theater is discussed with the local body of elected representatives. "The *Intendanten*** come in to discuss their programs with the cultural committee, which includes actors, writers, artists, the editor of a church paper—as well as workers particularly interested in culture," described Dr. Horst Oswald, Berlin's City Councillor for Culture. In addition to the elected members of a committee, "the council calls on citizens with a particular interest in that area to meet with the committee—they have a voice but no vote. The more broadly we work, the more democratic our work."

"This," as Gerhard Piens put it, "is the workers and farmers state in practice. We are the state."

Not only do cultural workers play an important part in this state, but most of the cultural workers we met have working-class backgrounds. "My father and mother were workers. All my ancestors were either workers or farmers from way back," said Piens. Johannes Wieke was a "worker's child," an orphan who "didn't know my real parents." Dieter Klein's father was a worker and he himself was a toolmaker. Ruth Berghaus' father was a worker. Horst Oswald's father was a plumber, his mother a sales clerk; he himself was a machinist. Joachim Tenschert's father was a mechanic. Pilka Häntzsche's mother was a cigarette worker, her father a mechanic. Fritz Rödel comes "from a working-class family and I myself was a worker—carpenter, miner and construction worker."

Rödel, Piens and Tenschert attended the Workers and Farmers College, the post-war avenue to higher education for men and women with a working-class or farm background. "We had to give special help at that time to children of workers and farmers," explained Rödel. "We don't need this any more because now everyone has the opportunity to go from a regular school to a university."

The job security in the GDR doesn't mean that a person is tied down in one place if he or she wants to make a change, as the backgrounds of these same theater workers illustrate. Horst Seeger, for instance, was a music critic and then *Chefdramaturg* at Berlin's *Komische Oper*

*Overall director of a theater, feminine form.
**Plural form.

(Comic Opera) before joining the Dresden opera. Gerhard Piens taught dramatic history, held posts at a film as well as a drama school, and was a theater critic. And Dieter Klein's career illustrates how a GDR citizen has leeway in moving from one field to an entirely different one.

"How I came to be in the theater is directly related to our state and situation here," he said. In 1959 the twenty-three-year-old Klein was working in a dental equipment plant. In that year the movement of socialist work brigades was launched. (Today the workforce at each enterprise is organized into such brigades, collectives of workers whose aim is to "work, learn and live in a socialist way.") "Artists became part of these brigades," related Klein. Helene Weigel and Benno Besson, a director and now Volksbühne *Intendant,* joined Klein's brigade.

"I never lost contact with Besson," said Klein. "First I worked at the Volksbühne as a voluntary cooperator, and later as a full-time member of the ensemble. This is quite typical of the way many people developed."

The GDR, as Gerhard Piens said, is "the workers and farmers state in practice." And the democratic way the citizens of this state function often comes as a surprise to people from the West. Dieter Klein told us of an example:

Members of the Volksbühne were invited by the regional administration and the steel workers union in Terni, Italy, to conduct a seminar in a steel mill there. One of the subjects discussed during the sessions—attended by one hundred steel workers—was Brecht's *The Exception And The Rule.* "At the end of the two-week seminar," related Klein, "a steel worker who'd always voted for the Right said he'd learned a lot about social ideas from Brecht's play. And he said he'd also changed his ideas about the GDR. He felt the discussion was on such a high level, so democratic, that it must prove how things are done in the GDR—because no one could pretend for such a long time."

4. Conflicts On Stage and Off

For a number of years Ronald Holloway has covered theater in the Federal Republic of Germany and West Berlin for the British magazine *Plays and Players*. From time to time his *Plays and Players'* assignment also takes him to the GDR.

After Holloway goes to the theater in the FRG or West Berlin, he reviews the plays. After an occasional foray to the GDR theater, he reviews the system—always giving it a closing notice. Even when he finds something to praise in the GDR theater, he manages to interpret it as a reflection on the socialist state.

Of the GDR's celebration of its twenty-fifth anniversary in 1974, Holloway wrote:

... the East Berlin theatres let out all the stops. Chief among the festivities was the fortnight presentation, *Spektakel 2,* under *Intendant* Benno Besson at the Volksbühne; in a virtuoso display of 12 original productions by contemporary playwrights, every nook and cranny in this mammoth house was used in a "life experience" review of the past and present. Five visits would have been required to see everything; capacity crowds reaching a thousand nightly were richly entertained until the wee hours of the morning; and refreshments flowed like milk and honey to crown the festive occasion.[1]

One could hardly find a more enthusiastic response to a theatrical experience, nor a more striking contradiction to what usually emerges in the Western media as the "gray" existence of "East Germans." Still what Holloway gives with one or two sentences he tries to take away with his others:

A critical as well as a commercial success, one wonders why this noteworthy and evidently widely appreciated spectacle should vanish so quickly from the boards after the official celebrations passed. An experience that offers not only sober reflection on the past but also satirical chuckles on the foibles of the present, *Spektakel 2* deserves a revival if not a sequel.[2]

One can only wonder how any theater could continue a "virtuoso display" of twelve productions in "every nook and cranny" of a "mammoth house" till the "wee hours" indefinitely. And one must also wonder how it would be possible for the "capacity crowds" celebrating a special anniversary to keep coming to a theater till the "wee hours"— since those were crowds of working people and students.

Holloway, however, prefers to attribute *Spektakel 2*'s fortnight run to a sinister motive:

Satire and self-criticism in one bag provide a healthy sign of a stable government and free society, even if only for a fortnight.[3]

When Holloway alleges that "satire and self-criticism" appear on a GDR stage "only for a fortnight," he feels confident that his readers' only information about GDR theater comes from *Plays and Players* and other bourgeois sources—which somehow neglect to tell them that "satire and self-criticism" are integral features of GDR plays, and a satirical theater, the Distel, performs year-round in Berlin. As for the twelve plays produced for *Spektakel 2*, they were "the result," said Dieter Klein of the Volksbühne, "of our continuing cooperation with playwrights"—who were obviously encouraged to create works of "satire and self-criticism." And long before Holloway wrote that "*Spektakel 2* deserves a revival if not a sequel," the Volksbühne and other GDR theaters were planning great celebrations for May 1975, when the thirtieth anniversary of the liberation from fascism was observed.

ALTHOUGH IT's impossible to find out what's really happening in a GDR theater from Ronald Holloway, he does offer an occasional clue—albeit in distorted form. For example, he suggests that there's a revolutionary difference between theater in the socialist GDR and capitalist countries when he states:

Perhaps the main difference between East German theatre and its counterpart in the West is the audience: the dramatist there is writing for the *mass* public while the playwright here is serving only the elite . . .[4]

If one wishes to single out the "main difference" between GDR theater and its "counterpart in the West"—presumably in the FRG—one must recognize that it lies not within the theater but within the total society. The FRG is a capitalist society, and those who control it are the counterparts of those controlling the U.S. Like their U.S. equivalents, the FRG rulers bombard *all* sections of the public with racist, chauvinist, militarist, anti-Communist, anti-Soviet ideology. The social system in the GDR moves counter to this in every respect, and its creation of a "mass" instead of an "elite" theater public is just one reflection of this fact.

As for the theater directly: one cannot say that any single element accounts for the "main difference" between GDR and bourgeois theaters. If the GDR playwright writes for the "*mass* public," then the playwright's role has changed just as much as the audience's. *Each* facet of theater in a socialist country undergoes revolutionary change, otherwise there would be no "*mass* public" for the theater. Take, for example, the role of critics.

"Socialist society has changed the function of critics," commented Gisela May, the internationally known interpreter of Brecht's songs, and a member of the Berliner Ensemble. "We have a new audience now. In the past critics wrote for the intelligentsia only. Today a critic must stimulate an interest in theater-going among working people." But critics are only one aspect of a very broad process, which is in the first place the responsibility of theater workers themselves.

"Our theater has roots in social conditions that demand a new level of quality and inclusion of the public in our activities," said Dieter Klein. "At the Volksbühne we have friendship agreements with different enterprises—a lighting equipment plant, a housing construction combinate and an airport." All the theaters have such agreements—with plants, collective farms, universities and schools (theater-going is an intrinsic part of the educational program at each grade level, and several cities have a year-round repertory theater for children). These agreements are the basis for many activities: subscriptions, closed-house performances at the theater, performances at the workplace. Plays are also discussed at the workplace during rehearsal and after they open.

"The characters in *Weather For Tomorrow* are workers in an auto plant, and when we produced it the director and actors went to a plant that makes trucks," related Fritz Rödel at the Gorki. "They discussed it at length with the workers until they were sure their ideas for interpreting were right. The play was successful. The workers wanted to see it."

Playwrights, directors and actors also have their own individual relationship with a particular work brigade in a plant. "I have such a relationship with a brigade in a big cable plant," Gisela May told us. "The members of this brigade attend rehearsals at the theater, and after the play opens they discuss it with the other actors and with me. And together we worked out a program on Brecht's seventy-fifth birthday which was presented at the plant. These brigade members sang or played in a scene, some of them for the first time." Such experience is as valuable to artists as to workers. "It enlarges your outlook—you get new impressions," commented May. "And you hear reasonable, open opinions. They really are very frank in telling me what they think."

To refer to the "*mass* public" in the GDR, as Holloway does, is to imply that there may also be an "elite" public. In the GDR the "*mass* public" is the *only* one. All audiences are audiences of working people, including intellectuals allied to the working class. And as the relationship between audience and theater suggests, this is not only a new audience but an audience that plays a qualitatively new role.

"What Brecht called the art of the spectator plays a very important role in the revolutionary theater in a socialist society," said Dr. Ursula Püschel, editor of *Theater in the German Democratic Republic.* "In bourgeois societies, the contact between art and life—which existed in the Elizabethan age—is lost more and more. In our society the gap between art and life is closing more and more and sometimes the contact is very close."

FOR A BOURGEOIS critic to say that the dramatist in the GDR is "writing for the *mass* public," while the playwright in the West is "serving only the elite," is not to offer a compliment to the former. To such a critic, writing for the "*mass* public" means "writing down" to an audience—

an idea that turns up frequently in the U.S., where many intellectuals attribute the low level of mass-media writing to the dictates of the public.

Those who hold this idea fail to recognize that mass-media writers turn out not what audiences but corporate sponsors order. Although TV executives say their programming—racism, violence, sex, escapism—is what the public wants, one should be aware that in no area of U.S. life do the people get what they want. They get what the corporations give them—unless they react against it, compelling certain adjustments.

If the low level of the mass media could be ascribed to the mass public, then there'd be a sharp difference between the mass media and the theater, attended by an "elite" audience. This contrast cannot be verified by reality. But the "elite" audience (those with at least a comfortable income) won't demand change in the theater. Contrary to bourgeois thought, the level of the theater will rise through its ties with the people—which will develop as the people's movements fight for cultural alternatives.

Meanwhile, masses in the U.S. have been given no reason to expect anything at all of theater, or even to think of it. But the new "*mass public*" in the GDR does have real expectations of theater—and the theater is responsive to them.

"We create theater for the people—and not only to amuse an audience, but to give them the possibility of finding their way on questions of everyday life with greater understanding," said Christoph Funke, theater critic for *Der Morgen,* newspaper of the Liberal Democratic Party, author of books on the theater and a leader of the Association of Theater Workers.

"We see theater," he continued, "as an important stimulus in helping people to discover all the possibilities of their own personality, to sharpen their thinking, to develop their feelings more deeply—and to use all this for life and for constructing our socialist society." While developing socialist society is the common goal of GDR citizens, "individual paths leading to that goal can be quite distinct—and there are discussions and sharp differences about them. And individuals can encounter problems and conflicts on their paths that can become even tragic.

"Nevertheless," Funke emphasized, "the common conception for improving our existing socialist society is being carried out—and more so every day. And we must use all possible imagination, knowledge and spiritual power toward this goal. Within this great task the theater has an important place, its own specific place. But its place is within this task—not outside it."

Although the theater carries out this task in a variety of ways, its treatment of the conflicts of contemporary socialist life is of particular interest. A look at three plays in GDR repertories—*Laughing Pigeon, Campanella And The Commander* and *The New Sorrows of Young W*—will offer an idea of contemporary themes that absorb GDR theater workers and audiences.

FEW U.S. plays deal with the central subject of GDR drama: the lives, the conflicts of working people.

In *Laughing Pigeon*, by Helmut Baierl, the characters are a brigade of steel workers with a variety of human problems. One married worker is involved with another woman. Another worker, new to the brigade, served for years as manager of another plant. "For many years he managed a big steel mill, but because he made mistakes in his behavior toward people he's had to start all over—which of course he finds very difficult," related Fritz Rödel.

On one level *Laughing Pigeon* is funny, its humor satirical. The title character—a young worker nicknamed Laughing Pigeon simply because he laughs so much—is going to get married. But first he wants an apartment. "This is pretty difficult," said Rödel, "because usually you get it afterwards." But Laughing Pigeon has friends in the plant who make films. They go to the area housing office with him, set up their camera (which has no film in it) and tell the staff members they're making a film on a steel worker's life. Laughing Pigeon gets his apartment "because the people in the housing office don't want to appear to be bureaucrats."

The underlying theme of the play is, however, a serious one: the role of workers—the leading force in the new society—in decision making, co-determination, in the enterprises. "The question is: how big a part should workers play in management decisions," explained Rödel. "This question plays a big role in our literature because it plays a big role in our lives."

This is an historically new question: Before the founding of the Soviet Union, "there was no experience in socialist democracy. Of course, the working class did develop democratic forms in its struggles"—but only after the October Revolution was the working class confronted with the question of managing a state and its economy.

"This question," Rödel went on, "is very complex. In the management of the economic process, the manager in a plant must say the final word"—as the *Intendant* does in the theater. "But at the same time the possibilities must be created so that all the workers are included in making final decisions. Socialist society gives everyone the possibility of developing their talents, so everyone must also have the chance of applying them. Our society tries out all sorts of solutions for this problem—and that's why this question turns up again and again in our literature."

In *Laughing Pigeon* the conflict revolves around a decision to close down the steel plant. The problem created has no resemblance to what happens in the U.S. when a factory is shut down and workers are left jobless. In the socialist GDR, where every worker is assured of a job and opportunities for acquiring greater skills rather than being downgraded, the problem is that management made the decision to close without the workers' participation.

"The workers are angry—they understand that this is not the time for closing this steel mill," said Helmut Baierl, who spent six months in a steel plant before writing the play. "On the day they discover the plant is to be closed, the former manager of a steel mill joins their brigade. This man needs only one day to understand that he no longer has any authority. The workers integrate him into their brigade and use him—but not with intrigue—against their own manager, to criticize their manager and stop him from turning into what the former manager had been. What comes out is that the working class is the leading class, that management must be very sensitive to its special needs—and that no one can act against the workers' role."

What *Laughing Pigeon* indicates is that, contrary to unending allegations from the West, people in a socialist country have an unprecedented say over their lives.

TO GET AN idea of the diversity of questions dealt with in plays on life in a socialist country, "You shouldn't look just at the little GDR," said Jochen Ziller, *Chefdramaturg* of Henschelverlag Kunst und Gesellschaft, publishers in the arts. "You have to look at the whole socialist community."

Many plays from the other socialist countries are performed by

GDR theaters. One of these is *Campanella And The Commander,* by Soviet playwright Michail Shatrov, also author of *Weather For Tomorrow.* It probes the conflict that occurs when individuals try to put their ideals into everyday practice. This is not an old-style treatment of the conflict between ideals and reality—the individual's loss of ideals and acceptance of things as they are—but a treatment of the struggle to change reality in a way possible only in socialist society.

In *Campanella And The Commander* a group of students sets up a commune in a new territory in the Soviet Unon. Their commune bears no resemblance to U.S. student communes of the sixties. These Soviet young people aren't seeking "alternate life styles" in isolation from society. Society has given them the responsibility for carrying out an important construction task. The play's situation, however, barely suggests the scope of its concerns.

"The play's theme is the future of the human being in a socialist society," commented Fritz Rödel. "The central philosophical question is whether socialism should distinguish itself from capitalism only by new housing, etc., or also by a new kind of living together among human beings—and by developing the individuality of each person. These young people want to live according to the laws of the future in a perfect mini-society."

To carry out this plan, they take as their model an organizational form of the Russian Revolution: a commander and a commission. The commander in this case is "practical," while Campanella—who gets his nickname from an Italian utopianist—is a dreamer. The conflict between them involves such questions as collective life, socialist democracy, the responsibility of the individual.

Campanella And The Commander "deals with matters that really move the people involved in the development of our socialist society," stated Hans Dieter Mäde, who directed the Gorki's production of this play. He went on to say:

The play is about young people, but the questions it puts about our expectations for the future and our present-day actions, about ideal and reality, concern not only them. . . . the author confronts the ensemble and the audience with interesting situations which need a decision, because he raises genuine and intelligent questions and, above all, because he has created a whole number of colorful and contradictory figures. They are young people . . . who do not just complain. but who are active, argue a lot, insist on having fun, do not forget love and who discover how serious their responsibility is for the whole society.[5]

The Gorki drew in as production advisers for *Campanella And The Commander* Berlin university students who had been involved in a special project in Kazakhstan, USSR. When the students were asked how they felt in taking on this responsibility for the theater, one replied:

Of course we found this quite normal and took ourselves very seriously because we were familiar with the milieu and problems . . . However, we soon noticed that, while we were able to give the company advice, there was far more in the play than we had imagined.

You mean [said the interviewer] that the issue is not just one of opening up virgin land?

That was only the subject. The real issue is the future and what it should be like, and above all what type of human being we need to make this future reality.[6]

SOVIET PLAYS have had a place of special importance in GDR theater since its first days, when they helped develop the beginnings of socialist consciousness among the people.

"In the fifties it hadn't yet been decided if our population would go the way of socialism. Through Soviet plays both our actors and our public got to know about socialist life," said Klaus Pfützner of the Association of Theater Workers.

Most actors in the early GDR theater had come out of the theater in the old Germany, and "bourgeois actors can have anti-Communist prejudices. But because these were serious actors, they didn't just memorize their parts. They studied them. They didn't just deliver their lines. They tried to penetrate the characters' backgrounds. This was a first step for our actors and directors in learning about communism. Their prejudices were destroyed because these were great plays and they recognized them as true. Antagonistic actors became friends—not through reading newspapers or political schools, but because they had played these parts concerned with real life."

A particularly important Soviet play produced by the GDR theater was *Optimistic Tragedy,* described by Gerhard Piens of the Dresden State Theater as "one of the great plays of the Russian Revolution. It deals," he said, "with the transformation of a battalion of anarchists into conscious revolutionaries." Since the battalion's commander is a woman, *Optimistic Tragedy* helped people understand that women must play leading roles in all areas of socialist life.

Cement, a play by GDR writer Heiner Müller, is based on a great

Soviet novel dealing with the Soviet people's struggle to build up their country—which was devasted by World War I—after the 1917 Revolution and in the face of counterrevolution and imperialist military intervention, including by the U.S. "Müller took this theme and together with the fight against counterrevolution, he especially underlined the relationship between men and women," said director Wolfgang Pintzka of the Berliner Ensemble. Pintzka's own first experience with Soviet plays came about in an unforgettable manner.

"My father was Jewish—and the only reason I'm alive is that my father built racing cars for Hitler and later on tanks. When people asked Herman Göring how he could let a Jew build tanks, Göring said, '*I* decide who's Jewish.' I was lucky. My wife, who is also Jewish, lost eleven members of her family. They were killed in concentration camps."

The father's connections in high places weren't enough to keep the son out of the Nazi Army. "In 1945 when I was sixteen, I was lucky enough to be captured by Soviet soldiers. As a prisoner of war in the Soviet Union—where I met anti-fascist Germans in exile—I learned to think. And while I was a prisoner of war, I acted in a theater. On May Day 1950 I returned to Berlin—and I saw my first post-war play, *Mother Courage*. And in 1953 the next lucky thing in my life happened. I met Brecht."

The New Sorrows of Young W caused a stir in the GDR. It caused a stir of a very different kind in the West, where the media published rumors of an "East German youth rebellion," "dissatisfaction with the system," etc.

Ronald Holloway accorded *The New Sorrows of Young W* the honor of at least three reviews. By way of introduction to one of them, he tacitly acknowledged that satire *does* turn up in GDR plays for more than "a fortnight." But in Holloway's interpretation, satire in a GDR play is directed against the socialist system. Writing this time for a U.S. publication, he stated:

East German theater is imbued with a rich vein of humor intuitively directed toward a radical reformation affecting the future in ways the party's present grasp of the situation cannot.[7]

Although *Young W*'s direction is presumably beyond the "party's present grasp," it isn't beyond Holloway's. In this review he places it in the "radical reformation" category, in another he calls it a "revolutionary play." Although he's all for "radical reformation" and "revolution" in the socialist GDR, he never expresses any desire for revolution, "radical reformation" or even the *slightest* reformation in the capitalist FRG—making it clear that what he has in mind for the GDR is *counter*revolution.

That Holloway's view is from stage far right becomes additionally apparent when he attempts to explain why a play "affecting the future" in the way he claims would be performed in GDR theaters:

One should not be surprised that such activity thrives in a communist state, for, as Dietrich Bonhoeffer's *Letters from Prison* aptly illustrates, freedom is primarily a state of consciousness and not the conscious property of the state.[8]

When Holloway uses Bonhoeffer's letters to explain why *The New Sorrows of Young W* is produced in the GDR, he takes his place among those who equate socialism with fascism—since these letters were written while Bonhoeffer was a prisoner of the Nazis.

In asserting that "freedom is primarily a state of consciousness and not the conscious property of a state," Holloway ignores the distinction between freedom and the desire for it: Fascist state power could not confiscate the people's desire for freedom—but it could prevent them from exercising freedom. The U.S. is not a fascist state, but the state treats freedom as its "conscious property"—and the people must struggle continuously to exercise a degree of it.

Holloway overlooks this distinction for an obvious reason: if he didn't, he'd have to explain why Bonhoeffer's letters weren't published by the Nazis, while *Young W* is produced by the GDR's subsidized state theaters. Even so, Holloway feels the need to offer further reasons for *Young W*'s production:

... an educational process is going on in the theater; the state is allowing its citizens to grow toward fuller maturity—and the play demonstrates where the present limits are being set.[9]

Since for Holloway *Young W* is a play that aims at "radical reformation," one can only wonder: where *are* the "present limits" being set?

When Holloway finally gets to the play itself, this is his view of it:

This modern updating of Germany's revolutionary-minded classic *The Sorrows of Young Werther* features a long-haired Jesus figure backed up by a pop band . . . its attack on the local establishment is in the manner of "angry theater" and promises a bright horizon in the future.[10]

And:

... rebellious, sharp-tongued, long-haired, jeans-wearing youth grapples with the drawbacks of . . . living in a modern authoritarian, socialist society.[11]

And:

... [Young W] engages in a mocking game of finger-pointing, using Goethe's own text at times to put enemies in their place; such boat rocking has not been experienced since Holden Caulfield exploded on the American scene in the early '50s.[12]

In this portrait Young W emerges as a duplicate of the rebellious Western youth of the sixties—jeans-wearing, long-haired, "finger-pointing"—with a dash of Holden Caulfield, the fifties rebel-without-a-cause, thrown in.

But Young W lives in a socialist not a capitalist society, and so Holloway targets his "enemy" for him: the socialist system.

Knowing that other bourgeois writers will offer similar interpretations of *The New Sorrows of Young W,* Holloway proposes staging the play in the FRG where, he says, it would "draw attention to those writers in the East" who have "fought a lonely battle to preserve the freedom to dissent."[13]

It's true that the "battle" into which Holloway would like to recruit Young W—"dissent" against the socialist system—is a "lonely" one. It has few takers in the socialist countries. But has there been anything "lonely" about Young W's reception in the GDR?

The New Sorrows of Young W, by Ulrich Plenzdorf, had its premiere in 1972, and has been produced continuously since then. Eighteen GDR theaters have staged it, and at one time it was presented simultaneously by two Berlin theaters, the Deutsches and the Volksbühne.

As for the play itself: Young W (Edgar Wibeau) breaks away from his sheltered home to strike out on his own, to find a new path for himself. He goes to work in the construction field. He falls in love with a woman engaged to someone else. In his secluded home, he works secretly on an invention his construction brigade tried but failed to perfect. The invention blows up and kills him. The play begins just after Young W's death. From his spot "in eternity," he interrupts other characters to comment on the various stages in his life. In these comments lie much of the play's humor.

In the GDR the play set off what was described to us as a "very wide and very heated" discussion. Why? Was it because the play expresses a dissatisfaction among GDR youth with the social system?

"THIS IS complete nonsense," replied Joachim Tenschert at the Deutsches. "We who staged this play feel one thing must be understood (and we know it's difficult for bourgeois critics to understand it): A critical attitude is not a negative attitude. That's one thing we learned from Brecht."

"In *Young W*," said Dieter Mann, who played the title role in the Deutsches' production, "Plenzdorf was driving at a certain kind of unrest, which is not hostility to the system. Part of this unrest we've overcome, part we're just beginning to overcome. Plenzdorf used the legitimate device of putting these feelings into the mouth of a seventeen-year-old character."

Is the character of Young W a counterpart of rebellious Western youth?

"The theme of this play could have developed only on the socialist pre-conditions in the GDR," responded Tenschert. "Among young people here there's an attitude of searching. But one must analyze whether this is a search without consequences, without results—or whether it involves a critical attitude that helps bring about change. I come from the school of Brecht that considers doubt a very productive attitude. If you look at it philosophically, capitalism—especially in its last phase—has no use for critics because they question its existence.

"This play," he continued, "which has been a sensational success, shows a very young person, just starting out—trying to manage himself, his own life, to find himself as a person. It's up to the spectator to decide whether he does it by proper means or not: The play doesn't offer prefabricated solutions. Everybody can take something from it according to their own situation and experience."

Probing the reasons for Young W's special search—and why it could take place only on socialist pre-conditions—Tenschert said, "The generation of which Young W is a part has had—from their earliest childhood—no negative alternatives. Everything was available for them to become developed personalities."

A generation with "no negative alternatives"! In other words a generation—unlike any in a capitalist country—whose members have never had to settle for a dead-end job, a dead-end life! But an end to "negative alternatives" doesn't bring an end to problems. When young people are in a position to investigate positive alternatives—the various ways they can have a creative life—new conflicts arise. It was the play's treatment of these new conflicts that aroused such intense interest in the GDR.

Commenting on this point Christoph Funke said, "This play treats the problems of a very young person who's looking for his way within our society. He tries to find it at first by breaking out of all collective ties—that's what was at the center of all the discussion.

"I see in the special way of life of this young person," he went on, "a youth's very important attempt to become conscious of his own personality, to express the demands of the individual toward society—together with a recognition of the possibilities in this society for developing one's individuality."

Discussing what he called the play's treatment of "a very special problem that can exist only under socialism," Fritz Rödel said, "Young W is a gifted youth who gets along beautifully in school and has every possibility for the future. He rebels only because his life is so orderly—and leaves his family in order to live according to his own ideas. At first he's pretty anarchistic. When he tries to do something useful for society, he gets killed." The reason for the play's great effect in the GDR, he feels, is that "it evidently catches a certain side of the problems of our very young people. I'm of the generation that took part in great social upheavals. Now our young people are confronted with the question, 'What can I do?' They want to do things in their own way, things nobody tells them to do."

However, he emphasized, the desire "to do things in their own way" doesn't lead GDR young people along the bypaths taken by large numbers of youth in capitalist countries. "Of course, a few of our youth lose their way. But the overwhelming majority of our young people want to confirm their personalities in social life, want to have responsibility. I think this is what accounts for the play's great repercussions. Of course," he added, "this play doesn't show the full dialectics of the problem. It only touches on it."

Among the questions raised in the GDR's discussion of *The New Sorrows of Young W* were: "Is our young generation like the young people in the play? Is Young W typical or not? Is the play's emphasis in the interest of socialist development?"

The answer to the last question, many GDR theater workers feel, depends on how the play is staged. For example, does the staging place a distance between Young W and the spectator, or does it encourage uncritical identification? Are those around Young W made to appear solely responsible for his problems? Or can the spectator see that Young W shares this responsibility?

When the play was performed in the FRG, the manner of staging was, of course predictable. "A play dealing with such a situation is taken up immediately by certain people in the West," noted Rödel. "It was produced in the FRG to be used against us. We're confronted with the fact that our enemies are always looking over our shoulder." But the response in the FRG was sometimes quite different from what anti-socialist forces had in mind.

"I heard of one production in Nuremberg," said Rödel, "where when the curtain went up you didn't see any scenery—only a big GDR flag. The young people in the audience would start to applaud."

For GDR productions young people were invited to act as production advisers. The initial production, in Halle, drew on the opinions of local railway apprentices and students. That these young people were well equipped to help assure a truthful emphasis in the staging is attested to by the comments of one of them, a schoolgirl:

Young W has an urge to do something special, and I think this is general among youth. They are always going through a storm-and-stress period. . . . Plenzdorf did not want to criticize society as such, he wanted to show that young people can also be seen differently, that one should take their needs into account, but differently to the way one generally does this. To tell you the truth, at first I was completely for Young W. Now I'm suddenly with Young W against Young W. One just needs to discuss these things.[14]

OF THE QUESTIONS arising around *The New Sorrows of Young W,* the one of particular interest to us was: Is Young W typical of GDR youth?

From discussion and observation, our own answer would be yes and no.

In his desire to do "something special," Young W *is* typical of GDR youth. But the way he finds to do "something special" is atypical. His searching takes the form of "outsiderism." Overwhelmingly, GDR youth find that their society offers them a multitude of opportunities to do "something special" precisely because of the new relations among human beings. But Young W had not learned to distinguish between individuality and individualism.

To understand the duality of Young W's character, one must

recognize that the ideas of the old society enter the GDR constantly via FRG television and radio—including the idea that a capitalist society offers the individual the chance to "make it," to do "something special" entirely on his own. What the old society really offers young people is the "opportunity" to defer their dreams amidst the chaos of the struggle to survive—until the time comes when they must forget them.

But Young W is in a new situation. The solution of survival-level problems doesn't fall on him. Society has already solved them. As a result, not only does he have the chance to do something special, he can even choose *how* he'll do it. He would be spectacular not only in *what* he does, but the *way* he does it—all by himself!

That Young W can exert such choice in his life, such influence over his own path, is proof enough that socialism has brought life to a new stage. Although Young W's own search to solve the new problems becomes distorted, his odyssey has proved of value to the real life searching of GDR young people.

According to bourgeois critics, when people in a socialist country criticize certain aspects of social development, they are rejecting the social system itself. But what interests GDR citizens is not the allegations of hostile critics, but the search for solutions to new problems. In the GDR the discussion of *The New Sorrows of Young W* was understood to be within a socialist framework.

Although it's elementary that whatever comes out of a socialist country will be distorted by bourgeois ideologists, we nonetheless feel that certain limitations in the handling of its theme make *The New Sorrows of Young W* prone to misinterpretation in the West.

But whatever one's view of the play itself (positive, negative, or somewhere in-between), it seems to us there can be no doubt of the value of the profound, many-faceted discussion it provoked in the GDR—just one example of how "the gap between art and life is closing more and more" in socialist society.

5. U.S. Strategy To Assimilate Protest

Artists were hard hit by the McCarthyite repression of the fifties, as were working people in all categories. It was a time when the U.S. government's singling out of Communists for persecution, blacklisting and imprisonment led to nationwide persecution, blacklisting and imprisonment for people with a variety of political views. It was the time when the U.S. government executed Ethel and Julius Rosenberg despite a world outcry—that included the voice of Bertolt Brecht. It was a time when the great Black artist and leader, Paul Robeson, was barred from the concert stage and the mass media, and when his passport was revoked. After an eight-year battle, the ban on travel was dropped, but not the bars to performance. Thus U.S. government persecution forced Robeson into exile—but not isolation: he was welcomed in the GDR, the USSR, and by progressive people in many Western countries.

By the early fifties the curtain had been rung down on social theater in our country. But the desire for such theater—like the longing for freedom in even the most repressive circumstances—continued its unlimited engagement.

This desire was translated into a burst of activity during the civil rights and anti-war upsurges of the sixties. The Free Southern Theater, Black and white in its first years, an artistic branch of the civil rights movement, toured the South with full-length plays. New Black theater groups came into existence across the country. And street theater, which had vanished with the thirties, was alive once again. At anti-war demonstrations the gigantic figures of the Bread and Puppet Theater were an eerie presence. In the grape and lettuce fields, El Teatro Campesino, a Chicano troupe, performed as part of the United Farm Workers organizing drive. And theaters with such names as Rapid Transit, Guerilla Communications and SDS RAT* put in a feverish but brief appearance.

The war in Vietnam and the worsening crisis at home made the sixties a desperate time for masses of young people. In theater as in the movements for social change as a whole, radical youth cast about for ways to bring fundamental change in the society. They searched for a revolutionary ideology and revolutionary action. They wondered: Who is the enemy, who is the revolutionary force?

The mass media poured out answers. One day the revolutionary force was everyone under thirty. The next day it was those who took the newest, most popular "mind-blowing" drug. Many "revolutionary" forces were named—but the working class was not among them.

Big publishing houses put out books calling for "urban guerilla warfare" in the U.S., then arranged TV talk show appearances for their authors. Influenced by all of this, some young people also spoke of guns, but it was the government that used them—at Jackson State College, at Kent State College, and in Chicago when police assassinated Fred Hampton and other young Black militants.

As many young radicals became increasingly disoriented by this barrage of terror and pseudo-revolutionary ideologies, certain prominent figures moved in to criticize—not for clarification but to discourage any further search for a revolutionary alternative. One of those who played this role was Robert Brustein, dean of Yale School of Drama. In his book *Revolution As Theatre*, he addresses himself to those he calls "the radical young":

The evils of the present system are certainly obvious enough. The war in Indochina and the inertia of the country in face of serious domestic problems (oppression of the blacks, pollution of the environment, economic deterioration) have weakened our faith in the viability of American political institutions. And the Vietnam massacres, the police attacks on the Black Panthers, the gathering threat to rights and liberties, have expressed a side of our national character that we used to identify only with fascist regimes. These evils have been sufficiently denounced . . .[1]

*Students For A Democratic Society Radical Arts Troupe

Only by making such admissions about the "evils of the present system" could Brustein have hoped for a hearing from the "radical young." But he acknowledged "evils" only to short-circuit action against them, saying they have been "sufficiently denounced." Have they? Although the U.S. government was forced to end its genocide in Indochina, its military and economic might is placed on the side of reaction throughout the world, while the crisis at home continues to intensify. Evils have been "sufficiently denounced" only when they are ended.

And one cannot end evils only by denouncing them. One must also "denounce"—and struggle against—those responsible for them. Although Brustein attributes these "evils" to "our national character," this hardly seems a convincing enemy—particularly in view of the nationwide majority sentiment against the war in Vietnam. But Brustein goes on to warn the "radical young" against placing responsibility for "evils" where it belongs:

... [these evils] have been rehearsed so often lately that we are now in danger of producing a melodrama on the stage of American politics where the "Other"—an enemy invariably identified with the "Establishment"—is assumed to be uniquely guilty of cankers that may be ravaging us all.[2]

By asserting that the "Establishment" is not "uniquely guilty" of the "cankers that may be ravishing us all," Brustein is giving us yet another version of the "we are all guilty" refrain. If, as Brustein tells us, the people have no enemy but instead are their own enemy, then the Vietnamese victims of genocide and the assassinated Blacks share the guilt for being murdered with their murderers. In fact, for all practical purposes, the Vietnamese and Blacks become even *more* guilty since the genocidal attacks against them have already been "sufficiently denounced"—making Brustein available to come to the defense of the "Establishment," or more precisely, the corporate forces controlling this country.

Although "Establishment" spokesmen forever warn artists against "mixing" art with politics, they themselves never follow this dictum. This is demonstrated by Brustein, as he proceeds with his advice to the "radical young":

If we do not continue to preserve high standards for our art (regardless of charges of "elitism"), then we are merely exchanging one form of mediocrity for another; and if we do not try to purify radical politics through frank analysis and honest criticism, then the politics of the country will remain precisely the same, regardless of who takes power.[3]

It must have come as a surprise to the "radical young" to learn that we have to "preserve high standards for our art," since most radicals are aware that art must be rescued from the Neanderthal "standards" now perverting it. And standards in art cannot be changed without power. But when Brustein asserts that the "politics of the country" could "remain precisely the same, regardless of who takes power," he is attempting to convince the "radical young" that there's no relationship between power and what goes on in a country, including its standards of art.

It's true that whether a Nixon, a Ford or a Carter enters the White House, the basic "politics of the country" will "remain precisely the same." But when a Democrat or Republican takes office, he doesn't *take* power. He *represents* power: the power of those controlling the country. And Brustein wants this power to stay where it is.

This is why he tells the "radical young" that the politics of the country can remain precisely the same, regardless of who takes power. If this is so, the "radical young" have no incentive to fight for change— for the power of the working class and its allies to replace the class power of corporate monopoly. When Brustein speaks of the need for "frank analysis and honest criticism" in order to "purify radical politics," it is because he wants to "purify radical politics" of any idea of the desirability of a change in power.

Brustein goes on to say that if he is "harsh" in his "critique of the style of the young radicals," it is because "I feel closer to them than to their antagonists on the Right, and I am therefore more despondent when I see them failing their promise."[4]

Although claiming to be "despondent" when he saw young radicals "failing their promise," Brustein did all he could to assure failure. Attempting to split them from the very forces that can help them realize their promise, he duplicated what is said by their open "antagonists on the Right": The "greatest threat we face today is from totalitarian thinking—both from the right and the left."[5]

With these remarks Brustein became yet another prominent figure in the arts to equate right and left, to make it appear that the two opposites—fascism and socialism—are one and the same. This reflects the concerted effort by those controlling the arts, and society as a whole, to prevent emergence of an independent alternative in the arts, as in society as a whole. This effort takes many forms.

IT WASN'T difficult for Brustein to criticize the "radical young": They were vulnerable to attack precisely because they reflected the super-revolutionary ideas made available to them in so many ways by the "establishment." Ultra-left ideas accounted for the rapid demise of many organizations, including theaters, of the sixties and early seventies. But even after these groups were gone, the "establishment" found ways to help the ideas that killed them live on. Some of these can be found in *Guerilla Street Theater*, published by Avon Books, a division of the Hearst Corporation.

In this book in an article titled *"In Defense of Combative Theater,"* Charles Brover writes:

In 1970 I asked my students to read some modern drama from China, particularly some pieces written during the Great Proletarian Cultural Revolution. The students were disappointed by what they took to be the lack of sophistication of modern Chinese drama. Their sensibilities were particularly offended by what they perceived as "politically directed art."[6]

If Brover's students had been conditioned to accept the illusion of "art for art's sake," as is likely, their misapprehensions about art's social role could only have been confirmed by the caricatures of revolutionary art produced by Mao's disciples during the "Great Proletarian Cultural Revolution." (One's mind boggles at the effect on his students' "sensibilities" if Brover had told them that Mozart and Bach recordings were smashed during the "Great Proletarian Cultural Revolution.")

In the sixties and early seventies a strong influence was exerted over many radicals by, in the words of the authors of another article in *Guerilla Street Theater*, "the very important lessons Chinese revolutionaries learned and taught the world during the Great Proletarian Cultural Revolution."[7] Although these radicals didn't understand the "very important lessons" the Maoists taught, the controllers of the U.S. media instantly grasped their meaning—and promoted these "lessons" accordingly. "Mao is the greatest social revolutionary in history," wrote *The New York Times'* associate editor Tom Wicker. "He knows the only revolution is permanent revolution—against the society revolution creates as much as against the one it overthrows."[8]

Anything carried on *against* the "society revolution creates" is not revolutionary, but rather *counter*revolutionary, with the aim of overthrowing the new social order. That Maoism is indeed on the side of counterrevolution became clear to many radicals after the Maoists' recognition of the fascist Chilean junta and the Maoists joint action with the U.S. and apartheid South Africa in armed attacks against Angola's independence struggle.

How the influence of superrevolutionary ideas led to the breakup of groups with radical intentions can be gleaned from the remarks of *Guerilla Street Theater*'s editor, Henry Lesnick.

Lesnick was a member of a street theater that put on a skit in Chicago's Lincoln Park during the 1968 Democratic Convention "to dramatize the political repressiveness of the convention." Hours after the performance "thousands of police opened up, clubbing, kicking, macing, teargassing hundreds of demonstrators and passersby. They even attacked neighborhood people in their homes."[9] The next morning the members of the group concluded, "No art could achieve the drama, intensity or scope of the reality," and since "none of us saw any alternative function for guerilla theater . . . we abandoned it."[10]

Virtually all "guerilla theater" groups were abandoned because "We can't compete with the six o'clock news." Through TV news reports, states Lesnick,

Eyewitness accounts of US military atrocities, complete with photos, footage of Fred Hampton's blood-spattered apartment, worms coming out of the water faucets in Harlem, cops dealing dope, Kent State, Jackson State, Attica, are made a more immediate part of almost every American's consciousness than we could ever make them. The media have preempted this function of guerilla theater, and it is politically superfluous for us to pursue it.[11]

Since, according to Lesnick, the "media have preempted this function of guerilla theater," "guerilla theater" must assume another function:

. . . it has become clear that more is needed to effect change than informing the American people of the terrible facts of American life. Most people are already aware of them. What is generally lacking is a conceptual framework within which to understand these facts, an analysis of the causes of our social problems and the most suitable strategies for eliminating them. The development and dissemination of this analysis is the primary task of progressive theater today.[12]

It's quite true that simply knowing the "terrible facts of American life" isn't enough to make people decide to change them. Seeing horror after horror can also make people feel there's nothing they can do about it. But something even more dangerous is involved here.

According to Lesnick, media coverage of events is simply a raw presentation of brutal facts. But if the media present "terrible facts of American life" from time to time, it's only because the crisis in this country has made it impossible for them to continue to hide these "terrible facts." But the media have ways to compensate for any admissions of "terrible facts." They will show films of an Attica massacre within a "conceptual framework" that assigns responsibility for the murders not to Rockefeller but the prisoners. The media presentation of "terrible facts" is in a "conceptual framework" that not only immobilizes large sections of the people, but also influences large sections to move in a way disastrous to their own interests.

Contrary to Lesnick's view, progressive theater cannot leave the presentation of the "terrible facts of American life" to television. Progressive artists must transform these "terrible facts" into art—art that helps people see the possibility of basic social change.

But while Lesnick dismisses one aspect of the role of progressive theater, he preempts unto the theater a task not within its realm at all. It's not the theater but the people's movement itself that must develop "the most suitable strategies for eliminating" the "causes of our social problems." A people's theater must be part of a people's movement with a strategy for social change—and the theater's role within this strategy is much more fluid, many-sided and artistic than Lesnick's analysis indicates.

IN THE U.S. during the thirties people's theaters came into existence as part of a vast people's movement—with the working class, Black and white, as the leading force. These theaters were engaged in helping achieve the broad goals of this movement. Along with progressive theaters performing full-length plays, there were many street theater or "agit-prop" groups, as they were called. While the need for these groups was created by conditions in the U.S., inspiration also came from the German workers' theater of the twenties. (The first U.S. agit-prop group of the thirties was formed by a director from this theater.)

In the GDR we talked with a man who had been part of the German workers' theater: Peter Meter, now cultural director of the Committee of Anti-Fascist Resistance Fighters. Meter told us that during the twenties—a time of great economic crisis in Germany—"a famous Soviet agit-prop troupe came and played in all the big German cities." In the wake of these performances many German agit-prop groups sprang up. (Soviet films also had a revolutionary impact in Germany:

"In 1931 *Potemkin* was shown in the working class part of Cologne. When the film was over," said Meter, "a thousand people got up and marched through the city with red flags.")

Meter joined one of the new street theaters. "We performed wherever there was a platform—on trucks, at demonstrations, at meetings," he recalled. "There were workers' chorales, readings of revolutionary poetry, scenes from revolutionary plays. Brecht was already a well-known playwright and he wrote many plays for this kind of theater."

The workers' theater productions were innovative in form as well as content (their combination of films with live performances was the prototype for U.S. "mixed media" of the sixties), and their influence went far beyond their own ranks. "The workers' theater also fertilized the traditional German theater in a revolutionary sense," said Meter.

Only because the German workers' theater movement functioned as part of the German workers' revolutionary movement—not in isolation from it—could it play a role in the struggle to change society. "We've never pretended that theater itself can change society. Only the working class and its allies can change society," commented Fritz Rödel at the Gorki. "Theater can contribute to changing society if it's linked with the revolutionary social forces—but a revolutionary theater can develop only if there's a revolutionary movement behind it." Obviously, the fate of a people's theater is tied to the fate of the people as a whole.

"In Germany in the twenties the revolutionary theater was highly developed. But the far larger machine of bourgeois society absorbed the results of much of this activity," said Rödel. "And then the people's movement was unable to stop fascism from gaining power. So it's evident that a large number of facts must exist if theater is to have a revolutionary effect."

Those who control a capitalist society do all they can to prevent emergence of a people's theater because they know how powerful it can be—so powerful that even fascism couldn't burn away the influence of the German workers' theater. "The role of the revolutionary theater was very great in the German workers' class education," declared Rödel. "The theater in the GDR would be unthinkable without its influence."

To HEAD off development of a people's theater is a constant aim of U.S. corporate monopoly. But the attempt to carry out this aim requires a diversity of tactics. As the people's struggles mounted during the sixties, the outright repression of the McCarthy period was replaced by more subtle means—including the role of the corporate foundations in subsidizing the arts.

An insight into the purpose of these foundations is provided (despite his intentions to the contrary) by Herbert Blau, a recipient of many corporate grants and one of Joseph Papp's predecessors at Lincoln Center. In his 1964 book, *The Impossible Theater,* written while he headed the Actor's Workshop in San Franscisco, Blau stated:

The psychology of foundation grants is worth a study of its own. They are a peculiarly American phenomenon to the extent they have gone, in the theater and the academic world, to people like myself, who were brought up to believe there were three villains in the universe: Herbert Hoover, John D. Rockefeller and Henry Ford . . . Now we find it the natural condition of talented estrangement in our body politic to be catered to, financed, and sent on the Grand Tour. Or, as with our theater, provided with operating funds. If this is the new secret weapon of the Establishment, I prefer it to neglect, and if there is a Grand Strategy to assimilate protest, I am willing to take my chances.[13]

There certainly is a "Grand Strategy," if one wants to call it that, to "assimilate protest"—and Blau's remarks suggest certain of its essential elements: In stating that foundation grants have gone "to people like myself who were brought up to believe" the "three villains in the universe" were Herbert Hoover, John D. Rockefeller and Henry Ford, Blau was saying the recipients were apt to be individuals with "radical" pretensions who, the foundations knew, would conform to the "Grand Strategy to assimilate protest" because they "prefer it to neglect."

Continuing, Blau states:

My theater has received a series of grants from the Ford Foundation, and though that makes me no expert on the ulterior motives of capitalist beneficence, I can say this much: If the Foundation has—as people warned us—any intention of subverting our independence, then it has given no explicit evidence.[14]

Despite his denial of any Ford Foundation "intention of subverting our independence," Blau gives "explicit evidence" of his awareness that too much "independence" results in an end to corporate grants:

. . . when one wonders at what point in a theater's intransigeance support would be withdrawn or withheld, I would say that at this juncture even the Foundation doesn't know. For the Foundation is, like any other institution in this ambiguous period . . . trying to define its own character.[15]

Far from "trying to define its own character" in the sixties (or at any other time), the Ford Foundation's concern was how best to use its money and influence to "define the character" of the arts in the U.S. While Blau asserted that the foundation didn't know at what point of a "theater's intransigeance" it would withdraw support, not only did the foundation know—Blau knew too. Although the McCarthy era was presumably over when Blau's theater received its Ford grants, he gives "explicit evidence" of the McCarthyite standards the foundation imposed:

If it could be shown that our theater has a reasonable quota of what the Justice Department might consider fellow travelers, I suspect giving might be curtailed, as it possibly has been elsewhere.[16]

To make sure there would be no "fellow travelers" to cause "intransigeance," the foundation investigated all potential recipients of funds. The Actor's Workshop had no problem in passing through this McCarthyite sieve:

As for the Foundation, having investigated us with its usual care, it recognized us, we assume, for what we were and what we aspire to be. Our cards were on the table, our behavior out in the open, our principles in our program notes.[17]

What did the "principles in the program notes" tell the corporate investigators about the Actor's Workshop?

[We] were not attached to any social movement; we were a disassociated organism. We were not, like the Group [Theatre], surrounded by any ideological ferment . . .[18]

Lest there by any doubt about the Workshop's "principles," Blau elaborates:

Unlike the Group Theatre of the thirties, then, we were not prompted by social idealism . . . We had no "common cause with the worker," or—for that matter—identification with any class. No more than the young man of *Awake and Sing* did we want life printed on dollar bills—but we had a few more than he did . . .[19]

A theater that rejects "common cause" with the working class finds itself, despite denials, identified with another class—the one the Ford Foundation represents. This identity will be revealed in everything from the theater's productions to its director's views. Blau's views on the great issues of this country were compatible with the "Grand Strategy to assimilate protest." Commenting, for example, on the civil rights struggles, Blau stated:

Only in the last couple of years, with the Negro revolution, has the power of mass action become inspiring again. But even so, the spirit of gradualism rules over a possessed minority . . .[20]

When Blau attributes the "spirit of gradualism" to Black people, he has shifted it away from its true source: The "spirit of gradualism" can be traced to the *possessing* minority—the Fords, Rockefellers, Du-Ponts, etc. By contrast, the "spirit of gradualism" is anathema to the Black *oppressed* minority. (To speak of Black people as "possessed" is to conform to an old racist stereotype. Black people are not gripped by some eerie mysticism—but rather by the desire for liberation. During slavery, however, Black people were literally a "possessed minority.")

When Blau accused Black people of being "ruled" by the "spirit of gradualism," he was suggesting that he was more radical than they. This relieved him of any compunction to ally himself with Black people until their struggles met *his* specifications. For those who judge the oppressed instead of the oppressor, as the Ford Foundation well knows, the time for action never comes. Which, of course, is the purpose of the "Grand Strategy to assimilate protest."

ALTHOUGH THE "Grand Strategy to assimilate protest" became evident in the sixties, its inspiration can be traced to the thirties. At that time the people's movements fought for and won government subsidies for the theater, resulting in the Federal Theater Project.* Because of the strength of these movements, the Federal Theater could not "assimilate protest"—but instead became a theater of protest! This theater of protest was then attacked by the government that had been forced to subsidize it: The Federal Theater was killed off by congressional investigations, forerunners of the investigations of the McCarthy period—when, as Blau points out, there was "no subsidy to theater of any kind."

From the standpoint of the corporations, in whose interests the U.S. government functions, foundation grants offer basic advantages over government ones: While corporations are not immune to public pressure, they are less vulnerable to it than government. While the money dispensed through these tax-exempt foundations belongs to the people as surely as if it came straight from government, corporate

---

*The Federal Theater Project involved over 15,000 actors and other theater workers during its four-year existence.

auspices make this fact less obvious. Further, by creating foundation boards, the Fords and Rockefellers can make their disbursal of funds appear "non-partisan." They can also, when they wish, disclaim responsibility for the way money is channeled. However, despite these advantages, the "Grand Strategy" is not without contradictions.

The Actor's Workshop, as Blau put it, "was not attached to any social movement" but was a "disassociated organism." This was an asset when it came to getting foundation money. On the other hand, a theater without ties to the people has little leeway for "intransigeance." By contrast, the Negro Ensemble Company (NEC), which has also received Ford Foundation subsidies, is *not* a "disassociated organism" but has ties with the Black community. These ties do not make the NEC immune to Ford Foundation pressure, but they provide a base for greater resistance to it. The NEC has made very real contributions to this country's cultural life. But no thanks for this are due the Ford Foundation. It was the power of the Black people's struggles that made it possible for the NEC to come into existence, offering an opportunity for numerous Black playwrights, actors and directors to develop. (NEC director Douglas Turner Ward recently described plays dealing with "internal examinations of Black life" as a "mixed blessing." These plays, he noted, have "more commercial possibilities" than "overtly political ones"—for example, one such play traveled from the NEC to Broadway in 1975. But, Ward stressed, "We still need the Black Brechts."[21]

The advantages to corporate monopoly of foundation instead of government grants have become increasingly apparent in the recent period—when foundations slashed their grants to the performing arts without having to show even token accountability to the people.

To PRESERVE the continuity of their control, those who dominate this society try to create discontinuity in the people's movements by, for example, attempting to prevent the experience of one period from reaching a later one, except in distorted form.

This is why so few today have heard of the successful struggle to win government subsidies for theater and for artists in every field during the thirties—a fight that must be taken up once again. On the other hand, the art of the thirties is in the bourgeois media a subject of continuing abuse.

In a 1975 interview Joseph Papp stated:

I don't do protest plays—of the thirties. I receive plays about Nixon and Vietnam. They're one-sided. I'm not interested in political tracts. I'm interested in art—as a societal force.[22]

On the face of it, there's no need for Papp to say, "I don't do protest plays—of the thirties," since no one is asking him to. But playwrights *are* asking for production of progressive plays of the seventies—which Papp dismisses as "political tracts."

To discourage playwrights from moving in a truly radical direction, Papp selects as a terrible example the only period in our history when theater was identified with working people. Obviously, the plays of that time don't meet today's needs, socially or artistically. But one pays attention to the past in order to construct the future.

Papp says he's interested in art as a "societal force." So are the Rockefellers and Fords. The question is, what *kind* of "societal force"? When Papp warns writers against being "one-sided," he is telling them not to be *left*-sided. Artists who view art as a *revolutionary* "societal force" have always had to fight attempts to consign their work to the category of "political tracts." Real art is partisan in its allegiance, many-sided in its exploration of character, situation and society.

One who takes a very different view of the art of the thirties is Harold Clurman, a founder of the Group Theatre. In his book, *The Fervent Years,* a story of that time, he writes:

. . . in the thirties there developed to a high point of consciousness the hunger for a spiritually active world, a humanly meaningful and relevant art.[23]

That hunger persists, intensifies today. A great multi-racial, multi-national people's theater movement—doing complex, fully-rounded plays as well as mobile and other forms of theater—is one way that hunger will be met.

6. From Antagonism to Advocacy

Those who control communications in the old society not only strive to create discontinuity in the people's struggles by keeping the experience of one period from reaching later ones. Their most concerted effort is to keep the experience of socialist countries from reaching capitalist ones, except in anti-socialist form.

Although attacks on socialist society intensify in an openly conservative style—as when Papp speaks of artists being "pressured" into "fulfilling" the "aims and objectives" of "totalitarian society"— this type of phrasing severely limits the impact on those seeking a radical alternative in the U.S. This is why the same ideas now appear so often in "revolutionary" form.

For example, in an article titled "The Dialectics of Legitimation: Brecht in the GDR," David Bathrick, editor of *New German Critique,* a U.S. publication, writes:

Can a revolutionary theater forged as a means for transforming society remain true to its original intentions if used to affirm rather than critically change social conditions? Worded differently, what are the implications for revolutionary culture when it is forced to function as legitimation?[1]

When Bathrick speaks of "revolutionary culture" being "forced to function as legitimation," he too is saying that artists in a socialist society are "pressured" into "fulfilling" the "aims and objectives" of a "totalitarian society"—but addition of the word "revolutionary" makes his a "radical" instead of obviously conservative statement.

When Bathrick indicates that theater in a socialist society should "remain true" to the "original intentions" of revolutionary theater, he is saying the goal of revolutionary theater in socialist society should be the same as in a capitalist one: to establish a different social order. Thus Bathrick would have theaters in a socialist country apply *New York Times* editor Tom Wicker's concept of "revolution": "the only revolution is permanent revolution—against the society revolution creates as much as against the one it overthrows."

After reading Bathrick's statement, we wondered what GDR theater workers would have to say about it. We took it with us to the GDR.

"THAT'S A lovely mixture of pseudo-art and pseudo-dialectics," laughed Gerhard Piens at the Dresden State Theater after reading a German translation of the statement. He paused.

"'*Forced* to function'? Yes. Yes. But one must define this. One must imagine a human being with a sound brain who cannot act in two different ways. Yes, I'm 'forced to function'—forced by myself to work as I do."

"'*Forced* to function'!" exclaimed Erhard Schmidt at the Volkstheater Rostock. "*Who* forces us? Nobody! Our consciousness 'forces' us."

And Rolf Dieter Eichler, critic for the *National Zeitung,* newspaper of the National Democratic Party, said with a certain trace of irony, "I can't understand why anyone would think badly of socialist artists for expressing their ideas in their work. If freedom of opinion applies at this point, then socialist artists should be able to express their socialist opinions."

Only because socialist culture "affirms" socialist society, GDR theater workers stressed, can it carry out its corollary function: to "critically change" certain social conditions.

"What do we want to change? Not socialism—we built it! We're not going backwards, we wouldn't dream of it. What we still want to change—to continually develop—is the consciousness of the human being," declared Erhard Schmidt.

"There's a great revolution taking place in people's minds"—stimulated by the totality of developments in the new society. "But the development of individuals," Schmidt noted, "varies greatly." In playing its many-sided revolutionary role, socialist art must be concerned with *all* the people, "including those who are slow, who don't keep up with the rest, whose way of thought and feeling must be developed by art toward the more humane.

"What's happening to the consciousness of the people in the GDR and other socialist countries is a great revolution. To participate in this work is the revolutionary task of the theater."

By contrast, Bathrick's concept of the task of "revolutionary culture," said Gerhard Piens, "is very questionable. I suspect that when he says to 'critically change social conditions,' he really means socialism itself—that he'd like everything here to come tumbling down.

"But in our theaters we're trying to create socialist art, and the objective of socialist art is to 'affirm' socialist society. Of course, this means that socialist art is at the same time dedicated to developing socialist society. But we're creating art to *develop* socialism—not end it.

"There was a time in the GDR," Piens continued, "of certain restrictions." These occurred during the country's earliest period, when a bitter struggle was waged to prevent those who had ruled the old society from regaining control. "It was sometimes necessary then to restrict certain things—including things we wouldn't have restricted two years later. And mistakes were made—anyone doing something new makes mistakes. But so far as being 'forced to function,' that's just slander—pure and simple. Even in those times—which are way behind us—we tried to convince artists of what was necessary. No one ever said, you must do this or that!"

One of those who "forged" a revolutionary theater in the old German state is Peter Meter. Does revolutionary theater, we asked him, "remain true to its original intentions if used to affirm," to develop, the new society?

"We understand theater as revolutionary," he replied, "only if it helps to change the world through artistic and scientific means in the interests of the working class. No other revolutionary theater is possible. The GDR theater wouldn't have the slightest understanding of revolutionary development if it didn't participate in socialist progress, in changing and developing things in a socialist way."

MANY RADICALS are influenced by the idea, put forth by Bathrick and others, that revolutionary artists under socialism should play the same role as revolutionary artists under capitalism. There are many reasons for their susceptibility to this idea, including an historical one: The role of the progressive artist as antagonist of the existing social system is centuries old, while the role of the progressive artist as protagonist of the existing social system is brief, beginning only with the founding of the first socialist society, the USSR.

Each socialist society that has come into existence—from the Soviet Union to Cuba to Vietnam—has had to develop amidst ceaseless attacks from its enemies. Far from remaining aloof from the developing society, the socialist artist does all she or he can to assist it. The theater, for example, "tries to further all processes that will advance our society," as Fritz Rödel put it.

To "further all processes that will advance our society" means that the artist functions as the advocate of the new socialist state. But, again, many U.S. radicals reject this concept—influenced by the anarchistic idea that all states are bad per se, and artists must oppose them. This idea may sound "revolutionary," but it's helpful only to those who oppose existing socialist states and do all they can to prevent formation of new ones—including by armed overthrow of people's governments, as in Chile.

As Peter Meter said, theater is revolutionary "only if it helps to change the world" in the interests of the working class. But the basic reason many radicals do not distinguish between the artist's role in a capitalist and socialist society is because of their attitude toward the working class. Influenced by anti-working-class stereotypes and theories, it's difficult for them to recognize that workers are the leading force in creating a new society and the conditions for a new art.

Although Bathrick fails to mention it, revolutionary theater in the old society was "forged" through its ties with the working class and reemerged through these ties in the new society. Thus the artist's role in the new society would be the same only if the working class's role were the same. But in the old society the working class is the antagonist of the class in power. In the new society the working class *is* the class in power.

With emergence of the new society, everything is turned upside down—or rather, right side up. The former ruling class is now the enemy of the state and tries to regain power by any means possible—for example, by incitement to counterrevolution in the GDR in 1953.

The idea that the artist's role in the new society should remain what it was in the old, can pass as "revolutionary" only if it remains an abstraction. Analyzed in specific terms, its true meaning becomes apparent. For instance, did revolutionary German artists have the same relationship to the old German state as they did, or do, to the GDR?

The noted playwright Friedrich Wolf was one of those who "forged" a revolutionary theater as a "means for transforming" the old German state. When the Nazis took power, his work was banned and he was driven into exile in France. With the Nazi occupation of France, he was put into a concentration camp (where he worked on a play about the French revolution). Later he went to the Soviet Union.

When Wolf returned to his own land after World War II, it's absurd to think he could have remained "true" to the "original intentions" of revolutionary theater by acting toward the anti-fascists now in power as he had to the fascists who forced him into exile! It's a matter of record that Wolf did indeed "affirm" the new society.

GDR film director Konrad Wolf is Friedrich Wolf's son. He fought against fascism as a young soldier in the Red Army. Back in his own land, he could continue his anti-fascist struggle only by "affirming" the new society.

Socialist affirmation means conscious, active participation in the complicated struggle to build the new society. And affirmation has an indivisible corollary: honest criticism. To refrain from honest criticism is to be an impediment to socialist development. But artists, like all members of the new society, can criticize constructively and effectively only as protagonists of socialist development—as Konrad Wolf makes clear.

There are, he said, "many problems and conflicts" in building socialism and "one would not be a Marxist" if one expected the new society to emerge as "heaven on earth." Each artist, he believes, is obliged to "put for himself" the question of his or her responsibility to a socialist society. Basically, he feels, this is a question of whether "an artist can identify completely" with socialist development, and thus confront the problems arising during it—or whether the artist prefers to stand apart as a "kind of prophet." Many things in the course of development go very well indeed, yet things can always be done better. But, Wolf remarked, can an artist say only that development could be better—yet take no part in it?

Wolf himself has "taken the path of involvement," trying through art to help people see that problems can be overcome, encouraging them to take part in solving conflicts by "identifying with socialist principles." This, he believes, is the "main task" of the artist in socialism. And to carry out this task, he stressed, is difficult.

In a socialist society, "everything is new," and an honest artist can see problems in a way that differs from "general truth." "All this can happen," said Wolf, "but the artist must not stand apart from the normal course of development."

ACCORDING TO bourgeois ideologists, artists in socialist countries are true artists only if they "stand apart from the normal course of development." Every way in which artists express their affirmation of the new social system becomes a target for hostile reactions from the West.

One running point of attack is the artistic approach that enables socialist artists to express affirmation and criticism within that affirmation: socialist realism—portrayed by the bourgeois media as a narrow, rigid, posterlike, sloganeering non-art form imposed upon writers in the Soviet Union, GDR and other socialist countries.

If one's concept of socialist realism is based on information from such sources, it may come as a surprise to learn that a leading proponent of socialist realism (and one who placed his own work in this category) was Bertolt Brecht.

No, the artistic theory and method of socialist realism did not reach GDR writers by "edict." On the contrary, socialist realist art is linked with revolutionary German working-class struggles. Further, German anti-fascist writers in exile during the thirties were involved in one of the most complex and heated debates in literary history, and the subject was socialist realism—a phrase launched by Maxim Gorky in 1934 at the First All-Union Congress of Soviet Writers. The debate around socialist realism was international in scope. And among the central, as well as opposing figures were Brecht and Georg Lukács, a Hungarian. The question was not *if* socialist realism was a viable approach to art, but what was the most viable interpretation of socialist realism.

No debate in U.S. literary history can even be compared in intensity or scope with this one. Above all, it was not an esoteric argument but one with far-reaching consequences. Brecht's entry into the debate took place as follows:

In 1938 after reading an article by Lukács in *Das Wort,* a German emigré review, Brecht was prompted "to clarify his own views as to the problems of realism. In this way, two entirely different, even diametrically opposed concepts of socialist realism took shape. The whole further development of the theory of realism, especially in Germany, was deeply influenced by these two concepts," states Werner Mittenzwei, a GDR critic.[2]

It was Lukács's contention that Balzac and Tolstoy should serve as *the* models for socialist realist art. In this way he restricted socialist artists both as to precedents and innovation. Brecht, on the other hand, wrote, "Realism is nothing formal. One cannot take the form of one single realist (or of several) and call it *the* realist form."[3]

At the same time Lukács condemned the forms developed by certain twentieth century writers as "decadent." Thus Lukács was saying that form is content. Brecht, however, asserted, "The form of a work of art is nothing else but the perfect organization of its content, and its value depends entirely on that of the content."[4]

Whatever their original use may have been, Brecht felt that a great variety of forms could be used by progressive writers (even though detaching them from their original content is not a simple matter). Referring to the works of late bourgeois authors Brecht asserted, "socialist writers can get acquainted with valuable, fully-developed technical elements in these documents of disorientation, for they are able to see the way out."[5]

However, the differences in the Brecht-Lukács debate were not esthetic in origin. They were political, at bottom a question of class identification. Mittenzwei writes:

Using Balzac as an example, [Lukács] demonstrates how a writer can subject his own class to criticism without breaking with it . . . *What he wants is the critical stance, not the break with the ruling class.*[6]

This is the basis for the empathy a number of U.S. radicals have for Lukács. Such radicals do not consciously identify with the bourgeoisie; on the contrary, they consider themselves against it. Yet they do not identify with the working class either. And so on basic class questions they often share the positions of the bourgeoisie, even though they do so from a "left" stance.

Although such radicals do not function independently from the class in power under capitalism, they demand that artists function independently from the class in power under socialism. But revolutionary artists reject such "independence," since a revolutionary is identified by partisanship for the working class.

In his article "The Dialectics of Legitimation: Brecht in the GDR," Bathrick—asserting that revolutionary art cannot "remain true to its original intentions if used to affirm" the new society—expresses concern because Brecht's work is used to "affirm" socialist society. This is a strange concern since "legitimation" of the new social order was the purpose of Brecht's life and work. On the other hand Bathrick expresses no concern about U.S. "establishment" theater productions of Brecht that rob his plays of their anti-capitalist core. Yet in staging Brecht's plays, these theaters attempt to give themselves a "radical" image—and thus to "legitimatize" a society permitting such activity.

Since the "original intentions" of revolutionary art are to help create the new society, the revolutionary artist can "remain true" to these intentions only by "affirming" the new society once it comes into existence. Certainly Brecht affirmed the new society in his poem, "The Moscow Workers Take Over The Great Metro on April 27th, 1935":

> Where had it ever happened before that the fruit of the work
> Had fallen to those who had done the work
> And where
> Were those who had built it
> Not driven from the building?[7]

BRECHT WROTE extensively on socialist realism. In a complex definition of this artistic method he included these points:

Socialist Realism means realistically reproducing men's life together by artistic means from a socialist point of view. It is reproduced in such a way as to promote insight into society's mechanisms and stimulate socialist impulses. In the case of Socialist Realism a large part of the pleasure which all art must provoke is pleasure at the possibility of society's mastering man's fate.

And:

A Socialist Realist work of art shows characters and events as historical and alterable and as contradictory.

And:

A Socialist Realist work of art is based on a working class viewpoint.[8]

From this defintion it can be seen why socialist realism could have its origins in the work of socialist writers who lived in capitalist societies. But to come fully into its own, socialist realism needed not only artists who understood the laws of social development but the new society itself—whose members would collaborate as readers or spectators, critics and partners in production. And the central subject of this new art, the working class—formerly the subject of just a small minority of writers—could move from the wings to center stage only when the working class itself came to power.

In the past, progressive art was created in the face of active hostility from the class in power. In a socialist society progressive art develops with the active assistance of the class in power—with the aim of creating a literature not for a few but for a whole nation, a literature to help shape socialist personalities. To achieve this new artistic goal is obviously a complex matter.

"All the developments here—of the working class, of agriculture— have been dealt with in our art," related Jochen Ziller of the publishing house, Henschelverlag. And in each period there were outstanding works that caught vital aspects of the times. But there were also many problems in creating this new literature. In the theater for instance, "We had great difficulty for many years with portraying the working class. Our theoretical understanding was not deep enough. There was a time when we handled this in a way pretty close to naturalism—with the result that workers said, 'I've seen this all day in the factory and I'm not interested.'"

Contrary to what bourgeois critics allege, this semi-naturalist phase was not socialist realism itself—but a transition to it. And such a transitory phase is common to all new literatures in their early stages. "To throw the public raw statements of facts, artificially provided with tendencies," Brecht pointed out, "this happens in the first phase of a socially ascendant form."[9]

In capitalism, attacks on "socially ascendant" art originate from the ruling class within the society. In the new society such attacks originate from outside. "Our writers have experimented with many new things, and getting results has been a long difficult process," noted Jochen Ziller. "And of course the class enemy, in keeping with its political and esthetic views, points out that all these things aren't perfect. Our art has undergone constant attack from the standpoint of the capitalist class.

"But," Ziller stressed, "the Party and the various artists' associations have done a lot to help arm our artists to carry on this fight in a better way—this has been a very positive stimulus for us. We've also," he continued, "discussed the theory and practice of literature, of socialist realism, the special character of art—what it can do, what it can't do." As a result, "the artistic value of our plays has increased—and the development of certain playwrights has had a great influence on this process."

BRECHT WROTE that socialist art shows characters and events as "alterable and contradictory." And for GDR writers this question of contradiction and change is central.

"If the working class wins power something revolutionary starts in everyday life. Then you have to discover the things to be overcome in this new life and represent them in art in such a way that people recognize the possibility of changing them," said Horst Oswald, Cultural Councillor of Berlin.

In a capitalist society the socialist writer's starting point is the recognition that the "things to be overcome"—that is, the contradictions—*can* be overcome only by replacing the old social system with the new, because the contradictions in the old society are antagonistic, based on the exploitation of the majority by the corporate minority. In a socialist society there is no exploitation and hence no antagonistic contradictions. The new conflicts created by socialist development are of an entirely different nature than the old ones—yet they can be sharp and difficult.

"All of us want much more today and tomorrow than we can attain in line with our present economic possibilities," stated *Der Morgen* drama critic Christoph Funke. The GDR's great economic advances were attested to even by the scene of our meeting: the Volksbühne canteen, where we were surrounded by actors, directors, technicians, eating, talking, listening to music in their workplace. Yet many problems remain. "We would love to give everyone the apartment they'd like immediately. But we know we still need a number of years to reach this great goal. The tension between the basic possibilities of our social system and the hard demands of the present—where some must still wait for certain things—produces conflicts and problems."

As Funke indicated, the basis for resolving these conflicts is inherent in the socialist system—that is, the housing problem *is* on the way to solution. But in the U.S. the housing problem is getting worse—as are all material conditions for the people in a country where the wealth is poured into a budget geared to corporate profits, armaments and aggression.

The difference in the nature of the contradictions in the two societies is also apparent in every area of human relations. In the U.S. the status of women, for example, is characterized by unequal wages, lack of child care facilities, a culture that degrades them (and is particularly degrading to women whose skin is dark)—and these conditions are generated by the system itself.

In the GDR there is equal pay for equal work, extensive child care services, and a culture that helps move life in the direction of full equality for women. Yet survivals of the past still affect relations between men and women—although in a new way. GDR writer Susanne Statkowa comments,

> . . . new human relations do not proceed without conflict, any more than the new attitude to the role of women in society and family prevails automatically . . . It is quite illuminating that young men who are not raised in the parental home in the spirit of equality can easily get into conflict with an economically independent, self-confident young woman who is on the same educational level. Wrong attitudes which in old marriages are mostly tolerated and overlooked at the cost of the wife, now come into the foreground.[10]

It is conflicts such as these that present a challenge to the artistry and understanding of GDR writers.

"The writer's task in a capitalist society—unmasking the antagonistic contradictions—disappears in socialism. In our society the writer's task is quite different, although it's not an easier one," remarked Marianne Lange, who heads the Department of Culture and Education of the Party College.

"Conflicts and contradictions are quite natural in our development," she continued. "Artists can uncover these contradictions—ask real questions, make discoveries. Starting from a socialist standpoint, they have the possibility of dealing with all questions."

In socialism all aspects of life—including the writer's role—develop in the course of overcoming contradictions. "A writer must deal with real conflicts that move people," noted Lange. But in the past "writers were frequently expected to find a solution for whatever problems they showed." Some writers tried to handle this situation by inventing "pseudo-conflicts, as we call them." Through a process of critical analysis these distortions were overcome, and now the discovery of new conflicts is recognized as an important part of the writer's role.

"The contradictions in life are reflected in art. Far from being negative, these contradictions are a stimulus to our development. We have to discover them in order to overcome them, and this is one of the functions of art," said Eberhard Roehner, vice chairman of the Department of Culture and Education of the Party College. He added: "The question is from what standpoint these contradictions are shown."

The GDR, Roehner continued, "is a stable state, recognized all over the world. We can say that literature has accompanied the GDR on its path—many films, novels and plays have helped tell about socialism and the changes that have taken place." However, precisely because of the GDR's strides, "some now believe the function of art has changed: now it doesn't have to help develop socialism so much. We don't agree that the writer's role should be limited to critical aspects. We start from the constructive role of art—and artists must have a firm class position. It's not so much a question of what's shown, but the artist's point of view. We struggle in two directions: against misrepresenting reality by claiming we still have antagonistic contradictions—and against painting things rosy."

Treating non-antagonistic conflicts is an historically new task for artists and, as Marianne Lange stressed, a difficult one. At first "playwrights in the GDR found it easier to deal with the antagonistic contradictions of the past than the non-antagonistic conflicts," remarked Professor Dr. Ernst Schumacher, drama critic of the *Berliner Zeitung,* a regional paper of the Socialist Unity Party, and a professor at Humboldt University. "Then they shifted away from treating the contradictions of the imperialist world to the conflicts of the socialist world." But, Schumacher emphasized, "world historical topics must also be dealt with in the GDR theater—to avoid underestimating imperialism's world-wide influence."

Playwright Helmut Baierl, discussing this same question, said, "During the time when the GDR was not recognized, a whole generation of artists dealt with the discovery of this country, of the many outstanding things here. Then we wrote only for our own people. We must continue writing for them, but sometimes our horizon has been too small. Now we are making a new start so people in other societies will also understand what's happening here. Our horizon must be broadened—without giving up any of our own aims but with a greater consciousness of what's beyond."

Baierl feels there is no challenge to playwrights so exciting as that offered by the non-antagonistic conflicts, because this is new territory. "When Brecht returned to Berlin," Baierl recalled, "he wrote, 'The hardships of the mountains are behind us/ Before us lie the hardships of the plains.'

"At one time," Baierl continued, "we thought the hardships of the plains would be quite easy. But they are also difficult—people's conflicts, unhappiness, laziness. Sometimes we don't dare to say they're more complicated because we have such respect for those still engaged in a hard class struggle. Some day when exploitation has been ended everywhere, the whole world will be engaged in overcoming the hardships of the plains."

Going on to discuss the relationship of the playwright to his times, Baierl said, "Shakespeare lived in a transitional period and he caught his times in a way that caught all times. Brecht also lived in a transitional period—a time of bourgeois repression, but also a time when the October Revolution had taken place and when the struggle against fascism was going on. Brecht's best plays described this transitional period, and they will remain classics."

The present, Baierl noted, is also a time of transition—the revolutionary transition from capitalism to socialism. Today, in a large part of the world, "you have real, existing socialism. You have the organized character of the revolution—the storm has been turned into a march, a long march with millions of people joined together. In this battalion of millions you have all kinds of people—people who sacrifice their lives, and people who think only of themselves and that they sleep well.

"If we want to perceive this period we must do two things: First, with all artistic skill, we must describe this great battalion, marching, with all kinds of characters in it—who are sometimes no different from Shakespeare's. But we also have to describe the whole—the organized, scientific character that's part of this march. If you omit this, you'll have only figures who are not representative of the whole—characters who are standing outside and who give a false picture of the whole."

Of course, Baierl pointed out, a playwright can portray unrepresentative figures without distorting reality—so long as the playwright views these characters as atypical. "You may describe a character who is in a certain way ignorant—ignorant first of all of society. Nevertheless, he and his criticisms are part of social life, although he may not know it. You can compare such a character with someone on a ship—someone who's at the prow and then moves to the stern. If you describe such a person in art without describing the context, you conceal the fact that the ship is moving forward. In *Quiet Flows The Don,* Sholokhov wrote of the way a counterrevolutionary sees revolution—he's moving backward as the whole society goes forward."

Helmut Baierl, it is clear, has his own very distinct interpretation of socialist realism—as do other GDR playwrights and theater workers in general. These individual approaches bring to socialist realism what critic Rolf Dieter Eichler calls "the subjective factor."

"People with misconceptions about socialist realism think of it as a precise but dead mirror reflecting certain social conditions," he remarked. "Our theater proves that socialist realism doesn't only portray conditions and developments, but at the same time the views of the artists concerning these conditions and changes. This subjective factor is a very important part of socialist realism—and not only today but since Gorky, since Brecht."

Dieter Klein of the Volksbühne also commented on distorted concepts of socialist realism: "Everything we do, we feel, is socialist realism. And what we do is, we know, contrary to the interpretation of many in the U.S.—who say that socialist realism is strict and gray. On the contrary it's vivid. We very much follow Brecht who believed that theater must be a pleasure. In our theater you can see the liveliness of our contemporary lives—in everything from plays on what's happening here, to the German and world classics and Latin American theater.

"We," he emphasized, "are the ones responsible for this—and it's not always easy. It's not ordered from above, as some may think. It's the theater workers who are responsible. We are the specialists. We have our own opinions and ideas, and what's happening in the theater is the responsibility of those who work in the theater." He added: "As for those in the West who love to elaborate theories about socialism, but do nothing for it—we regard them in the same way as we do our theater work: It's one thing to talk about it, another to do it. Socialism is applied in the socialist countries and the best way to talk about socialism and socialist theater is to look at it where it exists."

"Brecht said, 'We are interested in the question because of the answer.' When our theater puts questions for society, it can't always give the answers because the answers must be found in life. But we put the questions in a way to point toward the answers—because we think the world can be changed," declared Fritz Rödel.

The questions that "point toward the answers" arise not only from the GDR theater's productions of contemporary plays but also from its interpretation of the classics.

"Marxist-Leninist philosophy frees all people who have been exploited and oppressed at the same time that it frees the working class—and so it will absorb all the progressive culture of the past into its own culture, all the human heritage," said Peter Meter. "This cultural inheritance is a bridge toward revolutionary culture.

"For me," he noted, "Thomas Mann is a great German author. He didn't write in a class sense but he was critically humanist. He was a writer who stepped upon the bridge, even though he didn't cross it." A great German writer who *did* cross the bridge, and who drew upon the cultural heritage to take this revolutionary step was Brecht. "He is a great author who not only drew upon the German classics but all the world classics—Shakespeare, Gorky, the Chinese classics. Goethe once said, 'My whole life is a collective work. I cannot pretend to be the only author.' Brecht's use of the classics was a new way of understanding literature. For instance, he took Villon's last poem into the *Threepenny Opera.* There you can see in what a sensitive way he penetrated the literature of the past—linking it with the revolutionary power and enthusiasm of a new class literature." An important part of the work of GDR theaters is interpreting "the literature of the past—linking it with the revolutionary power" of a socialist outlook.

"What we do," explained Maik Hamburger of the Deutsches, "is play the classics with full attention to their humanist contents and in such a way that they have significance for present-day GDR audiences."

The interpretation of classics has changed and developed along with all other aspects of GDR life. "In the beginning," commented Hans-Rainer John, editor of *Theater Der Zeit,* "the enlightenment factor—in the eighteenth century sense—was strongly emphasized in our theater to help people find an historical point of view in real life. But now people absorb a basic social understanding in school. Now personality has become much more the center of art. The individual is the great theme and the implications of this are far reaching." However, this stress on the individual doesn't lessen the importance of social circumstances.

Comparing two productions of the same opera, John said, "In the fifties Walter Felsenstein"—who headed the *Komische Oper* until his death in 1975—"produced *The Marriage of Figaro,*" placing primary stress on the social situation. "His production in the seventies was much different. It didn't negate the characters' social circumstances but it deepened their individual qualities." The same change occurred in GDR productions of *The Magic Flute.* "In early interpretations it was good against bad. With the Queen of the Night—everything was negative. Now they've changed the conception: In a world where women play a new role the treatment is a little richer. There are different shadings, corresponding more to Mozart's music."

One of the productions in the Deutsches Theater's repertory was the classic, *The Prince of Homburg,* by Heinrich von Kleist. "This play," said Ilse Galfert, a Deutsches' *Dramaturgin**, "is about a man who is fighting against inhuman laws and wants to revolt." Thus it offers a contrast between progressive action in old societies and socialist society. "It's a principle of our state that the individual can have his or her rights within the laws—and we keep exploring the possibilities for applying them better." She added: "I have many friends in the Federal Republic of Germany and West Berlin. When they come here for the first time and see our brilliant productions, they discuss how they are brilliant in spite of the fact that we are oppressed here. When they see a play like Besson's *Dragon,*** I say, 'Who do you want to save?' We're still a very young state and a state, you understand, that enjoys a certain love and pity it really does not need."

SUCH VISITORS as Ilse Galfert described reflect the confrontation policies of those who rule the FRG. And this confrontation is particularly acute on the cultural front, with FRG propaganda portraying a "united German cultural nation based on the common culture and destiny of all Germans." But there is no identity—cultural or otherwise—between the socialist GDR and the capitalist FRG.

"It would be inconceivable for us," said Horst Oswald, "to build a socialist society while maintaining some vague, ominous cultural link with the bourgeoisie. Our socialist foundations are diametrically different. Our entire life is different."

However, the FRG corporate forces who dream still of reacquiring what was once the Eastern part of Germany have a special reason for

---

* Literary adviser, feminine form
** *The Dragon* is a Soviet play, a social satire in fairy-tale form that has enjoyed a long run in the Deutsches' repertory. The production was staged by Benno Besson.

selecting the cultural arena as a focal point in their propaganda. "By now everybody understands you can't compare the politics, economy and social system of the GDR and the FRG. The only thing that remains for the FRG reactionaries to picture as 'one' is culture, since you can't measure it so exactly. They say we still have the same language, but in reality the content, the ideas—even the connotations of words—are changing," said Oswald.

As for art, the FRG reactionaries have always tried to use the bourgeois classics for their own purposes. But now they go further: "They're now taking up certain things in the cultural area that they denied before—such as the proletarian tradition from the beginning of the century through the twenties, including the tradition represented by Käthe Kollwitz. Until the mid-sixties they pretended this wasn't art," related Oswald. "But since we've carried on everything progressive in bourgeois art as well as the proletarian tradition, they couldn't pretend a unity of culture if they denied the proletarian tradition— which they now interpret in their own way." They also interpret in their own way a proper approach to classical bourgeois artists.

"In Hamburg there is no Heinrich Heine street or monument. In Düsseldorf the university should be named after him. It is not. They hate him 120 years after he died," declared Günter Klein, a journalist and deputy director of Panorama GDR, an organization that produces books and films on the GDR for other countries.

"Goethe," he continued, "they promote as a minister of state, a gentleman. But they don't mention the last words of Faust: 'I would like to see such a crowd, standing on free soil as a free people.'"

While the GDR conducts a sharp struggle against the "united German cultural nation" propaganda, it welcomes all efforts by the people's forces in the FRG to develop progressive culture—in the face of attacks from the bourgeoisie. "In the FRG, as in every capitalist nation, there are two cultures—that of the oppressed and the oppressor," said Peter Meter. "Here where the working class is in power, we develop the culture of the working class and its allies. But we have common elements in our goals with the progressive forces in the FRG who develop the culture of the oppressed class."

MOVING FROM the world of FRG fiction to the world of fact, one learns that the socialist GDR does indeed have close cultural ties with other states—that is, with the other members of the socialist community. Each of these countries encourages the full development of its own national culture, and at the same time promotes closer cultural ties with the other socialist nations—a process that enriches the socialist culture and national identity of each country while bringing them all closer together.

"The main international task of the Association of Theater Workers," said Klaus Pfützner, "is to enrich socialist art together with the other socialist countries. Our theater scientists go to these countries to study their plays and bring them to the GDR. We want to further integrate plays from the fraternal countries with the GDR theater."

In addition to the plays from other socialist countries in the repertories of GDR theaters, the GDR also stages a festival of plays from a different socialist country each year. Many of the plays from these countries deal with matters at the heart of socialist development. Others offer insights in different ways.

"In other socialist countries there are different ideas from ours on socialist realism," pointed out Pfützner. "At one time we had the dogmatic view that a play had to have a positive character in it. But you can't ask this of every play. The Hungarians never had this opinion. They've produced plays with petty-bourgeois characters only, characters with very un-socialist traits. At one time we wouldn't have put them on—we thought it wouldn't help develop socialist personalities. Now we feel we must play them—there are still petty-bourgeois survivals in people."

In the GDR, as Peter Meter said, "We understand theater as revolutionary only if it helps change the world through artistic and scientific means in the interest of the working class." And the plays produced in the GDR—whether contemporary, classical, from the socialist, capitalist or "third" world—are staged with this idea in mind.

At the Volkstheater Rostock, Erhard Schmidt said, "Young people don't know history through their own experience, and we want to develop this consciousness in them. Right now I think it might be important to stage something again about the war in Spain. Our young people know it from their history lessons, but the emotional impact of a work of art in forming this consciousness of history is still more important."

Gerhard Piens told us of a successful Dresden State Theater production on a "third world" theme: *The Glory and Death of Joaquin Murieta,* based on a poem by Pablo Neruda. "This is a ballad about robbers during the gold rush in California," said Piens. Although set in the past, the ballad has direct contemporary meaning: "Joaquin Murieta is a Chilean hero and the theme is the fight against imperialism in its earliest stages."

In the play a troupe of actors puts on a performance in a Chilean slum on election day to encourage the people to vote for Popular Unity candidates. "The actors ask the people who live in the slum to play the part of Murieta. They do so—and become more conscious of history and more class conscious." The play was staged after the fascist coup in Chile.

WITHIN THE principle of helping to "change the world through artistic and scientific means in the interest of the working class," the GDR theater itself has changed over the years.

"We had to start off by propagating the normal humanities, such as understanding amongst the people," Maik Hamburger pointed out. "But the aims of the theater gradually took on a more active direction. It was in the early fifties when our government set us the task of helping to build socialism. Of course the theater embraced this task as its central motivation."

Many in the West, we said to Hamburger, would consider this "central motivation" as inconsistent with artistic achievement.

"Of course," he replied, "there are bourgeois critics and ideologists who maintain socialist motivation is incompatible with artistic quality. The facts show this not to be the case—even the facts supplied by the bourgeois world itself. I think if you compare the situation of West European theater with the theater in socialist countries, you'll realize that constructive and continuous theatrical work is only possible if you have people who are driven by an inner purpose. Some theater people in Western countries with an inner purpose start theaters, but these last only a few years—until circumstances force them to cease."

By contrast, said Hamburger, "in the socialist countries where the inner purpose of theater artists—with all their diversity of individual styles and personalities—corresponds basically with the purpose of society as a whole, the quality of theater can boast of a continuity which you look for in vain in Western countries."

IN THE U.S., members of the Federal Theater, the Group Theatre and other ensembles of the thirties, as well as of the sixties, were "driven by an inner purpose." But after brief activity these theaters were forced to halt: Money problems, political repression and cooption brought their work to an end. This does not negate their value: Some of the light remains even though the candle flickered out. (However, in a basic sense more light was cast in the thirties by the Federal Theater than by the Group: The former had the participation of Black artists, although in far from sufficient numbers, while the Group was all white.)

Among the enormous barriers put up in our country to prevent emergence of a new people's theater movement are the false attitudes promoted toward socialist countries where revolutionary theater exists. As the people's movement in the U.S. becomes stronger and stronger—as the people's ability to perceive what is revolutionary at home and throughout the world develops—these barriers will be overcome.

7. Stronger Than the Night

He's a member of the National Democratic Party and I'm a member of the Socialist Unity Party," said the Volksbühne's Deputy *Intendant* Dieter Klein, motioning toward critic Rolf Dieter Eichler. "As to the goals of our state, we're certainly of the same opinion. But there's a lively discussion on how we should solve problems. Lively discussion is a part of socialism—and almost everything enters into this discussion."

Almost everything?

"We don't allow war mongering, we don't allow racism. They're not permitted, we don't want them," declared Klein.

And at the Volkstheater Rostock actor Erhard Schmidt, speaking of the work of GDR playwrights, said: "No one can write in favor of racism, fascism or war. But no one would try it. It's just not possible."

Differences on the GDR's prohibition of racist, fascist or pro-war expressions may arise between GDR citizens and visitors from the West. But it's not a point of difference among GDR citizens themselves: This is a long settled matter.

However, to many in the U.S.—including civil libertarians and even some radicals—a ban on this type of expression is an "infringement" of free speech. There must be no limitation, they assert, on "advocacy"—even if one advocates racism, fascism or war. To set up limits, they contend, puts free speech itself in jeopardy. Controversies around this question—particularly between those who defend the "right" to be racist and those who assert that racism contradicts freedom—occur time and again in the U.S.

In 1920, for example, film producer and director D.W. Griffith published a pamphlet titled, *The Rise And Fall of Free Speech,* in which he stated:

The right of free speech has cost centuries upon centuries of untold suffering and agonies; it has cost rivers of blood; it has taken as its toll uncounted fields littered with the carcasses of human beings—all this that there might come to live and survive that wonderful thing, the power of free speech . . .[1]

On one night in 1920, 10,000 people were arrested in the Palmer Raids as suspected "bolsheviks." And on the day the Armistice was signed in 1918, 1,500 opponents of World War I were still in jail. When these thousands of jailings took place Griffith made no protest against the infringement of the "right of free speech" and the "untold suffering and agonies" it caused. In fact, he had exercised his own "right of free speech" by making propaganda films demanding U.S. entry into World War I—films which portrayed "all Germans as loathsome."[2]

During the same post-war period in which Griffith issued his pamphlet, "rivers of blood" *were* flowing in the U.S. From 1919 to 1922, 239 Black people were lynched, some of them still in their army uniforms. (During the war itself 199 Blacks had been lynched.) In addition there was a great number of shootings of Blacks. And more "rivers of blood" flowed in the post-war period when "race riots" were touched off by mob attacks on Blacks in Northern as well as Southern cities—leaving large numbers of Black casualties. It was a time when Ku Klux Klan membership had grown nationally to an estimated five million. For this wave of terror—and the growth of the Klan—D.W. Griffith bore a grave individual responsibility.

In 1915 his *Birth of a Nation* had been released. The film's portrayal of the post-Civil War Reconstruction period (with Black roles played by white actors in blackface) is described by Donald Bogle, in his book on the treatment of Blacks in U.S. films, as follows:

"Lawlessness runs riot!" says one title card. The old slaves have quit work to dance. They roam the streets, shoving whites off sidewalks. They take over the political polls and disenfranchise whites. A black political victory culminates in an orgiastic street celebration. Blacks dance, sing, drink, rejoice. Later they conduct a black Congressional session . . . in which the freed Negro legislators are depicted as lustful, arrogant, and idiotic. They bite on chicken legs and drink whiskey from bottles while sprawling with their bare feet upon desks.

Bogle continues:

Matters in *The Birth of a Nation* reach a heady climax when the renegade black Gus sets out to rape the young Cameron daughter [of the former slave-owning family]. Rather than submit, the Pet Sister flees from him and throws herself from a cliff—into the "opal gates of death." Then the mulatto Silas Lynch attempts to force white Elsie Stoneman to marry him. Finally, when all looks hopelessly lost; there emerges a group of good, upright Southern white men, members of an "invisible empire," who, while wearing white sheets and hoods, battle the blacks in a direct confrontation. Led by Ben Cameron in a rousing stampede, they magnificently defeat the black rebels! Defenders of white womanhood, white honor, and white glory, they restore to the South everything it has lost, including its white supremacy. Thus we have the birth of a nation. And the birth of the Ku Klux Klan.[3]

Before its New York premiere, the film was shown at the White House for President Woodrow Wilson. Wilson lauded it, but was forced to disavow his praise as protests against the film mounted: The New York opening was picketed by the NAACP, which also led massive demonstrations when the film came to Chicago and Boston. Other organizations joined the campaign. With protest from Blacks and whites continuing, *The Birth of a Nation* was eventually banned in five states and nineteen cities. But it played in countless others. Donald Bogle states:

In the South, the film was often advertised as calculated to "work audiences into a frenzy . . . it will make you hate." In some regions, the ad campaign may have been effective, for in 1915 lynchings in the United States reached their highest peak since 1908.[4]

The Birth of a Nation continues to be reissued, with "artistic merit" usually offered as the reason: The film is frequently credited with introducing certain film techniques. Be that as it may, *The Birth of a Nation* definitely introduced to the screen racist stereotypes that—with whatever variations—still plague the U.S. cinema.

When *The Birth of a Nation* is rereleased, there is almost always protest. Occasionally it has kept the film from being shown. It was because of the original protest that D.W. Griffith wrote *The Rise And Fall of Free Speech,* with which he launched a long-running crusade against "censorship." Today Griffith's views on "artistic freedom" versus "censorship" are still maintained by the mass media.

On July 20, 1975, *The New York Times* ran an article titled "The Campaign To Suppress 'Coonskin.'" The writer, Stephen Farber, reported that a "controversy exploded" at a prerelease showing of *Coonskin,* an animated film directed by Ralph Bakshi. Several Black leaders present for the screening "vehemently attacked" the movie (whose racism even seeped into its title). One leader said, "It depicts blacks as hustlers and whores. It is a racist film to me, and very insulting." Another said, "The movie perpetuates racial disrespect. The black community does not need people like Bakshi who want to make clowns out of us. Every movie and TV show depicts blacks as comics, whores, pushers or pimps."

Black organizations initiated a campaign against *Coonskin,* forcing the original distributor to drop the film. Backed up by *The New York Times,* Bakshi seized on the "censorship" issue: "My freedom is being taken away from me . . . If I don't start fighting back, I'm going to lose." He added, "But I refuse to do non-political films that offend no one. I would rather give up animation." (This would be a real contribution on Bakshi's part, since he personally was responsible for *Coonskin's* grotesque animated caricatures of Blacks.)

When Bakshi and his producer found another distributor for *Coonskin,* one Black leader declared, "We charge them with high crimes against black people—stereotyping and degrading blacks." Black leaders who pledged to continue the campaign against showing this film were asked by the *Times'* Farber if "the attempt to block the release of *Coonskin* might not be considered a form of censorship." One leader replied, "We call it self-defense, not censorship. We're not going to give these film-makers license to exploit black people." Another declared, "If you try to stop a factory from polluting the environment, is that censorship? *Coonskin* is a form of mental pollution."

D.W. GRIFFITH's views on "freedom of the arts" are also shared by those who have formed a cult around the films of Leni Riefenstahl, the Nazi director. In 1974 a "festival" of her films was arranged in Aspen, Colorado. Riefenstahl travelled from Munich, FRG, to attend the event, held amidst picketing and other heated protests. And in 1975 a "hot debate" was touched off, *The New York Times* reported, when two Riefenstahl films were included in an Atlanta arts festival described by its sponsors as "a 'salute' to 'humanism' in society as portrayed by women artists." The *Times* went on to state:

A proposal to show two controversial Nazi-era films in Atlanta has divided this city's art community, probably the South's most active, and stirred hot debate about the fine line between art and propaganda, censorship and good taste and government support of and interference in the arts.[5]

The director of an Atlanta museum, one of the festival's sponsors, reacted to the protests by stating, "They put pressure on us very hard, but we will not be subjected to any form of censorship." He added: "As a matter of fact, there are several other films to be shown that also involve a political point of view, but again that is not our interest."

But the politics of Riefenstahl's films is of more than passing interest: One of the "humanist" films scheduled for the festival was *Triumph of the Will*, a 1936 "documentary" glorifying the Nazi Party. Hitler personally asked Riefenstahl to direct this film, which was distributed by his propaganda ministry. At a time when other German film-makers were driven into exile, imprisoned or murdered, Riefenstahl was presented the Nazis' film-of-the-year award for *Triumph of the Will.*

The other "humanist" Riefenstahl film scheduled for the Atlanta festival was *Olympiad,* on the Olympics held in Berlin, 1936. *Olympiad*—which was premiered in 1938 on Hitler's birthday, with Hitler himself in the audience—is frequently used as an illustration of the alleged separation between art and politics. The original version—which contained shots of Hitler's address to the Olympics, of prominent Nazi spectators and the awarding of Nazi victory medals—was edited for post-war distribution. Nevertheless, the fascist spirit remains intact in what one critic calls "the purified versions." This critic writes:

Leni Riefenstahl's films about the Olympic Games . . . are, even in their purified versions that evade mention of Hitler and other Nazi leaders, still outspokenly fascistic in spirit. The films celebrate sport as an heroic, superhuman feat, a kind of ritual. This is especially apparent in the narration, which constantly resounds with words like "fight" and "conquest" and also in shots, for example, of marathon races through the forest that are stylized in Nordic mystery . . . These few illustrations should suffice to demonstrate the difficulty of separating Leni Riefenstahl's seemingly "unpolitical" films from her blatant propaganda works. Both emanate from a unified mind.[6]

What do GDR artists think of the showing of Leni Riefenstahl's films?

"I find it terrifying that they're being shown again," replied novelist Irmtraud Morgner, born the year Hitler seized power. "A writer should say something you can touch—but there's very little I can say." She paused, then remarked: "They are using the fashion of nostalgia, especially to affect young people. For young people this past is far away, and they are using certain things from it to awaken the sensation of curiosity. This is a strange past, but on the outside it may seem harmless—the people wore peculiar clothes, the fashions were odd. They display this fascist past as one displays grandmother's kerosene lamp. It's as if grandmother said, 'I'll tell you now how things used to be and the bloody present will not be immediately noticed.'"

And Ruth Berghaus of the Deutsche State Opera said, "The propaganda apparatus of the Nazis was enormous—and showing these films has nothing in common with freedom. It's very dangerous. It's a question of tolerating fascism and war mongering. In the FRG there are also exhibitions of Nazi 'art'—and one can't apologize for any of this by calling it 'the cult of nostalgia.' You can only answer this with the last lines of *Arturo Ui*"—Brecht's parable of Hitler's rise to power—" 'The womb out of which he crept is still fruitful.'"

And writer Claus Küchenmeister responded: "That's a strange question to ask a GDR citizen. Here you can see such films for scientific purposes or research work. But poison and lies cannot be exhibited here unless they're so labeled—in chemistry if you're not warned to beware of poison you can be poisoned. If our film students see such pictures it's always with a commentary that unmasks the propaganda—the old lies and the new lies," said Küchenmeister, who with his wife Wera is the author of films, plays, librettos and children's books.

But when such films are presented for the general public as "art," he continued, "you 'objectivize' fascism: It becomes an historical phenomenon that is quite harmless and doesn't concern us now. A similar thing was done in the FRG when Goebbels' propaganda journal was printed in a newspaper without a commentary. This has a serious effect on young people. Every young man likes a certain circle of very close friends, and if his ideal is the SS it becomes a crime. Riefenstahl's films were made with a great deal of money and they have a certain effect on those who don't know that time, who may think the youth of that time were very lucky."

And Wera Küchenmeister said: "This is not just a media campaign for 'freedom of the arts' in connection with Leni Riefenstahl. I think the example of Riefenstahl must be taken very seriously, but one must not forget that her films are shown as part of a larger campaign—a large-scale strategy. The audiences that see such films absorb the hostile propaganda without realizing it." But given a certain "political constellation of events, what they've absorbed can come out. This is the purpose of propaganda. The ordinary audience is not to blame for absorbing this. One must blame the Western media and those behind them."

That the handling of Riefenstahl's films *is* part of a "large-scale strategy" can be verified by the U.S. mass media's treatment of related events in other fields. For instance, Shockley and Jensen—the current "theoreticians" of the "biological inferiority" of Black people—frequently speak on college campuses. When students picket and boo their appearances, they are charged by the media and university administrations with depriving Shockley and Jensen of their "right to free speech."

And in 1975 Judge Irving R. Kaufman also emerged in the media as a victim of "censorship." Kaufman, who passed the death sentence on Ethel and Julius Rosenberg, complained that he was suffering a "continuing pattern of harassment" because students booed him when he spoke on campuses. Judge Kaufman, it seems, has increasingly run into this difficulty since the Rosenbergs' sons, Michael and Robert Meeropol—backed by thousands of supporters—demanded the reopening of their parents' case. Although the Rosenbergs were officially convicted as "atom-bomb spies," large numbers of people now realize they were actually convicted as advocates of peace during the Korean War hysteria, and condemned to death in an era of raging anti-communism, racism and anti-Semitism. (Kaufman's selection as judge was a vain attempt to disguise the anti-Semitism involved in the trial. In fact, when Kaufman pronounced the death sentence, he reminded many people of the Jews who led other Jews to the gas chamber in Nazi Germany.)

THE HISTORY of film in the old German state eliminates any possible confusion between the "right" to advocate racism, fascism and war, and the right to freedom of speech. The Nazis (whose film industry was headed by Joseph Goebbels) not only made anti-Semitic films, but they also inserted, at random, anti-Semitic passages into films on other themes. In addition, they banned the showing of pre-Hitler films with "non-aryan" actors.

One of the films with an anti-Semitic theme, *Der ewige Jude (The Eternal Jew)* pictures Jews in a hideously repulsive manner, compares them with rats, and charges them with dominating the world economy. The film ends, as the official synposis puts it, with contrasting scenes of "German men and German order," which "fill the spectator with a feeling of deep-seated gratification for belonging to a people whose leader has absolutely solved the Jewish problem." Another notorious film, *Jud Süss (Jew Süss),* is reminiscent of *The Birth of a Nation:* It portrays a Jew brutally raping an "aryan" who manages to escape and drown herself.

And like *The Birth of a Nation* before it, *Jud Süss* illustrated the connection between racist propaganda and racist violence. The authors of an article titled "Jackboot Cinema," which appeared in the British magazine, *Films and Filming,* state:

The impact of [*Jud Süss*] on adolescents was enormous and devastating. For example, in Vienna an old Jewish man was trampled to death on a public street by Hitler youth bands which had just seen the film. Special mention must be made of the refined tactics of the authorities who looked the other way when such a film was officially classified "unsuitable for young people." The lowest instincts of mankind were appealed to. This is seen in a rape sequence, intercut with a torture scene, which was cleverly built up to a climax. Ferdinand Marian [the actor playing the title part] . . . made of Jew Süss a personified Satan.[7]

And like *The Birth of a Nation, Jud Süss*, was cinematically effective:

Without doubt, this film was the best propaganda film of the Third Reich due to the high level film technique . . . The fascination exercised by this film was twice as dangerous, since the insidious intention of this work was fully attained—the film was a great box-office hit.[8]

At Christmas 1940, *Jud Süss* was being shown in sixty-six theaters in Berlin alone. Himmler declared it compulsory viewing for all military troops at home and at the front, as well as for the SS and the police. It was also widely exported to those parts of Europe occupied by the Nazis.

In the book *Theater and Film in the Third Reich,* Josef Wulf states:

It is no coincidence that the three anti-Semitic movies *Die Rothschilds, Jud Süss,* and *Der ewige Jude* were premiered precisely in 1940. Unquestionably, Goebbels had those three films made and shown because of the planned and later actually executed "Final Solution of the Jewish Problem" . . .⁹

WHEN BLACK people charged the makers of a racist film with "high crimes"—and tried to prevent showing of that film—*The New York Times* called it "censorship." This form of "censorship" has been strictly enforced in the GDR—as demanded by the GDR Constitution which makes the propagation of racist, fascist or pro-war views a "high crime."

The New York Times' views on "freedom of the arts" are fully in line with the approach of the Western powers to this same matter after World War II. Under the pressure of world opinion, the U.S., British and French occupation powers were forced to try Veit Harlan, director of *Jud Süss,* for crimes against humanity. In 1950 they acquitted him for "lack of sufficient evidence." (It is understandable that these powers—each with a long record of racist oppression internally and/or colonially—would find *Jud Süss* insufficient evidence of crimes against humanity.) The freed Harlan promptly returned to his old occupation, and between 1950 and 1958 directed nine more pictures in the FRG.

"It all depends on what you understand by freedom," noted Ruth Berghaus. "There is no abstract or absolute freedom. As Hegel said, 'The truth is concrete.' Centuries ago the word 'freedom' was included in every sentence of the constitution in Germany. What was achieved by this is another matter. And I assume that those who manipulate the word 'freedom' today also want to achieve a certain objective.

"In our constitution we're very precise in handling this word. Racist acts are punishable by law."

AT THE END of World War II Irmtraud Morgner was twelve years old. The daughter of a railway engineer and a dressmaker, she had never been outside the working-class section of the town she was born in. "The end of the war," she recalled, "was also for me the end of a certain hierarchy. At the top of this hierarchy were the men, in the middle the women, and down at the bottom the children. The men had been soldiers in the Nazi army. Our teachers had also been men—they wore Nazi uniforms and oppressed us. The men had the worst consciences. The women were not quite so guilty. But now this pyramid was turned upside down and the kings all of a sudden were the children. Wonderful. Not only could one sleep because there was no more bombing— now there was tremendous freedom! Such beautiful things available, things I could never have touched before. Now I could touch litera- ture—have the courage to touch literature."

The hierarchy of the child's world had been overturned because the hierarchy of the real world was being overturned. Following people's plebiscites, the property of the war criminals and active Nazis—who had also been the owners of industry—was expropriated. Working- class men and women—at first hungry and cold and often without pay—began to operate those plants that had not been destroyed. The land of the Junkers, of the other big landowners and that of all active fascists was expropriated. War criminals and active Nazis were punished. Irmtraud Morgner's fascist teachers were removed: At the end of the war, over 28,000 of the 39,000 teachers in the Eastern part of Germany had been Nazi Party members. In the face of threats and sabotage, they were replaced by the "new teachers," young Germans who wanted to build a new life of peace and democracy. Most of these "new teachers" had little formal education, and were trained as they taught by anti-fascist instructors.

In the Soviet Occupation Zone the hierarchy was dismantled against fierce opposition from the same forces that prevented its overturn in the Western Occupation Zones. (For example, people's plebiscites in the West also voted for expropriating the property of war criminals and Nazis. But the war criminals and Nazis, backed up by the U.S. and other Western powers, prevented this from being carried out.)

Alongside reconstruction of the ruins in the streets went the struggle to reconstruct the ruins inside people's heads. New democratic mass organizations were formed among workers, women, youth, artists— all of which played a part in overcoming fascist ideology. One of these organizations was the League of Culture.

"From its formation in 1945 until 1958 the League's work was totally devoted to overcoming racism, anti-Semitism and national chauvinism by cultural means—to get all of this out of people's heads and replace it with a humanist culture," related the League's secretary, Gerd Haines.

"The League," Haines continued, "had a pre-history in other countries—where German refugees got together to develop their own cultural life during exile. This was not just for abstract cultural reasons but to make use of art as a weapon—understood as a weapon and applied as a weapon."

Two months after V-Day the League opened its offices in the British sector of West Berlin. "All the occupation powers had agreed to the League's formation. But when the Western powers (particularly the Americans) noticed that its members did not have an idyllic approach to culture—that they wanted to rebuild the country with the help of progressive culture—they were thrown out of their offices. They settled on this side in 1947." (There is also a League of Culture in the FRG but it continually faces government restrictions—"not because all the members are Communists but because all are progressive. To this day we have very good relations," said Haines.)

In carrying on the anti-fascist, democratic struggle through cultural means, "the main thing was to find a link with the cultural heritage interrupted by the Nazis," said Peter Meter, cultural director of the Committee of Anti-Fascist Resistance Fighters. "We had to prove that not all Germans were Nazi war criminals," declared Meter—who had plenty of experience with those who were: In 1933 he was arrested for doing "illegal work." Released from prison in 1935, he was rearrested in 1936. He spent nine years in a concentration camp.

"The greater part of the German people," continued Meter, "had been corrupted and taken along, but you couldn't talk to them as though they were Nazis. You had to reach them at the point where they stopped before the Nazis. Heine, Goethe, Schiller, Thomas Mann—all became of greater importance in a new sense. Now we had to prove that once upon a time Germans had been a people called thinkers and poets. And that meant Germans had to continue and develop this great tradition in the cultural field. We had to prove that to be German did not necessarily mean to be a barbarian, but could instead mean something humane and progressive.

"For me," said Meter, "Lessing, the author of *Nathan the Wise,* is a great example of progressive humanism. When I was in prison I stole a prohibited book from what the Nazis called 'the poison cupboard.' I stole this book just after I learned of 'crystal night'"—when the Nazis stormed into Jewish homes. The book was *Nathan the Wise*. "I understood it in such a deep way. I saw what a contradiction there was between the high demands of the best German cultural inheritance and the barbarism under fascism."

MOST OF the theaters in the Eastern part of Germany reopened with *Nathan the Wise*. Of this reopening Brecht wrote:

[After the October Revolution the] young Soviet Government, hard-pressed from within and without, showed touching care for the theater amidst war and starvation. Help was given in the form of coal, special rations, urgent tasks.

This was repeated 25 years later when the Soviet Commandant in conquered Berlin gave orders, in the very first day, that the theaters which Hitler had closed should be reopened. The enemy, defeated with such difficulty, was invited to the theater. The first things the victor did were to supply bread, ensure water supplies, and open the theaters.[10]

No more direct confrontation with fascist ideology—instilled through such means as *The Eternal Jew* and *Jew Süss*—could have been made than by reopening the theaters with *Nathan the Wise*. "There were many heads that still had fascist, racist poison in them. This criminal race hatred against Jewish co-citizens had penetrated their minds and we had to get it out of them," declared actor Erhard Schmidt. "Our theater confronted this problem: There were many plays dealing with this question. The whole field of culture worked on it. It's a different story today. Every spectator knows scientifically there's no such thing as a race question in terms of inferior races."

"The theaters went all out on this question in every respect," stated Gerhard Piens of the Dresden State Theater. "We especially dealt with anti-Sovietism and anti-Semitism"—which had led to the deaths of six million Jews and more than twenty million Soviet citizens. "The Party and the mass organizations worked intensively to eradicate these old attitudes and replace them with the new. We did this with all our strength." Piens, too, stressed the importance of the humanist bridge in reaching people whose thoughts had been deformed by fascism.

"There's an old humanist theater tradition in Germany and even during the Nazis, little islands of humanism survived. We had the good fortune that those who didn't want to learn anything went to the West, and we could start with people who were ready to bring humanism and anti-fascism to the stage. And by and by this included socialism. It was quite a fluid transition." He added: "Now we have a unified system of culture and education that includes all media." (Gerhard Piens was a direct part of the reeducation process: He served as one of the "new teachers.")

Bertolt Brecht's plays, which he staged himself, had a powerful effect in the struggle to change people's consciousness. "I could prove by my own experience how much those who saw his plays were helped by them—even bourgeois cultural workers who still retained remnants of fascist ideology. Brecht's plays influenced them at least toward anti-fascist, humanist thoughts—especially through Helene Weigel's interpretation of *Mother Courage*," said Ludwig Einicke, press and information officer of the Committee of Anti-Fascist Resistance Fighters.

As a youth Einicke was a metal worker. He joined the Communist Party, did "illegal work" after Hitler came to power, was arrested in 1935 and spent more than ten years in a concentration camp. During the Soviet Occupation he served as vice minister of education in a region including the Halle area. "After every theater premiere— whether it was a play by Brecht, an opera or a work by a traditional Russian author—our Soviet comrades organized a discussion evening." Present were the performers and other theater workers, cultural workers in mass organizations, educators, etc. "We discussed whether the performance had really brought out the humanist core of the play or opera.

"Our Soviet comrades," Einicke continued, "helped us develop a humanist, democratic culture in order to overcome the influences of fascism—and pave the way for socialist culture. Our Soviet comrades did this exceedingly well." He gave an example: "About two years ago I got a phone call from the Deutsche State Opera. I was invited to come to the opera café that night. When I arrived there was a surprise for me: About twenty-five or thirty of the actors and actresses who'd been in Halle were there with their husbands or wives. Then the Soviet officer who'd been in Halle during the occupation appeared." Some of the theater workers from his Halle days, Einicke said, are Party members. Others are not. "But all are absolutely at our side in building socialism. This shows how our theater work helped us tremendously in paving the way for the socialist future." He added: "Many people were poisoned by fascist and racist theories—and Brecht's plays especially were of tremendous help in overcoming this fascist mentality, in helping to free people from this poison."

The secretary of the German-Soviet Friendship Association, Herbert Grünstein, also recalled those post-war days: "After theater life was begun anew by order of the Soviet commandant, the first play, *Nathan the Wise,* made a terrific impact on the population." But the Soviet commandant not only made it possible for German artists to stage humanist works. Soviet artists also performed—with an astounding impact on the people who had been taught to hate them.

"The thing that changed the attitude toward the Soviet Union was the Alexandrov Ensemble of the Red Army," related Grünstein, who fought in Spain with the German Thälmann Battalion, and who served as the GDR's first secretary of state. "They appeared in a square in Berlin in August 1948 for an audience of almost a million and a half people. They sang old German folk songs, including the one by Heine, 'A boy saw a rose growing in a field.' This is the most popular German folk song of all—and for Germans to hear it sung by those 'Russian barbarians who'd come to destroy civilization' was overwhelming."

It was in this time of revolutionary social and cultural change that the child Irmtraud Morgner could "touch literature."

"There had been no books in my family. Neither my parents nor the larger family had any," she recalled. "The people I grew up among spoke very little. One didn't talk about one's feelings. There was a piano and I thought the secrets of the world could be expressed only by sounds." She had gone to the gymnasium, the school for working-class children. "And children who went to the gymnasium did not touch the classics. I was terribly surprised to learn that you could also express the secrets of life in words. Goethe's *Faust* looks strange inside the head of a young girl. It was like a storm or an earthquake for me."

The hierarchy of the child's world, and the entire hierarchy of the old society, had been permanently overturned. And this child, like many other working-class children, was on the way to a university, on the way to becoming a writer—something that would have been virtually impossible for the daughter of workers if the hierarchy had been allowed to stay in place.

NOT LONG after the reopening of the theaters, the Soviet commandant authorized the resumption of film-making. In fact, just two months after the war ended, a meeting of film-makers had been held. This event is described in the program notes for the Museum of Modern Art's 1975 festival of GDR films, as follows:

On November 17, 1945, the first post-war gathering of people in the movie industry was held in the ruins of the famous Hotel Adlon in Berlin. They were there to discuss the most urgent steps to be taken in order to build up an anti-fascist democratic film industry. With the help of the Soviet Military Administration, it was possible to start dubbing Soviet films as early as a few weeks after the end of the war.

In May 1946 DEFA, the film organization, was established. The museum's program notes state:

Colonel Tulpanov of the Soviet Military Administration emphasized, while handing out the license, that the supreme obligation of the German cinema had to consist in "aiding the democratic renewal of Germany, in educating the German people, particularly the youth, in a spirit of democracy and humanism in an effort to arouse respect for other people and countries."

DEFA began to carry out this responsibility with its first film, *The Murderers Are Among Us.*

The Murderers Are Among Us was one of the few DEFA films shown in the U.S. before the government—in an intensifying cold war and McCarthyite atmosphere—banned them. In 1948 *Cue* magazine described *The Murderers Are Among Us* as "a savage picture of Berlin in 1945, where people are trying to rebuild their lives among the ruins. Its realism and impact are heightened by the obvious fact that the producers know only too well what they are talking about." The film, *Cue* went on, concerns a

shell-shocked doctor's attempts to master his war-induced melancholia, and resume his post-war practice. He is aided and comforted in his struggle back to normality by a young girl liberated from a concentration camp.

The film's title, *Cue* pointed out,

refers to the Germans who ordered mass executions of civilians during the war, and part of the doctor's mental turmoil arises from his driving compulsion to hunt down and kill his captain, who had ordered such an execution one Christmas Eve. The film ends on a fine note of bitterness as the cornered murderer shrieks, "I am innocent" ... The fact that this mass murderer bears a marked resemblance to the late Heinrich Himmler makes the scene even more meaningful.[11]

A journal from the Eastern part of Germany, where *The Murderers Are Among Us* had been released in 1946, wrote:

[DEFA's] very first great dramatic film, produced under inexpressible difficulties practically from nothing within a record time, will—unless we are utterly mistaken—prove to the listening world that in the new, democratic

Germany . . . forces are at work which will not rest until those dishonorers of the German name, until the criminals of that war have been punished.

We have been warned: the murderers are still in our midst. Will the German people understand this exhortation and warning?[12]

This was not left a question in the Eastern part of Germany. By mid-1946 the first plebiscite on the punishment of war criminals and active Nazis had been held in one of the industrial centers, followed by the plebiscites in other areas. The political and economic power of these forces was being abolished. To carry on this struggle it was, of course, necessary that the people as a whole understand who were the murderers among them. Everywhere discussions were held "to explain the roots of the war. We were tremendously assisted in this by the great longing for peace, the wish that war would never come again," said journalist Günter Klein.

"After the war the feeling of 'never war again' was very widespread, even among nationalistically-minded people. A large part of Hitler's army had the feeling of having been defeated by a mighty Soviet Army and betrayed by the Nazis. The tenor of the books by former German soldiers who became writers can be seen in the title of one, *Betrayed Till The Last Day.*

"We started from this point: If you never want to be betrayed again on this soil where for the last three centuries there have been innumerable losses, then you must do everything to support all the steps for dispossessing the Nazi criminals. In this way we motivated people."

His own life had given Klein confidence that the people could be won to a new outlook. In 1940 at the age of eighteen Günter Klein had volunteered to join the Nazi Army. "All twelve boys in our class volunteered for the Wehrmacht. I look back on it today wondering, unable to understand." Klein's father, a skilled worker, was an anti-fascist. "My father said, 'If you ever come back with stars on your uniform, you'll no longer be my son.' It was very courageous of a father to say that at such a time."

Delving into the reasons for his enlistment Klein said, "A great part of the young people—including myself—believed the Nazis. There was such an atmosphere around the Versailles Treaty—and they took advantage of this." But Klein, who was sent into the air force, soon began to go through changes similar to those experienced by many U.S. soldiers in Vietnam. "It didn't take me long to wonder why we were fighting. I became older, more reasonable, and saw through my own eyes. I began to see how soldiers behaved in occupied territories. I also saw how rich sons did not go to the front—whereas I was sent first to the Western front, then to the East."

Klein was one of four members of a plane crew. The pilot was the son of a Catholic, anti-Nazi farmer. The radioman was a worker whose sympathies were with the Left. The mechanic was the son of a Communist murdered by the Nazis. "This boy's fate was especially tragic," recalled Klein. "He was taken from his mother when he was ten and sent to a Nazi school. The boys wore Nazi uniforms and were educated to be fighters—followers of the Nazi Party and the SS. This boy lived in a double world—remembering his father and his father's ideas—and on the other side of this world, remembering the long period he attended the Nazi school."

As the war went on, the crew saw many things. "We saw how they treated concentration camp prisoners who had to work at the airport. We four considered their treatment a crime. And next to the airport there was a camp for Soviet pilots who'd been shot down. Sometimes they gave them no food for weeks but forced them to work. We tried to give them food. This was punishable by death. But we did it with primitive human emotions. Maybe to quiet our consciences."

The crew members were sure that if they were ever forced down on Soviet territory they would be shot to death. "We thought they'd have the moral right to do this. We believed we belonged to an army of criminals." Flying over the Baltic, the crew considered escape to Sweden. "But all German soldiers who deserted to Sweden were returned and sentenced to death. We saw no way out of our misery."

In late 1941 the plane was shot down on Soviet territory. "When the plane landed, our pilot gave the order for us to shoot ourselves. He did this first. Then the mechanic—the youth who lived in a double world. The radioman, who was wounded from flak, did not pick up his gun. I hesitated—I was the youngest, not yet nineteen. I had my pistol at my forehead when a Soviet lieutenant, three and a half meters away, shot me in the arm. As my pistol dropped he said in German, 'What are you doing? Soon we'll both be dancing the tango in Berlin!' (The lieutenant did not get to Berlin. He didn't survive the war.)"

Klein was taken to a Soviet hospital "where we were cared for in the same way as Soviet people. The internationalist education of the Soviet people was so deep they couldn't understand how simple working people could fight the Soviet Union. From the beginning they asked, 'What are you doing here? What are you fighting for?'

"I did not answer, did not repeat Nazi propaganda. I started really to think." Released from the hospital, Klein was sent to a camp for German prisoners. "My fellow Germans nearly killed me because I believed this war a crime—that we had to stop it and get rid of the people responsible for it."

In the P.O.W. camp the reeducation of Günter Klein and other German soldiers began. Their teachers were Germans in exile who "answered all our questions" and gave them literature—from Thomas Mann to Marxist classics. Later Klein was sent to a "great anti-fascist school in Moscow where we studied day and night." Klein's reeducation was particularly intensive because "I applied to return to Germany—to fight together with the Red Army and the partisans."

By summer 1944 Klein was a partisan inside Germany, fighting with the resistance movement. "After the attempt on Hitler's life in July of that year, the Nazis attacked the resistance movement so severely that most of its members were killed. Many partisans were also killed. Today we reckon that three to four thousand came back to Germany as fighters with the Red Army and as partisans. About three to four hundred of us are still alive. And our story proves that every working person can be won to new ideas.

"In the first years after the war," Klein continued, "most Germans looked on us as traitors, guilty of the death of their sons and husbands. But we had seen those who fought for the youth of our country and who did not give up this fight in the hardest times. This confidence in the youth was handed over to us, and we were expected to educate the youth with the same principles used to reeducate us." He added: "Most of us never dreamed of the life we would later lead."

DEFA FILMS dealt not only with the horrors of fascist rule. They also portrayed the resistance to it. The resistance movement, which Günter Klein joined during the war, was organized at the time Hitler came to power. Among the movies made about resistance fighters in the prewar period was *They Called Him Amigo,* produced in 1959 from a screenplay by Wera and Claus Küchenmeister. It is the story of a fifteen-year-old boy who rescues a resistance fighter from a concentration camp. And *Stronger Than The Night,* made in 1954, centers around a Communist leader, a factory worker, who struggles to help organize the resistance movement. While *Stronger Than The Night* was being shown, a GDR writer examined the reasons why a "serious and shocking political film" had become a "public success":

The taste of a considerable part of the movie-going public, which goes out of its way to see a serious and shocking political film . . . is something that bears further watching. The oft-quoted expression, "The people wish to be left alone," is refuted by this film; the film is a public success. What are the causes of this success?

. . . *Stronger Than The Night* holds its audience spellbound. They experience again, as spectators, a period of time which they lived through as working people, employed or unemployed, which they survived by persisting or denying the reality of the situation. The public feels it urgent for its present life and existence to come to terms with this period.[13]

The public could not, of course, "come to terms with this period" without recognizing the part anti-Semitism played in it. And from the early post-war days DEFA dealt with the Nazis' treatment of Jews and the responsibility of those who allowed this to happen. While *Nathan the Wise* was being staged in the theaters, *Marriage In The Shadows* (1947) and *The Blum Affair* (1948) were being shown in the cinemas.

Of *Marriage In The Shadows,* which is about the marriage of a Jewish woman and an "aryan" man, the *New Republic* wrote: "[This film] proves once more that there can be no moderation in murder, and that no man may escape responsibility for the acts committed in his name." And the *New York Post* called *The Blum Affair* "an extraordinarily perfect picture . . . it was a local Dreyfus case, and all the elements that were to blossom so hideously under Hitler are shown in their earlier setting."

The Blum Affair, Marriage In The Shadows and *The Murderers Are Among Us* were the only DEFA films to be shown in the U.S. before the government ban, which lasted a quarter of a century. Since the end of the official ban, there has been commercial release here of just one GDR film, which had a brief and limited run.

DURING KONRAD Wolf's tour of the U.S., a screening of three of his films was sponsored by the City University of New York Doctoral Programs in German Language and Literature. One of these films, *Stars,* also deals with anti-Semitism under the Nazis. After its showing there was a discussion between Wolf and members of the audience.

"In the film production of the GDR," he said, "this kind of film is not an exception. This theme belongs to DEFA—which returns to it again and again." *Stars,* made in 1959, is the story of the love that develops between a young school teacher—one of a large group of Jews held prisoner before being shipped to Auschwitz—and a German soldier acting as a guard. In contrast to other German soldiers who are shown as thoroughly brutalized by the Nazis, this soldier struggles to regain his humanity. "It was important," Wolf commented, "to show the process of differentiation" taking place among Germans—even, as with Günter Klein, in the fascist army. Portraying this process, Wolf continued, helped give Germans who had lived through that period a "strong moral impulse."

"What was the reaction in East Germany to this film?" asked a student who said she came from Hamburg, FRG. "Was the moral impulse successful?"

"It's not a spectacular film. The people who saw it were in the main made very thoughtful by it," responded Wolf. The film is shown "again and again" on GDR television and the response continues to be "very strong."

"What about the response in West Germany?" asked the same student.

Stars was shown in small theaters in the FRG, replied Wolf. There was a "strong response from young people who learned something from the war." However, when it was shown in Munich, anti-Semitic inscriptions appeared on the walls of the theater. And when it was shown at the Cannes Film Festival, the official FRG delegation left under protest.

Most of the group discussing *Stars* were young. But an older woman, who identified herself as a German Jew, spoke of her "appreciation of this movie." In the thirties, she continued, "I saw a movie made by your father that also dealt with the persecution of Jews." The film was *Professor Mamlock,* based on the play by Friedrich Wolf and made while he was in exile in the Soviet Union.

"In 1961 I also made a film of *Professor Mamlock*," said Konrad Wolf—illustrating anew that DEFA returns to the struggle against anti-Semitism "again and again." This continues right up to the present. In 1974 DEFA produced *Jacob The Liar,* a film about Jews in a ghetto before they are shipped en masse to a concentration camp. It opened the 1975 festival of GDR films at the Museum of Modern Art.

KONRAD WOLF escaped from Nazi Germany as a child. He returned to Germany as a soldier in the Red Army. In 1968 he made the film *I Was 19* based on his war experiences. Günter Klein left Germany as a member of the Nazi Army. He returned as a partisan. In 1976 Wolf made a film, *Mama I Live,* based on Klein's experiences.

Kurt Gutmann fled Germany on the "children's transport." He returned with the British Army. "I was born in 1927 and I was just starting school the year Hitler came to power," related Gutmann. "Our headmaster was a Storm Troop officer and when we came in we were supposed to give the Hitler salute. When I didn't, they beat me with a stick." Gutmann was one of the few Jews in the school, "and on the playground the boys would beat me too. They'd come at me as a group—with one exception. The son of a Communist wouldn't take part.

"From year to year," Gutmann recalled, "it grew worse and worse. After 'crystal night' in 1938, the Jewish men were thrown into concentration camps, Jews were thrown out of windows, the synagogues set on fire. People asked, how far will they go? Up to then the Jews believed it was a pogrom. Then they must finally have realized what Hitler was after. Anti-Semitism was not only the way to draw people's attention from economic problems. It was also a way of brutalizing people—brutalizing the 'master race' for war against the Slavs and other peoples."

In 1939 "my mother had the opportunity to send me on the children's transport to an orphanage in Glasgow." But his mother and older brother didn't have the money to get out. "Of course, I kept on hoping that they had gotten through. But in 1945 I learned they'd been sent on a transport from which no one ever returned." They died in Auschwitz.

In 1942 when he was seventeen and still living in Scotland, Gutmann volunteered for the British Army. "I saw the Soviet Union was really putting up a fight against the Nazis, and I wanted to take part in the war against fascism." In 1947 Gutmann was still in the army, a guard in the British Occupation Zone in Germany.

"Once while I was on guard duty a group of youths went past singing a terrible Nazi song—'We'll go on marching, marching, till the whole world belongs to Germany.' I yelled for them to stop—then shot in the air. They were tried and got two weeks. Not because they sang a fascist song—but because they didn't stop immediately when ordered by a member of the Royal Forces."

And during a dance in the British Occupation Zone, a youth came up to a young woman who was with Gutmann and said, "Did you know you were dancing with a Jew? That's a racial shame." "I hit him," said Gutmann. On another occasion, "I heard someone say, 'It was really terrible what Hitler did to the Jews. But he should have killed all or none. Those left are taking revenge.'" No official steps were taken in the British Occupation Zone against such persistent expressions of fascist ideology. In 1948 when Gutmann was discharged from the British Army, "I returned to the East. I had nobody anywhere and I chose to come here." The differences between the West and the East were immediately apparent.

"I saw that films were being shown in the cinemas on the Nazi concentration camps—this was pressed on people. The older people would say, 'We didn't know.' The younger ones couldn't believe this." Even in the early post-war period great changes had already taken place in the young people's thinking. "In a revolutionary situation things are made very clear to people in just days and months. The young people were shocked by the German defeat. They'd been told terrible things about what the Red Army would do to them. But the soldiers who tried to run away from Hitler's army were shot down by the SS," said Gutmann, who is now a writer for GDR radio.

Despite the intensity of the struggle against anti-Semitism in the Eastern part of Germany, anti-Semitic incidents did not, of course, occur only in the Western occupation zones. The difference between East and West was in the reaction to them.

Lore Krüger is a Jew who escaped from Germany when Hitler came to power. During her exile she lived in a number of countries, including the U.S., and learned the language of each. ("Hitler made me a linguist," she says today.) After the war she returned to the Eastern part of Germany.

"The people here knew much but not all of what happened in the concentration camps to political prisoners and Jews. At first they didn't want to believe it, and they also wanted to convince themselves and others they weren't responsible for it," said Lore Krüger, who is now a translator of English classics into German.

"We explained to the people," she continued, "that racism was used to keep them divided in a time of great depression. At the same time we made very severe laws against racism and war propaganda. We weren't lenient with those who tried to start racism again. We sent them to prison." She gave an example: "Where I lived there was a family with a Nazi background. They made difficulties wherever they could—at elections, everywhere. One of their daughters worked in a factory and made anti-Semitic remarks there. She was put on trial and sentenced to two and half years in prison for racism." She added: "Some people continued to have anti-Semitic feelings but few of them dared to try and corrupt the young generation. They knew we wouldn't allow it."

THE STRUGGLE against old attitudes was a hard and sometimes bitter one. "Large sections of our population still have a completely capitalist way of looking at things. This is true even of parts of the working class," wrote Brecht in 1953.[14] This was the year an attempt was made to restore the old society.

The Nazi war criminals across the border—backed up by the North Atlantic Treaty Organization (NATO) base in West Berlin (which had set up a special staff for counterrevolutionary actions in the GDR)— aimed at regaining the territory they had lost. Because of the persistence of old attitudes these reactionaries were able to exploit certain mistakes made in the GDR's effort to accelerate its economic development.

"In Berlin this attempt at counterrevolution started with a strike of construction workers," related Günter Klein. "In 1945 many of the Nazis who'd been removed from their posts were sent to construction sites to build up what they had destroyed. Thousands of them were there, and most of them very angry—particularly because they saw that in the FRG their old colleagues had important posts."

The attempted counterrevolution was put down decisively. "The vast majority of the people did not take part in it. We isolated the Nazis and agents of imperialism who were behind it, and gave pardons to all workers who'd been misled into taking part," said Klein. "Many of these workers today have the title of Hero of Socialist Labor. And today the construction workers are among the most progressive in the GDR."

THE FIGHT against old attitudes was carried on in an affirmative way, as an integral part of the great effort to create a new outlook. One highpoint in this struggle was the Third World Youth Festival, held in Berlin in 1951.

"The enthusiasm of the young people there was unbelievable," recalled Kurt Gutmann, who at twenty-four was one of the participants.

"The young people from the entire world came here. They made a tremendous impression on young people here who had been hesitant about the new life," said Lore Krüger. "We had told them they could believe in a better world but they were skeptical, especially since the material difficulties were still so great."

Today the children of the GDR youth who participated in that festival are among those who have grown up under socialism. Their parents had been instructed in hatred by the fascists, but their own first books showed pictures of children of all races and nations dancing together. As they grew older, their teachers not only gave them a scientific understanding of race but also a feeling of identification with all peoples, especially the oppressed. As one result, "Our children don't know what it feels like to experience anti-Semitism," said Lore Krüger.

And what is the view of the children themselves?

"I myself have never been religiously inclined in any way. I know very little about the Jewish religion—but I know about Jewish history," responded eighteen-year-old Elke Gutmann, daughter of Kurt, a twelfth-year student planning to specialize in economics.

"It's natural that scientifically educated youth are non-believers, and that they discuss religion from a scientific point of view. But," she emphasized, "young people who are members of a religious community are not second-class citizens, not outsiders in society. Their personality, their achievements are recognized and accepted just as any other member of the collective." She added: "We don't wonder about anyone's religion."

We heard variations of this comment from a number of Jews in the GDR: People here, they said, don't wonder whether someone "looks Jewish" or "has a Jewish name." But, we said, Jews in the U.S. frequently have the experience of "not being taken for Jewish." However, when the fact that they are Jewish becomes known, the reactions of others may inform them of their conversion from individuals into stereotypes. Do your fellow students, we asked Elke Gutmann, know of your Jewish background?

"My father spoke at the annual rally held at school in memory of the victims of fascism. He spoke of the problems of the past and everyone knew he was my father. The young people are very impressed by this—they have the greatest respect for what the anti-fascists went through. But they wouldn't ask me questions and say 'I'm sorry,' because they identify with and consider themselves the heirs of those who fought fascism."

Elke Gutmann and her classmates, she told us, had just staged a play (written by themselves) about a young Black woman in the U.S., a talented artist whose career is stymied by racism. "We didn't learn anything new from the play. It underlined the strong attitude we already had."

In the GDR we heard no discussions of the kind frequently held among whites in the U.S. about the alleged characteristics and capabilities of Blacks and whether "they" should do this, that or the other thing. "We talk about the forms in which racism is expressed in other countries—this disturbs and enrages us. Just a few days ago," Elke related, "we heard a report about a doctor in the States who treated a fourteen-year-old Black boy for a cut. When the boy couldn't pay, the doctor opened the cut again. The father took the doctor to court and the doctor was *fined twenty dollars!*"*

It is through such individual experiences that one learns of GDR citizens' attitudes toward racism. We talked, for example, with Hannelore Mensch, a city councillor and secretary of the Berlin City Council. We told her that a plan to forbid a candidate in New York State from making racial attacks on another candidate had just been declared unconstitutional, an infringement on "free speech," by the U.S. Supreme Court. As an elected official, we asked, what did she think of this?

For several moments she said nothing. She seemed stunned by the question. Finally she replied, "I grew up in a socialist society." After another pause she said, "I must say I cannot even imagine that anything like that could happen here."

What, we pressed, would happen if anything racist occurred at a GDR event?

"There are," she responded, "anti-Semitic attacks on Jewish citizens in West Berlin and the FRG. If in a public event here a racist phenomenon would occur—because people from racist countries were present—all the GDR participants would disassociate themselves, spontaneously, vocally."

□ □ □

THE GDR's remarkable struggle to overcome racism and instill humanist attitudes has impressed many visitors from the West. One of

*This incident occurred in Uniontown, Alabama, in 1976.

them, Raymond H. Boone, editor of the Richmond *Afro-American,* wrote after a recent trip:

Perhaps the most easily-identified example of the GDR's desire to match words with actions in its drive to eradicate racism is the prominence it gives to Paul Robeson—the American great whose name is a household word in the GDR while being vaguely familar in America, largely because of a hostile white press that ignores his greatness.

GDR publishing houses also produce books by a long list of popular black American authors . . . [15]

The GDR's publication of "a long list of popular black American authors" is accompanied by publication of the works of many African writers—all part of a great effort to acquaint GDR people through cultural means with the lives and struggles of oppressed peoples.

But, we have been asked in the U.S., how does this jibe with production in the GDR musical theater of *Porgy and Bess?* Isn't this a contradiction? Yes, it is—and an ironic one.

Porgy and Bess is staged in the GDR for the same reasons that "a long list of popular black American writers" is published there. This is certainly ironic since two of the most popular Black playwrights, Lorraine Hansberry and Joseph Walker, author of *The River Niger,* are among the many many Black artists who have denounced *Porgy and Bess.*

Although outside this country *Porgy and Bess* has acquired the reputation of a folk opera, it is rejected by the folk it presumes to portray. To be specific, Black people, as well as anti-racist whites in the U.S., have rejected *Porgy and Bess* because of its stereotypes. To understand the contradiction in the staging by GDR theater workers of *Porgy and Bess,* it is this question of stereotypes that must be explored.

The stereotypes that turn up in *Porgy and Bess* were engendered by the racist conditions in the U.S. These old-style stereotypes are still with us, but the mass media have reacted to pressures for social change by introducing new ones—or, more accurately, old ones in new forms. Because these figures so endlessly appear in one or another variation in the mass media, it is difficult for whites to recognize them as stereotypes. Instead of rejecting them as racist stereotypes, huge numbers of whites accept them as characteristic Black figures.

There are also difficulties in recognizing stereotypes in the GDR—but for very different reasons. GDR people are highly aware of the struggles of Black people in the U.S. and in Africa. But they themselves are not a part of the struggles inside countries where class and national oppression exists and takes multiple forms—including racist stereotypes. In the GDR racist stereotypes cannot originate in any form: There the roots of racism have been destroyed and the overwhelmingly successful fight against survivals continues. Stereotypes can enter such an anti-racist, pro-human environment only if introduced from alien sources. Thus, when this happens there can be problems in detecting them. To GDR theater workers and audiences the figures in *Porgy and Bess* are likely to appear simply as idiosyncratic characters, which abound in dramatic literature—and certainly the musical theater.

Unlike the folk art of Black people, *Porgy and Bess*—which was pieced together from racist myths by its white creators—reflects not a trace of the struggles of Black people. GDR theater workers obviously perceived this lack: In staging *Porgy and Bess* they introduced elements unknown to U.S. productions in an attempt to dramatize the oppression and resistance of Black people.

GDR theater workers realized something was missing in *Porgy and Bess*—but they didn't recognize what was already there. If one recognizes that *Porgy and Bess* revolves around stereotypes, one can only conclude that efforts to transform it into an anti-racist statement are contradicted by the very nature of the work itself.

In the U.S. we have also been asked: Isn't it a contradiction that blackface is used in the GDR theater to portray Black characters?

Yes, it is—and the way this contradiction arose also requires exploration.

First of all, one reacts to dark makeup as blackface only if one is familiar with the racist use of dark makeup in the U.S. Blackface dates from the days of slavery, when white performers first smeared their faces with burnt cork to caricature Black people in the minstrel shows. Blackface was used in the theater and later in films for the same purpose—and for additional ones: to prevent physical contact between Black male and white female performers, and to employ white instead of Black actors.

In the GDR dark makeup has no such associations for people. Thus it has seemed to be a solution to casting problems in a country whose population is almost entirely white. (Black performers have also appeared in various GDR productions.) Dark makeup—which is applied in a way that simply darkens skin tone—has been used not only in staging *Porgy and Bess* but works of an entirely different character such as *Raisin In The Sun.*

But to discuss *why* GDR actors use dark makeup is not to say that its use, in our opinion, serves the goals of these theater workers. While dark makeup has no more intrinsic meaning than white makeup—which is to say it has no intrinsic meaning at all—it has acquired racist connotations because of its history in the U.S.

GDR actors stand not only in a national but an international spotlight. When they put on dark makeup, they appear in the view of many in the U.S. to identify themselves with the context and associations of blackface. Thus dark makeup serves to obscure the anti-racist commitment of the theater workers of the GDR.

RAYMOND BOONE visited the GDR as a member of a group of sixteen editors and publishers of Black journals, including *Jet* magazine and the *New York Voice.* Other members of the group also published their opinions about the GDR in a series of reports in *The Afro-American*—revealing the striking difference between attitudes in the GDR and those in the FRG, as well as in the U.S.

Sherman Briscoe, then executive director of the National Newspaper Publishers Association, described what happened when the group missed its connecting flight and landed in West Berlin instead of Berlin, GDR:

The only hint of racism to confront our delegation of 16 black editors and publishers in a weeklong trip to the German Democratic Republic was at the airport stand in West Berlin.

There, Briscoe continued,

Dr. Carlton B. Goodlett, president of the National Newspaper Publishers Association and the head of our group, inquired of an airport official about three cabs.

Without batting an eye, he said, "Impossible. There is no way to get that number of cabs for you."

"What can we do?" Goodlett asked.

The West German merely hunched his shoulders.

By then, wrote Briscoe, the hour had grown late:

We had left Kennedy International in New York the night before . . .

Everybody is tired and hungry and short-tempered and looking askance at Dr. Goodlett, who has brought us all this way to meet the kind of Jim Crow we left in Mississippi a decade ago.[16]

Meanwhile, GDR representatives were awaiting the delegation at the Berlin airport. Finally, Dr. Goodlett was able to reach them by phone and arrangements were made to meet at "Checkpoint Charlie" in West Berlin. But the taxicab problem recurred:

Taxis are few and far apart, and German travelers are grabbing them . . . . We tried hailing down three or four of them, but they passed right by and picked up Germans a car length away.

Briscoe concludes:

At Checkpoint Charlie we met our wonderful guides who took us to our hotel and a good dinner at 12:30 in the morning.

For the rest of our trip we experienced not one scintilla of racism, and we went everywhere . . .

But when our tour was over, we headed out of the German Democratic Republic for Copenhagen, looking back occasionally, as if we could not believe that some West German racism had not slopped over the Berlin Wall.[17]

In his article, Raymond Boone also commented on the new human relations in the GDR. He pointed out that there is

. . . evidence of race on the wide, tree-lined main streets of East Berlin. Black students from African nations are frequent faces among motorists and pedestrians. It is not uncommon to see black male students strolling hand in hand with young blondes—without a glance from passersby.[18]

Obviously, GDR citizens do not turn their heads at the sight of an interracial couple because—by any rational standard—such couples are neither more nor less interesting than other couples. What causes such undue fascination (and sometimes violence) on the part of some U.S. whites is not the sight of two human beings whose skin is of different colors, but the racist fantasies such whites project onto others.

In another article in the *Afro-American* series, William O. Walker, editor-publisher of the *Cleveland Call and Post,* wrote: "The German Democratic Republic . . . has done a phenomenal job of physical restoration and human rehabilitation."

After discussing the immense strides in housing, education, etc., Walker concluded:

All of us were greatly impressed with what we saw in the German Democratic Republic; its form of government seems to be working.[19]

IT IS CLEAR that in the past thirty-odd years the consciousness of the people in what was the Eastern part of the former German state has been transformed. This is all the more remarkable when one realizes that influences of the past cannot be eradicated completely in so short a time, but can still be communicated. Further, the GDR is not sealed off from racism; it is, in fact, penetrated by FRG television channels. But such influences cannot corrupt the anti-racist, pro-human attitudes instilled in the GDR.

In the FRG (as in the U.S.) *anti*-racist racist views conflict with the state and its entire apparatus. In the GDR any expression of racism or chauvinism would contradict the socialist state, the media, the educational system and the masses of the people.

It is quite true that at the beginning some Germans had to be "pressured" into "conformity" with the anti-racist "aims and objectives" of the new society. (Black Americans, as well as conscious whites, look to the day when racists from Ralph Bakshi to George Wallace will be "pressured" into "conformity" with the "aims and objectives" of a new, anti-racist U.S.A.) But the overwhelming majority of the people responded to the "aims and objectives" of the new society.

"When the GDR was established in 1949, even the most wildly mixed up people didn't demand 'freedom' for war mongering or racism because we have had our very special experience of both," declared Horst Oswald, Berlin City Councillor for Culture. "From our own history we know that racism and chauvinism are intensified when the ruling class has a situation it can't cope with and is looking for a culprit. For a certain time Hitler was able to distract people's minds with the so-called Jewish question and the 'sub-humanity' of Soviet citizens—to hide the fact that monopoly had created the economic and social problems."

In the U.S. also the "ruling class has a situation it can't cope with"— and here the "culprit" is the Black and other oppressed minorities. Today most whites may still believe that what happens to Blacks doesn't affect them. A good many may even believe that Black advances threaten whites. But while some whites were protesting minimum admission quotas for Blacks as "racism in reverse," college tuitions were escalated, teachers fired—and admissions for all pared away. As whites protested the "forced busing" of their children to interracial schools, the budgets for teachers, books, recreational programs and school maintenance were slashed. White construction workers, fearing for their jobs, have denied Blacks admission into unions; meanwhile, more and more of the national wealth is poured into military spending—and construction slows down nationwide. As for arts programs, they are down at the bottom of a long list of what used to be called "priorities."

But people by the thousands have joined the wave of demonstrations against the cutbacks, the closings and the firings. They are beginning to see who the real "culprit" is.

More and more artists, particularly young ones, are also recognizing the real "culprit"—a system that allows theaters, operas and symphony halls to close while performers are turned out on the streets. It is this system that protects "free speech" for the Bakshis and the Riefenstahls—while trying to deny it to artists and all others who fight for desperately needed changes.

8. The Other Side of Advocacy (I)

Criticism is the other side of advocacy. If only by implication, one advocates what one does not criticize and vice versa.

In the U.S., generations of children have been taught that this is a "free country" whose citizens have the right to criticize anything they please, in contrast to "totalitarian countries" whose citizens are not permitted to criticize anything at all.

Millions of those children who have become adults now question at least part of what they were taught: They are far from sure they have the right to criticize. Even if they are ready to risk saying what they think (which can be very dangerous—often leading at the very least to loss of a job), where will they say it? The ordinary people of this country have virtually no access to the press, television or radio, and those who do are not there to voice the dissatisfactions of the ordinary people.

As a result of the exclusion of the people's views from the media, another form of criticism exists—which finds its organized expression in meetings, picket lines, and demonstrations. The majority of people whose dissatisfaction with life in this country is very deep still do not participate in this form of criticism, but the number who do grows by the day. Many who participate even in this organized criticism may still believe the system is capable of correcting its injustices, if only it will. But those who control the system rightly view such criticism as inherently a challenge to the system itself. They try to frustrate it in myriad ways—refusing permits for speaking and marching, banning picket lines, issuing injunctions. They also seek to make it a high-risk venture through the threat and/or use of violence and reprisals such as loss of job.

By contrast to the masses who make their criticisms outside the system's established channels, a relatively few individuals bear the formal designation "critic." Functioning through the mass media, they are advocates of what they do not criticize: the system. They are among those designated by the mass media to deflect criticism of the status quo into criticism of an alternative to the status quo. (Even when the mass media are forced by public pressure to reflect certain criticisms, they use this mild airing of grievances to sustain the illusion that a system permitting such criticism is capable of correcting itself.)

Although these critics are few in number, their power is great—and has many effects. In *The Season* William Goldman tells of a conversation between NBC-TV sports reporter Kyle Rote and drama critic Edwin Newman, who had just given a 70-second review of a Tennessee Williams play:

[Newman] goes into a washroom and takes off his makeup. Kyle Rote comes in. "I guess you put some more people out of work tonight," Rote says.[1]

The point may be made that when this critic "put some more people out of work tonight," he meant them no harm. He was just doing his job. But the fact that the critics function against the performers' interests not only as a by-product of their role but also as part of their role itself can be seen when the antagonistic conflict between performers and their employers comes out into the open. During the strike of the Musicians Union in 1975, Martin Gottfried, then *New York Post* theater critic wrote:

The theater is not merely a business. The musician is not merely a worker. A union, while necessary for protection, cannot feel the individual life flow that goes into the creation and sustenance of a musical. It must understand that a show cannot close and open like a factory.[2]

A show "cannot close and open like a factory"—but it does, and for the same reasons. Although the performers through their union "cannot feel the individual life flow" that goes into a musical, the producers presumably can: They look at the box-office receipts and if the show isn't making at least its weekly "nut," they will decide the "life flow" is insufficient—and close it.

And a show, like a factory, closes if the workers go out on strike—in which case the media put pressure on them to return at once, and not on management to assure livable wages and conditions. Theater, in other words, is a business when it comes to making a profit, and performers are workers when they are hired or fired. They become "artists" only when they go out on strike!

The critics' identity with management's point of view is equally apparent in their reviews. And this becomes blatantly obvious when an issue of importance to the forces controlling this country is at stake—as was the case with *Coonskin*.

Except for those aware of its racism, *Coonskin* was soon forgotten (at least on a conscious level). Although the mass campaign was unable to halt its release, the "life flow" at the box office did not warrant a long run. But this was through no fault of the critics—who hailed it as a "masterpiece." *Coonskin*'s producers—who were charged by Black leaders with "high crimes against black people"— featured quotes from these rave reviews in their ads:[3]

Coonskin is a rarity in contemporary American film making. A shatteringly successful effort to use a nearly new form—cartoons and live action combined . . . It is Mr. Bakshi's third full-length animated feature, it could be his masterpiece.—Richard Eder, *The New York Times.*

Coonskin is Bakshi's richest and most mature work. The world he creates invites us to laugh irreverently.—Joy Gould Boyum, *Wall Street Journal.*

Brilliant! *Coonskin* is funny, ingenious, inventive and entertaining.—Gene Shalit, WNBC-TV.

Coonskin is an angry movie, extraordinary and brilliantly realized . . . Bakshi is a genuine artist in film, and original—we just don't have enough like that anymore.—Arthur Knight.

But the media's promotion of *Coonskin* did not end even with these reviews. Interviews with Ralph Bakshi appeared in the press and on TV, with Bakshi emerging as a martyred artist persecuted by Black bigots. *Coonskin* also received a special follow-up article in the *Times'* weekly "Arts and Leisure" section, in which critic Richard Eder called the film "a work of brilliance and innovation" and condemned the protest against it:

The campaign argues that *Coonskin* is a savage and unfair caricature of the black community.

Coonskin clearly is savage and a cartoon clearly is a caricature. But it seems stupid and blind not to see that Bakshi is making a most serious and difficult kind of artistic commitment in trying to capture black Harlem's human condition by heightening rather than softening its miseries.[4]

There is no doubt that *Coonskin* had the effect of "heightening" the "miseries" of the Black community. This is because its "savage" edge was turned not against those responsible for these "miseries"—but against the victims. This is a direction approved of by the critics, who are part of a total operation designed to stop any work whose "savagery" is aimed at the oppressors. (And, one must note, when Eder calls Black people "stupid," he becomes an explicit part of the massive institutional effort to perpetuate the myth of Black "inferiority.")

Of all the mass media critics reviewing *Coonskin* from coast to coast, not one was Black. None of the mass media TV, film or book critics are Black either. Nor are any of the critics for academic, literary or liberal publications. At the height of the civil rights struggles in the sixties, there were occasional "guest" reviews by Blacks in a few newspapers. Although white critics have for centuries been writing about Blacks, these Black critics were not permitted to give their opinion of films, plays or books about whites, but were strictly confined to works dealing with Blacks. However, along with the turning back of the civil rights gains, there's been sharp retrenchment on any reviews at all by Blacks.

It's not difficult to see the relationship between Black exclusion from the critical system and films dating from *The Birth of a Nation* to *Gone With The Wind* to *Superfly*. And if the mass media had not excluded Native American Indian critics, would we have had decades of "cowboy and Indian" movies—where the reality of government genocide against Native Americans was reversed by white actors in red paint massacring the settlers? And how many "lazy Mexicans" and "wily Orientals" have been inflicted on us along with the barring of Asian-American and Latin critics?

In condemning the all-white critical system, we aren't saying whites are incapable of understanding the effects of racism (including on themselves), of having insight into Black-white relationships, or that they must necessarily be impervious to Black people's feelings. What we do say is that as long as Blacks, Chicanos, Puerto Ricans, Native Americans and Asian Americans are barred from the critical process, whites committed to the fight against racism and for social change will also be barred. And we'll be left with critics who condemn as "propaganda" all works "savage" to the oppressors, while welcoming as "art" those savage to the oppressed.

WHEN SUCH critics make adjustments to social change, it is only to hold it back. But they change surprisingly little. This becomes particularly apparent when they review the same play in different periods. This happened, for instance, with *Member of the Wedding,* whose two Broadway productions took place a quarter century apart.

This play, by Carson McCullers, had its premiere in 1950. Set in the Deep South in the 1940s, it deals with the relationship between a white girl in early adolescence, a little white boy, and a Black woman, a servant in the girl's family. The critics for New York's seven major papers—the *Times, Herald Tribune, Journal American, World Telegram & Sun, Daily Mirror, Daily News* and *Post*—lauded its "sensitivity," a quality they seemed ill-equipped to recognize: Not one of them said a word about the nature of Black-white relationships in a time and place when they were determined not only by white supremacist attitudes but "legal" segregation. Despite their lack of specific comment, these critics showed exactly how they stood: Their reviews were clotted with plantation-style references to the "Negro mammy" and the "colored mammy," whom they praised for her "lumbering, elemental compassion"—tributes placing her in a category reserved for "primitives."

When *Member of the Wedding* was revived in 1975, most of the New York papers that had reviewed the original production were dead. But their critics' ideas lived on. The critic for the *Daily News* spoke of "the black boy," when he was referring to an adult male character. And in the old racist tradition of assigning Blacks to one of two categories, the *Times'* Clive Barnes spoke of the Black woman's relationships with the "good black, T. T. Williams, and with her rebellious nephew, Honey."

The events between 1950 and 1975 forced the critics to dispense with their studied obliviousness to the nature of Black-white relations. Now they had a different approach. In his 1950 review the *Post*'s Richard Watts said nothing about the "racial problem." In his 1975 review he acknowledged its existence in the past only to deny its persistence into the present: "I didn't think [the play] was quite as moving as it had appeared to me a quarter of a century ago . . . At that period in our country's history there was a timeliness in the vogue of plays and novels about the rural South with its racial problem that has happily eased today . . ."

If the "racial problem" has "happily eased today," it is certainly news that should be moved from the theater section to page one— where it could run right alongside all the daily evidence to the contrary!

And in 1975 the white critic for the *Jersey Record* praised the white author of *Member of the Wedding* for the very quality they both lacked: "The racial hatred in the South," he wrote, "is handled with great understanding by the author. The late Miss McCullers wrote the script long before the struggle for equality in the 1960s." But what can be said of the "understanding" of a critic who thinks the "struggle for equality" dates from the sixties, when it actually began at the time the very first slaves were brought to this country and has continued unceasingly since?

In 1950 one "establishment" reviewer did reveal a flicker of understanding of the play's implications (whatever the author's intentions). That year the *Christian Science Monitor*'s critic wrote, "The Negro woman's own troubles are great and—in a white world—almost unnoticed." But when the same critic reviewed the same play for the same paper twenty-five years later, his glimmer of perception of what a Black person faces—not, to be exact, in a "white world" but a racist country— had given way to full acceptance of the play's "loyal mammy" stereotype. In 1975 he wrote of the "devoted black servant," praising her as a "woman of simple wisdom."

The white critics have had a mass-media monopoly on *Member of the Wedding* for over twenty-five years. Even such an event as the Civil War Centennial didn't break this monopoly—although it did bring about a radio symposium on a small listener-sponsored station that gave two Black writers a crack at the play. In this 1961 symposium Lorraine Hansberry and James Baldwin commented on a scene in the play that went unmentioned by the white reviewers: The nephew of the Black woman is being chased by a lynch mob. But the Black woman's concern is not for the Black man about to be lynched. Her preoccupation is with the little white boy she takes care of! "Now this doesn't say anything about the truth of Negro life, but it reveals a great deal about the state of mind of the white Southern woman who wrote it," declared Baldwin.[5]

And Lorraine Hansberry had this to say of the "devoted servant" stereotype that turns up in Faulkner's as well as McCullers's work:

... the intimacy of knowledge which the Negro may culturally have of white Americans does not exist in the reverse. So that William Faulkner has never in his life sat in on a discussion in a home where there are all Negroes. It is physically impossible. He has never heard the nuances of hatred, of total contempt from his most devoted servant . . .[6]

The mass media critics didn't see what was in *Member of the Wedding*. Instead they saw what wasn't there ("sensitivity"). They also saw what wasn't in Lorraine Hansberry's own plays. And for the same reason. Commenting on a review of *Raisin In the Sun,* Hansberry wrote:

My colleagues and I were reduced to mirth and tears by that gentleman writing his review of our play in a Connecticut paper who remarked of his pleasure at seeing how "our dusky brethern" could "come up with a song and hum their troubles away." It did not disturb the writer in the least that there is no such implication in the entire three acts. He did not need it in the play; he had it in his head.[7]

As LORRAINE HANSBERRY implied, such reviewers are so deeply imbued with racism they frequently reflect it unconsciously. But they are in the first place a *conscious* barrier to social art, and in many cases on an extremely sophisticated level. On the New York theater scene reactionary ideology is particularly potent because it goes hand-in-hand with concentrated power. In fact, these two characteristics come packaged in the person of one reviewer, the critic for *The New York Times.*

Producer Robert Nemiroff, who was the husband of Lorraine Hansberry, describes this critic's power:

... the general crisis of the theater itself [arises] from its commercial nature: the fact, for instance, that given the skyrocketing costs of production and operation, and the resultant exorbitant price of tickets which makes theatergoing a luxury, the number of plays that most people can afford to see is severely limited—and the number of *serious* plays (as distinct from musicals and comedies) even more so. Within this context, a very simple factor operates which most critics tend to pass over inasmuch as it touches on the efficacy of their own positions, yet nine times out of ten one need not look beyond it to determine whether a production will live or die. One might call it Sulzberger's Law, after the publisher of *The New York Times*: the fact that, given the situation described, no *serious* play can withstand a cool review from the daily reviewer of *The New York Times*. (Which is not the same thing at all, it should be noted, as saying that a *good* review can assure success.) For no matter how enthusiastic his colleagues may be, it is to the *Times* that the brokers, the businesses, the large commercial and organizational accounts who together make up the major slice of Broadway box-office—and for whom a "prestige" ticket is but commerce in another form—turn first. ... In the past decade it is difficult to think of a single exception to Sulzberger's Law.[8]

"Sulzberger's Law" killed Lorraine Hansberry's last play, *Les Blancs*. It opened in late 1970, more than five years after her death, "to an audience so personally involved, so visibly affected that if one closed one's eyes one might have imagined that this was not the Broadway of the seventies—the Broadway of the lethargic listeners— but the impassioned theatre of the thirties. Or perhaps the Abbey Theatre of Sean O'Casey," declared Robert Nemiroff.[9]

The critic for the *Village Voice,* Arthur Sainer, described this opening night scene:

Much feeling at the Longacre Sunday night . . . A sense of emotional investment throughout the audience—black, white audience—partly a celebration of the spirit of the playwright, partly a response to the nature of the material. Much cheering ... some scattered heckling, and a disturbance at the back of the house ... At best, an audience feeling something at stake ... [in a play] that manages to speak where the century is discovering it lives.

Sainer added:

What is best about *Les Blancs* is the intelligence of Lorraine Hansberry, the passion and the courage. The playwright suggests no absolutes, with the exception of a moral imperative which moves like a brushfire through the action—the necessity to become free.[10]

And Clayton Riley, a Black "guest" reviewer for *The New York Times,* called *Les Blancs*

. . . an incredibly moving experience. Or, perhaps, an extended moment in one's life . . . not easily forgotten . . . in a commercial theatre that takes such pains to protect us from knowing who and what and where we are in 20th-Century America . . .[11]

Riley gave this reason for the passionate response to *Les Blancs*:

The play divides people into sectors inhabited on the one hand by those who recognize clearly that a struggle exists in the world today that is about the liberation of oppressed peoples, a struggle to be supported at all costs. In the other camp live those who still accept as real the soothing mythology that oppression can be dealt with reasonably—particularly by Black people . . .[12]

There were other critics who fervently admired *Les Blancs*, as well as some who detested it (John Simon, writing for *New York* magazine, did not even attempt to disguise his racist attitude, calling the play "a malodorous, unenlightening mess"[13]).

But none of this made any difference at the box office. All that counts there is the opinion of the *Times'* regular reviewer. The play soon closed because, as Nemiroff pointed out, "Clive Barnes did not like *Les Blancs*."

Writing on the morning after *Les Blancs* opened (unlike guest critics whose reviews may appear a week or two later), Barnes stated:

The major fault of the play is the shallowness of the confrontations. The arguments have all been heard before . . .[14]

Have they? Where? On what U.S. stage or screen have the "arguments" around the dramatic liberation struggles of the African peoples "all been heard before"? What private theater did Clive Barnes attend? What secret films or television plays did he see? Why did he keep all this hidden from the public?

By claiming that "the arguments have all been heard before," Barnes was attempting to make his readers feel sated and jaded with a theme most of them have never been impelled to confront.

Barnes went on to assert: "Too much of it sounds like political propaganda rather than political debate . . ."[15]

In reading Barnes's reviews one learns that (in his opinion) the difference between "political propaganda" and "art" is determined by the playwright's point of view. Through *Les Blancs'* characters Hansberry presented a diversity of views, and in a highly complex manner. But the play did not emerge as the "political debate" Barnes wanted because the audience knew where the author stood. She was not interested in a "political debate" about liberation and social progress—to which she devoted her life and all her work. What Barnes disapproved of as "political propaganda" was the playwright's own commitment.

MORE THAN three years elapsed before Clive Barnes could give a repeat performance in his crusade against "political propaganda." The time lag was not due to any lack of vigilance on Barnes's part, but because of the dearth of productions with even a remote resemblance to social commitment.

Barnes had his chance to go all out again when *The Freedom of the City,* by the Irish playwright Brian Friel, opened on Broadway. It had been successful in London and Dublin but it didn't last long in New York. Barnes is on the side of the class in power in the U.S. and his native England, and when this play on Irish liberation arrived in this country in early 1974 he gave it treatment remarkably similar to that he accorded *Les Blancs.* Barnes wrote:

Unfortunately, for Mr. Friel, the play is . . . perfectly predictable. Here within five minutes of the play's opening we know exactly what is going to happen.[16]

The "arguments," in other words, "have all been heard before"! But where? Where are the U.S. theaters that have made us so familiar with the contemporary Irish liberation struggles?

Freedom of the City concerns two men and one woman who flee the military violence against a civil rights march in Londonderry, Northern Ireland, to seek refuge in the town's Guildhall. When they leave the hall—unarmed, hands held high above their heads—they are shot to death by British troops.

According to Barnes, what happens in the play is "perfectly predictable." But if we know what will happen in the play it's only because we know what *has* happened in life. Yet Barnes contradicts his "perfectly predictable" theme by denying that what happens on the stage could have happened in life. When the rumor is circulated that as many as fifty "terrorists" are massed inside the Guildhall, the Royal Forces mobilize outside. But, asks Barnes,

Can we really be expected to believe that the British Army could mobilize against these three people 22 tanks, two dozen armored cars, four water cannon and "a modicum of air cover"?[17]

Even aside from the fact that the play's technique is far from naturalistic, yes, we certainly can be expected to believe this! We have seen all too many armed military mobilizations against such "terrorists" as the civil rights marchers in the South of this country and the students in Soweto, South Africa.

As Barnes pointed out, the play ends with "the white-washing of [the killings by] the British Court of Inquiry." In Barnes's opinion, "The final finding of the court is far-fetched, indeed, impossible." But if the court's white-washing is "far-fetched, indeed, impossible," how can we know "exactly what is going to happen" within "five minutes of the play's opening"?

Clive Barnes wanted to have it (or us) both ways.

OF COURSE, all of Clive Barnes's reviews weren't negative. He came up with raves too. And in fall 1975 he really outdid himself. It was for a play called *Travesties.*

"Best Reviews In B'Way History" ran the headline over a full-page ad promoting *Travesties.*[18] Quotations from the reviews of more than two dozen critics crowded the page. And topping them all, in extra-large type, was the word from Clive Barnes:

A razzling, dazzling effervesence that erupts and bubbles throughout the evening. A remarkable play, as iridescent as a rainbow, clever, adroit and ultimately moving, encrusted with puns, garnished with verbal extravagances, madcap fun. For once the entertainment offered is not just illuminating but actually dazzling.

The other critics joined in the ecstasy:

Travesties glows . . . A smash hit!—Richard Watts, *N.Y. Post.*

An enthralling evening!—Caspar Citron, WNYC-TV.

It's brilliant, stunning, a miracle!—Alan Rich, *New York* magazine.

Brilliant, theatrical masterstroke. Crunchingly witty with a thousand laughs and nine hundred thoughts.—Jack Kroll, *Newsweek.*

Terrific! A wonderful, very funny, fabulous tour-de-farce. On a scale of 1 to 10, I rate it a perfect score of 10!—Pat Collins, CBS-TV.

Blazing with wit, exhiliratingly, diabolically clever. Amen and God Bless!— T.E. Kalem, *Time* magazine.

Funny and brilliantly witty.—Hobe, *Variety.*

What the play was about was impossible to grasp from this, the first of a series of full-page ads for *Travesties*. And it seemed strange that a play with the "best reviews in B'way history" should need so much advertising (not customary with hits). The ad aroused further suspicion by stating, "Seats now at box office & by mail"—without giving mail-order instructions to "list alternate dates," as is customary with shows making even a pretense of being a hit.

A check of *Variety* confirmed what the ad copy suggested: *Travesties* was far from a sellout. And what was quoted from *Variety's* review in the *Travesties* ad was far less interesting than what went unquoted: "The celebrity-studded first night audience," wrote critic Hobe, "was responsive and audibly amused at the start of both acts, but attention waned after a while. A few people left at intermission and others were seen nodding at times."[19]

Why the raves for a play that left people "nodding"?

The answer was supplied by English author Tom Stoppard shortly before his play opened. "*Travesties,*" he explained in an interview, "asks whether the words 'revolutionary' and 'artist' are capable of being synonymous or whether they are mutually exclusive."[20]

Actually *Travesties* doesn't so much ask as answer this question— the first part negatively, the second positively. One of the characters in the play is "Lenin." "Lenin" specializes in quoting Lenin out of context, twisting Lenin's meaning to the point where "Lenin" says what Lenin's enemies (right up to the present) claim Lenin said. In this same vein Stoppard arranges for Lenin's views to be "defended" by a "revolutionary" who attributes the ideas of Lenin's enemies to Lenin! (Of course, if a character in a play affirmed the ideas Lenin actually held, Barnes would not have crooned "iridescent as a rainbow" and "ultimately moving." He would have howled "political propaganda"!)

And the play's central character, clearly speaking for the author, offers the following critique of Marx:

By bad luck [Marx] encountered the capitalist system at its most deceptive period. The industrial revolution had crowded the people into slums and enslaved them in factories, but it had not yet begun to bring them the benefits of an industrialized society. Marx looked about him and saw that the system depended on a wretched army of wage slaves. He drew the lesson that the wealth of the capitalist was the counterpart to the poverty of the worker and had in fact been stolen from the worker in the form of unpaid labor. He thought that was how the whole thing worked. That false assumption was itself added to a false premise . . . Marx predicted that they would behave according to their class. But they didn't . . . in all kinds of ways and for all kinds of reasons the classes moved closer together instead of further apart.[21]

As the "celebrity-studded first night audience" watched *Travesties* on that fall evening in 1975, New York was on the brink of default—its fate hanging between a president who wanted it to go bankrupt and a section of the bankers who thought it might be bad for business if it did. Though there was this certain difference of opinion among the big businessmen and among their representatives in government, all agreed that "aid" to New York would be forthcoming only if thousands of additional jobs were done away with, more libraries closed, more hospitals shut, more children stuffed into already overflowing classrooms and more people on welfare turned out into the streets.

And outside—among the millions in New York who didn't have the money to walk inside any theater—many were drawing "the lesson that the wealth of the capitalist was the counterpart to the poverty of the worker and had in fact been stolen from the worker in the form of unpaid labor."

Stoppard—backed up by Barnes and a chorus of other critics—had picked a fine time to announce that the classes had "moved closer together instead of further apart"!

LESS THAN a month after he reviewed *Travesties,* Clive Barnes was once again ecstatic. He had just seen a "most absorbing and beautiful play." Titled *Ice Age,* it had, according to its program notes, created a "storm of protest throughout Europe." Barnes objected: "Some critics abroad," he said in his review, "have accused *Ice Age* of being apologetic for Nazism."[22]

This was hardly surprising since the real life counterpart of the play's protagonist was the writer Knut Hamsun. At the time the Nazis invaded Norway, Hamsun issued a proclamation to his fellow Norwegians: "Throw away your rifles and return home. The Germans are fighting for us."

In denying that the play is "apologetic for Nazism," Barnes succeeded only in placing himself in urgent need of defense against the same charges:

Ice Age is based on the last years of Knut Hamsun, one of Norway's major novelists . . . Always of a right-wing persuasion, and possibly with something of an anti-Semitic bias, in 1940 he wrote acclaiming the German invasion. In 1945, true to his last, he wrote a laudatory obituary of Hitler, knowing precisely what he was doing.[23]

One mustn't overlook the admirable aspects, Barnes insists, of writing a "laudatory obituary" of Hitler: "A curmudgeon of a man then—stubborn, bitter but with great courage."[24]

After praising Hamsun's "deeply felt political convictions," Barnes tells us that

... in any human situation, even in any crime, however heinous, a real person is involved—a person with a character, motives and problems.[25]

This is exactly the view of the spate of books coming out of the FRG designed to "humanize" Hitler and other top Nazis.

Barnes also gave the play's author, Tankred Dorst, a peculiar defense against charges of sympathy for the Nazis:

Mr. Dorst, who is 50 now, and went through [World War II] as a German soldier, shows no sympathy at all for Nazism . . . He has created a most delicately poised play that is scrupulously fair to this old man . . .

"Fair" is hardly the word:

Why Mr. Dorst finds Hamsun interesting is precisely the reason why an audience will find Hamsun interesting. He was not your common or garden bigot. He was a man of great intellect and character. He never joined the Nazi Party, and his support for Hitler was ideological rather than practical, theoretical rather than real. Yet undoubtedly the moral and intellectual weight of his name did the cause of Norway and the free world great harm in its darkest hour.[26]

No matter. The subsidized Chelsea Theater Center of Brooklyn which staged this play is now one of the "great companies of the world." Barnes's only regret was that because of its large cast, *Ice Age* "could not be produced commercially nowadays." *Ice Age,* concluded Barnes, "is one of those productions that convince me that the Chelsea Theater is America's window on the theatrical world."[27]

As the *Times'* drama critic, Barnes himself stood at "America's window on the theatrical world" for a decade. From this vantage point he acted as a sniper, ready to cut down anyone advancing across the terrain bearing ideas in opposition to his own. Now the *Times* has a different drama critic. The change in individuals has little importance. What is important is that The New York Times' drama critic— whoever he is—must conform to the "aims and objectives" of the most influential media representative of those who rule this country.

The role of The New York Times' drama critic, it can be said, dramatizes the role of critics in the United States.

9. The Other Side of Advocacy (II)

How does the role of the critics in the GDR compare with the critics' role in the U.S.? Is the critical process in the GDR confined to their opinions? What's their relationship to the theaters? Are they as influential as U.S. critics? Do they have the power to make or break plays?

"Of course we don't have such power," declared *Der Morgen* critic Christoph Funke. The "structure of the critics' work," he emphasized, is based on "cooperation with the theaters."

"We don't work against theaters but together with them so that the public can have the greatest possible artistic experience. We think of ourselves as theater artists, scientific cooperators—intermediaries between the theater and public who do our part so the theater's work will be brought in a living way to the public—although, of course, the critical attitude is there."

In their role as "intermediaries between the theater and the public," the critics do indeed help to carry out the "aims and objectives" of the socialist state, asserted Funke: "It's a fact that both the theaters and the critics work to carry out the basic cultural goals of our state. There are no antagonistic differences of attitude concerning the basic questions of our cultural work."

But, we remarked, many U.S. theater workers would say that the absence of such differences between the state, the theater and the critics is proof of the absence of freedom, of multiplicity of choice for the individual.

"Only in a socialist society does the possibility exist so that the individual *can* develop freely," replied Funke. "In a socialist country the individual can work to build society in a voluntary alliance between a very definite personality and the state for a common goal. We think a personality can develop only when exploitation no longer exists, when there is an opportunity for all-around education without financial worries, and where an individual's development depends only on his or her own capacity."

Although there are no antagonistic differences between theaters and critics, the reviewers' "critical attitude," as Funke said, "is of course there."

"I've often been confronted with a situation," stated *National Zeitung* critic Rolf Dieter Eichler, "where my criticism of productions wasn't related to the artistic level of staging but to questions left unanswered by the plays, even if they were comedies. And I said so in my reviews. But other critics had completely different ideas.

"I say this to show that socialism, real socialism, can have substantial differences of opinion. But the entire range of our discussion is productive because it's based on a common outlook of socialist goals. That's why we don't allow our enemies to mix in in any way."

Although he commented first on the social aspects of his criticism, Eichler went on to stress the esthetic side as well. "I know from many discussions with audiences how multiple their cultural needs are. And I know how seriously GDR theaters are striving artistically, on a socialist basis, with great enthusiasm to bring out the different possibilities of theater." Turning to the Volksbühne as an example he said, "I think this is one of the Berlin theaters whose special character emerges in both current and classical plays: The very personal handwriting of each director and of certain actors around the director is very evident. You recognize that they're trying to create real pleasure for the audience, they're addressing themselves to all senses. Some casts—I don't mean theaters, but specific casts—overemphasize dialogue. But the casts at the Volksbühne really use everything that can be mobilized, including the floor."

Dieter Klein, the Volksbühne's deputy *Intendant,* listened to Eichler's remarks and smiled. "I couldn't have made that interpretation. That's the critic's job."

ROLF DIETER EICHLER singled out the Volksbühne for particular mention. Other GDR critics may well feel a special empathy for other theaters. But the relations between critics and theater people are not characterized only by empathy. The conflicts existing in a society where all sections of the people have the same basic goals are also reflected in very specific ways in the theater.

"We say the critics don't help the actors enough," declared actress Barbara Dittus of the Berliner Ensemble. "We feel this way particularly about TV critics. There should be artistic as well as social criticism, but if the TV critics like the play or film then the artists are good too. They should make a greater distinction if the meaning is good and the artists are not very good." Even theater critics, she feels, "should help artists more. They don't watch the development of an actor enough over many productions."

Playwrights too have their criticisms. "The bad thing about criticism is that it goes only one way, from the critic to the author and not back," declared Helmut Baierl.

"I would say there are non-antagonistic contradictions between critics and authors. The critics themselves are quite lovely. And if they are my colleagues I must accept them as people and they must accept me. If such a relationship exists, they can be very strong and acute in their criticism. It's possible in a friendly way to say it's a very bad play. But at times this relationship can lead to reviews that are too compromising."

On the other hand, Baierl said, problems can occur in the opposite direction. "I once got such bad, incorrect criticism I wanted to criticize the critic in return." However, he added, such unproductively negative criticism "seldom occurs."

And no matter how much the critics may dislike a production, they can't close it. "In the old Germany there was a bourgeois critic who was known as a 'pope,'" said Baierl. "If he called a play bad, it was usually closed. And I see that's still the case in your country."

It's certainly not true in the GDR, agreed Rainer Kerndl, critic for *Neues Deutschland,* national paper of the Socialist Unity Party. "I can't look at myself as a pedant because I don't have that kind of power. I don't want to idealize this because people would tell you there's a lot of truth in what I said.

"Critics and theater people," he continued, "have a common front because all have more or less the same starting point and the same intentions. This was not the case at the beginning. It's the result of years of development and it's certainly very beautiful. But it can blunt the necessary weapon of criticism. If you have too much agreement from the beginning, the critic can become the co-defender of theater people. And there are occasions when this has happened." To avoid this, Kerndl emphasized, the critics should maintain a "certain distance":

"Of course, everyone wants a socialist theater. But not everyone understands the same thing by this. Critics are partners of theater people in the sense that we are socialist contemporaries. But in order to play their role, critics must keep a certain distance—because on the landscape of the GDR theater we have some real problems."

Kerndl cited examples of these problems—among them, the difficulty in distinguishing between innovation and formalism. "One thing young people are afraid of is convention. I've seen Gorky's *Lower Depths* played in a way that if you didn't know it was Gorky you wouldn't know. You can't renounce everything of the past—I think bourgeois theater has given us much without which we couldn't exist." On the other hand, "repetition of the formalist experiments of the late bourgeois theater is for us completely unnecessary." (Criticizing this kind of experimentation, Brecht wrote of "unknown sensational effects, which are however of a purely formalist kind: That is to say, they are forcibly imposed on the work, on its content and on its message. . ."[1]) Kerndl added: "It's sometimes difficult to find a common language with young theater people. But I'm convinced we're overcoming this problem."

Problems have also resulted from certain interpretations of Brecht's theater theories. For instance, "Brecht emphasized the social functions of personality—these had to become evident. This was very important for the theater of the German language." However, for some theater workers this "became a goal in itself. They showed only the social function of personality, not the interior richness of personality. This brought about a certain impoverishment in the work of some theaters and a later generation of actors, now thirty to thirty-five years old, felt this."

Theaters may also face problems in maintaining an appropriate balance in their repertory of contemporary socialist plays, classics, and contemporary plays from the West and "third world." While specific theaters may not achieve this at a particular time, "if you take the sum of our theaters as a whole," Kerndl feels, "you can say we have an acceptable balance."

The greatest audience demand, however, is for plays dealing with contemporary socialist life. This has sometimes resulted in plays that are "written very fast and don't have the proper quality. They don't show the full depth of the problem," declared Kerndl.

On the other hand, as the treatment of the conflicts of socialism becomes deeper and more complex, interpretation takes on a new importance. "At first in our plays we showed only good and bad characters," noted actor Alfred Müller of the Gorki Theater. But as theater literature developed, characters often became "very complicated. You can see them from this side or that side—and the enemy can use this. It's important to stage these plays from a class-conscious standpoint."

But sometimes even a strong production can't prevent misinterpretation. "In general, plays can be misinterpreted, that you must risk," commented Helmut Baierl. "But playwrights naturally express different shades of opinion and some plays will be understood better than others.

"At the same time you must remember that in the ideological area we carry on the class struggle. But some writers may see only things that should be criticized. They write only for those who are ideological friends and who know the ship is moving forward. They may think everyone knows this. But if you assume everyone knows the ship is moving forward, you also assume the class struggle has been decided almost everywhere."

PROFESSIONAL CRITICISM in the theater is not limited to media drama critics. First of all, there are the ongoing critical discussions within each permanent company. "We have strenuous discussions, and they're not always a pleasure," said actor Dieter Mann, who is also a leader in the Cultural Workers Union. "But they are necessary for our profession. When you have different viewpoints, you should have a frank exchange. And struggles take place, because if you're convinced quickly you can't have had a firm standpoint to begin with."

"In the theater," said actress Ursula Karusseit, a member of the Volksbühne ensemble, "we talk things over as they do in the plants. Just yesterday we had an argument about a play we're staging. It had nothing to do with production—there were political questions. The discussion was against the author, the *Intendant* and the director—and for the author, the *Intendant* and the director. If that's not democracy, I don't know what is."

There are also continuing discussions between the ensembles and theater scientists from the Association of Theater Workers. "We have twenty-two theater scientists, people with many years of theater experience. They have the capacity to analyze plays and they can work with people," related Klaus Pfützner. "They're ready to listen, to accept the opinions of others—and they can explain positions in a convincing way from a class standpoint."

The Association may meet with members of a theater after the ensemble has decided to produce a certain play. "We'll discuss with the artists which ideological problems will arise if the play is staged in such and such a way, how it can be produced to win people, what the accent should be." Or the Association may meet with theater workers after their play has opened—with results that sometimes lead to changes in interpretation.

"Sometimes people say, 'We have to think it over, you may be right,'" said Pfützner. On other occasions the talks have immediate impact. "One director said, 'If you saw the play and feel that way—that's a catastrophe. The production didn't express what I wanted it to.' The assistant director said, 'We need more rehearsals, we must change it.'" Other directors, Pfützner noted, may not agree so readily—if at all. "But these are normal problems." (Normal, that is, in a socialist country. Hardly so in the U.S.: When reviews decide a production's fate, how many plays can have a second chance?)

The critical process in the theater, Pfützner pointed out, has changed greatly over the years. "At the beginning there were artists who didn't have enough political understanding to care about the social results of their work. We talked very harshly with these people because we had to bring about a new way of looking at things. The theater had to play its part in the struggle against survivals of fascist ideas."

Now, however, "we'll invite people to watch a play and we may discuss it for three or four hours. What's important is not one discussion, but the process. Because of the reality of socialism, our ideological work is in many ways easier now: We can show the relationship between ideology and our material and human progress."

Nevertheless, Pfützner emphasized, "the struggle still takes place under the influence of the class enemy. It's a very hard, very bitter, very subtle struggle. The frontier we have in this city forces us to have this political discussion. There are three FRG television networks, tourists and family ties."

"The FRG puts on television programs to project its positions over the border into our territory," said Horst Oswald, Cultural Councillor of Berlin. "We're always conscious that we must show our real situation as understandably as possible because they tell people to react in an entirely different way."

Ursula Karusseit had just seen a film that told people "to react in an entirely different way." "The other day I saw an anti-Cuban film on an FRG channel. It was an American-French coproduction about a spy and it took place in diplomatic circles. The Cubans are shown as a people with no culture, no education—a spitting people. Only the Americans work with their brains. This anti-Communist movie showed those who are positive as negative and vice versa. The film was very dangerous because it was well made, with a very good actor in it. If you turned it upside down it would have been a good movie."

However, bourgeois ideology also arrives in the GDR in a far more sophisticated form. "The political-ideological struggle," said Klaus Pfützner, "also takes place on esthetic questions that seem apolitical. There's a theater publication in the FRG, for instance, whose critic writes that the best theater in the world is in 'East Berlin' and Moscow. But this man is interested in admiring certain things only to use them against us. He welcomes in order to divide."

And *Berliner Zeitung* critic Ernst Schumacher observed, "Reaction has chosen new tactics—I follow this closely. The naked, raw polemics are over. Now when they praise certain things that should be criticized they also praise things that deserve praise—to give what they're doing the appearance of objectivity. This is how they try to exert influence on us, indirectly—to disorient our own assessment. This means our artists and critics must have an independent point of view."

The reasons for developing such an understanding among GDR theater workers are not only related to the current situation: They can be traced back to theater in the old Germany. For many years before

Hitler came to power, Max Reinhardt (who was also to become famous in Hollywood) headed the Deutsches Theater. "Reinhardt took the Deutsches into his own hands so that he—as one man—could apply his own personal esthetic ideas," said Deustches' *Dramaturgin* Ilse Galfert. "While Reinhardt was developing a romantic, pompous theater, fascism was already emerging. In 1933 he was flabbergasted, like a child in a thunderstorm when lightning strikes. He had closed his eyes to what was happening and suddenly he had to emigrate.

"When Brecht returned from emigration his first productions were at the Deutsches—*Mother Courage* and *Puntilla And His Servant Matti*. From the beginning we've produced plays not only for esthetic but political reasons."

IN THE U.S. the critical process is in the hands of a few because power is controlled by a few. This is why the people find it increasingly difficult to express their criticism. In the GDR, power is in the hands of the working people—who play an ever greater role in all aspects of life, including the critical process. This is reflected in the theater: The critics views aren't decisive because the audience's views carry so much weight.

All sections of the population are involved in critical discussions— workers, intellectuals, young people—and all have the same basic goals. But again, there are many different opinions on how to reach these goals. And this fact presents a daily challenge to theater workers.

"It's a great responsibility for artists to decide how they'll treat each internal question of socialism, because reaction is always searching with a microscope for a little hole to seep into," said Jochen Ziller, Henschelverlag's *Chefdramaturg*. "In the last few years," he continued, "we've seen our country's social and economic development recognized on a world scale. But at the same time the ideological struggle gets sharper. Through attacks on our art and its interpretation of reality, reaction tries to gain influence in our country. Our artists are constantly confronted by our enemies just across the border."

At the same time, Ernst Schumacher stressed, enemy distortions can't be taken as a reason for avoiding criticism. "Because we're at the threshold of two worlds, we've sometimes been inclined by necessity to accentuate affirmative elements. And sometimes we've been a little hesitant to present ourselves critically because the enemy is watching us with thousands of eyes. But we must not be misled by this into underestimating the importance of continual critical evaluation."

Another complication in treating "each internal question of social-ism" is the fact that millions of young GDR citizens have no basis for comparing their problems with those of people in capitalist societies. To these young people unemployment and lack of educational oppor-tunities are matters of the imagination. Further, the early struggles in their own country are not a part of their own direct experience. Thus, bringing them a consciousness of their own history as well as world history is also a task of art.

"We must draw young people's attention to the incredibly difficult development and hard personal conflicts we all had to go through to reach our present level and the world place we occupy today," commented Christoph Funke. "The point is not to look at our present as something to be taken for granted, but as the result of a difficult process, full of conflicts, over a period of thirty years."

At the same time the new stage of development brings many conflicts of its own, and how they are resolved affects both the happiness of individuals and overall social progress. "The young people don't remember the difficulties and it is necessary to appreciate the successes we've had," said actress Barbara Dittus who, like many other cultural workers we talked with, grew up under socialism. "But there are still some people with narrow ideas—who say we built socialism here and who speak only of our successes. But it's not enough to speak only of successes. The young people have new wishes and new problems. We have our problems and we have the right to speak of them."

Again, *how* to speak of these problems through art is, as Jochen Ziller said, "a great responsibility for artists." Although Western media would have us believe responsibility negates freedom, the opposite is true.

The abstract freedom of which bourgeois ideologists speak doesn't exist in any society. When it comes to publication of books and production of plays, there always has been and will be selectivity. The point is, what's the decision-making criterion?

In the U.S., esthetic questions have little relevance. With few exceptions the criterion is: Will it make a profit? Will it promote or at least avoid conflicting with the "aims and objectives" of the state? In the GDR where the profit motive for production does not exist, the criterion is: Will the work in some way encourage through artistic means the development of socialism, of socialist personalities? But this is an immensely complex criterion to apply.

"Appearance and essence are sometimes very difficult to distinguish," noted Ilse Galfert. "One can't always discern immediately if a particular critical attitude is positive or destructive in a certain situation."

"The question of criticism and self-criticism is very complicated. What helps, what doesn't help—this must be decided every day," said Alfred Müller.

"In discussions around a play," said Rainer Kerndl who is a playwright as well as a critic, "the actors may sometimes tell the author, 'You don't have the entire truth.' All of the artists involved feel themselves dedicated to socialist society, but they have very different ideas on how to interpret it. There is hard contact and sharp discussion.

"In my own case I have my point of view and I try to live and work accordingly. But one must watch not to become opportunist. Writers always have to deal with this question according to their sense of political understanding and artistic responsibility—and every time anew. This is a very complicated problem, and I've written a play on it." The play, *Night With Compromises,* had its premiere at the Volkstheater Rostock.

Since each theater has wide latitude in selecting its repertory, the decision-making criterion may be applied in a variety of ways—or sometimes misapplied. "I remember three or four years ago," said Kerndl, "when certain plays were not produced in the theater in one city. The *Intendant* would have loved to stop the *Dramaturgen* even from reading these plays if he could have. But in the next city—twenty-five minutes away by car—these plays were considered examples of the best contemporary socialist work and were produced with great success. It's just as easy," Kerndl noted, "to have narrow stiff reactions as the opposite kind." He added:

"We have great possibilities—but we're not playing with them. They have to be used, not misused. We have the political task of challenging the reality of socialist democracy to prove itself. It's really a new land for us to explore and if we don't develop it, it will not develop."

As part of this overall development of socialist democracy, the approach to criticism undergoes continual change. "The need to criticize is really a socialist need. Without criticism nothing moves," declared Helmut Baierl. "In my plays I check the extent to which criticism is accepted by society and how things can be changed by this criticism.

"But it may happen that my criticisms are not accepted by others. Then I must decide who is more likely to be right, I or the others. This is a conflict every writer has to settle with himself, by himself. As artists we are not only the 'conscience of mankind' that the bourgeois critics are always speaking of. We fight on the ideological front. I have to decide whether I am uninterested in the present day and write only for 'posterity'—which means that what I write will automatically be seized upon by the bourgeois media."

However, if Baierl remains convinced of his views in the face of differing opinions, "then I must be strong enough to convince others." This involves the relationship between the individual and the collective. "Of course there are contradictions in this. But developing the relationship between the individual and the collective is also a process.

"Freedom always has boundaries arising in the daily class struggle. But the more intelligent our cultural policies, the more possibilities we have. And now we have a broader freedom. A higher degree of consciousness contributes to a higher consciousness of responsibility—and therefore to greater individual freedom."

A socialist artist's concept of consciousness should not be confused with the perversion of consciousness often developed by writers in capitalist countries: the self-censorship leading them to make mental deletions before their fingers hit the typewriter—so the work of the sellers won't be rejected by the buyers. Revolutionary artists consider the social effects of their work. They reject the illusory concept of art for art's sake and recognize art's ability to affect social development, for better or worse. By increasing their consciousness, their understanding of the total society, writers in a socialist country are able to have a greater impact on the consciousness of others. And through their participation in the collective, writers themselves are for the first time in history a part of the decision-making process affecting their own work.

As Helmut Baierl pointed out, contradictions occur between the individual and the collective. This can certainly include disagreements between the individual and the collective where the individual is right. And the opposite can happen. This proves only that no method of decision making is infallible. But this method, which ends the writers' isolation from the social processes affecting them, is the only one giving the writer the opportunity to win the collective to her or his point of view or vice versa. Applying this method is in itself a difficult process, as are all other aspects of socialist development. But it is an altogether different process from that portrayed in the bourgeois media.

In 1955 Brecht wrote, in a piece that was read at a theater conference in the FRG, "It will hardly surprise you to hear me say that the question of describing the world is a social one. I have maintained this for many years, and now I live in a state where a vast effort is being made to transform society. You may not approve of the means used—I hope, by the way, that you are really acquainted with them, and not just from the papers."[2]

Unfortunately, more than twenty years later most people in the West, in and out of the theater—and including many radicals—are not "really acquainted with" the means by which socialist society is developed except "from the papers." Although one would not expect radicals to believe everything they read in the papers, many still do when it comes to socialist countries.

Ruth Berghaus, of the Deutsche State Opera, has talked with a number of these radicals, including some "who always tell us what mistakes we're making. I like to listen to them—although it's rather strange they don't recognize that the socialist community's existence not only gives moral encouragement to people in capitalist countries, but also changes the relationship between the bourgeoisie and the workers.*

"Anyone who does anything," she continued, "makes mistakes—and it's always easier to criticize than to do something. Coming up with ideas is not the problem. What's difficult is the daily struggle to advance inch by inch, with all the people together if possible.

"The individual of course develops more slowly than society as a

---

*How the socialist community changes "the relationship between the bourgeoisie and the workers" was illustrated by an incident that occurred at a hearing of the U.S. Civil Rights Commission in October 1976 concerning layoffs. Edith Glidden of the New York City Commission on Human Rights—asserting that layoffs had been "devastating" for Black, Latin and women workers—pointed out that she was attending the hearing in place of the commission's director, Eleanor Holmes Norton, "who left today on a mission to the Soviet Union where they don't have any layoff problems."[3]

whole. Out of this comes many contradictions—and out of these contradictions much advice comes from abroad. This is not always meant in a negative way, although it frequently is." The critics with negative intentions want to "break us away from socialism, separate us from this society."

By contrast, there are many radicals who certainly do not share the intentions of these hostile critics but are nonetheless influenced by them because, again, most radicals are not "really acquainted with" the process of development in socialist society.

"The most important thing is the existence of the productive forces controlled by the people so that those who create the material values can live in the most human way," said Ruth Berghaus. But many from the West "don't see that the development of art and culture must go parallel with social development. In bourgeois societies culture is for the few. But no one should be denied the right to live in a cultural environment—and in a socialist country culture is created for the masses. But to do this is difficult and—I think of this often—there can sometimes be a certain feeling of superiority that could lead to separation.

"To satisfy economic and social needs is possible—difficult, but possible. You can plan it, you can see it. But to satisfy intellectual and cultural needs—this is an endless process. And a very contradictory process. Goethe said, 'If I say this is final, then it's reactionary.'"

"THERE'S A contrast between what progressive artists in capitalist countries want and what we want: We don't want to change our social system—we want to make it continually better. We are socialist people, we think our system is okay," declared Gisela May of the Berliner Ensemble.

However, this contrast between the artist's role in capitalist and socialist societies is not yet apparent to many radicals in the U.S. In their opinion, artists who "affirm" society—any society—abdicate their role in helping to "critically change social conditions." To those who hold this view, artists are revolutionary only if they are primarily critics, artists only if their criticism is without boundaries.

"I know many radicals are of the opinion that revolutionary art can't be affirmative," commented Dr. Ursula Püschel, editor of *Theater In The German Democratic Republic*. A certain historical conditioning, she pointed out, often leads to this belief.

"Art as long as we've known it has been class art. And because humanist art in capitalist societies had to learn to say no, we carry on our shoulders the centuries old art of saying no. But since 1917 a society has existed to which one should not say no, but yes. Saying yes to socialism—the task of socialist art—is linked with the responsibility of criticizing at the same time. But when socialist art says no, it doesn't give a total no. Socialist art criticizes backwardness and lack of development, and it recognizes that problems in a socialist society keep changing.

"If one thinks art can't be revolutionary when it confirms society, one has a wrong idea of revolution—starting from the notion that revolution is nothing but a change of power, then it's over. Communism is a movement. As for the esthetic consequences of this development, there are no recipes. Discussion always continues."

And an integral part of these discussions is the humanist art of the past. Although this art "had to learn to say no," its value, pointed out Dr. Püschel, was not determined by negation. "Brecht said it is the works that show the way to a 'growingly stronger, tenderer and bolder humanity' that have been preserved. That's why it's so important for us to analyze this art for our daily life, for our work, and for developing an affirmative art which also has the responsibility of saying no."

Yet the role continually projected from the West for socialist artists is not affirmation and criticism directed toward development but negation of the society. The bourgeois media that deny time and space to dissenting artists in capitalist societies continually demand "dissent" from artists in socialist countries, both in their art and in their lives. This idea was seized upon by FRG author Günter Grass who wrote a play condemning Brecht for not being a leader of the 1953 attempted counterrevolution, which in real life Brecht actively opposed.

"Revolutionary playwrights fight for socialism. When they have it, why should they demand that people go into the streets to protest the power of the working people—of which they are a part?" declared poet and film writer Paul Wiens.

In the view of some in the West, "a revolutionary is a critical person so a revolutionary in a socialist society must criticize socialism, criticize the whole society. The reason they fall into this," Wiens noted, "is that after a socialist revolution the new society is not readymade.

The revolution continues—but not in the sense of a fight for power. That's been decided, the people have the power. It's revolutionary in the sense that things are advancing and changing.

"But there are also conflicts. Old opinions are outmoded, but many people aren't yet aware of this. For some, they're just the 'good old ways.' Among the playwrights there are those who see the conflicts, who show the new and fight for the new. Sometimes you have something really new—but there can be fights against it. Some people have ideas that are hard to change. But sometimes you have something that seems new but is really something old in a new form. Then there are discussions: What is the new thing? What has outlived its usefulness?

"The fact that life is so full of conflicts—although they aren't antagonistic in socialism—is used by our enemies, especially in the ideological field. In the cultural field this is very complicated."

Although some radicals believe that affirmation of socialist society negates criticism, scientific socialists see it otherwise. "It's not a contradiction to be for socialist society and to be critical at the same time," said Ernst Schumacher. "Marxists use every means to see that socialism is developed and strengthened. But together with this affirmative step, Marxists recognize that the new society may show reactionary features from the past or negative trends—and these must be stubbornly fought. Criticism is an integral part of Marxism-Leninism.

"In the theater, everyone can strengthen socialist development and criticize this development. In the best plays of the Soviet Union the society is seen critically from a fundamental socialist standpoint. And the development of socialism toward the Communist stage is enhanced by this."

"IN A SOCIALIST society," said Helmut Baierl, "one criticizes to change and develop the present situation—not return to old conditions. That's why we understand criticism not only as blame but also as praise—not in the moral sense, but in an esthetic sense. Criticism in a Marxist sense—not for the abolition of existing socialism but for its further development."

However, the implications of this view are precisely what many from the West, including some advocates of socialism, take issue with. In their opinion criticism should extend to the "right to dissent," that is, the right to challenge the existence of the socialist system itself. But, as Baierl emphasized, what one criticizes is what one wants to change.

"Criticism of the system itself—if it were successful—would abolish the system, and also the criticism. Solzhenitsyn criticized the system and it turned out that he wanted to go back to Czarist Russia. When this became evident, many of the bourgeois writers of the FRG disassociated themselves from him."

Nevertheless, some advocates of socialism continue to assert there can be no real freedom in the new society without the right to challenge the system as such.

"But if one can challenge the system as a whole," said Ernst Schumacher, "one assumes there's an alternative to socialism. But the next stage, communism, isn't an alternative to socialism. They are two stages of the same thing, and one creates the first to get to the second. Those who call for 'dissent' have no alternative to offer—because the alternative would be the restoration of capitalism."

Those who demand the "right to dissent" under socialism assert that this right exists in capitalist societies and to eliminate it under socialism is a retrogression from bourgeois democracy. What they overlook is that the bourgeoisie doesn't *permit* dissent. Those in power in the U.S. have never voluntarily allowed the advocacy of socialism. When it takes place, it's because they're unable to stop it. The extent to which the right to dissent exists under capitalism depends on the strength of the people's movement.

Historically, the working class fights to succeed the bourgeoisie as the class in power. But this fight doesn't stop when the working class does come to power. The old ruling class can then be depended upon to try to regain its former position—and the working class does not reverse its historical role by allowing it the chance to do so. Instead, the new class in power recognizes that the old corporate rulers will try to dissent with everything from words to arms—and that the people must be prepared to defend their revolutionary advance.

"I can of course understand," said Rainer Kerndl, "that people from different countries, with different social and historical circumstances, must find their own way to create a socialist society. Such differences exist among the nations of the socialist community—and they are differences one cannot ignore. On the other hand," Kerndl emphasized, "I don't believe certain principles can be renounced.

"I don't believe it's possible to create a socialist society without having the ability to keep it intact—without a certain power it will not be possible." So far in history, Kerndl pointed out, the new society has had to use its power to prevent restoration of the old—as happened when counterrevolution was attempted in the GDR. "Those who speak of the leading role of the working class as bypassed by history, and who call for the 'right to dissent' against socialism—I think they take counterrevolution into the new society. This might seem simplistic but it must be proved to the contrary. Many in the West speak of what they're going to do under socialism. Not what they've done. I'm talking of reality."

Barbara Dittus also spoke of reality: "As long as you have imperialism, antagonistic contradictions, you can't have freedom for everyone. Look what happened in Chile. And Portugal is dangerous too.

"If you don't make changes, if the plants are taken away from the people—you can't build socialism. If you put it in a very primitive way, you can say that if the capitalists are allowed to keep on doing what they did before, there can't be any socialist development—big or small. Some socialism if the capitalists can do what they want—what they did before!"

The tragedy of Chile occurred because the working class—which had not yet come to power, but was still fighting for it—was unable to stop the armed "dissent" of the junta. But in the GDR, from the beginning, the working class was in power. Advocacy of the old system was barred, together with the racism, fascism and war-mongering with which it had been maintained.

"The working class doesn't give away any position of power it has won," said Ruth Berghaus. "This isn't a principle we've had since yesterday—many have fought and died for this reason. It's a big responsibility we have."

THOSE WHO call for dissent under socialism—that is, the "right" to oppose the system—fail to distinguish between dissent and criticism. When socialism comes into being, the need to dissent in the old antagonistic sense passes into history, while the need to criticize remains.

"Criticism is necessary—we have many things to criticize. But no one has the right to call for a step backward into history," declared Barbara Dittus.

"You can only discuss in the sense of development. And if the people have questions, that's a positive thing. Brecht wrote 'in praise of doubt.' But I would wonder about anyone who wanted to take away the successes of our society. It's ridiculous to think the workers would demand to go back to having the right not to work—to be unemployed!"

And Ilse Galfert said, "There's an old German tale about a land where chickens roast themselves and arrive in people's mouths ready to eat. No social formation will ever be such a paradise. But socialism gives you enormous space for ideas, for their application and for a feeling of responsibility."

And novelist Irmtraud Morgner said: "There are plenty of things we must tackle in our art, in our life. But we're doing it on a new foundation. People don't ask the old question: Capitalism or socialism, which is better? People know. Now our real work has begun."

□ □ □

OPPOSITION TO the social system in the GDR comes from beyond the country's borders to the West. Opposition to the social system in the U.S. comes from within.

There are already millions in the U.S. who consider the system itself responsible for the people's plight. But there is a far larger number whose bitterness is presently directed against what they consider the abuses of the system rather than the system itself. And this feeling, at least, is likely to be expressed at gatherings of any section of the people—including in the cultural area.

In the spring of 1975 (not long after returning from our second trip to the GDR) we attended two programs in a series titled "Who Wrote The Movie?" sponsored by the University of California at Los Angeles. Each program consisted of a film, a guest speaker (a writer or director), and audience discussion. The series was presided over by critic Arthur Knight.

At the opening of one program, "Writing The Socially Conscious Movie," Knight apologized: He had been unable to locate a socially conscious movie. However, he said, "rumor has it" that the film to be shown "might have some remote relationship to our topic." Well, maybe it did. The film, *Lepke,* starring Tony Curtis, did reveal what might be called a social commitment—that is, to the most Neanderthal forces in this society.

Lepke was allegedly based on the life of the gangster who headed Murder Incorporated in the thirties. The hero of the movie is the FBI, but in this same spirit Lepke is portrayed as not-such-a-bad-guy after all. In real life Lepke was hired by the owners in the fur and garment industries to "persuade" the workers through violent means to stop demanding higher wages. In the movie, Lepke demands that the bosses pay the workers higher wages, while the workers plead with him not to—fervently attesting to their satisfaction with the status quo. *Lepke* came to an end amidst wild laughter and derisive shouts of "Author! Author!"

Lepke's author was fortunately not on the premises. The guest speaker that evening, Abby Mann—author of the film *Judgment At Nuremberg*—revealed why it had not been possible to find a "socially conscious" U.S. film to show. Dismissing *Lepke* as a "vile cartoon," Mann went on to speak of his own experiences in film and TV. Recently, he said, he'd had a good one: a TV script he'd written about a Black youth who'd been framed and finally proved innocent had been produced. (What a rarity a "socially conscious" TV program is can be attested to by progressive viewers who may watch thousands of miles of tape before coming upon anything remotely within this category.) The producer of this TV show, Mann related, had said it was "important enough to take chances" to do this script. But such a producer is as rare as a "socially conscious" production. Mann offered an example of typical producer/author relations: He'd recently been working on a TV series and the producer tried to bar him from the set. "There must come a time," the producer said, "when the writer relinquishes the script."

Mann also told of his experiences with the producer of a TV documentary on Ethel and Julius Rosenberg. Interested in writing the script, Mann had examined the trial record. "I didn't find one scrap of evidence against them." But the "only thing" the producer dared put in question almost twenty-five years after the Rosenbergs' execution, related Mann, was the death sentence. "I don't give a damn if they were innocent or guilty," said the producer. "I want to play it down the middle of the road."

And artists who speak up for progressive causes in their role as citizens face the same pressures. The media have, for instance, frequently sniped at Marlon Brando for championing the rights of Native

Americans. "People criticize Marlon because of his feeling for Indians," remarked Mann. "I think it's wonderful for an actor to fight for something besides billing."

Some time later, Mann himself was to come into sharp criticism of a different kind, when associates of Dr. Martin Luther King, Jr. denounced Mann's treatment of King in a film for TV. To date the film has not been shown for the public, but one fact is already beyond dispute: It was written and produced by whites only.

UNFORTUNATELY, Abby Mann wasn't present at another session in the series when Lonne Elder III, author of the play *Ceremonies in Dark Old Men* and the film *Sounder,* was guest speaker.

The title of that program was "Responsibilities of the Black Writer." (Since there was no program on the "Responsibilities of the White Writer," one could only assume that in the view of the major university sponsoring the series, whites have no responsibility for ending the racist-imposed inequality of Black people.)

Presented that night was a film about Black people—written, directed and produced by white people. "There's an arrogant notion that Blacks can't write about white people but whites can write about Black people," declared Elder.

It was clear from Elder's remarks that Hollywood's treatment of Black writers parallels the treatment of Black people as a whole by government and big business. The Black writer, said Elder, "is basically denied involvement" in the "so-called important films," "kept from participation in the mainstream of picture-making." When Elder condemned "the freeze on price for films for Blacks," he got a rebuttal from Arthur Knight. If these films have low budgets, declared Knight, it's only because they "must reach to a wider than Black audience to get back their investment." In just one sentence Knight had endorsed both the profit system as the criterion for film subjects and simultaneously implied that realistic films about Blacks would be of interest only to Black people.

Elder castigated the *Shaft* and *Superfly* movies in which Blacks "reside in a comic strip world of violence, pimps and whores." (Knight was to endorse this racist "comic strip world" only a few months later when he called *Coonskin* an "extraordinary and brilliantly realized" movie.)

The film industry, Elder went on, "hasn't even begun to recognize my struggle to survive. When the adventures of a Beverly Hills hairdresser* are more important than my struggle to survive for 400 years, they haven't recognized a thing."

Arthur Knight, however, could see only hopeful signs of "change" on the Hollywood horizon. "Isn't the darkness beginning to dissipate?" he inquired of Elder, citing "just your being here" as evidence.

"The darkness is not dissipating," responded Elder. Besides, "I don't know how long I'll be here making these statements."

Although there were no signs from the film industry of the "darkness beginning to dissipate," there were certain indications from the audience that glimmers of light were piercing the media-induced fog. When one young white man condemned the film shown that night for carrying on the "welfare cheat" stereotype (the Black woman on welfare who allegedly lives in affluence), there was strong applause from the predominantly white, student audience.

On the other hand there was evidence that heavy fog still remained. "What's the theme of *Ceremonies in Dark Old Men*? Do you consider it important?" inquired another young white man. Elder made it clear that he certainly does consider the theme important. "Basically all of my work deals with Black survival through ritual and ceremony. Why did my mother press my clothes every morning so I'd look good? Why didn't she just give up? Why didn't we go crazy?"

A number of aspiring young white authors were anxious for Elder to endorse their efforts to write about the "Black experience."

"I've written about a Black theme that moves me," asserted a young woman. "Would you try to discourage me?"

"I wouldn't try to discourage you," replied Elder. "You'd have a better chance of getting it on the screen than I would." But she might as well know, pointed out Elder, that this is a "dangerous undertaking" for a white writer. He likened it to crossing the Hollywood Freeway at high noon.

"Why can't a white writer write about the Black experience?" countered a young white man.

"He's writing about me day and night," replied Elder. "The fact is he's so arrogant he thinks he knows more about me than I do. That means I know more about him."

However, Elder made a distinction between a white author writing about Black people "from where he's at" and one writing about the

---

*A reference to the film *Shampoo*.

"Black experience." But no white writer expressed a desire to write about Black people "from where he's at"—that is, of the relations between Black and white and how they're affected by racism. None of them, in fact, mentioned racism at all. One wondered, how could white writers even begin to understand the "Black experience" if they had not yet recognized racism's role in it? And what accounted for this urge to write about the "Black experience" but not about racism? Could it have been the marketplace, whose stalls were accepting fictitious accounts of the "Black experience" and rejecting realistic ones? "In the atmosphere of the Hollywood community," Lonne Elder remarked, "it is rather difficult for a white writer to accomplish honorable ends and goals—so many things in the culture and environment fight against it."

Elder concluded by speaking of "change." Not as Arthur Knight had, as if the change had already taken place. Elder spoke of the change that has to come. "All this," he said, "has got to change. There's no way in the world it can stay the way it is. It has got to come. I believe it's going to come, just like I believe judgment day is going to come."

10. Brecht in Two Worlds

The first production in the U.S. of a Brecht work—*Lindbergh's Flight*—took place in 1931. The play, with music by Kurt Weill and Paul Hindemith, was written not long after Lindbergh's flight across the Atlantic in 1927. (When Lindbergh later identified himself with fascism, Brecht changed the title of the play to *The Ocean Flight* and renamed the main character "The Flyer.") The U.S. production took place at the Academy of Music in Philadelphia, with Leopold Stokowski conducting the orchestra.

For almost a quarter of a century thereafter—including the years Brecht spent in exile in the U.S.—productions of his plays were a rarity in this country. By the mid-fifties this neglect had been transformed into a deep interest in Bertolt Brecht—a change brought about by the interaction between two sets of circumstances.

Brecht's theater, the Berliner Ensemble, founded in the GDR in 1949, had become world famous—establishing his reputation internationally as a foremost playwright of the twentieth century. During the years Brecht's international reputation was growing, changes occurred in the U.S. that created a new atmosphere: The Korean War had

163

been brought to an end in 1953, and the era of civil rights struggles—
that broke the McCarthyite ice age—was launched when Rosa Parks
refused to move to the back of the bus in Montgomery, Alabama,
1955. This changed atmosphere produced a receptive audience for
Brecht in the U.S.

In 1954 *The Threepenny Opera* was an off-Broadway hit, and soon
recordings of "Mack The Knife" soared to the top of the charts. But
Threepenny Opera was one of Brecht's early works. A more significant
breakthrough came in 1956 with the production of *Mother Courage,*
considered by many to be Brecht's greatest play.

Whether the first U.S. production of *Mother Courage,* directed by
Herbert Blau, was an artistic success is open to question. But it made a
success of Blau's theater, the Actor's Workshop, and launched Blau
himself on his trip to the theatrical moon—at the time, Lincoln
Center.

Blau's journey to Lincoln Center had been preceded by other
significant travels. For instance, he took a European tour—on a Ford
Foundation grant—highlighted by what he called a "pilgrimage" to
the Berliner Ensemble. In his book, *The Impossible Theater,* Blau
writes:

. . . I was in Berlin several years ago, calling on Helene Weigel-Brecht at the
Berliner Ensemble. Weigel, primly potent in a black ankle-side gown, her
glasses breasted on a chain, served tea. Then she picked up the phone and
called Elizabeth Hauptmann, Brecht's secretary and collaborator, to come
over and meet me. We had corresponded briefly. When Hauptmann arrived,
Weigel introduced me as the director of the first American production of
Mother Courage. Hauptmann, recalling, smiled. Then Weigel said, "And he is
here on money from the Ford Foundation." End smile. Severe Prussian set of
jaw, proletarianized. "Any strings attached?"[1]

Blau's odd descriptions of Weigel and Hauptmann reveal nothing
more than his bias toward those with a socialist outlook. What *is*
revealing is Blau's admission that the question "Any strings attached?"
came not only from "East German" sources. "I have since learned," he
went on to say, "you don't have to go to East Germany to be asked that
question." That Blau was asked this same question in the U.S. when
his theater "received a series of grants from the Ford Foundation" was
a reflection of the developing radicalization in this country.

The Impossible Theater was written during the early sixties, a time
when criticism could no longer be stifled by repression. But the
increasingly critical attitude of young people toward this social system

could be channeled into a dead end if they were made to feel hopeless about the possibility of an alternative. This is why the Ford and Rockefeller foundations began to show a particular interest in individuals who combined criticisms of this country with assertions that things were even worse in the "totalitarian" states. Blau did exactly that in *The Impossible Theater*. For example:

The Age of Obfuscation had reached its political apotheosis, and took its toll on the theater. It was the end of 1951—the atmosphere having grown so paralyzing in New York—that [*New York Times'* drama critic] Brooks Atkinson remarked we were emulating the totalitarian countries by yielding our cultural life "to the Yahoos and hoodlums" . . . But it was a strange period. For as Atkinson was writing this passage about the American theater, we were confronted with the irony of Brecht and Felsenstein developing two of the greatest theaters in the world in one of its most repressive sectors, East Berlin.[2]

Great theater in a "totalitarian" society? That would really be the "impossible theater"! Great theater never appears in a totalitarian state. A totalitarian state is well aware of the challenge that would emanate from great theater, and so uses its power to suppress it.

Great theater can arise in a capitalist country only when the people's forces are ascending. But the basis for great theater to develop consistently can exist only in a country where the people hold power. In the GDR a government composed of what Atkinson called "yahoos and hoodlums" subsidized a culture that took masses poisoned by fascism and educated them in the spirit of peace and democracy. At a time when the atmosphere in the U.S. theater was "paralyzing"—a paralysis induced by the U.S. government—the GDR government "set us the task of building socialism," as Maik Hamburger of the Deutsches Theater put it, adding: "Of course, the theater embraced this task as its central motivation."

IF ONE INVENTS an "impossible theater," one must also invent an "impossible" audience. Blau does just that—starting with the German workers' theater of the twenties. At that time, Blau claims, Brecht's plays had to be presented in a "labored" manner for the benefit of "uninstructed" workers. But Brecht did not consider his workers' audience "uninstructed." (The distance between Brecht's and Blau's attitudes toward working people may be gauged by the fact that Blau in his book urges actors to work without salaries[3]—expressing an attitude echoed a decade later by Joseph Papp.)

Brecht recognized and respected workers as the revolutionary force that would lead the way to a new society. But he also knew that "instruction" of workers in a capitalist society comes from a bourgeois educational system and the bourgeois media. Brecht's plays, along with the workers' own lives and struggles, countered that "instruction."

After inventing an impossible audience for the German workers' theater, Blau does the same for the GDR theater. In the GDR, he asserts, it's not necessary to play Brecht in a "labored" manner because "even in the proletarian East Berlin," audiences have become "more bourgeois and informed."[4]

A line about working people becoming "more bourgeois and informed" is best reserved for the "impossible theater." If workers are under bourgeois influence, they are misinformed from the standpoint of their own interests. Only the bourgeoisie can be "bourgeois and informed" to its own advantage.

Certainly GDR audiences are informed. This is because the working people comprising this audience have grown up without the influence of bourgeois ideology, except insofar as it enters their country from the FRG and Voice of America. Instead they have access to the culture created by socialism as well as the cultural heritage previously the province of the bourgeoisie—which they have the ability to interpret from a working-class point of view. Only because GDR audiences are so informed can they move in opposition to the bourgeois influences of racism, national chauvinism and anti-Semitism that enter their borders from alien sources.

THE GERMAN workers' theater interpreted Brecht for an audience fighting for a new society. The GDR interprets Brecht for a people building that new society. Blau interpreted Brecht for those who subsidize theater in order to keep audiences locked within the ideology of the old society.

According to Blau, "*Mother Courage* is a revolutionary play, precisely because it can't be appropriated without misgivings by any particular cause."[5]

It's certainly true that there have been efforts to "appropriate" *Mother Courage*. But there is one "particular cause" that doesn't have to "appropriate" *Mother Courage,* since it was written—without "misgivings"—for this "particular cause": peace, equality and socialism. It is Brecht's commitment to this particular cause that makes *Mother Courage* a revolutionary play.

"I don't believe [*Mother Courage*] leaves the audience in a state of objectivity (i.e., dispassionately balancing pros and cons)," stated Brecht.[6] The "question of choice of artistic means," he went on, "can be only that of how we playwrights give a social stimulus to our audience (get them moving)."[7]

But the director of the first U.S. production of *Mother Courage* was not trying to "get them moving." He writes:

If Brecht urges us to take a stand, many of the plays we have been doing [at the Actor's Workshop] have warned us that it may be impossible to take a stand: that in an atomic world fission is a property of belief as well as matter. Beware of ideology.[8]

Blau is not warning against some nebulous "ideology." He is warning against a *particular* ideology: Brecht's ideology, Marxism. "Brecht's ideology," asserts Blau, "no more exempted him from the doubts that we all share, and the contradictions, than it overthrew the artistic integrity of his work."[9]

In other words, according to Blau, Brecht had to protect himself against his ideology in order to maintain his "artistic integrity." That Marxism can "overthrow" a writer's "artistic integrity" is, of course, a longtime allegation of bourgeois critics. Since these critics can't deny the achievements of Brecht and other Marxist artists, they assert that Marxist artists are artists *despite* their Marxism!

As for Blau's implication that Marxism was of no use to Brecht because it didn't "exempt" him from "doubts" and "contradictions": If Brecht had expected this of Marxism, he would have been rejecting the philosophy he advocated. Marxism helped Brecht understand contradictions—and use doubt productively, as those who worked with him attest.

In 1926, when Brecht was only twenty-eight, his collaborator Elisabeth Hauptmann wrote:

. . . Brecht obtains works on socialism and Marxism and asks for lists of the basic works he should study first. In a letter a little later from holiday he writes: "I am now eight feet deep in 'Das Kapital.' Now I want to know all the details."[10]

Through Marxism Brecht came to "take a stand"—on a lifelong basis—for revolutionary change. But Blau—who advises us that in an "atomic world" it "may be impossible to take a stand"—time and again denies the revolutionary essence of Brecht's work.

Mother Courage, according to Blau, is "disturbing because it impugns us all."[11] Thus Blau (like Robert Brustein and so many others) is telling us we have no enemies, we are all the enemy. The class that subsidized Blau wants us to believe this. But Brecht tells us it isn't true.

Brecht is not part of the we-are-all-guilty chorus. Brecht does not "impugn" people who struggle against war. He impugns those responsible for it (while calling on those who *should* be fighting against war to do so—a call all the more urgent in today's "atomic world"):

> General, your tank is a powerful vehicle
> It slashes down forests and crushes a hundred men.
> But it has one defect:
> It needs a driver.
>
> General, your bomber is powerful.
> It flies faster than a storm and carries more than
>   an elephant
> But it has one defect:
> It needs a mechanic.
>
> General, a man is very useful.
> He can fly and he can kill.
> But he has one defect:
> He can think.[12]

WHEN INTEREST in this country in Brecht became increasingly apparent, corporate foundations and bourgeois publishers reacted: As part of their strategy to keep radicalized young people from recognizing what is revolutionary in art and in life, they saw to it that anti-socialist interpretations of Brecht's work and life became widely available.

Blau states:

Let us not be mistaken: the ground we cleared for Brecht was negligible beside the bulldozing of belated recognition. Books on Brecht, essays on Brecht, Brecht on Brecht, David Merrick on Brecht—if the propaganda mills behind the Iron Curtain were to expend all their subversive wiliness on behalf of Brecht, they could hardly achieve what paperback saturation . . . [has] done in the last few years . . . Consumption is not conspicuous. It is voracious.[13]

When one reads lines about the "subversive wiliness" of the "propaganda mills behind the Iron Curtain," one might think the author is deliberately parodying the style of anti-Communist comic books. Far from it. This is typical of the way Brecht "experts" write on Brecht, the GDR and real socialism in general.

Although Blau speaks of "the ground we cleared for Brecht,"

accuracy would have required him to speak of he way he and many others used Brecht to clear the ground for their own careers—supplying the "books on Brecht, essays on Brecht" that meet bourgeois requirements. One of these suppliers is Eric Bentley.

Bentley, who has written on Brecht over a considerable period, shares Blau's antagonism to Brecht's views—as revealed, for example, in the following:

"Brecht's Communism," says Bentley, "will not appear as unplausible as it does to many of his readers in America today" if they "remember that an artist will accept almost anything if it seems to offer a future for his art. Brecht accepted Communism as Pascal advised accepting supernatural religion: as a bet according to which you have everything to gain and very little to lose."[14]

In 1961 when Bentley wrote this, it may well have been that "Brecht's Communism" appeared "unplausible" to many U.S. readers. But today what many thousands of Brecht's readers in this country find "unplausible" is not "Brecht's Communism" but Bentley's anti-Communist interpretation of Brecht.

To assert that Brecht "accepted Communism" because he had "everything to gain and very little to lose" is a strange way to speak of an artist who "accepted Communism" during the grim period of anti-fascist struggle in Germany—and continued to assert his convictions when this meant exile for him. Those artists willing to "accept almost anything" were the ones who accepted fascism.

By staying true to his beliefs, Brecht did have "everything to gain"—but not in narrow personal terms. He had "everything to gain" only if one considers that remaining part of the struggle to change the world is "everything."

ANOTHER BRECHT "expert" is Robert Brustein. Writing three years after Bentley presented a picture of Brecht as a split personality, Brustein took the same concept several steps further:

... [Brecht] comes to terms with life only by continuing to reject it—by drifting with a political tide, he overcomes his spiritual horror and nausea. And this is the only synthesis of Brecht's double revolt. Only by merging with evil did he feel he could still function for good; only by embracing the destroyers could he still join the ranks of the creators. The chicanery and compromises Brecht accepted for the sake of the survival of himself and his art are not always very attractive. And no modern playwright better exemplifies the dwindling possibilities of revolt in an age of totalitarianism, war, and the mass state. But if Brecht sometimes sacrificed his personal integrity to a collective falsehood, then this was in order that his individualism could still be secretly expressed.[15]

When Brustein claims Brecht was "drifting with a political tide," he is saying what Bentley said—and consequently evokes the same reaction: Was Brecht "drifting with a political tide" in Germany when he struggled against fascism? Was it "drifting with a political tide" that earned Brecht a summons from the House Committee on Un-American Activities during his exile in the U.S.? Was Brecht "drifting with a political tide" when he returned to a territory poisoned by years of fascism in order to be part of the struggle for a peaceful, democratic German state—and of the struggle to build socialism?

And one must ask: How can an artist "join the ranks of the creators" by "embracing the destroyers"? Those artists who embraced the fascist destroyers left forever the "ranks of the creators." Artists who drift with the political tide—as the lives of those who "embraced the destroyers" attest—cannot overcome but are overcome by "spiritual horror and nausea."

It is evident from reading Brustein (and Bentley) that no accusation is too derisive, too lurid to be applied to Brecht. When Brustein, as is typical of him, identifies socialism with "totalitarianism," he is simply repeating a stock generality of anticommunism. But certain of Brustein's (and Bentley's) allegations against Brecht seem to be quite specific. Brustein, for example, accuses Brecht of "chicanery and compromises," of sacrificing "his personal integrity to a collective falsehood" so his "individualism could still be secretly expressed." One wonders: How can "individualism" be "secretly expressed" from the stage of a theater?

According to Brustein, Brecht's life "exemplifies the dwindling possibilities of revolt." If this were true, it wouldn't be necessary for bourgeois writers to engage in endless attacks on him. What Brecht's life "exemplifies" is that socialist revolution opens up unlimited possibilities for artists. Since this is hardly the conclusion bourgeois ideologists want readers to draw, they have seen to it that an altogether different portrait of Brecht emerges in capitalist countries.

In writing about Brecht, Brustein and Bentley seem to base themselves on identical facts. These "facts"—as well as the Brustein and Bentley interpretations—originate from a single source: a book called *Brecht: The Man And His Work*. This is by far the most widely available biography of Brecht in the U.S. Brustein, Bentley and Blau all refer to its author, Martin Esslin, as one does to an authority. According to Bentley, this book is "the best thing yet written about Brecht in any language."[16]

In 1967, for an issue of *The Drama Review* devoted to Brecht, Martin Esslin wrote:

On February 10, 1968, Brecht would have celebrated his seventieth birthday. It makes one realize how young he died on August 14, 1956, and how rapidly, since he died, he has acquired the status of an established international classic; and yet, ten years earlier, in 1946, he was little more than an unknown and neglected German exile tramping the streets of Los Angeles and New York in search of recognition.[17]

At first glance this paragraph appears to contrast with Esslin's customary approach to Brecht: It seems quite sympathetic. In reality, these lines contain the clue to Esslin's distortion of Brecht's life and work.

The Brecht Esslin describes would have been no different from those thousands of writers who were "in search of recognition"—and willing to write whatever might bring it. If Brecht was "in search of recognition," it is all the more to his credit that he never adjusted what he wrote to win it.

In exile in Los Angeles Brecht wrote:

> Every day, to earn my daily bread
> I go to the market where lies are bought
> Hopefully
> I take my place among the sellers[18]

What Brecht wrote was not, in this instance, what Brecht did: He was quite unable to take his "place among the sellers" of lies. During his six years in Hollywood, Brecht sold only one screenplay, *Hangmen Also Die*. It was a story with an anti-fascist theme. "But the final product bore little resemblance to Brecht's outline and he disassociated himself from it," Martin Esslin admits.[19] This means Brecht refused screen credit. Strange behavior for one "tramping the streets of Los Angeles and New York in search of recognition"!

An incident in the autobiography of Salka Viertel, an actress in pre-Hitler Germany who became a screenwriter in Hollywood, reveals why Brecht was unable to take his "place among the sellers." Describing her collaboration with Brecht on what was intended to be a commercial screenplay, she writes:

Brecht bit into his cigar and assured me that we could write our story in such a way that they would not notice what a highbrow masterpiece it was. But we had to proceed scientifically, soberly and objectively. I felt that his suggestion was prompted by his desire to help me and to cheer me up, and I was very moved.*

The first thing we promised each other was never to consider anything from an ideological or "artistic" viewpoint. We had to be shrewd and invent situations and characters for the Hollywood market. We must begin with a survey of stars who needed "vehicles."[20]

After completing their survey of Hollywood stars, Brecht and Viertel decided:

... we had to have the story first, then worry about casting. Whatever ideas we tried, whatever subject we broac ed, we always came back to the war, and finally our main character emerged as a heroine of the French Resistance ... Before leaving [occupied] Paris a vengeful SS officer had shaved the young woman's head to make her appear as a "collaboratice" ... Brecht had insisted that for the larger part of the film the actress playing the role remain hairless. I pleaded that at least she wear a scarf and reminded him of our pact, but his only concession was that at the beginning we see her brushing her long hair. The more we discussed it the more stubborn Brecht became about the clean-shaven scalp of the leading lady, and soon I also got used to it, comforted by the thought that as the film went on, the hair would grow at least half an inch.[21]

The outcome? "In due course, we discarded our basic agreement" not to be "ideological" or "artistic," and "it turned into a good story and we believed in it. Alas, no studio wanted to buy it and no star could be induced to shave her head."[22]

Again, this was strange behavior for a man supposedly tramping the streets of Los Angeles in search of recognition! It was also strangely uncompromising behavior for a man allegedly guilty of "chicanery and compromises"!

Today, Salka Viertel goes on to say,

Books about him are written in many languages and his plays are performed everywhere in the East and West. It was not so in Hollywood. Life was hard.[23]

A dramatist can write in hope of future production. An actress can do nothing without a production. If life was hard for Brecht in Hollywood, it may have been even harder for Helene Weigel. Viertel writes:

Hollywood actresses who met Helli at the Chaplins' or in my house were amazed when I told them that she was their distinguished colleague. "She

*Salka Viertel was going through personal and financial difficulties at the time.

certainly doesn't look it," concluded the flighty ones, after they had scrutinized her face and straight hair pulled back in a tight knot.[24]

Although the Weigel story did not end in Hollywood, one might almost say that it included a Hollywood ending:

Fifteen years later, in Paris, I saw her play *Mother Courage* with the Berliner Ensemble. The Sarah Bernhardt Theater was packed and after the last curtain the audience stood and cheered. When I went backstage, Helli, in the dressing room of the great Sarah, was sitting in front of a huge gilded mirror, press photographers crowding around her clicking their cameras. The room was filled with French, German and English-speaking admirers and many who were curious to meet an actress "from behind the Iron Curtain." She saw me, extricated herself from the crowd and embracing me, exclaimed: "I am glad you could see that I can do something else besides bake a *Gugelhupf* . . ."[25]

AFTER BRECHT returned in 1948 to what had been the Eastern part of Germany, he said, "I don't have my opinions because I am here, I am here because of my opinions."

But Esslin's Brecht is a man who never formed an opinion except on the basis of the narrowest personal considerations. According to Esslin, this is what accounted for Brecht's opinions of capitalist society:

. . . [it cannot] be said that Brecht's experiences in the West during his exile gave him a real chance to change his opinion of the sterility of bourgeois society and its neglect of the artist. His lack of financial or critical success seemed to confirm his most pessimistic view about the philistinism and contempt for values in a commercial society. Of course, what he blamed the Western world for was his personal lack of success . . .[26]

What Esslin doesn't mention is that Brecht formed his opinions on the "sterility of bourgeois society" *in* a bourgeois society, pre-Hitler Germany—where he had no "lack of success." But Brecht's success as a playwright did not change his views on the "sterility of bourgeois society."

The real reasons for Brecht's "personal lack of success" while in exile, asserts Esslin, were not understood by Brecht himself:

can he be expected to have realized that this was largely due to the language barrier and the strangeness of his views and background in countries with an utterly different tradition?[27]

If Brecht's lack of recognition while in exile was "due to the language barrier and the strangeness of his views," why is it that he "acquired the status of an established international classic" only a short time after leaving the U.S.? The answer is that language proved no barrier nor did Brecht's views seem "strange" when his plays were performed by the Berliner Ensemble to cheering audiences in countries with a "different tradition."

But Esslin makes no connection between Brecht's recognition as an "established international classic" and the existence of the Berliner Ensemble—a theater made possible by a society with the highest regard for Brecht's work. Instead Esslin produces a sinister interpretation for the founding of Brecht's theater:

When the East offered him the most lavish means to put his ideas into practice, to work and to experiment to his heart's content, he accepted . . .

By accepting the East German government's offer he put himself at the disposal of one of the most cruel and heartless regimes in history and must bear his share of responsibility for it.[28]

What a Brecht biographer would call "cruel and heartless," one would think, is the fascist German regime that forced Brecht into exile—or the reactionary U.S. regime that drove him out of this country. But to Esslin the "cruel and heartless" state is the one that offered Brecht "the means to put his ideas into practice."

Of course, if it had been up to Esslin, Brecht would never have been permitted to "put his ideas into practice." Esslin is so utterly opposed to Brecht's views that he even claims Brecht was unable to understand Nazism! To "substantiate" this charge, Esslin writes:

Brecht's Communist views hindered rather than helped him to penetrate the true nature of National Socialism; he regarded it as a kind of conspiracy of the rich against the poor . . .[29]

For those millions throughout the world who view fascism as "a kind of conspiracy of the rich against the poor," it would be difficult to grasp how "Brecht's Communist views hindered rather than helped him" understand fascism's true nature. (Those too young to have witnessed the "conspiracy" that led to the takeover of Germany had the opportunity to see what happened in Chile.)

Although Esslin neglects to mention it, Brecht had "Communist views" toward the GDR. This is why Brecht said, "I don't have my opinions because I am here, I am here because of my opinions." But Esslin doesn't tell us this. Instead he informs us that Brecht put himself "at the disposal of one of the most cruel and heartless regimes in history"—and got a theater in return. As for the "regime"'s end of the bargain, "The East German authorities regarded the winning over of such a famous playwright as a major propaganda victory."[30]

The anti-Communist attacks against Brecht that continue long after his death began very early in his career, dating back to the time when he first became a Marxist.

In 1931, for example, Brecht collaborated on a film portraying the lives of workers during a terrible depression. In 1932 the censors declared that the film, *Kuhle Wampe*, "endangered the state." According to the state's charge, *Kuhle Wampe*

... offends against the vital interests of the state ... The frequently repeated summons to solidarity . . . is nothing but a summons to violence and subversion. This summons to solidarity runs like a thread throughout the film, and culminates in a summons to change the world.[31]

Brecht's lifelong "summons to change the world" is what accounts for the unabating anti-Communist attacks that span so many decades. Today only the forms have changed.

In times past, anti-Communists said Brecht "endangered" the capitalist state. Now anti-Communists claim the socialist state "endangered" Brecht. Therefore, they assert, Brecht became the antagonist of socialism as it was being developed in the GDR. This is Martin Esslin's theme and the theme of bourgeois Brecht "specialists" in general. GDR cultural workers are well acquainted with these accusations.

"There's a continuous effort to separate Brecht from the GDR—to separate Brecht the great poet from a Brecht who was supposedly a small politician. Brecht's writings and his actions show his art and politics were inseparable," declared Wolfgang Pintzka at the Berliner Ensemble.

"They have never forgiven Brecht for coming here," said Peter Meter, cultural director of the Committee of Anti-Fascist Resistance Fighters. "Brecht is one of the most eminent playwrights, writers and thinkers in the world—they can't admit he was a Communist and lived in the GDR because he wanted to. That's why they try to discredit him in every possible way.

"For years," continued Meter, "they tried to break Brecht away from his unity with the working class. But Brecht was always for real, existing socialism. He didn't come here looking for a workers' paradise. He knew that building socialism is a very difficult thing.

"Now that Brecht's dead they think they can do what they want with him. Since he's a poet who represents what's human and humane, they pretend he's a great human spirit beyond the Party. They want to absorb him in this way, take him over for their own purposes. That's why they try to discredit his partisanship to socialism by pretending he was a partisan only so he could do his theater work—but that in reality he always fought the Party."

Werner Hecht, who has written extensively on Brecht and who edited Brecht's *Work Journal,* also commented on the misrepresentation of Brecht's role in the GDR. "They give him a special role," noted Hecht. "They say he's a special Communist who wanted a special communism for himself. They interpret this communism in such a way that Brecht's books could be put into the libraries of the owners of industry." The "main characteristic" of the anti-Communists' treatment of Brecht in the GDR, said Hecht, is "the invention of a confrontation between Brecht and the Party." Hecht is familiar with the anti-Communist attacks against Brecht from their earliest stage: At the time we met, he was codirecting a film concerning the events around *Kuhle Wampe.* "Our film shows the very sharp anti-Communist moves against Brecht in Germany in 1932," said Hecht—moves taken by individuals who soon became "good Nazis."

According to Esslin and other bourgeois writers, confrontations with the Party left Brecht so "tired and worn" that his years in the GDR were a period of artistic "sterility." In reality these years were for Brecht a time of great creativity.

"I knew Brecht," stated playwright Helmut Baierl. "The first thing he wanted to do here was stage his plays. During his years in the GDR Brecht founded a world theater, developed the manner of staging his plays—and staged them for the world."

During this same eight-year period, Werner Hecht pointed out, Brecht was productive as a writer: He wrote two plays, *Turandot, Or The Congress of Whitewashers* and *The Days of the Commune,* "about 500 poems and five volumes on the theater and the art of acting."

Oddly, while Esslin claims battles with the Party left Brecht "tired and worn," he also states that Brecht took to "the controversy" like "a duck to water and seemed to enjoy it all tremendously."[32]

Brecht *was* involved in sharp discussions on cultural policies in the GDR and he *did,* said Peter Meter, enjoy this involvement. "Brecht was a man who liked to discuss, to argue. A Western journalist once said to Brecht, 'Isn't it incredible that a government will spend six hours discussing your plays with you?' Brecht replied, 'Can you tell me of another government that would be willing to discuss my plays with me for six hours?'"

In these discussions, Meter continued, "Brecht made very helpful criticisms. His critique of certain things in our socialist state was really positive, creative. Sometimes he said very disagreeable things—and I say he was often right.

"Brecht was really able to understand differences in the cultural field—while at the same time recognizing that real socialism is much larger than culture. He understood that the continuous improvement of social conditions for every worker is more important than certain blown-up cultural differences."

Werner Hecht also spoke of Brecht's ability to put differences on culture in their proper perspective. The debate on socialist realism, pointed out Hecht—in which Brecht and Lukács emerged as central and contending figures—began in 1938 among German writers in exile. "For this reason Brecht didn't publish his differences with Lukács at that time. Although Brecht was very strongly against Lukács's opinions, he felt that anti-fascist unity among those in exile was more important" than debating cultural differences.

When the debate was resumed in the GDR, Brecht expressed his sharp disagreement with the Lukács position. "That," commented Hecht, "shows nothing more than the fact that Brecht believed socialist development must take place through discussion. Brecht fought—and this is the point bourgeois critics misuse. They don't see that socialism develops through such conflicts. They see contradictions only as they exist under capitalism."

In 1955 Brecht discussed the question of socialist development with a group of students. Hecht, who was one of those students, said, "Brecht pointed out that the dialectical principles of development apply to all phases of a society's development—and a dialectician must understand that things will not happen without conflict under socialism. In socialism, in communism and in the phases following that, there'll always be the fight of the new with the old."

ALTHOUGH Peter Meter often agreed with the "very disagreeable things" Brecht sometimes said, he did not always agree with Brecht. He had differences, for example, with certain views Brecht expressed in his *Brief Organon for the Theater.*

"In the *Brief Organon* where Brecht asks that his audience follow him in a purely rational way, where Brecht says he tries very hard not to create emotions, and if he does to control them by reason—at this point, one must criticize. Especially," stressed Meter, "in a country where all possible means of reaching people must be used—as was the case here after the war.

"What Brecht does in the *Brief Organon* is a sin—I almost said against the holy spirit. One must include in theater the tremendous strength feeling can give. The fascists knew this very well. All this so-called ideology of racism, anticommunism, anti-humanism is based on brainlessness. On feelings only—and primitive feelings at that.

"People talked to Brecht about this. They told him his theory didn't correspond to life because human beings are both feeling and reason—and at the beginning of their development more feeling than reason."

In the discussions involving Brecht, two distinct trends emerged. In the debate between Brecht and Lukács, it became clear that what lay beneath the advocacy of different methods was a divergency in goals. On the other hand, what became evident in Brecht's well-known dialogue with Friedrich Wolf is that different means can be used to pursue identical aims.

One aspect of the Brecht-Wolf dialogue revolved around the very complicated question of approach to emotion. Wolf said:

Your theater appeals in the first place to the spectator's power of understanding. You want to set out by arousing the audience to a clear recognition of the relationships in actual and possible situations . . . and so to lead it to correct conclusions and decisions. Are you unwilling to address yourself in the same way directly to the feelings and emotions—to the sense of justice, the urge to freedom, the "sacred wrath" against the oppressor? I am deliberately putting the question simply: in this spirit . . . do you think it better not to offer present-day audiences such an historical chronicle as Schiller's *Götz von Berlichingen* (. . . which addresses itself above all to an emotional experience)? Do you feel that the Hitler period with its avalanche of perverted emotions has so discredited such works that we have come to treat them as *a priori* suspicious?

Brecht replied:

It is not true, though it is sometimes suggested, that epic theater . . . proclaims the slogan: "Reason this side, Emotion (feeling) that." It by no means renounces emotion, least of all the sense of justice, the urge to freedom and righteous anger; it is so far from renouncing these that it does not even assume their presence, but tries to arouse or reinforce them.[33]

That a common goal can be pursued by different artistic methods is

particularly evident in the Brecht-Wolf exchange on *Mother Courage.*
Wolf said:

... I think *Courage* would have been even *more* effective if at the end the
mother had given her curse on the war some visible expression in the action (as
Kattrin did) and drawn the logical conclusions from her change of mind. (I
might add that the same Thirty Years' War saw peasants banding together and
defending themselves against the soldiery).

Brecht responded:

As you quite rightly say, the play in question shows that Courage has learned
nothing from the disasters that befall her . . . But even if Courage learns
nothing else at least the audience can, in my view, learn something by
observing her.[34]

Commenting on the dialogue between Brecht and his father, film
director Konrad Wolf said, "Of course there was a difference of
opinion, especially concerning methods of work." But he likened the
two playwrights to "two different military strategists" who are not
confronting each other "but stand on the same side." One strategist
suggests a "frontal attack," the other an "encircling maneuver." From
military science," Wolf stated, "we know both methods have a right to
exist." He added: "So far as I'm concerned, Brecht and Wolf had an
impact on each other."

THE "CONTINUOUS effort to separate Brecht from the GDR"—to
counterpose Brecht against the policies of the Socialist Unity Party
and the state—has many ramifications. For instance, if Brecht's
alleged hostility to these policies is to appear justified, it's necessary to
make the policies themselves appear contemptible. This is just what
Esslin undertakes to do.

During the fifties in the GDR, he states, there was a "return to
violent chauvinism" in order to "win over the masses who were still
largely conditioned by National Socialism."[35] With this statement
Esslin makes a "violent" departure not only from fact but from even a
pretense of logic: How could "violent chauvinism" have been used to
"win over the masses" to socialism—when "violent chauvinism" is
what had been used to lead the masses into fascism and war?

Esslin makes no attempt to document his allegation of chauvinism,
"violent" or otherwise. He can't. Chauvinism is always reflected in
culture, as the Nazis proved with their anti-Semitic, anti-Soviet, pro-
war films. During the fifties GDR film-makers were involved, as

the Museum of Modern Art's program notes for its GDR film festival put it, in an "exploration" of the "reprehensible results of a politics of racism." And not even Esslin would dare tell his readers that *Mother Courage* and *The Resistable Rise of Arturo Ui* (which was in the Berliner Ensemble repertory for fifteen years) are evidences of chauvinism!

Since Esslin describes this period as a time of "return to violent chauvinism," he can portray Brecht as one who stood aside from a state with such policies—except when he was "bitterly critical" of this state. But the portrayal of a Brecht who was either aloof from or actively hostile to developments in the GDR suffered a particularly devastating blow with the publication of Brecht's *Work Journal.*

"Now that the *Work Journal* has been published, they can no longer claim Brecht didn't participate in activity in the GDR," said Werner Hecht. "In his *Work Journal* Brecht expresses his opinions about the state—and even the most reactionary critics have had to take this fact into account." Hecht paused to note: "I personally am one of the people in the world most attacked by Esslin and other bourgeois critics because I edited Brecht's writings dealing mainly with political questions. They don't find in these writings what in their opinion Brecht should have written—so now the editor's the culprit."

Far from standing apart from the state, Brecht was an adviser to the Ministry of Culture. He was also a vice-president of the Academy of Arts and had a "great responsibility" in the Writers League. Brecht took these responsibilities "very seriously, he did a lot," emphasized Hecht.

"Brecht's political work," pointed out Wolfgang Pintzka, "was above all ideological work—he fought on the ideological front of politics. It's well known that he reacted very fast, very directly—not only in the arts but to all political events." One of the events to which Brecht "reacted very fast, very directly" was the attempted counter-revolution of 1953.

"When the West Berlin reactionaries penetrated with the intention of starting a coup, Brecht was at his country home," related Hecht. "When Brecht heard these events were taking place he returned immediately to Berlin." As a leader both in the theater and of important organizations, Brecht "called a meeting of his colleagues. He came back in order to help fight against these events."

At this time Brecht expressed his support to the Party: "I feel the need of writing to you at this time to express my alliance with the Socialist Unity Party."[36] He also called for the harshest measures against the provocateurs who had seized upon errors for anti-socialist purposes, and he spoke of the need for discussion of these errors.

Since Esslin and other bourgeois critics identify with the attempted counterrevolution (which to them is "revolutionary"), they castigate Brecht for not doing the same. There is a class basis for this identity, which most bourgeois critics try to obscure. Esslin, however, reveals it. For instance, Esslin states that because of "Brecht's Communist views"—which "hindered" him from penetrating the "true nature of National Socialism"—Brecht

... completely overlooked the genuinely revolutionary ... side of the Nazis, who were by no means merely the stooges of the generals or the industrialists whom they used and also ruthlessly betrayed.[37]

It's true that Brecht's "Communist views" "hindered" him from seeing the "genuinely revolutionary" side of the Nazis—because what Esslin calls their "genuinely revolutionary'" side was the Nazis' counterrevolutionary misleading of desperate masses in a time of terrible depression. It's also true that Brecht's "Communist views" "hindered" him from seeing that the "industrialists" had been "ruthlessly betrayed" by the Nazis: In Brecht's opinion the "industrialists"—who supported the Nazis' rise to power—had "ruthlessly betrayed" the people.

These same "industrialists" (that is, corporate monopolists) were behind the attempted counterrevolution in 1953. Since Esslin reflects their views, he insists that Brecht should have been a leader of the counterrevolutionists. At the same time Esslin (and other bourgeois writers who share his position) seize upon Brecht's criticism of mistakes—hiding the fact that he made it from a position of commitment to the socialist society.

"Brecht experienced the most difficult phase of the new socialist society," pointed out Konrad Wolf. Although he may have had differences on certain questions, Wolf noted, "even during this very difficult time, in the very complicated situation in 1953, Brecht never thought of leaving the GDR or turning his back on the GDR."

As Frederic Ewen, author of *Bertolt Brecht, His Life, His Art, and His Times*, states, everything Brecht did was "undertaken within the framework of the Socialist state in which he was participating, and for which he was working. He was not to be taken in by the jubilant cries from the Western camp . . . He was not ready to join in what they imagined were the imminent obsequies of the German Democratic Republic."[38]

To those in the West who said he was unable to recognize his real friends, Brecht replied:

> Softly, my dear fellows
> The Judas kiss for the artists follows
> Hard on the Judas kiss for the workers.
> The arsonist with his bottle of petrol
> Sneaks up grinning to
> The Academy of Arts . . .
>
> Even the narrowest minds
> In which peace is harbored
> Are more welcome to the arts than the art lover
> Who is also a lover of the art of war.[39]

Many times over Brecht made his own allegiance clear. "It isn't true," he told a Swiss colleague, "that I have set myself down on two chairs. I am already sitting on one. And that one stands in the East."[40]

"I HAVE been accused of wanting to 'denigrate' Brecht,"[41] exclaims an outraged Martin Esslin in a foreword to a 1960 edition of his book. Esslin then goes on to denounce as "grotesque" and "misrepresentation" the stinging criticism that met an edition published the previous year.

In the years since 1960 more and more of Esslin's readers have come to recognize who is responsible for the grotesque misrepresentation of Brecht. In a time of growing radicalization many have gone beyond the point where they can be influenced by Esslin's crude allegations.

But the increasing rejection of Esslin's misrepresentation doesn't mean misrepresentation of Brecht is ending. It means that in a time of change misrepresentation changes too. This is why misrepresentation of Brecht is now available also in "revolutionary" form—as in the *New German Critique* article, "The Dialectics of Legitimation: Brecht in the GDR," whose author objects that Brecht's work is used to "affirm" and "legitimatize" socialist society. But, as GDR theater workers pointed out, Brecht's purpose was to "affirm" and "legitimatize" socialist society—and his criticism was consistent with this aim.

"Our theater in the GDR has always been a theater of critics—of 'new German critics,'" noted Ruth Berghaus. "As for the question of legitimation," she continued, "this didn't arise after the founding of the GDR. This was the central question of Brecht's creativity from the 1920s on —legitimation of the revolution. So in that respect it's wrong to construct a break in 1949." Brecht felt, "if the revolution had its theater his plays would be realized"—as they were with the founding of the Berliner Ensemble in 1949.

"We view theater in the GDR as a theater of permanent social change. We develop only through struggle"—but not as struggle develops under capitalism. "That is excluded," emphasized Berghaus.

Commenting also on the "revolutionary" misrepresentation of Brecht, Konrad Wolf noted that the pseudo-radicals and right wing "meet as in a circle." Their concern, he said, is "not constructive criticism" but to "eliminate socialist society and replace it by— nothing—by capitalism, which would be the outcome.

"With Brecht," he went on, "they constantly carry on a demagogic struggle." Not only do they select from Brecht's writings "the parts where he expresses himself critically on certain questions in our society. They also try to turn Brecht upside down, to turn his critique of bourgeois society against socialist society."

In his own work Werner Hecht sees how the pseudo-radicals and the right wing "meet as in a circle." From all over the world questions on Brecht come to Hecht—both from those honestly seeking information and those seeking new ways to distort Brecht. "As for the different groups that falsify Brecht—as Marxists we see their anti-Communist connections with each other. It's quite interesting," Hecht remarked, "that these different groups quarrel about Brecht. The pseudo-radicals quarrel with the right—but both are anti-Communist."

But the misrepresentation of Brecht can't stop the genuine and growing interest in Brecht as a truly revolutionary artist, a protagonist of existing socialism. "I can't remember ever having a discussion about Brecht in a capitalist country that didn't become a purely political debate—because Brecht's views in his poems and plays are always political," said Hecht. He added: "I think nothing better can happen to Brecht."

CONFIRMATION OF the real Brecht, the Brecht hostile critics try to hide, is to be found throughout his writings. When Brecht comments on theater, it is as an advocate of socialism.

"Providing fresh insights and socialist impulses"[42] is the task of the theater, stated Brecht. To carry out this task, GDR theater workers turn for assistance to Brecht—whose work continues to provide "fresh insights and socialist impulses."

At the Berliner Ensemble, "we analyze Brecht constantly," said Wolfgang Pintzka. "We think his work offers tremendous reserves—artistically, philosophically, politically. We constantly find new things—we discover the possibilities for new impulses according to present social reality."

Because of continuous change in social reality, the Berliner Ensemble seeks to apply the "fresh insights" it finds in Brecht's writings both to its interpretation of new plays and Brecht's own plays. Discussing why the interpretation of, for example, *Mother Courage,* would change from period to period, a Berliner Ensemble *Dramaturg,* Friedrich Dieckmann, said, "This play was written in 1939 and produced ten years later—for Germans who had gone through the first world war and been misled into starting a second world war because they hadn't learned anything. The 1949 production here showed these people who had just come through this second world war a reflection of themselves.

"Brecht and Wolf," he remarked, "expressed their different opinions on *Mother Courage* from one and the same outlook. But I think neither Wolf's questions nor Brecht's answers would be valid for all time. You have to think about these questions each time you produce a play. You always have to analyze the situation and the public, because the scale of socialist theater is very large."

At the same time that the Berliner Ensemble interprets Brecht for a contemporary socialist audience, the theater works with young playwrights—as Brecht himself did. These new playwrights draw upon Brecht for "fresh insights" but also introduce their own particular experience into this theater of social change.

"Brecht was in favor of change even in regard to himself," stated Manfred Wekwerth,[43] shortly after he became *Intendant* of the Berliner Ensemble in Spring 1977. Brecht "wanted to change not only the world but also the theater," emphasized Wekwerth, who worked with Brecht and is an internationally known director. "If you talk about Brecht, you talk about change. This refers to everything: the artistic means as well as the interaction between theater and public, which has been subject to considerable change."[44] Things have changed to such an extent, Wekwerth remarked, that "the question today is no longer socialism or no socialism. The question is where the possibilities lie for everyone to develop their personality in a socialist setting, collectively with others."[45]

Discussing the relationship between tradition and change, Wekwerth said, "It is of course possible to break with tradition. We wouldn't be Marxists if we didn't say that Marxism is the greatest break with all continuums and at the same time the greatest continuum itself. But I think that the goal of the theater must remain its productivity in social matters."[46]

A THEATER devoted to providing "fresh insights and socialist impulses" is, of course, unacceptable to bourgeois critics. Those who portray Brecht in a role entirely different from the one he actually played also project an entirely different role for the Berliner Ensemble. Among this group is the British critic Kenneth Tynan who, antedating Herbert Blau, was one of the first to make the "pilgrimage" from a Western country to the Berliner Ensemble.

Although one rarely sees a Tynan byline in the U.S. today, in early 1976 his name surfaced anew—atop an article on the front page of *The New York Times'* Sunday "Arts and Leisure" section. Tynan had just returned from another "pilgrimage" to the Berliner Ensemble.

"I went to Berlin," he wrote, "to examine the current condition of the Berliner Ensemble."[47] As is characteristic of representatives (official or otherwise) of capitalist states when in a socialist country, Tynan had conducted his "examination" for anti-socialist purposes: This was revealed when he called for the Berliner Ensemble to take a different course—one that would make it impossible for the theater to carry out the socialist role Brecht envisioned. To understand why Tynan did this, one must first "examine" his record.

In the early fifties Tynan was a pioneer on the route taken by those who proclaimed an identification with Brecht to provide the "radical" image so helpful to achieving bourgeois theater success. His vociferous advocacy of Brecht's work together with his stinging theater reviews brought Tynan wide attention in that period—culminating with an invitation to come to the U.S. in 1958 as drama critic for the *New Yorker*. Whatever a backward glance might tell about them, Tynan's *New Yorker* reviews—coming after a long drought in socially oriented criticism—were welcomed by many in the U.S. interested in social theater. And Tynan's social outlook ranged beyond the stage: He supported the "fair play for Cuba" movement that sprang up when the U.S. government began to threaten that revolutionary country.

Nevertheless, there was a disquieting contradiction in Kenneth Tynan: While professing a deep interest in social theater—by definition a theater of humanist concern—Tynan wrote vitriolically of any actor unfortunate enough to incur his displeasure.

The paradox created by Tynan's apparent concern for social theater and his utter lack of concern for the human beings in the theater was soon resolved. In 1960 he was subpoenaed by the Senate Internal Security Sub-Committee, which was investigating "subversive" activities. Describing his reaction upon receiving the subpoena, Tynan stated: "Economic fears swelled up. Supposing I was publicly smeared, would my American earnings be jeopardised?"[48] In his appearance before the committee Tynan—collapsing like a cardboard carton under the weight of a jack boot—spilled out apologies and recantations.

Tynan returned to England, where he became literary manager of the National Theatre—which he left to produce *Oh! Calcutta!* An early arrival on the sex/nudity scene, *Oh! Calcutta!* hardly enriched the theater but did perform that function handsomely for Kenneth Tynan. Further, the Broadway production of *Oh! Calcutta!* brought the former angry young critic back to the U.S., this time in the avant garde of the pornographic invasion of the arts.

Today in the U.S. one is likely to come across Tynan's name in only one place: on the cover of the current edition of Esslin's book, which Tynan endorses as a "brilliantly perceptive study" of Brecht.

TYNAN'S ARTICLE on the Berliner Ensemble, consistent with Tynan's embrace of Esslin's anti-socialist attitudes toward Brecht and Brecht's theater, is a declaration of opposition to the Ensemble's role as a theater devoted to providing "fresh insights and socialist impulses."

Reporting on a conversation with an individual identified only as "dramaturg," Tynan writes: "The dramaturg says the company is trying to find new ways of staging Brecht."[49] Parenthetically, Tynan asks: "What was wrong with the old ways?" He then states:

Ever since Brecht died, people have been warning the company against what seems to be generally accepted as the most horrible fate that could befall any institution: namely, that of becoming a museum. For my part, I fail to understand why "museum" is such a terrible word. We urgently need museums to keep the best of the past alive . . .[50]

Ironically, not long after Tynan demanded that the Berliner Ensemble be turned into a museum, another English critic reported on the sharp criticism that arose when Laurence Olivier, with Tynan as his literary manager, made the National Theatre into a museum. Benedict Nightingale, theater writer for the *New Statesman,* declared:

[Olivier] wanted to be the curator of a sort of living museum . . . Catholicity would be the criterion, and that meant (as Olivier's literary manager Kenneth Tynan pointed out) that each play "would be presented in the style appropriate to it." The model was to be the Schiller Theater in West Berlin or the Royal Dramatic Theater in Stockholm, rather than the Berliner Ensemble or even the Comédie Francaise.

As a result of this policy, said Nightingale, there were "accusations":

Olivier was said to be insufficiently interested in discovering and developing new dramatists; he lacked a social conscience, and paid too little attention to the political problems of the day; he tended to avoid plays that might distress the British establishment.[51]

That Tynan had no disagreement with this policy was clear: He left the National not to produce social theater, but *Oh! Calcutta!*

Still further irony accompanied Tynan's call for the conversion of the Berliner Ensemble into a museum: At the very same time, another English critic, Ronald Bryden, was expressing his alarm because the British theater's involuntary servitude as a museum had turned it into a near-corpse. Bryden—whose theater background also includes five years as a play adviser to the Royal Shakespeare Company—wrote:

The myth of the Fabulous Invalid, always on the brink of mortality yet always miraculously recovering is only a myth . . . the invalid the British theatre brings to mind this winter is General Franco. Take away the blood transfusion, heart-pacer, kidney-machine and intravenous feeding-tubes and what you have left is a corpse.

Continuing, Bryden states:

. . . we seem doomed to a decade of Francoesque half-life which could lock the theatre forever into its present class structure. By preserving a theatre of the Hundred Essential Masterpieces to maintain a desert-island morale through the coming economic hurricane the Government will in effect preserve the bourgeois theatre of the nineteenth and early twentieth century. It will, all too fatally, preserve the Britain we know so well: a culture of inequality.

Bryden adds:

. . . we can see [the theatre] playing safe, retreading last year's models, packaging them in mock-morocco and imitation gilt as cultural totems and tourist souvenirs. If the present Government really wants a culture of equality, it ought to want a theatre which is not just a museum of bourgeois master-pieces but a stage of conversation, journalism, popular debate and millenial visions; a theatre of hope for the whole nation.[52]

The living theater Bryden advocates doesn't fall into the category of "millenial visions." Yet it can be realized, even in part, only against the British government's resistance. For the British government does *not* want a "culture of equality." What it wants is a culture that will keep not just the theater but the whole nation locked into the "present class structure."

But the GDR has no need for a theater that will "maintain a desert-island morale through the coming economic hurricane." For the socialist community there is no "coming economic hurricane": there is continuing economic and social progress. As a society moving toward a classless future, the GDR has a theater that advances a "culture of equality." Not only does the GDR reject theater as a "museum of bourgeois masterpieces," but it also rejects theater as a museum of revolutionary masterpieces. To produce socialist classics as museum pieces would first of all violate Brecht's own continuously innovative approach.

To interpret bourgeois and socialist classics for a contemporary audience, to stage new plays on socialist life, as well as plays from the capitalist countries and "third world," is a tremendous challenge to GDR theater workers. The Berliner Ensemble, as the major interpret-er of Brecht, has a unique role in this creative process. Its development involves experimentation—finding "new ways of staging Brecht," as well as producing new plays. And experimentation naturally entails complexities, difficulties and differences of opinions—all part of the struggle to advance socialist culture.

Tynan, however, doesn't see things this way. He's obsessed with the idea of turning the Berliner Ensemble into a museum. "With the right curator," he insists, "it could not only preserve the Brechtian past but open new windows on the future."[53]

It's not hard to guess what kind of "new windows" Tynan would like to see opened in the GDR. His anti-socialist attitudes—as expressed in his endorsement of Esslin's book—make it clear that he would like the Ensemble not only to "preserve" Brecht as a museum piece—but to help bring back the capitalist past Brecht condemned! A "curator" who would open such "windows on the future" cannot be found in the GDR theater.

11. Women: USA/GDR (I)

HE: You are free. Free to do what you want. Be what you want. Build a whole new life.

SHE: I'm scared.

HE: Your marriage made you weak. Let your divorce make you strong.

(During the agonies leading to her divorce, she sought consolation in food but attained obesity instead. Now she is slim again. He wheels in a richly loaded pastry cart. She looks at it with shock; then temptation mingles with horror. After a long pause:)

SHE: That's not what I want.

HE: That's what I've been waiting to hear.

SHE: I am strong. I am free now.

HE: One more thing, Joanne. You are very, very beautiful.

(Closeup: A beatific look spreads over her previously tortured face.)[1]

Satire? Parody? Comedy? No. Nothing funny ever happens (at least not intentionally) in television's world of daily serials. Spanning the hours when husbands and school-age children are out of the home,

TV's daytime image of women enters the heads of millions of women from 10:30AM to 4:30PM, Monday through Friday.

As this dialogue suggests, the world of soap opera reverberates with distorted echoes of the real world. In these serials women's liberation comes back to us as an image in the fun-house mirror: Something about it seems vaguely familiar, but so grotesquely out of shape that it's threatening instead of reassuring.

To give the appearance of "relevancy," soap operas have been garnished with a sprinkling of women lawyers and doctors, as well as a sculptor and an architect.

(Scene: A young executive is asked to interview an architect for a job. "I'll be glad to interview him," he replies. But when he is informed that the architect is not "him" but "her," the expression on his face changes, followed by a fadeout—symbolizing TV's adroitness at leaving a problem up in the air.) But these women's professional interest in their careers is less than minor. The woman architect, it seems, isn't after a job—but a male architect in the same firm. The woman sculptor doesn't really need a studio for sculpting (considering the little time she devotes to it), but a place for becoming involved with the male sculptor who shares it.

On the soap shows, it turns out, woman's liberation is indistinguishable from "sexual liberation." Extra-marital affairs, teen-age pregnancies, rape—all these are now staples of the daytime serials. Although abortion is also a commonplace, it is not shown as having any connection with a woman's right to control her own body but as an "it's the woman who pays" consequence of the "sexual revolution."

The difference between women's liberation and "sexual liberation" is the difference between freedom and license—and the only change the latter permits is new forms of the status quo. This is confirmed when one realizes there's been no change over the decades in the main characteristics of women on the daytime serials: They are still powerless, dependent on men, and in competition with other women. A woman says to her errant husband: "How did you spend our wedding anniversary? Gambling? With another woman? What difference does it make? One is as much a mistress as another." A woman says to another woman: "No matter what I want. It's what Steven wants." Together with the self-sacrificing women and the wronged women, there are the jealous scheming women—plotting to break up their sons' romances or to steal their daughters' lovers. But the schemers lose out too. Women must suffer. And the source of their misery lies in dependence on the wrong man—while their salvation lies in dependence on the right one. Time and again we are shown that talk of a woman's being free ("Free to do what you want") means nothing. All that counts is winning a man's approval ("You are very very beautiful").

The image of women on the daytime serials is interrupted every few minutes only to be reinforced by the image of women on the commercials. Here women are sneered and jeered at by husbands and sons for making poor coffee, soggy cake, thin spaghetti sauce and for leaving "ring around the collar." Their only decision-making power lies in switching brands—a move guaranteed to win male approval.

In the commercials a woman does nothing for her own sake. When she tastes a food it's not for her own enjoyment, but to serve as a surrogate palate on behalf of the future pleasure of her husband and children. Even when she uses "health products," it's not for herself. "When you're Pete Rose's wife, you take care of your health," exclaims a woman whose identity has been wiped out to the point where she doesn't even have a name of her own. When Black women appear on commercials (and these appearances are little more than token compared to the actual proportion of Black women in the population), they are generally assigned the same role as white women. But sometimes the white-woman stereotype gives way to a racist stereotype, as when an elderly Black woman exults over fried chicken made with a certain cooking oil.

Whether in commercials or on the programs as such, whether on daytime or nighttime TV,

Woman is spelled out as a second-banana mind. And what is even more frightening is the fact that the average house watches this travesty every day of every week for an average of six and a half hours a day. In the first four years and first two children of her marriage the typical woman is bombarded by millions of such TV impressions. And whether she averts to it or not, she absorbs this image subliminally. Worse—the message is picked up, stored and handed on down to her children.[2]

By 1975 women made up 40 percent of the U.S. work force. But a study done that year on "prime time" television revealed that out of a sample of 1,095 characters, 823 were employed—yet only 22 percent of the ones who worked were women.[3] And most of the working women characters had "stereotypic" jobs—for example, 95 percent of the clerks were women.* "The major roles of women," the study emphasized, "are usually in the home."

But it's not only a matter of the roles women nominally portray on TV. Even more important is *how* a particular role is portrayed. Although the "major roles of women are usually in the home," most TV homes and the women in them are alien to most of the women sitting in front of the home screen. Except for nurses and secretaries, most characters in the daytime serials are upper middle class or professional. Unlike the women who watch them, they don't worry about paying the rent or losing a job. And although they are constantly in hospitals, they don't give a thought to the bills!

When one network executive was asked why housewives are not portrayed honestly on TV, he replied:

We couldn't make it dramatic—and honest. Most of a housewife's life is too humdrum. If you showed it honestly, it would be too dull to watch . . . no one would believe it. Everyone knows how dull the life of a housewife really is.[4]

But corporate-owned television avoids honest treatment of the lives of housewives and other ordinary people not out of a fear of dullness, but because honest dramatic treatment of their lives would impel ordinary people to *change* their lives. Television programming is designed to maintain the status quo, not change it. And this becomes particularly evident on those rare occasions when a social question is touched upon:

Consider the way some soaps have come to handle members of the groups my upstairs neighbor refers to as "those people." CBS's *Search For Tomorrow,* for example, introduced a black orderly, developed him . . . and established a polarity between him and a wealthy respectable bigot out to get him fired. But after the writers have set us up for weeks, the orderly is revealed to be a talented Vietnam-trained paramedic who saves the bigot's life while all the doctors are out at lunch.[5]

ON NIGHTTIME TV programs aimed especially at male audiences, women are employed in their most traditional media occupation: sex object. On these shows where emotional violence is accompanied, if not outpaced, by physical violence, they serve also as objects of violence and objects to be defended from violence. In the past at the program's end, the hero would express his love for the woman, as well

---

*Although clerking is a "stereotypic" job for white women, there are other stereotypic jobs for Black women. The study does not take note of this difference.

as his desire to marry her. Today, courtesy of the "sexual revolution," the violent victor may simply head for the scene of his next conquest, the bedroom.

But on some shows, TV offers "equal opportunities" to women. The women's movement demands new professional openings for women, and TV responds by casting them as policewomen, detectives and undercover agents who are permitted to be almost as violent as their male counterparts: They not only toss the bad guys around with karate, they kill them. And the "new equality" isn't limited to violence. On one episode of *Serpico,* an undercover policewoman has an affair with a crime magnate to get information from him. Serpico, an undercover policeman, is condemnatory: "You sleep with the pig!" She retorts: "Haven't you ever slept with a woman to get information from her?" Still, she does have one regret: "I slept with that man and felt nothing." What we are supposed to regard as an assault on the double standard is really an invitation to women to become as callous toward sex as men are traditionally conditioned to be.

And when TV casts Black women in police roles it reacts to the dual demands for more roles for women and more roles for Blacks with a dual perversion. Commenting on the series, *Get Christy Love!,* whose title character was a Black policewoman, Jean Carey Bond states in *Freedomways:*

First of all, one hardly needs to cite the sexism ingrained in the role of this dusky policelady—it's so blatant. Never mind that Christy one-ups her co-workers a good bit of the time and dazzles us all with her sharp wit and supercompetence. The camera never fails to play on her glossy lips and swinging hips, and the script and camera constantly conspire in attaching sexual overtones to Christy's professional relationships with her all-white male colleagues at the precinct.

And "sexism" in regard to a Black woman, as Bond points out, can never be separated from racism:

. . . was it mere coincidence that in the series' first episode, we found Ms. Love masquerading as a prostitute to catch rapists? I think not, seeing as how the white males who bring us the Christy Loves are extremely cosy with the image of Black women as prostitutes.

But, Bond goes on to say, *Get Christy Love!* had "an even more insidious function":

This character is being used to cosmeticize one of the most notoriously repressive police forces in the country—an agency whose officers' guns are loaded with dum-dum bullets; an agency that saw fit to barbecue alive six, albeit misguided, human beings (Black and white) who could not possibly have held out given the forces that had been marshalled to subdue them; an agency whose officers have whipped more Black heads for no good reason than you could shake a nightstick at. That is the reality of the Los Angeles police force. In view of that reality, *Get Christy Love!,* armed with its sexy Black goddess, is perpetrating a cruel hoax.[6]

Television's nighttime violence is accompanied by nighttime comedy, which in its own way may be just as violent. After the sun goes down, the same elements that spell catastrophe during the day are frequently twisted in another direction to furnish grounds for hilarity. Everything from disastrous man/woman relations to homosexuality may be treated as one big joke. Even suicide is good for a laugh. *Maude* is a sit-com whose title character is a middle-class housewife. In one episode a welcome home party is held for her husband, who has been confined to a mental institution after attempting suicide. A stream of gags is touched off by the nuts, bananas and fruitcake awaiting the guest of honor.

The innumerable TV series with white characters are variously classified as serious, comic, adventurous, etc. But the few series with Black characters are strictly for laughs. Even when the problems of Black people are hinted at (as they are only rarely), they are used as set-ups for gags. Since the days of the minstrel shows, the white majority has been taught to laugh at the oppressed Black minority—but television has added a massive new impact to this racist phenomenon.

Commenting on the ideas behind these shows, Jean Carey Bond states:

The sexist side of the TV idea-man dictates that one sex must prevail over the other. His racism dictates that, in the case of Blacks, it must be the female over the male. Where Black media images are concerned, sexism and racism are two sides of the same coin.[7]

This is why, Bond points out, "Each of the female lead characters [on two "Black" sit-coms] fully embodies the *myth* of the Black matriarch served up on a sociological platter by Daniel Patrick Moynihan." Because the Black "matriarch" must have a male foil, she will be shown bossing around an ineffectual Black male caricature, who will take revenge in stereotype fashion.

For instance, on TV, white women characters are insulted by the presumably complimentary use of such terms as "babe," "piece of fluff," "pantyhose," etc. The reverse side of this occurred on *Sanford and Son*, where a Black male character continually called a Black woman character "your ugliness," "something from Western Union— an ugly-gram," etc. In a society where a woman is valued no more highly than her looks, the supreme insult is reserved for a Black woman.

On *The Jeffersons* the Black wife is portrayed in usual fashion as a "matriarch." But the producers sought a new twist for caricaturing the husband, who is so bigoted he is known as the "Black Archie Bunker." This series also contains the only interracial married couple on TV— Black wife, white husband (TV still holds to a total taboo on Black man/white woman marriages). But this slight concession to portraying the normal, everyday relationships existing between many Black and white people is outweighed by another factor: the white husband's behavior is as close to normal as anyone ever gets on a sit-com, which only makes the Black husband look that much worse.

"When you consider that the images of Black people that are projected are those with which the people who control television content are most comfortable, you perhaps can understand why many Black feminists feel compelled to focus primarily on what these images convey about Black people as a whole, rather than exclusively on what they say about Black women," notes Jean Carey Bond. This point was illustrated by the actresses on the "Black" sit-com *Good Times* (who may or may not consider themselves feminists).

"There are some bad times at *Good Times*," reported *Ebony* magazine.[8] "The crux of it all seems to be a continuing battle among the cast members to keep the comedic flavor of the program from becoming so outlandish as to be embarassing to blacks," stated *Ebony* writer Louie Robinson. According to "one of the show's observers," the cast was "overwhelmed by some of the garbage they have been asked to play."

Voicing her protest to white executive producer Norman Lear, then lead actress Esther Rolle declared: "Am I going to have any say about this show? Remember, I've been black longest."[9] As this remark implies, Esther Rolle's fight wasn't only for the role she herself played. Speaking of the character who is supposed to be her son, she declared: "He's 18 and he doesn't work. He can't read and write. He doesn't think." She added: "I resent the imagery that says to black kids that you can make it by standing on the corner saying 'Dyn-o-mite'!"[10]

"She fights every week for the characters," said co-star Ja'net DuBois of Esther Rolle. "How can you tell a black woman how to portray a black woman when she's been one all her life? I think we should have a little more to say about what we do because only we know how we feel." DuBois, who is also a playwright, producer and director, noted that *Good Times* "pays the rent, but there's got to be something that says more about the real me. I'm about love and I'm about feeling. Don't make me insensitive to life. Everything is no joke."[11]

Black actors and actresses continually fight with white producers to give Black characters some resemblance to reality. At times the producers may make certain concessions to this pressure. But they will continue to set all the rules—until there is a massive fight to change the rules, a fight that must have the support of whites as well as of the Black and other oppressed minorities.

The demands for true representation of these minorities both in terms of numbers and of characterization must be intensified. This is particularly urgent because TV is finding added ways to use the medium against the people: for instance, by making the appearance of Blacks on predominantly white shows the occasion for an injection of racism, instead of a wedge against segregation. And white women may be assigned their special (and traditional) role in this. On one white sit-com a Black couple attends a birthday party. They appear to be treated "just like anyone else," until they offer to take home a white woman who's had too much to drink. As the Black man helps her on with her coat, she tipsily calls out her pet name for her boyfriend, "Blue eyes." She turns, looks up with consternation and exclaims, "Oh—brown eyes," as the studio audience roars. At other times, however, the sexual aspects of racist mythology take on a more openly sinister form. On one serial, a criminal Latin character suddenly tries to rape a white woman—who is "saved" by the series' hero, a white policeman.

Another way in which the medium is being used against the people is through the sit-coms whose main characters are white working-class women. One of these is *Alice,* whose characters are waitresses—or to be exact, the waitress stereotypes handed down to TV from the movies: One is vacuous, another the cliché sexy talker, a third rolls her eyes as the clue to her stupidity. In *Laverne and Shirley* the young title characters are supposed to be assembly-line workers. This, of course, has nothing to do with the sit-com. In one typical episode, Laverne and Shirley—who are portrayed as the intellectual peers of the waitresses on *Alice*—concoct an elaborate and exhausting scheme to win a contest whose grand award is a television set. At the end of the episode they are seated in front of their prize. Shirley asks: "What are you gonna watch?" "Who cares," replies Laverne.

The network executive who defended TV's false portrayal of the housewife's life by saying, "If you showed it honestly it would be too dull to watch" could be expected to give the same rationale for TV's depiction of the lives of women workers. But a fear of dullness is hardly the reason the networks prohibit honest treatment of workers' lives. Realistic dramatic treatment of waitresses and assembly-line workers—the long, hard monotonous hours they put in, their struggle to make ends meet and all the personal problems that go with it—would not be dull. It would be explosive.

The people's mood is already far too explosive for those who control TV. In this period of mass radicalization they make constant efforts to freeze the people's consciousness, to divert them from a search for real alternatives. A sample of this was to be seen on one sit-com whose lead character was a young photographer. She spoke against the Vietnam War and Richard Nixon, and in general was supposed to give the impression of being a "liberated" woman. But her lover was a confirmed reactionary, while her own "radicalization" was kept within the bounds of confirmed support to the Democratic Party.

On the other hand, when the media controllers want a character to be taken for a "revolutionary," this is typical of the technique used: "How many workers have to die by inches just so corporations can get bigger!" exclaimed a character on the dramatic serial *Executive Suite*. Since a speech is always identified with the speaker, the character these lines were assigned to was a young woman terrorist. This, in other words, is an example of TV's efforts to influence masses of viewers to connect anti-corporate, pro-people sentiments with negative, pseudo-radical forces—instead of with advocates of mass struggle.

Even when TV reacts to mass pressure by dealing with social questions, it finds ways to discourage people from doing anything about them. A case in point was the two-hour TV film, *Nightmare in Badham County,* the story of two women college students—one Black, one white—who are framed up while on a vacation in the South and sent to a prison farm, where the most brutal conditions prevail. A source of cheap labor, the prison farm has the backing of local and state authorities. During the film the Black woman is raped by a white sheriff (this is "equalized" when a white girl is raped by another official), and finally shot to death trying to escape (the white girl commits suicide).

At the point when the two women are desperately plotting to escape, they receive the sympathy of Black inmates—but no encouragement. "Ain't no white man gonna help you, ain't no Black man *can*," declares one Black woman prisoner. Time and again the characters, Black and white, assert that things will stay as they are because "all the people want it that way." *Nightmare in Badham County* is set in the present, but listening to its characters talk one would think the great civil rights struggles of the sixties had never taken place! The film's message to viewers is that injustice and oppression—as well as the poor—will always be with us.

THE MOST sophisticated of TV's many products designed to stymie the development of people's consciousness was a show with a woman as the main character—*Mary Hartman, Mary Hartman*. This nightly series, its producers told us, satirized the daytime soap operas. But the main characters in the daytime serials are upper middle class and professional, while the main characters in *Mary Hartman, Mary Hartman* were working class (Mary's husband Tom was an auto worker). The actress who played the title role commented in an interview that Mary Hartman "is not aware of herself in time and space." Put in less existential terms, this meant that the show's producers knew what they were doing with Mary Hartman and the other characters, but the characters themselves were unaware of what was happening to them. The joke, in other words, was on the working class.

Mary Hartman, Mary Hartman was heralded as an unprecedentedly daring TV taboo smasher. During the series' most successful phase, Mary was having an affair with a police sergeant who also pursues other women, including Mary's sister, who in turn is involved with many other men. Tom is an alcoholic; although impotent he too is having an affair. Mary's grandfather is arrested by Mary's lover for indulging in his favorite pastime, "indecent exposure"; when the court assigns a social worker to rehabilitate the eighty-three-year-old man, he has an affair with her. Mary's father, a union official, is photographed in a hotel room with a prostitute during a union convention. Mary's twelve-year-old daughter threatens to bring American Civil Liberties Union suits against her mother. Mary is held hostage by the town's first teenage mass murderer. Mary is induced by a mother to try to break up her son's affair with another man. Mary is visited by the local basketball coach; high on liquor and drugs, he passes out in a bowl of Mary's chicken soup and drowns. Mary calls information to find out if she exists. Mary's sister enters Mary in a "Typical American Housewife" contest. Soon Mary is on the David Susskind show where she is asked her opinions on topics of the day, including woman's role. She is barely able to understand what her questioners are talking about. She goes into a frenzied soliloquy on her life, which culminates in a nervous breakdown.

Since we can do nothing with a nightmare but submit to it, the media controllers tried to make us believe we share Mary Hartman's surreal world. They tried to make the line between illusion and reality that did not exist for Mary Hartman disappear for us as well. This could be seen in the way they pressed Mary Hartman upon us, urging us not only to accept her as real but typical. On Election Day 1976, this was the lead on a front-page story in the *Los Angeles Times*:

Today's presidential election may be decided by a confused Midwestern housewife who is married to a low income blue-collar worker and who is not very interested in politics. In many respects, she resembles the character Mary Hartman on the nighttime television soap opera.

Because the working people in *Mary Hartman, Mary Hartman* were shown as helpless to change their circumstances, this supposedly taboo-shattering series left the media's paramount prohibition intact. The following—one of the numerous analyses of the series that cropped up in academic and literary publications as well as the mass media—offers a philosophical justification for *Mary Hartman, Mary Hartman:*

Mary Hartman may be living in the Year of the Woman—but what difference does it make? It is not so much that it has all passed her by—in fact, it hasn't . . . But the real life of Mary Hartman and of everyone else on the show—and all of us who watch it, too—takes place in a realm far distant from the historical present. Truly, America's psychoanalytic soap opera proves its point over and over: what we do and what takes place around us can scarcely affect what we *are*. This notion, this idea of the intransigeance of human fate may appear to be a rearguard one in our own peppy age, but it is also a profound and terrifying point of view. The adoring response the show has met with rather proves that many of us believe in our own helplessness—are, in fact, helpless to believe otherwise.[12]

The "idea of the intransigeance of human fate" is indeed a "rearguard" one—and "terrifying" if one accepts it. But it is hardly "profound." Our consciousness does not exist apart from our circumstances, and we remain helpless in the face of these circumstances only so long as we believe we can do nothing to change them. Certainly those who own the media would like us to feel we live in a "realm far distant from the historical present"—back in a time when the "intransigeance of human fate" seemed an incontrovertible idea to the masses of people, a time before it had been proved that working people could take their fate into their own hands.

The fate of women cannot be decided apart from the fate of men—and vice versa. Mary's "helplessness" is not shown in a "realm far distant from the historical present," but in the here and now. And Tom's "helplessness" is also demonstrated in very contemporary circumstances indeed.

Tom becomes "radicalized." This is surely not unusual for an auto worker today! (In November 1976, for example, 5,000 workers—men and women, Black, Chicano, Native American and white—lined up at a General Motors employment office in Detroit during a piercing cold night for jobs available, according to a company announcement, the next morning. Workers were trampled in the rush for application forms. But there were no jobs. Instead of jobs, GM had squads of police on hand with fire hoses, ready to deal with the anger of the crowd.) After Tom's "radicalization," he is nominated for union office by the "militants." He wins. When he carries on in his usual alcoholic stupor, management fires him. At a time when industrial workers are fighting against layoffs, speedup and right-wing union officials, TV concocts a "militant" who can be fired for alcoholism instead of union activities!

WOMAN ON the silver screen is in just as much trouble as woman on the home screen. And it's the same kind of trouble. Women have demanded liberation, but what they've gotten in film as well as TV is "sexual liberation"—with predictably bizarre results.

"Sexual liberation has done little more than reimprison women in sexual roles, but at a lower and more debased level," asserts critic Molly Haskell in *From Reverence To Rape,* her book on the treatment of women in movies. "The new liberated woman," she continues, has been

nowhere in sight, and what were we offered as the "strong woman" of the seventies? Raquel Welch as travesty-male, a pinup or roller-derby queen. In every case we got not only less than we might have expected and hoped for, but less than ever before: women who were less intelligent, less sensual, less humorous, and altogether less extraordinary than women in the twenties, the thirties, the forties, or even the poor, pallid uptight fifties . . . There were, instead, amoral pinup girls, molls taking guff from their gangsters that would have made their predecessors gag . . .[13]

It becomes particularly obvious that the "new liberated women" is "nowhere is sight" when one sees such a self-designated "woman's liberation" movie as *Alice Doesn't Live Here Anymore*. Alice is a housewife married to a truck driver. He is killed on the road, but his Neanderthal attitudes toward women (a standard part of the media stereotype of workers) make his death no great loss. Alice, yearning to be a singer, takes off with her son. She finds a job as a waitress and becomes involved with one of the customers. This man is also a worker. Because of the "sexual revolution" she is permitted to go to bed with him so quickly that she has no chance to learn he's a psychopath—who beats his wife and threatens Alice at knifepoint. Alice's problems are solved when she meets "Mr. Right" in the person of a prosperous ranch owner, who has all the qualities the worker caricatures in her life lacked. Not only can he offer her security, he is "supportive" of her singing aspirations. But security is, as ever, more important to a woman than sensitivity, particularly since the audience is made aware that Alice will never be a success as a singer.

Alice Doesn't Live Here Anymore pretends to champion women's liberation while actually keeping its heroine on a tradition-worn path. But another self-designated "women's liberation" film, *Lipstick*— about a woman who is raped and seeks vengeance—opens up a path to women previously reserved for men only: vigilantism. In a review for the *New York Post,* film critic Frank Rich stated that *Lipstick* is one of the "first films that promote sexism by exploiting feminism."[14] *Lipstick,* he goes on to say, is among those films "that lavish unusual attention on the women's movement, and at times even appear to champion it, when their real intent is to misrepresent that movement and wound its cause." This was apparent in the rape scene which Rich describes as a "grueling, extended episode in violent sex designed to turn on men—and, if anything, the sequence feeds a male audience's fantasies about committing the very crime *Lipstick* pretends to abhor." But, he points out, the "real payoff of the movie—and the innovation that turns it into the first feminist exploitation film—comes in its final section," when the heroine "takes the law into her own hands by tracking down the villain and emptying a double-barrelled shotgun into his groin."

If one believes that a policewoman's going to bed with a criminal for "professional" reasons represents an assault on the double standard, one might also believe that permitting women to be vigilantes is a step toward equal rights—instead of encouragement to the ultra-right.

Total "sexual liberation" in the movies has been just slightly out-paced by the total unleashing of violence, but the two are close enough together to proceed hand in hand. Molly Haskell is precisely accurate when she says that today's screen "molls taking guff from their gangsters" would have "made their predecessors gag." And audiences have undergone a similar metamorphosis. In the thirties when the gangster in *The Public Enemy* pushed a grapefruit in his moll's face, audiences were shocked. In the seventies when the gangster in *The Long Goodbye* smashed his moll's face with a jagged Coca Cola bottle, it was just another incident.

"The closer women come to claiming their rights and achieving their independence in real life, the more loudly and stridently films tell us it's a man's world,"[15] declares Haskell. If the U.S. film industry most blatantly tells us it's a "man's world" through the respective roles assigned men and women in the outright sex/violence exploitation movies, the same message is nonetheless communicated in even "the great women's roles of the decade."

... the great women's roles of the decade, what are they for the most part [asks Haskell]. Whores, quasi-whores, jilted mistresses, emotional cripples, drunks. Daffy ingenues, Lolitas, kooks, sex-starved spinsters, psychotics. Icebergs, zombies, and ball-breakers. That's what little girls of the sixties and seventies are made of.[16]

Hollywood also tells us it's a "man's world" through films that relegate women to unimportant roles or omit them altogether. And film actresses are "claiming their rights" by protesting against this. "There are no parts. I love to work, but there's nothing for me to do," said the young actress Carol Kane, who drew attention for her performance in *Hester Street*, in an interview.[17] "There just aren't enough scripts, and when there are scripts the roles are supporting." The reason?

"We think of films as entertainment, and I'm finally realizing films are made by banks. Only two women in America are financeable—whom the banks will take a risk on—Barbra Streisand and Liza Minnelli. Lately I'm beginning to think that one of the reasons script writers won't consider large roles for women is because the banks won't consider them. The attitude is, 'I would like to write a woman's film but I won't get any money for it.'" If she had her way, Carol Kane would play a woman "who's had some kind of vision to pursue."

MOLLY HASKELL speaks of women coming closer to "claiming their rights and achieving independence." Although women can "come closer" to "achieving independence" only by "claiming their rights," there's a big difference between "claiming their rights" and actually "achieving independence." Women can't do that alone. U.S. films tell us "it's a man's world," but we don't have to believe it. Molly Haskell apparently does: Throughout her book, she speaks of "male power," "male authority," and even "male imperialism." Those who see *men* in power—instead of a corporate monopoly *class* in power in the U.S.—necessarily see women "claiming their rights" in a battle against men. And usually the women they have in mind are white.

When Haskell called her book *From Reverence to Rape,* she could only have been thinking of white women. In the first influential U.S. film, *Birth of a Nation,* "reverence" was expressed for white women by protecting them from rape by Black men (that is, white actors in blackface). But the birth of this nation—long before the Declaration of Independence—was accompanied by slavery and the wholesale rape of Black women by white slaveowners.

Haskell also had white women only in mind when she wrote, "Sexual liberation has done little more than reimprison women in sexual roles, but at a lower and more debased level"[18]—because she doesn't mention that Black women have always been imprisoned in "sexual roles" at an even lower and more debased level than white women. Because the pressure was not great enough to force the media to drop these racist sexual stereotypes, it was possible for them to further debase both white and Black women.

But Haskell doesn't recognize this relationship between the treatment of Black and of white women. This is why she can write, "At present the industry, such as it is, is giving women the same treatment that it gave blacks for the half-century after *Birth of a Nation:* a kick in the face or a cold shoulder."[19] On the other hand, she goes on to assert, things are getting better for Black women:

Apart from the violent genre films, the fate of black women in film is a reversal of the downward drift of women in general. Whereas the portrayal of blacks from the silents to the sixties is one extended blot on the white conscience, with Hattie McDaniel and her ilk playing maids and happy darkies, the recent story of black women—Cicely Tyson in *Sounder* and *The Autobiography of Miss Jane Pittman*, Diahann Carroll in *Claudine*, Ellen Holly and Vonetta McGee as reflective genre heroines—is more optimistic.[20]

Such "optimism" has not been expressed by Black actresses, including Ellen Holly—who wrote an article titled "Where Are The Films About Real Black Men and Women?" In it she states that Black people's "hunger for alternatives" to "blaxploitation"-type films is so great that "films such as . . . *Claudine* are heaped with more praise than they deserve and heralded as events that would pale The Second Coming."[21]

"Most 'black' films," Holly goes on to say, "have been mired in the rut of a single formula—the so-called action film which deals with marginal anti-social elements in the Northern urban ghetto. These films have been subjected to a tremendous amount of criticism." Not, however, from Molly Haskell: Although she criticizes the treatment of Black women in these movies, it's for an odd reason indeed:

. . . a sort of cartoon reversal of the damsel in distress and of the supermacho black and kung fu hero, the action heroine popped up in . . . [the] black superwoman epics, *Cleopatra Jones* and *Coffy,* that were the tail end of the blaxploitation genre. A sort of revival of the old Pearl White tradition, these were women who could function in a violent way, but compared to the magnificent Shaft, they were more superbland than superblack.[22]

Haskell not only speaks approvingly of such a "blaxploitation" character as Shaft, but finds fault with his female counterparts who could "function in a violent way"—but not violently enough compared to the "magnificent" male original.

Black people, however, have found nothing "magnificent" about the "blaxploitation genre" (which even yet has not come to its "tail end"). As Ellen Holly points out, "Black citizens who are not gunslingers, dope pushers, pimps or prostitutes have been rightly and understandably enraged that the prevailing black image in most films has been one that is so grossly at odds with their own."

Haskell, however, goes on to discuss the other "magnificent" qualities of the "black genre" movies:

There, romantic and heroic values still hold sway, along with a comical but real sexism, in which bunnies and playgirls pop up like ducks in a shooting gallery—and get shot down as fast.[23]

It's paradoxical that Haskell condemns violence against white women but finds it "romantic and heroic" when Black women are shot down "like ducks in a shooting gallery"! And she also finds something "comical" about "real sexism"—but only when applied against Black women.

Black women themselves, however, find nothing "comical" about "sexism." "When racism doesn't get us, sexism does," declare four Black women—Inez Turner, Dorothy Robinson, Deborah Singletary and Margo Jefferson—in an article titled, "No More Sapphires or Black Pearls: Self Definition Is Where It Starts."[24] Far from being a "reversal of the downward drift of women in general," the "fate of Black women in films" and the other media has been qualitatively more oppressive. These four Black women state:

We could seldom turn on the television set and see a Black woman whom we could identify as mother, sister, co-worker or neighbor—there was no one any of us had ever seen in the flesh. The only familiarity we had with Black women on the TV screen was that we had seen the same tired stereotypes depicted on larger screens in movie-houses and walking across the stage in theaters.[25]

While Molly Haskell recognizes Black stereotypes in some of their old forms, she does not yet recognize them in the new. But these four Black women say:

We reject the old stereotypes and the new ... We are all the things humankind has ever been; and we are alive and aware and ready; ready to write our own books and command our own ships. We are ready to grow without the restraints of racism and sexism. We are ready to fight ... so that our daughters and granddaughters will be set free ... [26]

THE GREATEST influence on the ideas about women and the women's movement held by people beyond that movement has come from TV, movies, and the press. But the greatest influence on women who identify with that movement has come from books.

This began in a large-scale sense in 1963 with a book that spoke of a "strange stirring, a sense of dissatisfaction, a yearning that women suffered in the middle of the twentieth century in the United States."

This was *The Feminine Mystique,* by Betty Friedan. This book hit hard against the Freudian "anatomy is destiny" idea, against "sex-directed" education orienting women to be housewives, and "sex-role stereotyping" that bars countless doors in the arts and professions to women.

Betty Friedan worked on her book as the civil rights struggle surged in the South. And she reflected its influence when she acknowledged the interrelationship between freedom movements: The "battle to free women," she wrote, "was fired in the nineteenth century by the battle to free the slaves."

In the twentieth century the civil rights struggles helped fire a massive revulsion against McCarthyite conformity, including a new desire to look in forbidden directions. Betty Friedan reflected this too when she wrote, "Whenever, wherever in the world there has been an upsurge of human freedom, women have won a share of it for themselves." One such upsurge, she stated, brought about the "over-throw" of the "Russian Czar." And she registered an awareness that a basic change she demanded for U.S. women had already become a reality for Soviet women:

Not long ago Dr. Spock confessed, a bit uneasily, that Russian children, whose mothers usually have some purpose in their lives besides motherhood—they work in medicine, science, education, industry, government, art—seemed somehow more stable, adjusted, mature than American children, whose full-time mothers do nothing but worry about them. Could it be that Russian women are somehow better mothers because they have a serious purpose in their own lives?[27]

The Feminine Mystique was read on a huge scale: Two million copies eventually went into print. But millions of women who only heard about the book also responded to the idea that they had a right to be more than "just a housewife." Yet *The Feminine Mystique* contained contradictions that were a foreboding of trouble to come in the women's movement.

Betty Friedan spoke of "a yearning that women suffered in the middle of the twentieth century in the United States"—but, as it turned out, her perspective was limited to middle-class white women. In the book's first paragraph, she wrote:

As she made the beds, shopped for groceries, matched slipcover material, ate peanut butter sandwiches with her children, chauffered Cub Scouts and Brownies, lay beside her husband at night—she was afraid to ask even of herself the silent question—"Is this all?"[28]

Certainly middle-class housewives have every right to fulfill their aspirations, to do something worthwhile with their lives. But in Friedan's vision, their "silent question" can be answered—that is, they can enter the arts and professions—without anything's being done to answer the "age old material problems" of millions of women of all races and colors:

It is no longer . . . possible to dismiss the desperation of so many American women . . . I do not accept the answer that there is no problem because American women have luxuries that women in other times and lands never dreamed of; part of the strange newness of the problem is that it cannot be understood in terms of the age-old material problems of man: poverty, sickness, hunger, cold. The women who suffer this problem have a hunger that food cannot fill.[29]

It is quite true that women's problems "cannot be understood" *only* in terms of the "age-old material problems." But if there is a "hunger that food cannot fill," there is also a hunger that food *can* fill. And the working class and oppressed women who have fought for "bread and roses" suffer *both* kinds of hunger. Only if the "age-old material problems" are solved can women's special problems be solved.

By the mid-sixties large numbers of women who had experienced the civil rights and student struggles were looking for a deeper analysis of women's special problems than was to be found in Friedan's book. This search brought them to a book Friedan had referred to, a book which was to have a strong influence on many radically-minded women: *The Second Sex,* by Simone de Beauvoir.

No one writing on social questions has displayed a greater ability to make old ideas sound freshly discovered than Simone de Beauvoir. Like Hollywood movies, de Beauvoir tells us "it's a man's world"— only she has retitled it "the male universe":

The sphere to which [woman] belongs is everywhere enclosed, limited, dominated, by the male universe: high as she may raise herself, far as she may venture, there will always be a ceiling over her head, walls that will block her way.[30]

In this "male universe,"

. . . men compel [woman] to assume the status of the Other. They propose to stabilize her as object and to doom her to immanence since her transcendence is to be overshadowed and forever transcended by another ego . . .[31]

Since women are "enclosed, limited, dominated, by the male universe," where men "compel" them to their present status and "doom" them to be "forever transcended," women must fight this male enemy. It's the old war between the sexes but translated into seemingly socially advanced terms: "All oppression creates a state of war. And this is no exception." This conflict

... is no longer a question of war between individuals each shut up in his or her sphere: a caste claiming its rights goes over the top and it is resisted by the privileged caste.[32]

Thus, according to de Beauvoir, the demand for women's rights is "resisted" not by the class in power in capitalist societies, but by men—the majority of them working men who, together with their corporate employers, form a "privileged caste."

That women can't win anything in a battle against men is implied by de Beauvoir's use of such terms as "always," "doom," "forever transcended," etc., when describing women's status. Yet women *have* made advances, so de Beauvoir must try to account for them:

The fact is that oppressors cannot be expected to make a move of gratuitous generosity; but at one time the revolt of the oppressed, at another time even the very evolution of the privileged caste itself creates new situations; thus men have been led, in their own interest, to give partial emancipation to women.[33]

In a world ruled by a male "privileged caste," women can have no ally in the working class—and thus no enemy in the corporate ruling class. Therefore, women's historic advances have come about not through struggle but because of the "generosity" of the "privileged caste"—which in this case must refer to the capitalists, since working-class men had nothing to give away: They could only fight for their own and women's liberation. But de Beauvoir specifically discourages women from putting up this kind of fight:

... women's effort has never been anything more than a symbolic agitation. They have gained only what men have been willing to grant; they have taken nothing, they have only received.[34]

Lest this declaration of futility prove insufficient, de Beauvoir takes it one step further. Sounding very much like the bourgeois men who say "women should stay out of politics," she advises women that "It is for man to establish the reign of liberty in the world of the given." But, as de Beauvoir could see, women haven't been taking such advice for a long time. Therefore, she tries to discourage them from revolutionary struggle in yet another way: She warns women in capitalist countries—who increasingly connect their oppression with the system—

not against capitalism, but socialism. The conditions necessary for women's emancipation, she asserts, "have been realized nowhere, in Russia no more than in France or the United States."[35]

The influence of de Beauvoir's ideas soon began to show up in the writings of some of the women calling themselves "radical feminists." In these writings serious analysis of women's problems in this country was not forthcoming. Nor (as a logical corollary to this) was there any attempt to discover why Soviet women have "a serious purpose in their own lives." On the contrary, there was escalating "battle of the sexes" rhetoric, coupled with escalating attacks on the alleged condition of women in socialist countries. This kind of writing may have reached its frenzied peak in a document called "The Fourth World Manifesto," published in 1970 during the genocidal U.S. aggression in Vietnam.

"No anti-capitalist, working class" movement "will ever free women," exclaimed the manifesto, because males "define and control all the institutions of all national cultures—including every purportedly socialist nation that has ever existed." As the bombs dropped on Vietnamese men, as well as Vietnamese women and children, this document informed its readers that war is a "male institution," and the "demand for an end" to "male imperialist domination is a real attack on the masculine citadel of war." That "male imperialism" had nothing to do with U.S. imperialism in Vietnam was made even clearer when the manifesto went on to attack "the anti-imperialist women" who, "like the rest of the anti-war and anti-imperialist Left movement," do not "see imperialism and war in their deepest aspects as male supremacist institutions in *all* societies."

It would be wrong to assume that this document went no further than a small audience of "fringe" groups. Although originally issued by such groups, the article was reprinted in *Radical Feminism,* published in 1973 by Quadrangle, an affiliate of the New York Times Company.

In another article in *Radical Feminism,* one of the book's editors restates a de Beauvoir idea ("It is for man to establish the reign of liberty in the midst of the world of the given") by asserting that unless men "give up their domination over us," women will "not fight for their revolution, work for their revolution." What could be more desirable to *The New York Times* than a boycott by women (and men) of struggles for social change!

The forces behind the media, now highly skilled in disseminating reactionary ideas in radical guise, recognize that the ideas in "The Fourth World Manifesto" cannot influence a mass audience when written in the style of "The Fourth World Manifesto." Of course, they do everything possible to promote these views in their original form (*Radical Feminism* was issued in paperback as well as in hardcover). But their great interest lies in books that present the same ideas in a manner with appeal for the mass market, since these books can be manipulated into best-sellers.

"Supremely entertaining, brilliantly conceived, overwhelming in its arguments, breathtaking in its command of history and literature," exclaimed *The New York Times* in a review that helped make the first of these best-sellers: *Sexual Politics,* by Kate Millett.[36]

What made *Sexual Politics* "supremely entertaining" were, apparently, Millett's lengthy analyses of pornographic excerpts from Norman Mailer, Henry Miller, etc. In fact, these analyses only enhanced "the supremely entertaining" attributes of the originals.

The phrase "brilliantly conceived," however, must have been meant for Millett's addition to the portrayals of a "male universe." To Millett, every existing society has a "patriarchal government"—that is, the "institution whereby half of the populace which is female is controlled by that half which is male."[37] Therefore, in Millett's opinion, class is unimportant to a woman. Women, she asserts, "tend to transcend the usual class stratifications in patriarchy."[38] Why? "Economic dependency renders [their] affiliations with any class a tangential, vicarious and temporary matter."[39] Does it? If an economically dependent woman breaks up with a working man, what happens to her? Do her previous class "affiliations" disappear as she soars into the upper class—or does her situation get worse when she finds herself forced to get an unskilled, low-paid job or go on welfare?

In Millett's "brilliantly conceived" view, what will free women from economic dependency is not an assured opportunity to earn a decent living, but the "sexual revolution." "A sexual revolution," she declares, "would require, perhaps first of all, an end of traditional sexual inhibitions and taboos, particularly those that most threaten monogamous marriage: homosexuality, 'illegitimacy,' adolescent, pre- and extra-marital sexuality."[40] The "sexual revolution," Millett concludes, "would bring the institution of patriarchy to an end"—that is, bring down the institution of government. Although this society's sexual taboos co-exist with the continual breaking of them, it's had no known effect on government. No matter. In Millett's view government in a capitalist society doesn't threaten women: The threat comes from government in a socialist society.

The reason why *The New York Times* deems *Sexual Politics* "breathtaking in its command of history" can be found in a chapter titled "The Counterrevolution," whose subhead reads: "Reactionary Policy—The Models of Nazi Germany and the Soviet Union." By equating socialism with fascism, the "radical" Millett performed especially for the women's movement the service others before her had undertaken in the arts, sciences and professions. Clearly, times had changed since the brief period when a best-seller could mention, even in passing, that Soviet policy had brought women into "medicine, science, education, industry, government, art"—giving them "a serious purpose in their own lives."

Sexual Politics went into massive printings. It was a Book-Of-The-Month-Club selection. It made the *Times'* best-book-of-the-year list. Millett herself made the cover of *Time*. "The Women's Liberation Movement," exclaimed *Cosmopolitan* magazine, "has found its ideal spokeswoman!"

But the "establishment" couldn't allow its "ideal spokeswoman" to practice the "sexual revolution" it encouraged her to preach. When Millett announced her bisexuality, the news was picked up by *Time*, and the "ideal spokeswoman" was deposed from her pedestal. The "establishment" now sought an "ideal spokeswoman" who would differ from Millett only in the matter of sexual orientation.

Such a "spokeswoman" was forthcoming in Germaine Greer, whose book, *The Female Eunuch*, was already a best-seller in England.[41] Greer was jetted in from London to promote U.S. publication, which was announced with full-page ads asserting that the author was "a feminist leader who admittedly loves men." She didn't, however, like women very much. "*The Female Eunuch* is shallow, anti-woman, regressive, three steps backward to the world of false sexual liberation from which so many young women have fled," declared a woman critic.

Greer was reportedly an actress with a Ph.D. in Shakespearean comedy, but only the talents she acquired as an editor of the pornographic journal *Suck* were applied to help insure *The Female Eunuch's* rise to best-sellerdom. But Greer was also in tune with the times in another way; she didn't fail to insert a radical-sounding "analysis" of women's condition: "Women represent the most oppressed class of life-contracted unpaid workers, for whom slaves is not too melodramatic a description. They are the only true proletariat left."[42] This "true proletariat," she declared, must "challenge the masters." How? The "most effective method"—in a time when masses of women in the U.S. and England are desperate for jobs—"is simply to withdraw our labor in building up a system which oppresses us, the valid withdrawal of our labor."[43]

Greer also dutifully offered her version of the treatment of women in the Soviet Union: "Female construction workers in Russia are taught no skills and given no tools."[44] (One can only wonder how construction workers without skills or tools could have "a serious purpose in their own lives"!)

Far from disqualifying her from media attention, these ludicrous views were among the reasons she got so much of it. And while the author appeared on the cover of *Life* and on TV talk shows (where she described herself as "really just an intellectual superwhore"), *The Female Eunuch* began its massive publication cycle: seven hard-cover and five paperback editions.

The Female Eunuch had little influence on the thinking of women's movement activists. But in line with a long-standing media objective, it encouraged men to laugh cynically about women's liberation. At the same time Greer's (and Millett's) nihilistic, anti-family views were disquieting to large numbers of women desperately trying to hold their own families together against great social and economic odds.

IN CONTRAST to *The Female Eunuch*, a more recent mass-media promoted "women's liberation" book has had a serious effect within the women's movement as well as far beyond. This is *Against Our Will: Men, Women and Rape*, by Susan Brownmiller. Hailed as a "classic" and a "landmark," this book made every best-seller list in the country, as well as the *Times'* book-of-the-year list. The author, publicized as a "radical feminist," got $250,000 for the book's paperback rights alone. She was chosen by *Time* magazine as a woman of the year.

Along with all other portrayers of a "male universe," Brownmiller asserts that ideology is unrelated to class; what exists is "male ideology." But Brownmiller supplies a new twist: a "male universe" where "male ideology" is enforced by only one means: rape—which is "nothing more or less than a conscious process by which *all* men keep *all* women in a state of fear."[45]

Since "male ideology" is antagonistic to women, a "woman's *pol-*

itik," Brownmiller declares, "operates independent of traditional male forces of left and right." Brownmiller demonstrates the fantasy of this assertion by associating her own *politik* with the "traditional" ultra-right. Although violence has historically been initiated by the forces trying to turn back social change—who accompany other types of violence with rape—Brownmiller makes it appear that the danger comes from the other side. "Uprisings" and "revolutions," she states,

... have provided an outlet, and sometimes even an ideological excuse for men to practice rape on women.[46]

By warning women against revolutionary struggles instead of counter-revolutionists, Brownmiller sets the stage for her reversal of world history: She conjures up a scene in which the crimes—from rape to genocide—of the Nazis against Jews and Soviet people, white colonialists against Black Africans, and the U.S. government against Native Americans fade into insignificance. Brownmiller then proceeds to assign the role of oppressor to the right-wing's traditional villains: Soviet, African and Native American men. This historic reversal is by way of buildup to her most immediate preoccupation.

In *The Birth of a Nation,* Brownmiller writes, D.W. Griffith "sympathetically dramatized" the Ku Klux Klan's "sworn compact to 'protect' Southern womanhood from the black menace." In *Against Our Will,* Susan Brownmiller has "sympathetically dramatized" these same racist myths about "the black menace" and "white womanhood." She states:

The recurrent nightmare in the eighteenth-century slaveholding South had been the white male dream of black men rising up to rape "their" women, and in the second half of the twentieth century the black man in his fiercest rhetoric seems intent on fulfilling that prophecy.[47]

Rape *was* a "recurrent nightmare" in the South—but for the slaves, not their owners. The slaveholders' "recurrent nightmare" was not of Black men "rising up to rape" white women. This was the fictionalized version of their *real* nightmare: Black men and women rising up to claim their freedom—as they did time and again.*

*In her famous *Journal of A Residence on A Georgian Plantation,* the English actress Frances Anne Kemble told how she herself found out about the slaveowners' "recurrent nightmare." Describing a visit to Charleston, South Carolina, 1838, she wrote of "a most ominous tolling of bells and beating of drums, which, on the first evening of my arrival in Charleston, made me almost fancy myself in one of the old fortified frontier towns of the Continent, where the tocsin sounded, and the evening drum beaten, and the guard set as regularly every night as if an invasion were expected. In Charleston, however, it is not the dread of foreign invasion, but of domestic insurrection, which occasions these nightly precautions."[48]

As "proof" that Black men today "in their fiercest rhetoric seem intent on fulfilling" the slaveowners, "prophecy," Brownmiller cites the "fiercest rhetoric" of a confessed rapist, Eldridge Cleaver. (The Cleaver who once called rape an "insurrectionary act," and then replaced this rhetoric with a call for "urban guerilla warfare," is now extolling the glories of the "American way of life.")

Brownmiller speaks of the Ku Klux Klan's "sworn compact to 'protect' Southern womanhood from the black menace." But it would not be in keeping with Brownmiller's self-applied "radical feminist" label to advise women to turn to men for "protection." Instead she calls for them to take up "self-defense."

Very few women will act literally on Brownmiller's call for vigilantism. But this is unimportant to the media controllers who have built up her book. Their interest is related to its racism which can influence white working women—and men—from joining together with Black and other oppressed minorities against their real and mutual enemy: corporate power. And the book's anticommunism serves the same purpose.

In one of many attacks resurrecting the "fiercest rhetoric" of the McCarthy years, Brownmiller alleges that the left "excoriated" white women. Why? Because the left, Black and white, led struggles to save Black men framed on rape charges by the slaveholders' descendants. (The most famous of these struggles won the release of nine Black youths facing death sentences in Scottsboro, Alabama, in the thirties.)

What the left "excoriated" was the racist system. And the system, not white women, is what Brownmiller's book protects. White women *do* need protection—in the form of jobs, equality and the all-round right to a decent life. But white women can never win this by themselves. Their allies must include women of the oppressed minorities—who need the same things but find them doubly hard to get because of racism.

The media's ideological influence has certainly had a seriously disorienting effect on the women's movement (accentuated by the media's promotion of a bizarre assortment of diversions—everything from the conversion of personal sexual preferences into "revolutionary" issues to a cry for vigilantism). But the media have displayed undue satisfaction with their handiwork.

Since the mid-seventies they have featured such articles as "Does The Women's Movement Still Have Clout?" and "Women's Movement Going Nowhere Fast." This assault reached its nadir when a national magazine showed on its cover a mourning veil—illustrating the main article: "Requiem for The Women's Movement."

The media always play requiems for the people instead of the people's enemies.

The *real* news is that with every passing day more women throughout this country are gripped by the idea of their right to equality.

---

12. Women: USA/GDR (II)

Castro's historic speech last year denouncing *machismo* in Cuba and some programs being started in East Germany show the beginnings of awareness of a woman problem in the Communist regimes. I don't suppose that women in any part of the world can be isolated from the germs of women's movements spreading from the West," says Betty Friedan in her second book, *It Changed My Life.*[1]

While the "germs" of any people's movement originate within, not outside, each particular country, it is also true that the people's advances in any part of the world speed progress in every part of the world. But whether the "germs" of liberation, in this sense, are "spreading" from capitalist countries to socialist ones—or vice versa—can be determined in only one way: by comparing the "Communist regimes'" awareness of women's special problems with the "awareness" of the capitalist ones, as revealed in what the respective "regimes" are doing about them.

When Friedan speaks of "the beginnings of awareness" and "some programs being started in East Germany," she implies a grudging Johnny-come-lately reaction on the part of the socialist states—and ignores what she wrote more than thirteen years earlier: that is, Soviet women "work in medicine, science, education, government, art," and have "a serious purpose in their own lives."

It's simpler for Friedan to ignore this statement than attempt to refute it. Instead she now makes such allegations as "the women's movement and feminism are threatening to Communists" because they "put too much emphasis" on a "woman's right to control her own body and her own destiny." To make such claims is to assume they will be accepted—a reasonable assumption considering what U.S. readers have been conditioned to believe about "Communist regimes."

Perhaps Friedan's interest in "the germs of women's movements spreading from the West" has something to do with her role, in the words on the jacket of her latest book, as "foremost spokeswoman for women's rights in the world." She has in fact behaved as a global emissary on the woman question for some time now. (Whom she represents is another matter.)

"The women's movement is no longer just an American possibility," she wrote in 1973. Obviously, the women's movement was *never* "just an American possibility." But to speak as Friedan did in 1973 was not only presumptuous but ironic if one recalls the increasing disarray of the U.S. movement at that point—which was certainly apparent in the National Organization of Women founded by Friedan. "I've been asked to help organize groups," Friedan went on, "in Italy, Brazil, Mexico, Colombia, Sweden, France, Israel, Japan, India, and even in Czechoslovakia and other Socialist countries."[2]

Friedan didn't say who asked her to "help organize groups" in "Czechoslovakia and other Socialist countries." It certainly wasn't anyone interested in socialism, because the "foremost spokeswoman for women's rights in the world" places her faith in capitalism:

Sure, sex discrimination was profitable—still is for some companies. But for the economy as a whole—yes, even under rotten old capitalism, which may or may not have the power to regenerate itself—equality between the sexes, participation of women, with all the rewards thereof, is becoming one of the main sources of new energy.[3]

It would certainly surprise the millions of women in unskilled low-paid jobs to learn of their "equality" and "participation" in "the economy as a whole" with "all the rewards thereof." It might also come as a surprise to the U.S. Census Bureau.

In 1964, reports the bureau, women's incomes were 64 percent of men's. By 1976 the gap had widened to the point where women's incomes were only 57 percent of those of "comparable male workers." (These overall figures do not reflect the even greater income gap experienced by women of the oppressed minorities.) Although most women are in deadend jobs, the income gap applies even to those who are not. Women doctors, for instance, earned only 57 percent as much as their male equivalents, the "same percentage gap as that for all workers."[4]

Great as the income gap is already, it is expected to widen in the next decade, reports a United States Office of Education study.[5] Although women are expected to make up an even larger share of the workforce by 1985, low-paying clerical and service jobs are forecast for most of them, with breakthroughs in traditionally male jobs predicted in isolated instances only.

Clearly, "sex discrimination" is not only profitable for "some companies" but for the entire capitalist economy. That's why the corporations welcome the "new energy" they're getting from women. But the ones who need the "new energy" are the mothers of young children who've been forced into the labor market. While Friedan has nothing to say about the problems these women face, she obviously feels her assistance would be valuable in "Czechoslovakia and other Socialist countries."

It seems clear that whoever invited Friedan to "help organize groups" in "Czechoslovakia and other Socialist countries" was interested in assisting capitalism to "regenerate itself" within *socialist* countries. Such proved to be the case. In 1976, three years after announcing her invitation, Friedan told who had extended it: "My old friend Hilda Scott," she said, "asked me to come" to Czechoslovakia in 1967.[6] (In early spring 1968, the press reported on numerous prominent figures in U.S. industry, commerce, banking, etc., who were then in Czechoslovakia. No doubt they too had been asked to "help organize groups," since counterrevolution attempted to "regenerate" capitalism shortly after their Prague sojourn.)

Her "old friend Hilda Scott," Friedan went on to say, had written a "cogent, brilliant book" on the "plight" of women in Eastern Europe. It was titled, *Does Socialism Liberate Women?*

Does Socialism Liberate Women? was first published in 1974, with a paperback issued later. (Neither edition gives any information on Scott's identity, except that she is from the U.S. and lived in Czechoslovakia for "many" years. The reasons for her stay there are not indicated.) This timing on publication was not accidental: Radicalized women were going further in their search for answers to women's special problems; in fact, many "radical feminists" were now calling themselves "socialist feminists." It was clear that the media controllers intended for Scott's book to have the same effect on women with a growing interest in the socialist alternative as de Beauvoir's book had on women seeking radical alternatives in the sixties. *Does Socialism Liberate Women?* was promoted accordingly.

"The most important text on the role of women in society since Simone de Beauvoir's *The Second Sex*," trumpets an endorsement on the cover of the Scott paperback. *Does Socialism Liberate Women?* is without a doubt a lineal descendant of *The Second Sex*. But, as frequently happens, the descendant takes things one step further than the forebear.

When in 1948 de Beauvoir wrote of a "male universe" and a male "privileged caste," she was telling women that whatever the nature of the society, men—not a class—hold power. And when she alleged that women's emancipation has "been realized nowhere, in Russia no more than in France or the United States," she was warning that socialism offers no more hope than capitalism. But since that time, socialism's advances have been so tremendous that if one simply expresses a generalized despair with both systems, one cannot even expect to dampen the great interest aroused in the socialist alternative.

Therefore, although Scott's terms—"man's world," "male policymakers" and men who hold "political, financial and ideological power"—are remarkably similar to de Beauvoir's, Scott applies them almost exclusively to the socialist world.

In the movement for women's emancipation, Scott begins, there have been "two lines of development." One has involved "gradual legislative reform," while the other has "adopted Marxism as its guiding principle and found the origins of women's inferior position in the private property system." Both "existing answers," she asserts, have "disappointed their advocates." However, she gives no examples of why reformism has "disappointed" its advocates. Her critique is devoted exclusively to the socialist alternative.

"It is," Scott writes, "not easy for women in capitalist countries to visualize the socialist solution in action." True enough. But the reason it's so hard is because the media prevent women from getting the information they need to "visualize the socialist solution." The media create this problem not because socialism has "disappointed" its advocates, but because it alarms its opponents.

Since Scott recognizes how difficult it is for women in capitalist societies to visualize socialism, one would think she'd help them do it by comparing the conditions of U.S. women (since she herself is from this country) with those of women in socialism. Scott doesn't do this. Yet from whatever point one makes this comparison, one finds that it helps solve the visualization problem.

For instance, in the U.S., where the means of production are privately owned, it's considered a purely private matter if a woman works. If a woman is a professional or in some other better paid category, bourgeois society assumes she's working because she wants to; therefore it's up to her to provide for her children's care. If a woman works because her husband's earnings are inadequate, it's still a private affair because she has failed by marrying a man who can't "take care of her." Society takes no responsibility for child care—although this means that vast numbers of women who desperately need a job can't even look for one. This is one of the factors accounting for the following: In 1975 alone, the Census Bureau reports, the number of people living below the "poverty level" increased by 2.5 million—with a "disproportionate number of the poor" in families headed by a woman only.

In the GDR where society encourages a woman to work, society makes it possible for her to do so. Her decision to work is made with the socialist state, which assures her free training and employment in her chosen field. While a woman can choose to be "just a housewife," few women in socialism are interested in this retreat into the past. Child care is provided, and "affirmative action" programs are available to all women so they can continue to upgrade their skills and pay.

The same contrasting principles apply to motherhood in the U.S. and the GDR. In the U.S., motherhood is considered a personal matter, although in truth it is not. Millions of women can't make a personal decision about motherhood because they can't afford contraceptives, let alone abortion, or are compelled by religious pressures to have one baby after another. Although motherhood is all too frequently not a personal decision, it is always a personal responsibility, for society does nothing to help care for the child or to assure the child an equal start in life. Women are in fact penalized for having children from the time they are pregnant, when they are very likely to lose their jobs (and are almost sure to lose them if they aren't married).

And women are certainly penalized when lack of money stops them from having a child. Relatively few women can get any maternity benefits from their jobs. And at a time when the cost of normal delivery in a private hospital had climbed to about $2,000, the Supreme Court ruled that employers may exclude pregnancy from insurance plans. (Why are maternity costs so high? They have "climbed because each birth pays in part for all that technology and manpower, regardless of whether the birth was routine, requiring relatively little attention." Further, maternity departments are being shut down "because maternity proves itself to be an unprofitable business.")[7]

In the GDR, motherhood is a personal decision: Contraceptives and abortions, which are performend in hospitals, are free. And while motherhood is a personal decision, it's a social function: Children are wanted by both parents and society. A pregnant woman cannot be dismissed from her job, but she has the right to lighter work if she wants it. Her job will be held for her one year after she gives birth. Every woman receives twenty-six weeks paid maternity leave, and a woman with more than one child will receive a substantial monthly sum for the balance of the year if she remains at home during that time. Since 1975 the rate of abortion has gradually declined, while the birthrate has increased—trends related to a steady upgrading in social measures.

There is one difference in approach to unmarried mothers: They get *preferential* treatment because they need more assistance.

IF HILDA SCOTT had wanted to help women in capitalist societies "visualize the socialist solution in action," she had an added way of doing so: She could have offered a comparison of the lives of women in socialist countries before and after socialism.

In the GDR there are still millions of women who have experienced both societies. One of them is Brunhilde Hanke.

"I come from a working-class family," she told us. "My grandmother had fifteen children and she also had to work. The children had to be on their own—even when they were sick she didn't have time to care for them. She even washed dishes in restaurants at night to earn a little more money.

"My father," she continued, "was a turner in a factory and my mother worked at different jobs from the time she was fifteen. As a child, I cared for my younger sisters and brothers—there were no kindergartens for working-class children." After the defeat of fascism in World War II, "I went to work in a garment factory." Here the difference between her own life and the lives of her mother and grandmother began.

"The trade union said, 'Workers' children are needed for studies, and we have chosen you.' I felt I was much too stupid for studying. I was a girl. Boys could handle studying, I couldn't. Today girls don't have such problems. It's natural for girls and boys to be delegated for advanced studies. My daughter will soon be taking her final exam for her university diploma."

Brunhilde Hanke overcame her feelings of inadequacy and took the opportunity to study that capitalism had denied her. Today she is Mayor of Potsdam.

But hers is not the "success story" of capitalism: the lone individual from a poor family who against all odds wins fame and fortune. Nor is she a "token" woman in a leading position. (One out of every five GDR mayors and one out of every three judges are women.) Although her own personal qualities played a great role in her becoming a mayor, hers is much more than an individual success story. It is a success of the working class, a part of the rise of the masses of women in socialism.

"Only after the working class has gained power is it possible to solve the social questions involved in women's emancipation. In 1945 when the working class in the Eastern part of Germany had been liberated, it involved women in the struggle to extend its political power and economic base; at the same time this contributed to the emancipation of women," said Mayor Hanke—whose remarks indicate a Marxist-Leninist approach to women's emancipation.

But as Hilda Scott tells it, the Marxist-Leninist approach sounds quite different:

The socialist countries tried to make of the observations and proposals offered by Marx, Engels and Lenin—far-reaching in their implications but still touching only certain aspects of woman's total problem—a complete theory of emancipation to which nothing could be added and from which nothing could be taken away . . . They have belatedly realized the irreconcilability of this theory with certain realities of life, but because they do not feel able to change the theory and cannot change the realities, they are forced to perpetuate the myth that the two can be successfully synthesized, and that this is, in fact, what liberation means: to make it possible for woman to combine her role as wife and mother, as the dominant figure in the home, with her role as worker. In this concept, one less-skilled, less-rewarding, less-prestigious job plus home-making contains the same potential for equality as one better-paid, more interesting, or at least less tedious job by itself . . .[8]

The Soviet Union, GDR and other socialist countries certainly do base their views of women's emancipation on the theories of Marx, Engels and Lenin. And while these countries have not revised these theories, they have never taken the attitude that "nothing could be added," since Marxist-Leninist theories present a guide to action, not a blueprint. The reason they do not "change the theory" is because the theory has made it possible for them to do what Scott says cannot be done: "change the realities" of women's, and men's, lives.

Scott claims that in the Marxist view of the socialist countries, liberation means "to make it possible for woman to combine her role as wife and mother" with "her role as worker." The socialist countries recognize that at this stage women do have a "double burden." This double burden is not the creation of socialism, it is the legacy of capitalism. And while this double burden is in the process of being overcome in socialism, it's being intensified under capitalism. In fact, the double burden of working women in capitalist societies (and women without jobs have the even greater burden of economic dependence on a man) and its survivals under socialism really cannot be compared.

Working women in capitalism not only carry the burden of jobs—usually at low pay and with miserable working conditions—plus the burden of home and children. They carry a third burden: worry. They worry that they'll be without a job. They worry about paying the rent. They worry about medical care for their families and themselves. They worry about their children's education and whether their children will find jobs. In socialism these worries exist only in the memories of the older generation.

Further, in discussing women's double burden in socialism, it becomes necessary to make a distinction between *burden* and *respon-sibility*. Since women in socialism understand that their work is both for themselves and for society, work becomes a responsibility and a challenge rather than a burden. And since love for children is not distorted by fear of how much they cost, children are more and more a creative responsibility instead of a burden. The housework that must still be done by individual families is, of course, a burden. Lenin had some "far-reaching" proposals on this matter, which socialism is putting into practice.

Marx and Lenin did not create the "myth" that the meaning of "liberation" is that "one less-skilled, less-rewarding, less-prestigious job plus homemaking contains the same potential for equality as one better-paid, more interesting, or at least less tedious job by itself." The author of this myth is Scott. Lenin wrote:

The chief thing is to get women to take part in socially productive labor, to liberate them from domestic slavery, to free them from their stupefying and humiliating subjugation to the eternal drudgery of the kitchen and the nursery.

This struggle will be a long one, and it demands a radical reconstruction both of social technique and of morals. But it will end in the complete triumph of communism.[9]

The struggle Lenin called for—which explains why the biography of the Mayor of Potsdam is not an isolated success story—was begun in the Eastern part of Germany right after liberation from fascism.

WORKING WOMEN! Remember that fascism takes away your rights, rights you have obtained for yourselves in a bitter struggle . . . Remember that the Third Reich wants to degrade you to be man's slave and a machine for bearing children. Don't forget the courageous women, the fighters whom fascism holds in its prisons.[10]

This appeal to German women was made by Clara Zetkin, a Communist, a leader of the German and international working-class women's movement, and a friend of Lenin's. Thousands of the "courageous women, the fighters whom fascism holds in its prisons" were to die in those prisons. But many survived. And immediately after liberation, these women resistance fighters became active in the struggle for a peaceful, democratic Germany. One of their most important contributions was the formation in 1945 of anti-fascist women's committees.

"These committees were formed to help get women involved in reconstruction. This meant the committees had to help reshape women's political outlook—to make them understand the meaning of fascism, to overcome the devastating racist and anti-Soviet ideology of fascism," said Christel Büchner, a national leader of the Democratic Women's Federation (DWF), founded in 1947.

It was terribly difficult to convince German women to become involved in the struggle for a new Germany. "They'd been politicized and organized under fascism and they felt, 'We've been cheated by fascism and we'll never touch politics again.' They'd never had any part in co-determination and we had to convince them that what they had to say mattered. But there was a great incentive for women to think politically.

"In 1945 the population in the Eastern part of Germany was more than two-thirds women. The women had to work because the men hadn't come home."

In 1946 the Soviet Military Adminstration introduced the first legal basis for women's equality: equal pay for equal work. "This decree met with resistance from many men, including managers of firms. But the real battle," Büchner said, "took place when the men came back from the POW camps. It was vital for the women to work the first year, and their outlook had been somewhat changed by the time the men came back. The husbands were astounded to discover this change. They made their presence felt—and many of the women stopped working." But the husbands' views did not prevail.

"We made it clear to women that working was an essential part of equality," related Büchner. When the DWF was founded—with the overall aims of peace, equality for women and progress—"we had one plank: co-responsibility, co-knowledge and co-determination for women. The DWF won women to work for the first five-year plan— both for themselves and for the economy. But many legal and practical steps had to be taken to make this possible." The measures for women's emancipation adopted in the GDR had been pioneered in the Soviet Union. And because of its alliance with the Soviet Union the GDR could move rapidly to begin to put them into effect.

According to the laws of the former German state, it was "the prerogative of the husband to decide in all matters," while it was "the obligation of the wife to manage the joint household." These male supremacist laws were immediately abolished in the Eastern part of Germany, together with discrimination against unwed mothers and "illegitimate" children. In 1949 the GDR's first Constitution provided the legal basis for women's equality in education, work, social and economic life. In 1950 further significant legislation provided for constructing kindergartens and nurseries, financial allowances for children, and for promoting women in managerial and administrative activities.

To begin to translate legal equality into reality required winning the support of a people just emerged from fascism. An early struggle was around the nurseries and kindergartens that made it possible for women to move into economic and social life while their children's well being was assured. "Over a number of years the DWF worked to persuade both men and women that nurseries and kindergartens were vital," said Christel Büchner. "Although the women's organization was primarily involved in this, the overall policy of the Party and government saw to it that men were also influenced toward supporting these steps." Strong male resistance came "from doctors and intellectuals mainly. Their argument was that the child needs the mother's loving care"—an argument still widely used in the U.S. against women who want to work. "This struggle went on throughout the fifties," while kindergartens and nurseries were built and went into operation. "Social reality helped us overcome the resistance. People saw the children growing up happily."

It wasn't, of course, only the attitudes of men toward women that had to be changed, but the attitudes of women toward themselves. "At the beginning of socialist construction," said Büchner, "women naturally still had a traditional view of their role as mother and housewife. They couldn't overcome this by themselves—it was a long and difficult process." However, at all stages women were changing far more rapidly than was acceptable to many men. And the resistance from men in agriculture was much sharper than that of men in industry.

"The final victory of socialist production came with the collectivization of agriculture," stated Büchner. "The DWF did many things to persuade women farmers this was necessary. The struggle then was to convince both men and women to join the cooperatives, because equality for women works out only if women as well as men are members. This meant a fierce battle with men who wanted to keep their wives on a private plot, while they themselves profited from the collective. It wasn't until 1963-64 that most women had become members of the cooperatives."

That men as well as women have changed is clear. Today one out of every three members of the executive boards of the cooperative farms is a woman. The significance of these figures can also be gleaned from this: In the agricultural areas of the old Germany, the big landowners would say of the peasants, "There's one ox in front of the plow and another behind it." If this was the attitude toward men, one can only imagine the attitude toward women!

It was from this kind of existence that the women who participated in constructing socialism were liberated—women whose own lives were changed completely as they helped change completely the life of the country.

ALTHOUGH THE Soviet Union, the GDR and other socialist countries began to create the material preconditions for women's emancipation in the first stages of their existence, Hilda Scott writes:

There is no crash program to improve services or establish ideal nurseries because . . . the need for these facilities is not felt by the predominantly male policy-makers who allot funds. There are (and always will be) enough other projects which seem more vital to the economy and which need money.[11]

In only two sentences Scott makes a number of basic allegations about socialist society that, however, she does not attempt to back up. This is understandable, considering the facts.

We asked Liselotte Thoms-Heinrich, editor of *Für Dich*—a weekly publication for women with a circulation of one million—about Scott's charge of "no crash program to improve services or establish nurseries." She agreed with it.

"It's true," she said, "we have no crash program. We've always had a *continuous* program for improving services and establishing nurseries. We have statistics: We occupy first place in the world for the percentage of children who can go to nurseries and kindergartens." The saturation point for places in kindergarten will soon be reached (it's already been attained in rural areas) and nursery facilities continue to be expanded.

Although child care centers in the U.S. have existed mainly on a custodial level, and are now being shut down rather than expanded, Scott demands "ideal" nurseries in the socialist countries. (It's ironic that the less the Scotts and Friedans ask of capitalism, the more they demand of socialism.) Although there's no such thing as "ideal," since people's demands continue to rise, U.S. parents would certainly consider GDR nurseries ideal. Open from early morning till 7PM, they offer hot meals, educational games, medical care. Since the specialists in charge aren't worried about losing their jobs, they can devote themselves to caring for and educating the children. The atmosphere is a warm and loving one, and this is apparent in the children's response. Nursery care is free except for a nominal monthly charge for food.

Nurseries are provided not only for children of working people but of students. University dormitories are equipped with apartments for couples or single mothers, and there are nurseries for the children. In keeping with policy, first preference for a place in these facilities goes to unmarried mothers.

(The GDR's special assistance to unmarried mothers should be contrasted with treatment of unmarried mothers in the U.S., who in 1975 gave birth to 14 percent of all children.[12] As a rule education for young unmarried mothers in this country stops when their child is born, if not before. In New York in 1976, for instance, there were plans to shut down the special schools for pregnant teenagers. When these teenagers applied at regular schools, the principals told them to go to the special schools. The principals at the special schools refused to accept them, saying these schools would soon be closed. "From all parts of the city I hear that principals are performing like George Wallace when he blocked the doorway at the University of Alabama to thwart school integration," declared a city councilwoman who accompanied a delegation of the teenagers in a protest to City Hall.)[13]

That socialist "policy-makers" allot funds to free women of old burdens is evident in other ways too. "We're working to transfer housework out of the home and put it on society's shoulders," stated Thoms-Heinrich. One tremendous advance has been made in regard to meals. In most homes cooking needs to be done only on weekends, since working people and students have a hot meal at their workplace or school.

Scott's assertion that socialist "policy-makers" don't allot funds for nurseries and services because "other projects" always "seem more vital" is clearly disproved by the facts. But in addition to her assertion, Scott's statement contains an implication: The "other projects" are alien to women. This too is clearly disproved by the facts: Women benefit just as much as men from these "other projects"—modern housing, increased production, educational and cultural facilities.

In a socialist society funds must be allocated to meet the people's varied needs. (This is no consideration under capitalism: The corporate "male policy-makers" simply estimate what "project" will generate the most profits and invest accordingly.) Besides allocations to fill general needs, funds must be properly allocated to meet women's special needs. This doesn't happen automatically. Within this process, women play a special role.

And this role, pointed out novelist Irmtraud Morgner, is very different from the role working women must play in capitalism—where their enemy is the class in power. "In a capitalist society," said Morgner, "a woman who wants to enter history—who wants to become a human being—should first enter politics and learn who her allies are. Her allies are the workers' movement with which and in which she must take the revolutionary economic steps—and all the other steps that will follow."

In a socialist society the working class is in power—and within it and with it women continue to take revolutionary steps. "In a socialist society," Morgner continued, "there are a whole lot of small revolutions—such as the laws we have that are very pro-women." In bringing about these "small revolutions," women's special consciousness plays a part. "One cannot wait until presents fall into one's lap," declared Morgner. "One must do something about that."

And in a socialist society women are in a position to do a great deal about that because the "policy-makers" are female as well as male. In 1976 in the GDR's highest legislative body, the People's Chamber, 168 of the 500 members were women. (The highest legislative body in the U.S. is the Senate. It has 100 members, none of them women. And in the House in 1976, only 18 of the 435 members were women.)

The trade unions are a vital force in GDR life. Forty-seven percent of the members of the National Executive of the Confederation of Free German Trade Unions (FGTU) are women. From 40 to 53 percent of leadership at every other level of the FGTU are women—for instance, 43 percent of the shop stewards are women. (Contrast this with the almost all-male leadership in U.S. unions!) At a recent FGTU convention over half the delegates were women (most U.S. conventions, including most union conventions, are virtually all male). Both the FGTU and the DWF have their own groups in parliament.

Through the Party, the mass organizations and all elected bodies women play their part in advancing the status of women—and socialist society as a whole.

IN THE U.S. women who must get a job—any kind of job that will pay the bills—are confronted not only by the general unemployment crisis, but also by the employers' prejudices against hiring women, except where they can be used to replace men at a lower wage. And now the forecast is that conditions for working women will get worse. To prevent this predicted downward spiral from becoming a reality, working women must engage in a battle—with the support of working men—against corporate employers, who are backed up by the state.

A particularly dramatic example of this battle against the corporations was the suit for pregnancy benefits brought by women workers against General Electric—whose position was backed by twenty other corporations. When the corporations maintained that medical coverage for pregnancy would cost them $1 billion a year, the state, through its Supreme Court, ruled in their favor—with one judge saying, "Pregnancy is, of course, confined to women. But it is in other ways significantly different from the typical covered disease or disability."[14]

In the GDR the status of women is on a upward spiral: With the support of the state, of society as a whole, they are continuing to advance. And this advance involves solving the non-antagonistic but complex contradictions of socialism.

For instance, the law has served as an impetus to women's equality; in fact, certain aspects of inequality, such as the heritage of unequal pay for equal work, were abolished by mandate. But other phases of inequality could not be overcome by legislation alone. Legislation could lay the groundwork for advancing women in industry, but it could not do away with the fact that in the old German state most of the women who worked were unskilled. As the construction of socialism began, men had a huge accumulation of skills that capitalism had prevented women from acquiring. Socialism has fought stubbornly, and with great success, to overcome this legacy.

"The heritage capitalism left to the socialist state was women who did the most unskilled jobs," said Liselotte Thoms-Heinrich. "In the older generation this heritage was overcome as far as possible, but not entirely conquered. But in the younger generation, 99 percent of the girls graduate with a trade or profession. Girls get the same training on the shop floor as boys do."

"The leading class in our society," stated Christel Büchner, "is the working class, women and men workers. We want the *whole* class to consist of highly skilled people who can cope with the tasks of the present and the future. The need for unskilled workers is being reduced, and more and more highly skilled workers will be needed. Turning unskilled into skilled workers has been a special problem among women in those age groups that did not get vocational training. We have helped these women to raise their qualifications so they could become skilled workers." By the end of 1976, 70 percent of all women in the workforce were skilled.

In the U.S., women who want to become skilled workers face vast difficulties. Women form 40 percent of the workforce but have only 2 percent of the places in skilled training programs. In 1977 women's organizations demanded that steps be taken so that women's placement in federal apprenticeship programs would begin to reflect their numbers in the workforce. "Absolutely impossible," retorted the deputy administrator of the U.S. Labor Department's Bureau of Apprenticeship and Training. "We are opposed to setting such a goal." Why? The "system couldn't absorb it."[15]

In a socialist society women don't have to fight the system to upgrade their skills. On the contrary, the system itself provides the means for women to acquire skills. "In our opinion," said Charlotte Bombal who heads the 600,000 member Textile, Clothes and Leather Workers Union and is also a member of the National Executive of the FGTU, "it's the task of industry to see that women qualify for skilled work."

To carry out this responsibility, industry offers advanced training to women in workplace academies. Further, women who have completed vocational training may be delegated by their plants for still more advanced studies. If a woman can't study full-time because of family responsibilities, she's released from work to study two or three days a week, while being paid at her regular rate. Full-time women students get 80 percent of their earnings. When these women return to their plants, their work and pay is upgraded in line with their new skills. Women college graduates are also delegated by their firms for advanced studies. The enterprise must give the woman a promotion contract in advance, insuring her future assignment and material security.

"The proof that we want women to work at all levels is what we do so women can qualify," said Uwe Rosenkranz, who heads the Free German Youth's Department of Professional and Vocational Training. "Men have to qualify after working hours, but qualification courses for women only have been created on paid time. And the manager of every plant is bound by law to work out a development plan for women with the trade unions. And," he emphasized, "the trade union organization in each plant includes a women's commission."

There are over 13,000 of these commissions, elected bodies whose chairperson is always a member of the trade union leadership. "This guarantees that the special problems of women are discussed continuously by the plant management," declared Regina Zwanzig, editor of the newspaper at VEB* Köpenick Radio Works.

"We are not afraid our problems won't be heard—we raise them emphatically. We don't have any antagonistic conflicts to handle—no unemployment or layoffs. We're interested in solving social problems, further education and training for women, improving working and living conditions, child and health care, developing women's political consciousness—these are the most important areas for us. The special field of advanced training," she stressed, "has created many possibilities for women to qualify themselves."

This opportunity for qualification is available in a great number of areas: Trades closed to women in the old German state (and still virtually closed to U.S. women) are open to GDR women. "In Germany it was impossible for women to go into the building trades," said Uwe Rosenkranz. "Today women who go into this field are very much esteemed. And," he pointed out, "50 percent of the architectural students are women." This advance is typical of GDR women's progress in fields that largely exclude them in capitalist countries.

By 1974 half those receiving vocational training in the chemical industry, 46 percent in electrical engineering and electronics, 31 percent in machine tool and machine building, and 32 percent in general mechanical farm and automotive engineering were women. The majority of college and university students are now women, and the percentage is especially high in the field of economics, including engineering economics. All graduates, whether with a trade or profession, are guaranteed a place in their field.

Although the percentage of women in areas formerly closed to them grows every year, the workforce in certain industries is still predomi-

*These letters signify that the enterprise is owned by the people.

nantly male or female. "This is a question that must be dealt with historically," remarked Charlotte Bombal. "Typically feminine industries came about because physical work in many industries was very hard in the past. We've always oriented ourselves on science and technology to ease the work. But there is no woman in the GDR who works in the mines." Women doing heavy, dangerous work "is not the sense of equal rights."

Some forces in the U.S. women's movement might disagree with this. Not because they really feel women should do work that's too heavy for them or dangerous to their reproductive systems, but because they believe special protective measures for women are misused to keep women from doing jobs they are physically able to do. This is not true in the GDR and other socialist countries.

For other reasons this is essentially not true in capitalist countries either. Corporate employers always use excuses for keeping women in the lowest-paid jobs, and the claim that a job is "too much for a woman" is among them. But if employers succeed in keeping women in low-category jobs, it's not because of protective legislation. Quite the contrary. In the early days of industrialization, before the workers' movements had won any protective legislation, employers were totally successful in keeping women in the worst jobs. What brought about changes in women's status were the struggles of working women and the working class as such. And it is these struggles that will win more job opportunities for women as well as better health protection. Men want better health measures too, as witness the miners' fight for protection against Black Lung disease. In the socialist countries health and safety standards for men as well as women are on a continually rising plane.

In the GDR men who do heavy, physically dangerous work are paid extra. But this doesn't alter the fact that the historic differential between men's and women's earnings on an overall basis is being overcome, and at an increasingly higher level of pay for both. "You can't say that the degree of heaviness of work is our only criterion for evaluating the work," pointed out Charlotte Bombal. "That would mean wages and salaries would go down as automation increased. But that's not the case." As this statement suggests, automation has an opposite meaning for workers in capitalist and socialist countries.

Women workers in the U.S. are among those who particularly fear automation because it means less jobs. But in socialist countries, where no one worries about being unemployed, technology opens up countless jobs to women that were too heavy for them to handle in the past. It also speeds their upgrading. As Marlis Allendorf, a GDR writer, points out, "the training and retraining of women makes the best progress where the modernization of factories, and rationalization and automation of the processes of production make the biggest demands for up-to-date staff."[16]

Yet another factor contributes to the upgrading of women's incomes in socialist countries. In capitalist countries the most skilled jobs, even in industries where women predominate, are handled by men. "I just came back from two weeks in England where I visited the weaving mills," said Charlotte Bombal. "I saw that there were no women at the weaving machines—that's the main production machine. Women there are excluded from it completely. But we have no textile branch without women."

The same principle applies to other areas—for instance, the health field. In the U.S. almost all nurses are women while almost all doctors and dentists are men. But in the GDR 46 percent of the doctors and 45 percent of the dentists are women.

In the U.S. women are denied opportunities to advance. In the GDR women have tremendous opportunities to advance—but problems must still be overcome so they can take full advantage of them. "Much has been achieved during the last few decades in the training of women, more than many would have believed when the difficult uphill struggle began," notes Marlis Allendorf. Nevertheless, "there are still too many women" who have "not yet [been] able to overcome the obstacles in the way of full training." Older women, denied an education by capitalism, often need to be convinced of their ability to take up studies. With younger women the question of educational background has been solved—but to advance in their fields they must keep up with scientific and technological changes. The problem for these women, points out Allendorf, is "to go on studying in spite of their often heavy responsibilities to household and family."

At the VEB Housing Construction Combinate of Berlin, Alexandra Martin, who is in charge of cadre instruction for a group of 1,500, discussed this problem with us. "If women take on added responsibility, yes, it becomes more difficult for them. The pre-conditions are there, but the time—they're worried that starting new studies will leave them too little time for their families. But we fought for equal rights, for responsibility, and we must use them." She added: "I took my chance—I didn't just wait for it."

IN THE U.S. many married women who want to work still face resistance from their husbands. In the GDR husbands' attitudes have been transformed since the time the men came home from the POW camps and demanded that their wives stop working. Today, said Irmtraud Morgner, "A man with a bit of self-respect naturally has a wife with a job—that is practically a matter of honor. Wives who are simply housewives may make life more comfortable but are not held in particularly high regard by men."

This transformation did not come about by itself. The international socialist movement has carried on a long struggle for women's equality—in which Fidel Castro's historic speech assailing male supremacist attitudes and practices was not an unprecedented step but a dramatic highlight. At *Für Dich* headquarters we learned of an incident highlighting the Socialist Unity Party's struggle to change traditional male attitudes—a vital part of the struggle for women's complete equality.

"We went to a large plant to investigate men's attitudes on women's equality," related Dr. Ursula Hafranke, deputy editor. "We took with us Party documents from 1950 to 1960 stressing that men, especially Communist men, must stand for the equality of women. Men who didn't were sharply criticized."

The documents detailed certain male supremacist prejudices: Women are human beings of the second category; they can't think creatively; it's not worthwhile to give them advanced training because they can't carry on both family and professional duties; they don't understand technical things—at least not as well as men.

"We talked with a brigade of young workers, made up equally of men and women," continued Hafranke, "and we asked them 'What's left of these attitudes today?' They said, 'Nothing's left—except one thing: The argument that women can't understand technical things as well as men.' It was a brigade where the women did an excellent technical job—but one of the thirty women members didn't understand as well as the men and that was enough to keep the myth alive.

"In the end the men admitted it. They said, 'If one man doesn't understand—that's the exception. If one women doesn't, that's the rule.' "

The journalists visited another brigade in the same plant, a repair team for machine tools. "A year ago women became members of this brigade for the first time," said Hafranke. "The men were rather angry. They said, 'Machine toolmakers are the crown of the metal trade.' But these women were well-trained and the men became convinced the women could do the job. Now these men say, 'It's better to have women in the brigade. The most impolite men are more polite, the atmosphere is more friendly, and we don't only discuss soccer.' All the men agreed, 'Mixed work brigades are better.'"

Editor Thoms-Heinrich added: "Twenty years ago the men would probably have made so many traps, the women would have preferred to leave."

Of course, the cultural residue from centuries of male supremacy can't be expected to disappear overnight. While many prejudices have been overcome, certain others have reappeared in more subtle form. For instance, so many women have proved their leadership ability that resistance to the principle of promoting them is unlikely to be express-ed, points out Marlis Allendorf. But "newer objections have arisen with the growth of women's equality." Because women take time for maternity leave, to care for sick children and because women with three or more children get a shorter but fully paid work week, "Might it not be more logical, the argument goes, to employ only men in leading positions?"

It might be easier, Allendorf says, "if one does not look beyond the interests of the individual firm." But a socialist outlook must consider "the whole of society," and therefore every enterprise "has the duty of building up women to take leading positions, and of overcoming along the way those difficulties arising from women's particular prob-lems."[17]

That the enterprises, backed by society as a whole, are helping women to overcome these difficulties is confirmed by the facts: One out of every four leadership positions in GDR industry is now held by a woman. And while special problems must be solved so women can advance, women have proved that in many leading roles their contri-bution not only equals a man's but is a special one.

"We've found that for the development of cities and communities, it's an advantage to have women at the head," said Mayor Brunhilde Hanke. "Women don't see things from higher up, they know people's problems—because in a family women face problems in a different way from men.

"We had to do a lot," she continued, "so women could undertake these important activities—many material conditions had to be created. And if you see this as a process of thirty years of development, the accomplishments are impressive. The further advancing of women, including at the highest levels, depends largely on our own work."

Although the majority of GDR women in leadership positions are at the middle levels, many hold top-level posts. The next stage, as Mayor Hanke suggested, involves their full representation at the highest level. However, when one considers what's been achieved— that not only one out of every five mayors, one out of every three judges and one out of every four industry leaders is a woman, but every third elected representative is also a woman—one realizes in only thirty years GDR women are already well along on a journey that still lies ahead for U.S. women.

ONE NEED not talk with GDR women long to learn about their attitudes toward women's equality.

"I know that in the GDR women's level of consciousness of their role shows an awareness of their own value. I've never heard any girl or woman say, 'I'm only a woman,'" declared Elke Bitterhof of the FGY's Departments of Culture and International Relations, who is in her twenties.

"I have no fear of not being able to play my part or of not being an equal to men," said eighteen-year-old economics student Elke Gutmann.

"And this is proven every day in school," agreed one of her teachers, Annette Meinherz.

"We're not satisfied to sit home and take care of children and the house," asserted Gisela Kanus, twenty-four, who was home in the GDR on vacation: She had been in the Soviet Union as a member of one of the youth brigades constructing the Friendship Pipeline that will carry oil through the socialist nations. "We've gotten used to the idea that men should share household duties so women can function in society, improve their knowledge and training and exercise their equal rights in reality."

Young GDR women's interest in a career by no means implies an intention to sacrifice motherhood. "Women in the West are confronted with the question of either working or giving up their work to have a child. A society that confronts a woman with those alternatives is inhuman," said Irmtraud Morgner. "Here even if a woman is alone with a child she is not treated in a second-class way. She can be absolutely sure of getting special help from the state. One really has a feeling of security based on these facts."

Nor does combining a career with motherhood make motherhood less important. "The important work in a society is not only done in the plants and political life but also in the home and family," noted Morgner. "This is done for human beings, small human beings, who need the feeling parents have for them, the feeling that they are taken seriously. You need strength to have the patience to answer questions. And also time. If all this is not done well, children do not grow up in a healthy way. I find it very good in women that the norm men have acquired over centuries—which is a load on their shoulders and has deformed them—that women don't really recognize this norm. Women don't want to acquire this traditional male norm and consider children less important." What is required, of course, is a new norm.

To achieve this new norm, "it is again necessary to forget old ideas about man's and woman's place in life," states Marlis Allendorf. "So far the greatest share of looking after children rests on the woman's shoulders. Yet these children are as much the father's, and equality of the sexes demands that both partners share the joys and sorrows of child-rearing."[18] One of socialism's most complex tasks is bringing about this new norm.

Except where physical strength is a consideration, there is no vocation or profession a woman cannot handle as well as a man. On the other hand, a man can do everything a woman can do, except have babies and nurse them. But it's much easier for women than men to recognize the difference between innate and acquired characteristics, because women want to do things once considered the province of men only. But men are not so readily convinced of their equal ability to do "women's work." While socialist society asserts there is no such thing as "women's work," the voices of the past are not easily stilled. Yet a new norm *is* being brought about—based on a socialist concept of personality.

Dr. Herta Kuhrig, deputy chairperson of Women in Socialist Society, an advisory council of the GDR Academy of Sciences, states:

For the socialist society it is not in the first place a question of bringing up "girls" or "boys," but of developing socialist personalities conscious of their rights and responsibilities in all spheres of public life and acting ever better in accordance with the objective laws of nature and society. In this way one more important contribution is being made to the equality of women.[19]

Steps toward realizing this concept of personality are begun in a child's first years.

"There's no difference whatsoever as to boys' and girls' roles in the whole life in kindergarten. Every child can take every toy—boys don't take only locomotives or girls only dolls," said Erica Strube who heads a Berlin kindergarten/nursery. "And there's no difference in regard to work—the boys set the table the same as girls."

Of course, the child's education doesn't proceed without conflicts. "There are still effects on children from parents and grandparents, even sometimes from young parents," commented Doris Wetterhahn of the Ministry of Education. "It's astonishing what an effect it will still have on a child when the parents or grandparents say, 'A boy doesn't cry' or 'This isn't a toy for a boy.' Survivals sometimes live on for generations. We have to fight against them all the time, as well as influences from the West." The results of this struggle are clearly discernible.

"Today there are a lot of things we take for granted that we had hot discussions about in the past," said Mayor Brunhilde Hanke. "Twenty years ago a man would have felt ashamed to push a baby carriage or take a child to the nursery under the eyes of others. Now men do both."

Young Elke Gutmann sees this development in much the same way. While she feels considerable progress has been made with the older generation, "the young men are more advanced—the idea of equality is deeper, it has expanded more. The younger men feel more responsibility for the children than the older ones did. We're making progress toward sharing."

That fathers are playing a much greater role in the child's education can be seen in the composition of parents committees: They are now 50 percent male (as contrasted with the mostly female makeup of parents committees in the U.S.).

In the U.S. it's assumed that if children get sick, mothers take care of them. But GDR law guarantees that either parent may stay home for this purpose without loss of pay. If a U.S. mother had this assurance (instead of running the risk of being fired), she might well prefer staying home to going into a hateful job. But with the fusion in the GDR between working for one's own and society's benefit, more and more women want their husbands to share in caring for a sick child. "But it's very complex to convince him," pointed out Liselotte Thoms-Heinrich.

Nevertheless, men are beginning to share in this responsibility. And a special role in bringing this about is played by women in leading posts. Although it's hard to imagine the mayor of a U.S. city showing any concern about who'll stay home with a sick child (it's easier to think of him firing mothers for "absenteeism"), this is a matter that interests Mayor Hanke.

"In the past only the mother stayed home with a sick child, no matter what responsible work she did. Today it's often discussed in the family," stated Hanke. "The wife of our chief architect works as assistant manager of a drug store. In case their child is ill, they've decided the wife will stay home one week, the husband the next."

How do male managers react when a husband wants to stay home instead of a wife? "Some managers have old-fashioned ideas," responded Hanke. "They'll ask, 'Why are you staying home? Your wife can do it.' But that's changing."

One of the factors accelerating change is "the initiative of the individual—the laws are there but you have to use them," noted Ruth Berghaus of the Deutsche State Opera. "If the man is aware enough of the importance of the work the woman does he says, 'I'll stay home.' There are many men in the theater who take turns with their wives in caring for a sick child.

"The conditions for empancipation," she emphasized, "have been created. And emancipation isn't only for women. If the husband loses his job while caring for a sick child, he can't be emancipated."

As THESE steps toward co-responsibility in raising children suggest, the changes in society as a whole are reflected in the home—where family ties of a new kind are coming into existence.

"Patriarchy is giving way to a new relationship which might be called 'biarchy,'" states Soviet writer Yuri Ryurikov.[20] Formed from the Latin "bini" (both) and the Greek "arche" (ruling), "biarchy" means the rule of both sexes. "Biarchic changes in our country are part of the Communist revolution. They affect every man-woman relation in economic, family, social and sexual terms," points out Ryurikov. The number of families with biarchal relationships is "on the increase," signifying that biarchal famlies are "the families of the future in the Soviet Union"—and in the other socialist countries as well.

The biarchal family is supported by socialist law, as this GDR law shows:

The equality of husband and wife decisively determines the character of the family in socialist society. It binds husband and wife to shape their mutual relations in such a way that both are able fully to exercise the right to develop their abilities for their own benefit and for that of society.

Other GDR laws stipulate equality of responsibility for raising children, for assisting a marriage partner in pursuing educational and career goals, etc.

A prerequisite for the biarchal family is the woman's economic independence—which assures that a woman can marry for love. "I wouldn't think of accepting a man for economic reasons," declared Elke Gutmann, expressing a view typical of women in socialist society.

At the outset, then, marriage in socialism is on a different plane from marriage in bourgeois society—where even marriages entered upon for love are continually broken up by economic difficulties. (On the other hand countless marriages in the U.S. are held together for economic reasons only. "When a husband goes, he takes his credit rating, his medical plan, his insurance and his pension," the president of the National Association for Divorced Women points out.[21])

Since socialist marriage is on a different plane, so are the conflicts. "The old conflicts have been overcome and the new ones appear," noted Ursula Hafranke. "In the past man was king. Even when he was silly he was considered the talented one in a marriage. Today the wife may be recognized as the more talented one. A woman doesn't care if a man is better developed, but many men still care very much if it's the other way around."

At the same time, "There are now quite a few men who don't resent having a wife with better qualifications," pointed out Liselotte Thoms-Heinrich.

A woman's desire to work and advance in her work also creates conflicts in other ways. As Thoms-Heinrich said, socialist society is working to transfer the maximum amount of housework "out of the home and put it on society's shoulders." Much progress has been made toward this goal, and it's continuing—step by step.

Yet at this stage much work remains to be done in the home. Therefore, "It can hardly be stressed often enough," states Marlis Allendorf, "that sharing the 'slavery' is very necessary for the time being, with each member of the family encouraged to play a part." To "halve woman's work at home," she points out, is "not just a matter of righting a wrong" . . . "much bigger issues are involved. The creative power of millions of human beings must be freed to allow them to live a fuller life."[22]

Young GDR women in particular accept the idea of "halving the work" quite literally. "I know many men who say, 'Of course I help my wife do the housework.' But I've never heard a wife say, 'Of course I help my husband do the housework,'" declared Elke Bitterhof.

Although millions of working women in capitalist society wish their husbands would share in the housework, few expect it to happen. It is certainly not put forth as a reason for divorce. Yet in the GDR, said Irmtraud Mornger, "where 70 percent of the divorces are initiated by women" among the reasons most frequently given for this step is "the man doesn't share the housework with the woman."

Socialist women don't enter into marriage for economic reasons, nor do they stay in a marriage for such reasons. "Women are not fond of serving their husbands—that's why we see divorce not only as a negative symptom. We have more independence, more self-confidence—this is the explanation for most divorces," said Regina Zwanzig at the radio plant.

"Although we've made lots of progress in this respect, we must admit we still have certain men with some of the old attitudes," said FGY leader Uwe Rosenkranz. "The reason for our divorces is not that we're worse people or worse marriage partners than others, but because it's possible for a woman to break with a man when she feels he's not ideal. In the past many women wanted to get out of a marriage but couldn't."

And Liselotte Thoms-Henrich said, "The demands made of a marriage partner by working women have risen. A woman appreciated on her job will not tolerate a backward husband. For hundreds and hundreds of years women were forced to stay in unhappy marriages because they couldn't earn a living for themselves and their children. The marriages in the old society kept together for economic reasons were worse than prisons. Now women are economically independent and there is quite a percentage of divorces. At one time we looked on this as a bad chapter, but we came to the conclusion that its roots are progressive."

In the U.S. unhappy marriages are frequently said to be kept together for the sake of the children. "In the GDR we're naturally concerned about how children are affected by their parents' divorce," stressed Thoms-Heinrich. "But for them to grow up in an unhappy family would also be harmful." She added: "Lowering the divorce rate—this is a process."

What this process involves is overcoming the conflicts that occur as women and men move out of the shadow of patriarchy into biarchal relations. And far from weakening family ties, these new relations strengthen them—since biarchal families are held together by love not by economics or outdated concepts.

"Abolishing the hierarchal family structure in a society that exploits people—in my opinion that's impossible," commented Irmtraud Morgner. "Only in socialism, which liberates everyone from exploitation, can the emancipation of women be attained. The most important thing," she went on, "is producing a new kind of living together among people. Relations in the most intimate sphere, where the women still do most of the housework—that is what has to be changed. If you think something that took thousands of years to develop can be changed only with words. . .It must be done in a creative way, there must be a growing agreement." In many families this agreement *is* growing.

IN THE EARLY days of the GDR, couples who shared family responsibilities equally served as an example for a society just starting on the road toward putting these relationships into practice on a mass basis.

"A woman has good luck if she has a husband with emancipation in his innermost heart. I have been lucky enough to have a pearl of a man who was all out for emancipation and participated in household chores," said Berliner Ensemble Cadre Director Pilka Häntzsche. Her husband, a professor of film science, has been a Party member for fifty years. "We tried to educate our son to participate in this same way." Today the son, a doctor of artistic science, "shares in cooking, shopping, cleaning, and taking his child to school."

Today the mass media are an important factor in encouraging couples to share family responsibilities. "You can see the difference between our TV commercials and the ones in the FRG," noted poet and film writer Paul Wiens. "On their soap commercials the husband or son says, 'My shirt itches.' The mother says, 'I washed it but maybe I should have used such and such a soap.' In our commercials you see a man standing at a washing maching with the very best soap and putting it in to do the laundry."

Für Dich, which goes into every fourth home and is read not only by women but many men (one-third of the letters to the editor come from men), helps overcome old ideas about "women's work" by featuring stories on men who participate in household tasks. "For example, in the shopping centers we see many husbands—with their children—doing the shopping," said Liselotte Thoms-Heinrich. "By praising men who play a good role we advance the understanding of others." Although "we prefer to acknowledge rather than criticize," *Für Dich* will sometimes encourage criticism.

"We got a letter from a woman whose husband did nothing in the home. We published it without her name—and we got a huge number of letters. Fifty percent of them were from men. First these men swore at the husband who did nothing. Next they described how they organized housework and solved problems. They gave this woman advice on how she could get her husband to begin to help. We published these letters over a period of weeks to stimulate discussion. Then we brought the letters to this woman and her husband. He couldn't believe they were real. But at least he started to think."

IN ADVANCING women's equality there's an important link between the workplace and the home.

"With women qualified for more and more responsible jobs, there must be a new way of thinking about women," said Hannelore Lehrmann, director of economics at VEB NARVA, a lighting equipment plant with 10,000 workers. "At the plant we continue to reappraise our thinking—and there must also be a change of thinking in the family. Higher responsibilities for women not only mean more money for them. It's the question of implementing equality at all levels, in all aspects of our life.

"At home there was no difficulty in the process of rethinking when I took over an executive position," said Lehrmann, who has five departments under her direction, and has been a member of parliament for almost a decade. "I have two sons, fifteen and eleven, and all three men in our home must do more work. There's a certain strain if I'm away for a week, but no conflicts. It's very hard for a woman to carry out her responsibilities if the waves go high at home. . ."

Since women's equality is more advanced in the workplace, its influence may be used directly to advance equality in the home.

"It's easier for women to have equal rights on the job because there's the Party and the trade union. But it's more difficult at home because women don't have the Party and the trade union there," said Dieter Neumann, a trade union leader at the Berlin Housing Construction Combinate. "If problems arise in a family when a wife is trying to qualify, we see it as our responsibility to go with our cadre instructor and talk to the husband—so that he'll support what his wife is doing, instead of coming home, demanding supper and sitting in an armchair. But," he admitted, "sometimes I'm also an egoist at home."

"Husbands forty and fifty years old and older are lazybones," exclaimed Cadre Instructor Alexandra Martin. "And wives will do everything for these husbands without complaining. But my twenty-seven-year-old daughter won't give her husband supper if he doesn't shop. Once he came home without potatoes. The store was too crowded. 'Will it be any less crowded,' she asked, 'if I shop there?' They went to a restaurant."

Commenting on a man's role in bringing about biarchal relations, FGY leader Heinz Schuldt said, "I think I have a good attitude toward women's equality. My father? Not so good. But not entirely bad. Once he thought it beneath the dignity of a man to peel potatoes and dust. Now he does it. As for me, if I have a good attitude, I have to try to live accordingly. My wife and I have a plan at home, who does what job— cooking, cleaning and taking care of our son."

The dynamics of a wife's advancement in her profession also speed equality in the home. "My wife is a dentist who must continue her studies for five years so she can specialize," said Joachim Brueckner, a member of the FGY's International Department. "My main task is to help her complete her studies. We have a three-and-a-half-month-old son, this means additional problems. In six months he'll have a place in a nursery. If he gets sick, we've decided I'll stay home. My wife and I must help each other very much." He paused, then added, "I'm not trying to show my personal development or achievements." What he did show is that the GDR laws obligating husband and wife to assist each other are taking effect because of people's growing consciousness.

A similar development could be seen in what Wolfgang Reuter, of the FGY's Department of Culture, told us. When his wife went to the Soviet Union to study for six months, "I had to do everything— laundry, cooking, shopping. I lived fifty kilometers from my job and it was very difficult."

But he wasn't without help. In each GDR residential development there's a house committee. "They were wonderful—they picked up my daughter at kindergarten and took her home and put her to bed. Otherwise I would have had to go home ten times a day. During this time I changed many of my attitudes. Now I understand how difficult these things are, and I do much more at home. But I'm thirty-three and I'm of the opinion that the younger generation is already better than mine—they've absorbed the idea of equality from infancy."

WE MET MEMBERS of this younger generation during a rehearsal at the Cable Workers Theater. The cast was workers and students, but the director and *Dramaturg* were professionals from the Deutsches Theater. They interrupted their rehearsal of *Valentin and Valentina,* a Soviet play about the problems of a young couple in love, to discuss the real-life relations of women and men.

"I think it's right for a woman to have any profession according to her abilities," said Birgit Letze, seventeen, an apprentice in construction drawing. "But she has the same profession as a man and she does the housework too. Many men are not yet developed in this respect."

"The men say it's okay if you work. But as to housework, they sometimes carry out the garbage can and dry dishes on their days off," declared Sigrid Hoelzke, twenty, who does technical work for a magazine.

There were the sounds of sharp disagreement.

"I think that's nonsense," exclaimed Fred Zeige, twenty-one, a specialized worker in equipment machinery. "I live with my girl friend. I clean the kitchen. We do everything together. I see the same thing happening in her family. Her father does the cooking all the time. I'm sure other people do the same. On the streets you see men with shopping bags. I think you're very pessimistic."

"I also think you're very pessimistic," said Ellen Pultke, twenty, a skilled equipment worker at the cable plant. "If you teach the man or boy properly, if you take arrangements into your own hands—without nagging him—then he'll understand and share in the work through his own agreement."

"I wasn't thinking of the youngest," conceded Birgit Letze. "They may have changed. My father—men of his age—they're not that developed. Of course, my father is exceptional. He helps. There are four children in our family and we couldn't get along if he didn't."

"Men who don't help at home—it still does exist to a degree, but not as much," decided Sigrid Hoelzke. "It also depends on how parents educate a boy. If he's not taught from the beginning to do housework, he'll expect things to be the same with his girl friend or wife."

"With the youngest it's already different," said Fred Zeige. "Even in the movies and on TV you see more and more husbands helping. Both husbands and wives have more free time if they help each other."

"I think the development is good, but there are contradictions between present conditions and tradition," said Ingeborg Rovó, a young woman from the Deutsches' public relations department, a branch of dramaturgy. "There are problems arising from the just demands of women for full equality. A woman who's married may insist on studying, and there can be difficulties. She'll demand equal time to spend on her profession. It's a problem till both sexes harmonize. It's a question of development."

"I think it is too," said Deutsches' director Manfred Schwiering, who is in his thirties. "This question of equality is at the forefront of our social system. But it's a long process—and many women are demanding that it go faster. But there is a problem with the man—who must get used to the new situation in his own family. Still," he added, "I know many women a little older than me who are very satisfied. And even young ones."

"That's not right!" exclaimed Fred Zeige.

"It's not enough to be satisfied with for a lifetime," said Ellen Pultke.

That night at the Cable Workers Theater we saw one more example of the process of biarchy, which has entered every area of socialist life and is on its very difficult but sure way to center stage. Through relationships in a biarchal family, inequalities in the home are overcome—giving a great new impulse to women's equal participation in every area, on every level of public life.

And in this great development art plays its own special role.

"IT'S QUITE natural that in a socialist society what Engels calls the reintroduction of women into public industries takes place. He was speaking not only of the plants, but of a process that takes place in many ways, with many reflections," stated Dr. Ursula Püschel, editor of *Theater in The German Democratic Republic.* "Although this process is directed by socialist law, this alone can't do away with centuries of patriarchy—especially in the emotional sphere, where survivals will persist for a long time. Engels said that in patriarchy both men and women lose something." Helping to redefine women's new role and to overcome these patriarchal survivals is an important role of socialist art.

An early work with a revolutionary attitude to women is *The Mother* (Brecht's play is based upon Gorky's novel of the same name). "This deals with the relationship between mother and son—and in a way that can also be applied to other relationships between men and women," continued Püschel. "Brecht said they lost themselves as mothers and sons always lose themselves, but found each other again in a common undertaking—mother and son found each other in work for a better world. This touches upon Engels's statement on the reintroduction of women into public life. There were a number of plays in the GDR after we took the socialist way that treated the new role of women." This new attention to women was, in fact, initiated right after the war.

"Our film company, DEFA, has a long tradition of showing women's development," related Gabrielle Mylius, a national leader of the Cultural Workers Union. "The first DEFA film, *The Murderers Are Among Us,* was about a woman's fate. This was only natural because so many men did not return."

GDR television from its earliest days has also dealt with women's new role. "The very first play for TV, in 1960, was *The Decision of Lena Mattke,*" pointed out theater critic Rainer Kerndl. "This was about a woman in a small village, where it was even more difficult for women to realize themselves as personalities than in the city. Lena Mattke was shown as a woman who had the courage to break out of her marriage and the village."

In the late sixties "one of the most impressive plays on the new role of women was done on television," related Ursula Püschel. This play, *Ways Across The Country,* was performed in several parts with Ursula Karusseit of the Volksbühne Theater in the leading role.

"The fact that there are so many women in responsible positions— *Ways Across The Country* is one of the plays that helped bring this about by showing women in responsible roles," pointed out Karusseit.

Ways Across The Country, which begins in 1938, deals with "the fate of a servant who lives in a hut with her mother on a rich peasant's farm. She has an affair with the son of the house, hoping to marry him and get out of her misery. She doesn't succeed. She's pregnant but he doesn't want her or her baby and tells her to get rid of it," related Karusseit. The play traces this woman's life through the war—her experiences with the Nazis, her relationships with men, with her adopted children—to liberation and the bitter struggle to collectivize the farms. It ends in 1953 with the former servant now the head of a cooperative farm. "She marries a Communist and starts a new life—which he says will not be easy."

After *Ways Across The Country* was shown, "there was a tremendous amount of letters from viewers. So many women had gone through a similar fate—and had taken a similar path—that they really identified themselves with this woman. And people always identify me with *Ways Across The Country*." In fact the following incident, which occurred at an International Women's Day event, could have happened to Ursula Karusseit:

A peasant from a collective farm who had just received a decoration noticed a famous actress and went up to her on the spur of the moment. "We know each other," she said. Actually the two women had met for the first time, but the peasant woman had seen the actress play a peasant woman's part in a television film, and this made her think: this woman knows me well, my life, my joys and my sorrows. And I know her. In many ways she must be similar to me, things close to her heart are surely close to mine. And the actress understood the peasant at once, and agreed happily: "Of course, we know each other."[23]

In a socialist country, as this incident implies, women's identification with an actress and her roles is entirely different from this phenomenon in capitalism. Actually, U.S. women now seldom identify with the roles played by actresses—since these roles are neither realistic nor enviable. When identification occurs, it's more likely to be with a fantasy of the actress' off-screen life—indicating how the media induce audiences to descend further and further into illusion. But successful socialist works help audiences gain added insight into their own lives.

At each stage of socialist development, GDR art has treated the new conflicts confronting women. For instance, the TV play *One Day in The Life of Regina B.,* produced in the late sixties, dealt with a woman's conflicts when presented with new opportunities. "This woman works in a plant. She isn't married but has a child and three boy friends," described Rainer Kerndl. "She's a wonderful woman, not idealized—she's real, healthy and a little vulgar. She has the strength of an average woman. She is a good worker and is offered the opportunity to be an engineer. She has the ability to do it. But she thinks it over for a whole day and through an evening—and she understands she cannot do it. The realities of her everyday life are stronger than the possibilities. But the spectators could see that such possibilities were already there for women. It was very honest, very successful—and many people could identify with it."

In the Soviet play *Weather For Tomorrow,* produced by the Gorki, a woman is shown in the kind of role Regina B. was not yet in a position to cope with. "This play takes place in an auto plant, and there's an interesting figure of a woman in it," said Ursula Püschel. "She's not a part of management, she's a brigade leader, and as a brigade leader she really carries out her part in co-determination. What this woman does, what she's for and against, does play a role in decision making."

Another play, *I Met A Girl,* by Rainer Kerndl, shows a very different aspect of a woman worker. "This is about a young girl who works in a plant and who once heard a poet read his poems," related Püschel. "She takes him at his word—she takes everything seriously— and she travels to meet him. They don't know each other but each gives the other something—the poet thinks he should change his way of writing, but she says he shouldn't, what he wrote meant too much." There is a mutuality of exchange between the two characters because, instead of a life of fantasy, the young woman leads an independent existence, and has a very real concern about advancing in her work.

In socialist art women as well as men may play heroic roles. "In 1971 my husband and I wrote a film called *The Red Orchestra,* about an underground anti-fascist group of intellectuals," said Wera Küchenmeister. "We tried to show how important it is in the struggle for men and women to work together, to act together."

"We showed the wife as the active co-fighter in life, not as a passive companion," pointed out Claus Küchenmeister.

"These were couples like the Rosenbergs—and many of these great couples also had to sacrifice their lives as couples," continued Wera Küchenmeister. "The most important and tragic of these couples were Hans and Hilda Coppi. She had their child in prison, where she was persecuted to death—as was her husband. Their child, who was also called Hans, never saw his parents. Today he's a young specialist in the GDR." She added: "Claus's father was also a fighter in the Red

Orchestra, and he too was executed. So this was a great and important work for us personally." The film was very popular with GDR audiences.

On the other hand socialist art may portray women with no obviously heroic characteristics. "The new film I'm making also has to do with agriculture, but the theme is different from *Ways Across The Country,*" said Ursula Karusseit. "I like it, but my role has to do with anything but emancipation. This woman stays with her husband in spite of his weaknesses. There are such women. I wouldn't like it if only emancipated women were shown."

In the earlier period works such as *Ways Across The Country* dealt with women's struggles to overcome great obstacles and play their new role. Now that they are playing this new role, attention has been turned to the new conflicts—including those around patriarchal survivals in the "emotional sphere." A film that deals in a most unusual way with a conflict of this type is *The Third.*

EVEN THOSE who admit [to other wrongs] will possibly join issue with us when we suggest as another wrong to women the rigorous social rule that from man only must come the first proffer of affection, the proposal of marriage.[24]

So wrote Eleanor Marx, daugher of Karl, and her husband Edward Aveling in "The Woman Question," published in the latter part of the nineteenth century.

And today, as in the nineteenth century, many supporters of women's equality would stop short of advocating woman's equal right with man to take the initiative in a relationship. Many of these individuals could be expected to laugh this aside as unimportant, thus helping to preserve the sanctity of freedom for men only in the emotional sphere. It is impossible to imagine this as a subject for a U.S. film, except as a farce. And yet it is a serious problem: The loneliness women face to a vastly greater degree than men is related to the restrictions imposed upon them. *The Third* deals seriously with these ancient restrictions, bringing into consideration on a mass scale a problem that plagues us in capitalism, but which we can hardly begin to approach except as individuals.

"The issue is sex equality in a sphere that has hardly ever with such frankness been brought into public discussion by a work of art," wrote one GDR critic. The equality provided by law for GDR women is, he said, "obstructed by centuries-old traditions and obsolete moral norms." *The Third* is a "film on the subject of love in our life, a film on how we should live in this time of ours."

Margit Fliesser, the film's central character, is in her thirties. Left alone after her mother's death in the post-war period, she completes her education and advances to a leading post in mathematics. She has been involved seriously with two men and less seriously with others. Now she wants "the third"—but is confronted with the problem of how to get him.

"My work is with computers. I'm involved in the scientific and technological revolution in socialism, but when I want a man I can't tell him," she says. "We fold our hands and wait and behave as we did in our grandmother's day. We have won all the rights except the right to tell a man we love him." She becomes ashamed of herself for exerting "feminine wiles," and finally tells this to "the third" man—whose reaction is in question till the end of the film.

"In *The Third*," said Barbara Dittus of the Berliner Ensemble who played one of the leads, "we tried to show the new problems in women's emancipation." Since socialism has "already solved" the economic and legal pre-conditions for women's equality, "this film could start at a higher level.

"With the new possibilities in socialism for women," she continued, "there are also the new problems of living together with men. Men haven't developed as quickly—I'm speaking now of people's consciousness. Even in socialism it's very difficult for many men to accept women's new development—at work it's easier, but at home there can be big difficulties. There are many aspects to this. To have a partnership in the home, the right of the woman to decide with the man on all questions, not just the man—this is very difficult.

"Many men think women become masculine by emancipation. It's hard for them to understand a woman's being independent because they've always been told they're the stronger sex. For a woman to have the right to find a man for herself—this is quite a normal development. It's very difficult for many emancipated women who are alone when they don't want to be. They need men—but they don't want a man in bed if his brain is not advanced as theirs."

In *The Third* "we wanted to show this woman faced with the problem of living alone. The question is not really that she took the initiative, but that she wants someone and how to get him. The other woman, Lucy"—the part Dittus played— "had the same kind of problem, but she is much more decisive. She is shown as a sex object for men," but when difficulties arise with the man she lives with, "she sends him away. Lucy represents the younger generation. We wanted to show that many people are afraid to decide such questions because of the fear of being alone."

In the opinion of another GDR film critic, the importance of *The Third* lies in "its analysis of the self-understanding obtained by people who live under a socialist system." This "self-understanding" was evident in Elke Bitterhof's reaction to *The Third*.

"There is real economic and legal emancipation for women," she said. "But women have been educated in a certain way for thousands of years. And Margit Fliesser—who is really emancipated—applies all the tricks her grandmother used. This is for the moment the difference we still have. We, the emancipated unmarried women, must get things straight with ourselves in order to get along with our partners. When Margit talks to 'the third,' she says that women have all the possibilities—but our feelings can't be changed so rapidly. I know many things theoretically, all my friends are helping me, but I myself must make the transition from understanding to acting accordingly." At the same time, however, one must remember that Margit Fliesser is hesitant to act because of apprehension about the reaction of "the third" man.

"Both men and women have to emancipate themselves," said Barbara Dittus. "It was mainly women who had to fight in the early years. Now there's the question of the next step. Men must take this next big step."

Confidence in men's ability to take big steps is based on the many changes in men that have already taken place.

"Emancipation is a process you have to pay for with many kinds of money—you have to pay by finding new attitudes and in many other ways," commented Dr. Püschel. "If I remember how the streets looked twenty years ago when we never saw a man pushing a baby carriage, and when I see what my son and son-in-law do in their homes today—these are real changes. But many things must still change emotionally."

And Mayor Brunhilde Hanke said: "We've created the legal conditions for women's equality and we must keep improving services. But you can't decree that on such and such a day you're an equal partnership. We can do a lot, but this partnership on the basis of equal rights must be developed by a process. And the most important thing is the ideological possibilities in socialism and women themselves—and the completely new relationship between men and women."

And director Ruth Berghaus said: "The social basis is what really counts. It depends on men and women, what they do with these preconditions. If society doesn't change, then men won't change. I can only say that men have changed. I see great changes, especially with the young men here."

□ □ □

"I THOUGHT of that old gentleman, who is dead now, but was a bishop, I think, who declared that it was impossible for any woman past, present, or to come, to have the genius of Shakespeare," wrote Virginia Woolf in *A Room of One's Own*.[25]

The bishop, she decided, "was right at least in this; it would have been impossible, completely and entirely, for any woman to have written the plays of Shakespeare in the age of Shakespeare."[26] She went on to imagine "what would have happened had Shakespeare had a wonderfully gifted sister, called, Judith, let us say." Judith was as "adventurous, as imaginative, as agog to see the world" as her brother. But unlike her brother, Judith "was not sent to school. She had no chance of learning grammar and logic, let alone of reading Horace and Virgil. She picked up a book now and then, one of her brother's perhaps, and read a few pages. But then her parents came in and told her to mend the stockings or mind the stew and not moon about with books and papers."[27] Shakespeare left for London where he "lived at the hub of the universe." Judith also had "a taste for the theater." She ran away to London and stood at the stage door, where "Men laughed in her face." Then an "actor-manager took pity on her; she found herself with child by the gentleman" and "killed herself one winter night and lies buried at some crossroads where the omnibuses now stop."[28]

Suddenly Virginia Woolf's power of sympathetic evocation is cut short by the class lines crisscrossing her mind: "It is unthinkable," she goes on to say, "that any woman in Shakespeare's day should have had Shakespeare's genius. For a genius like Shakespeare's is not born among laboring, uneducated"[29] people.

Yet, strangely, Virginia Woolf has suggested something quite different from what she seems to say—and this contradiction becomes more apparent in her next lines: Genius, she wrote, "is not born today among the working classes. How, then, could it have been born among women whose work began . . . almost before they were out of the nursery, who were forced to it by their parents and held to it by the power of law and custom?"[30]

What these lines imply, of course, is that genius may be born anywhere, but liberated only under certain circumstances. And this implication comes close to an assertion in Woolf's next statement: "Yet genius of a sort must have existed among women as it must have existed among the working classes. Now and again an Emily Brontë or a Robert Burns blazes out and proves its presence."[31]

From this parallel between the status of women and the working class, it is easy to draw a conclusion Virginia Woolf herself never entertained: The fate of women is indentified with the working class, since in capitalism the creativity of both is stifled by "the power of law and custom." If Shakespeare were born in the U.S. today as the daughter or son of ordinary people, as a child of workers or of an oppressed minority, she or he would have enormous barriers to overcome to realize her or his genius.

But in a society where the working class holds power, the "power of law" and of *socialist* custom is behind women as they progress toward full realization of their creativity, of equality in every way. (One gauge of how far women in socialism have come: Among the GDR representatives at the World Congress for International Women's Year, held in Berlin, 1975, were many women of the generation brought up to believe a woman's place is "children, church and kitchen.")

Even Hilda Scott is forced to make basic admissions about women's massive advances in socialism. "There are impressive facts," she states, "regarding women's legal rights, employment, nurseries and other benefits which still represent a maximum program in other countries."[32] Further, she acknowledges, women in socialist countries "take the right to economic independence, their legal equality, and their social benefits for granted, and expect an equal voice with their husbands in the family and in the household. The husbands accept this too . . . "[33] In addition, these women have shown "that a job is not just something a woman can do before she has children and after the children leave home; that it is possible, with society's assistance, to work and at the same time to bring up children as successfully as women who devote full time to mothering."[34]

Having made these admissions, Scott denies their importance. "All this," she states, "does not add up to full equality for women." What Scott would have us believe is that unless "instant" equality is achieved in every respect after centuries of inequality, the advances aren't worth the effort. Lenin saw it differently when he wrote, "This struggle will be a long one . . . But it will end in the complete triumph of communism."[35]

Those who deny the significance of women's advances in socialism are those who urge women in a different direction. When Betty Friedan was invited by her "old friend Hilda Scott" to come to Czechoslovakia to organize a women's movement, Scott knew what kind of a women's movement Friedan was interested in. In her second book Friedan condemns those who believe "the movement's main concerns need to be racism, poverty . . . everything and anything but the problems of white middle-class American women"[36]—whom she designates as "the majority of women in America." Thus, Friedan asserts that those who call for a fight against racism and poverty contradict the aims of "white middle-class American women" who want to advance in the arts and professions. Although Friedan neglects to mention it, women of the working class and oppressed minorities also have these aspirations.

Contrary to Friedan's claim, the majority of U.S. women are part of the multi-racial, multi-national working class—and women in the arts, sciences and professions can advance their own demands only by identifying with the interests of this great majority. (The need for unity of the masses of women becomes particularly clear in the face of sharpening assaults on the women's movement by racist, ultra-right forces. In the past these forces mainly attacked the movement from without—through their anti-abortion crusades, etc. But with their attempts to take over the government-sponsored conferences on women in 1977, they stepped up their disruption from within.)

Because the media seize on views such as those expressed by Friedan, and also because some sections of the women's movement have limited objectives, many regard this movement as of and for white middle-class women. Although Black and Latin women have played the leading role in, for instance, the fight to save child care centers, their contributions go largely unrecognized.

The facts of women's lives reveal just how vital these centers are: One-third of the mothers with pre-school-age children are in the labor force (one-half of those with school-age children are also in the labor force). The child care issue alone is enough to account for media blackout and/or distortion of news on women's conditions in socialist society. When women in capitalist countries learn of these advances, it spurs them in their fight to win such benefits for themselves.

It's easy to see why Friedan's views have received such media attention. The media are devoted to reversing reality. And this is what Friedan does when she alleges that the women's movement in capitalist countries is "threatening to Communists" because it puts "too much emphasis" on a "woman's right to control her own body and her own destiny." How can a woman "control her own body and her own destiny" without such a basic right as the right to abortion?

While free abortion is available throughout the Soviet Union, the GDR and other socialist countries, it is still illegal in many states in this country. And now that the Supreme Court and Congress have decided federal funds may be denied for abortion, the right of a poor woman "to control her own body" has been virtually nullified. (Asked whether he considered the Supreme Court ruling on this matter fair, President Carter replied, "there are many things in life that are not fair, that wealthy people can afford and poor people can't." But, added this well-known advocate of human rights, "I don't believe that the Federal Government should take action to try to make these opportunities exactly equal.")[37]

Further, although most sections of the women's movement have not yet put up a fight against forced sterilization, many poor women—especially of the oppressed minorities—find themselves its victims. In fact, in the U.S. colony of Puerto Rico forced sterilization is in use on a mass scale. Exactly how does this jibe with a "woman's right to control her own body and her own destiny"?

At a time when socialist countries are expanding maternity benefits as part of a virtually free medical system, the Supreme Court ruled to exclude maternity benefits from medical coverage. How can a woman unable to afford a wanted child "control her own body and her own destiny"?

Every move that denies women's special requirements is linked to the moves that deny the special requirements of oppressed minorities to overcome centuries-long inequality. Any step that endangers affirmative social action for women endangers affirmative social action for oppressed minorities, and vice versa.

Further, the Supreme Court rulings against pregnancy benefits and abortion funds tell us how the courts would interpret the Equal Rights Amendment. As this proposed constitutional amendment is presently worded, the courts would not construe it as the basis for equal legal rights. They would instead use it for striking down protective legislation and affirmative action programs for women—interpreting them as "discrimination against men." (This explains why such strange "allies" of the women's movement as the National Association of Manufacturers and the Chamber of Commerce back ERA.) We believe ERA should be passed with a resolution of intent stating that this amendment will not be used to bar affirmative action programs or laws benefiting women.

As IRMTRAUD MORGNER put it, "a woman who wants to enter history—who wants to become a human being—should enter politics and learn who her allies are." In the U.S. her allies are both the working class and the oppressed peoples.

While the media play their "requiem for the women's movement," new forces are emerging. And once in a great while a glimmer of this even gets into the press.

"An avalanche of women is pouring into the workforce," reports one paper. Among them was a young mother of three whose husband had left her. She went out and got a job, saying, "I guess women's lib had something to do with it." And, according to another story, "Once-docile airlines stewardesses, conditioned by the women's movement and frustrated by a glamorless job with a glamorous image, have emerged as a militant labor force." One of these stewardesses, who now call themselves "flight attendants," declared: "The battle is just beginning. We're fighting for money and respect." And on National Secretaries Day—when the boss traditionally takes his secretary to lunch and gives her gifts—secretaries held a protest rally: "Keep your lunch, keep your candy, keep your flowers," cried out a young secretary. "Give us a decent living wage, a job description that eliminates personal errands, the end of discrimination against women." At the Second International Festival of Women's films, women protested that screenplays by women are seldom bought by the film industry. "That's because women's screenplays aren't as good," retorted actor/producer Warren Beatty—whose remarks were met by what was described as "an uproar."

After the Supreme Court issued its ruling against pregnancy benefits, scores of national organizations formed the Coalition to End
Discrimination Against Pregnant Women—with Black, Latin and
white trade union women playing a leading part. And some time
before that a multi-racial, multi-national organization of blue- and
white-collar workers, professionals and artists—Women for Racial
and Economic Equality (WREE)—was formed to fight for jobs for
women, peace and an end to racism. And in the very same month that
"Requiem for The Women's Movement" appeared, union women
together with some union men met and issued an appeal for unity in
the fight for jobs for women, peace and equality. They called their
gathering a Conference for Bread and Roses.

---

13. "Not Life Printed on Dollar Bills"

Official reports told us there were 10,908,000 unemployed in
October 1932, and in the first two months of 1933 the number rose to
12,000,000. There were brutally shameless breadlines in Times Square
and Columbus Circle," recalls Harold Clurman in his book on the
Group Theatre and the thirties.[1]

Paradoxically, this time of nationwide misery was also a time of
great hope for the U.S. people. While the misery was supplied by the
economic system, the hope was awakened by the giant struggles of the
working class, Black and white, for a better life. The fervor aroused by
these struggles spread to the theater. It blazed up the night *Waiting for
Lefty* opened.

The first scene of *Lefty* had not played for two minutes [writes Clurman] when a shock of delighted recognition struck the audience like a tidal wave. Deep laughter, hot assent, a kind of joyous fervor seemed to sweep the audience toward the stage. The actors no longer performed; they were being carried along as if by an exultancy of communication such as I had never witnessed in the theatre before.[2]

When at the end of the play one of the taxi driver characters asked, "Well, what's the answer?" the audience responded with "a spontaneous roar of 'Strike! Strike!'"

It was the birth cry of the thirties . . . "Strike!" was *Lefty*'s lyric message, not alone for a few extra pennies of wages or for shorter hours of work, strike for greater dignity, strike for a bolder humanity, strike for the full stature of man.[3]

The aspirations of millions of young people of the thirties were shared by the Group actors. "When I try to summon a single phrase that might stand as emblem of their desire," Clurman says, "I think of the boy in *Awake and Sing* as he exclaims, 'We don't want life printed on dollar bills.'" Through its own work the Group tried to transform this desire into reality.

Aiming "freely to do" what is really wanted to do, the Group "never produced a play in anticipation of a 'wow,'" never chose scripts as "commercial bait," but instead for "the pertinence of what they have to say," knowing in advance that "some of the scripts chosen are by no means perfect." The Group's goal was to sustain a permanent ensemble, one that would not limit itself to the "customary four-week rehearsal period." In short, the Group actors "felt they had a right to ask for more than just the privilege of appearing in a successful Broadway play."

But the actors' rejection of "life printed on dollar bills" brought them into sharp conflict with the "almost absolute emphasis" (as Clurman puts it) on the "profit motive in relation to the theater." Penalized for its artistic and social goals by a lack of financial support, the Group Theatre was unable to offer its company even subsistence-level pay. Increasingly alarmed about the Group's future, the actors determined to do all they could to insure it.

Labor's great demands for the right to organize, strike, picket and protest spurred demands for democracy in countless areas of U.S. life—including the theater. This mood was voiced, in Clurman's words, by the "impassioned little hackie of *Waiting for Lefty*" who shouts "I gotta right! I gotta right!"

Although decisions during the Group's first years had been made by Clurman and the two other founding directors, the actors came to feel "I gotta right!" to jointly determine with the directors the theater's destiny. This "urge among our people toward greater participation," states Clurman, was "another sign of the times":

I call it a sign of the times even though . . . it was actually a natural outgrowth of the Group's history, aims and tendencies. In cold logic, nothing the directors had said when we got together necessitated giving the actors an official voice in the making of decisions. But reality is subtler than logic, and the ideals implied not only in the directors' talks but in their actual conduct of affairs slowly but surely brought about a conscious demand for an open recognition not only that the actors were an integral part of the organization but that they had every right to function systematically as such.[4]

An actors' committee was formed. At a time when circumstances had become particularly desperate, this committee drafted a "lucid, frank analysis of the Group's quandry," which concluded:

What's to be done?
First we must assure the Group actors a regular, predictable sustaining income. At least one half the Group receive what for them is not even a subsistence wage. Another third live on a debasing wage level . . . Year after year debts pile up. As it is today, the Group's continuance is impossible.
   Second, the basic personal need for all of us . . . is sufficient artistic exercise . . . We believe we must take immediate steps, now, to institutionalize ourselves as a Theatre. Next year, sweeping aside other desiderata, we must have our own theatre. With it, forty weeks of active and full production and performance . . . We have one tattered bond left between us all—a passionate concern for the Group idea.[5]

The Group never realized these aims. The actors and directors were unable "to institutionalize ourselves as a Theatre." Although, as Clurman points out, "there can hardly be any true theatre culture" without repertory theater, the Group could never present more than one or two productions a season, each of them subject to the instant hit or instant death syndrome. While classics are an essential ingredient of a permanent theater, the Group could never stage one; the money could not be raised because the company "lacked a star." Unable to attain its own theater, the Group was forced to rent Broadway houses. And it never came anywhere near providing its actors a "regular, predictable sustaining income."

While the Group was unable to solve the most basic economic problems of the theater, its members looked to it to solve problems that a theater, by itself, can only visualize. "The complete, the universal, the strong individual balanced by a feeling for the social unit," states Clurman, represented "Group ideals." But since capitalist society conceives of a "strong individual" as one who takes what he wants and to hell with the "social unit," Group members came to feel their ideals could be realized only in a "society within a society." The Group itself "had to become a protected unit, a utopia, an oasis within the city, in which one could work out one's life, career and salvation."[6] But this dream, like all utopian dreams, was painfully shattered by reality.

"Bitter disappointment, even hate, developed with the Group when the Group failed to furnish such a center."[7] These reactions intensified when certain Group members chose to work out their "life, career and salvation" by accepting Hollywood offers (some who condemned the early departures later took the same route.). But while various "personal failings of the directorate or individual actors were often held to be of paramount significance,"[8] these were not, Clurman stresses, the source of the Group's troubles.

The fundamental economic instability from which the Group suffered, its piecemeal, bread-line existence, accounts for its hectic inner life and explains more about its real deficiencies than any analysis of the personal traits of its individual members. There was hardly a single personal problem within the Group that could not easily have been absorbed in the normal functioning of the organization if it could have seen its path clear to the preparation of four or five productions a season undisturbed by acute economic worry . . .[9]

The legendary Group Theatre, after a decade of "acute economic worry," was forced to dissolve. The organizations that wanted it to continue were unable to give it consistent financial support. The U.S. government never gave it any subsidy whatsoever.

ALTHOUGH THE GDR has a population of only 17 million on a very small territory, this socialist nation subsidizes fifty-six year-round repertory theaters. In place of the lifetime of "acute economic worry" faced by actors in capitalism, this state provides its actors with lifetime contracts. Theaters in this socialist country have been freed from the necessity of producing plays as "commercial bait" or "in anticipation of a 'wow'"; instead plays are staged for "the pertinence of what they have to say." The old conflict between art and commerce has been ended altogether; artists are paid to produce their very best. No longer need actors renounce the theater to take advantage of TV and film offers. They can now be attached to a theater ensemble while also doing work in the other media. More significant, all media have social and artistic importance. And since personal problems and conflicts in GDR theater are not exacerbated by "fundamental economic instability," they can be "absorbed in the normal functioning of the organization."

When Group actors came to believe that their ideal of a "strong individual balanced by a feeling for the social unit" could be attained only in a "society within a society," they were just one step away from the belief that it cannot be attained at all. Yet socialist society as a whole is producing such individuals. And this has its own particular reflections in the theater.

"There's something in collectivity. One isn't lost in a crowd— instead personalities develop," declared Ursula Karusseit. "An actor can be good even if others aren't. But it's no fun. I'm against the star system," said Karusseit, who is one of the GDR's most prominent actresses. "Every actor is happy to be well known but not to the extreme where everything turns around him. We do a lot to discourage star thinking."

In capitalism artists must fight bitterly for the means to produce quality theater. In socialism this fight has been won: The means for producing theater of the finest quality are in the hands of theater people. This victory creates new obligations.

"The enormous possibilities that socialism puts at the disposal of artists must be used with a great sense of responsibility," commented theater critic Rainer Kerndl. "In our society masses of the most different kinds of people really feel a great need for art. They ask something of a theater. Theater artists must deal with the most varied ideas as an expression of the demands of a socialist society."

In capitalism actors seldom have the opportunity to be motivated by artistic commitment. "When I was in New York I saw musicals that had been running for two or three years," said Gisela May of the Berliner Ensemble. "I would see a matinee performance and I'd know the same actors would have to play the same parts again in the evening. They could not play with their full strength. Yet they played. They are driven to do it."

But in a socialist theater, "No one drives us. We can only drive ourselves," stated Ursula Karusseit.

Bourgeois ideologists, trying to provide a "moral" justification for the goading that comes from financial insecurity, warn that the security offered by socialism makes people lazy. "We have security in the theater, our plants are wonderful—but to sit down and become lazy, that's death to artistic work," declared Karusseit.

"There's a moral side to the permanent contracts under the Labor Code," said Ruth Berghaus of the Deutsche State Opera. "They don't make people lazy. Everybody wants to work."

"We produce as many plays as possible," said Gisela May. "Not to earn more money, our salaries are fixed—but because it's important for actors to produce and audiences want to see as many plays as possible. These interests correspond."

The permanent contracts have, however, produced real problems and how to solve them is a subject of much debate among theater people.

"One big problem is that the ensembles aren't flexible enough from an artistic point of view," pointed out actor Alfred Müller. "At the moment we're busy finding solutions to this problem. We must keep the social security of the artists while improving the effectiveness of our art."

Another problem that has developed with the permanent contracts is the rising age level of ensembles. But because society collaborates with the theaters to overcome difficulties, solutions are beginning to be found. "Artists of great merit who can't play the parts they did in the past now get honorary pensions so they can continue to work in the theater," said Ruth Berghaus.

Additional funds are provided by the state to pay these older actors so the theaters can employ more young actors. "This is a high moral achievement. Our older colleagues would be very regretful if at the age of sixty or sixty-five they couldn't go on playing. If you stopped careers because of age, you'd kill the old actors by taking away the meaning of their lives. On principle," Berghaus emphasized, "we must raise our artistic level. But not at the expense of people. This is a struggle we have to carry on every day."

THE GROUP actors longed for a permanent ensemble that would not be restricted by the "customary four-week rehearsal period." Socialist theater provides whatever time is needed for production. "What we are able to do I realized only when I saw how they work in the FRG," said Deutsches *Dramaturgin* Ilse Galfert, who described an experience she and a GDR director had as guest artists in a Munich theater.

"In the Munich theater a list of actors is put up and the director is told he must use them. Then the text is distributed and the director tells the cast his general idea. But when our director was there, he would spend two hours of a morning discussing the play with the cast. He also read poems the playwright wrote so the cast could get a feel of them." The director brought material with him—newspapers, photographs—from the period when the play takes place "so the set designer could see the whole picture in front of him. The FRG actors who usually go hungry artistically almost cried when they saw that diet."

Wolfgang Pintzka of the Berliner Ensemble also had a chance to compare the differences between theater in the East and West when he directed a play in a Scandinavian country. "The pressure there is terrific. Not even one single extra day on a production is possible. That's terrible. The possibilities we have here—it's something great we've created in the GDR."

By ending the crushing economic pressures that prevail in exploitative societies, socialism lays the basis for new human relationships in all areas of life. "Here there are the beginnings of a real socialist attitude toward the human beings of this world," said Pintzka. Despite difficulties, he applied this attitude in the Western theater.

"The manager of the theater told me that one very good actor was not so good for the role he was in. He said, 'Take him out, take another actor.' I said no, it will be a psychological and physical blow to him if we do that. I organized special rehearsals with this actor. It was my personal time. But he became wonderful."

The fact that socialist society makes it possible for theater workers to use time at their own discretion is a compelling reason why time must not be abused. "All the people in our Republic are called upon to achieve high quality and economize," said Ruth Berghaus. "Each theater has its plan and work must be carried on in a rational way to fulfill it. We set the time for each production in advance. We don't throw money around like a dead animal." But economy, by contrast with the U.S., is not achieved by speeding up actors. "The entire production plan must be approved by the trade union. No one can set a rehearsal schedule without the union's approval."

The great desire of the Group Theatre actors for "sufficient artistic exercise" has become a reality for actors in most GDR ensembles.

They work virtually all the time. But in some of the biggest theaters solving one problem has created another.

It's a real achievement to maintain ensembles large enough so that a variety of plays can be cast from within a permanent company. But keeping a maximum number of artists active in these large ensembles calls for great resourcefulness. "At the Volkstheater Rostock they use seven or eight facilities, including small chamber theaters. The actors there are constantly engaged," pointed out critic Ernst Schumacher. "And when the Volksbühne did *Spektakel 1* and *Spektakel 2* in the style of the Italian theater, they used twelve stages every night. The most important thing was not that they had twelve performances every evening but that all the members of the ensemble had the feeling there was a great need for them."

WITH THE old problems of the theater solved, new problems have appeared in GDR theater in other ways as well. For example, capitalism's speed-up rehearsals have been ended. Now, some theater people feel, in certain instances too much time is spent on rehearsals.

"These non-antagonistic conflicts are real problems for us. One must have strong self-discipline," commented Rainer Kerndl. "If rehearsals go on for months and months, some actors just don't work. This doesn't improve artistic quality. If a writer doesn't write for two years, later he may do something that bears the fruit of his thinking. This isn't so with actors. They must keep working."

Kerndl also questions whether a very lengthy production period improves the quality of the play in rehearsal. "Some people explain the long rehearsal periods of certain directors by saying it's a matter of high quality. I wonder whether quality always corresponds with long rehearsals."

Ursula Karusseit, for one, doesn't think so. "If a director extends his rehearsal time beyond measure, he can say the play is difficult—but I think he hasn't prepared himself. If a director goes too slowly, you can feel the people on stage getting bored."

To justify long rehearsal periods, it is sometimes said this was Brecht's method. "But this is not correct," stated Wolfgang Pintzka. The famous production of *Mother Courage,* for example, "took only two months." Although Brecht rehearsed *The Caucasian Chalk Circle* over a period of nine months, "this was because of interruptions due to illness. It's not true that Brecht produced his great classics in long rehearsals. It was after Brecht's death that rehearsals took so long."

At the Berliner Ensemble the relationship of quantity to quality in production must be worked out against a very special background. "In the period after Brecht's death," related Pintzka, "there were productions of *Coriolanus, Days of the Commune, Arturo Ui.*" Although each production was outstanding, there were so few that "the results were negative for most of the actors. The actors with the main roles played permanently, but two-thirds of the company were almost paralyzed.

"If you spend a tremendous amount of time on *Arturo Ui, Coriolanus* and *Days of the Commune,* all the new plays have to be ignored. You move away from reality. This was the time when the Berliner Ensemble was called a museum, a glass house, a pantheon. Between 1963 and 1969 there was only one premiere a year. Then the goal became three premieres a year. Not everyone could come down from the sky, but we wanted to do new productions and give opportunities to three times as many actors, scene designers and directors."

The Berliner Ensemble has increased its annual number of premieres, "and we must continue to go this way. Both society and opinion within our theater demand this. This is our art—to balance time and quality."

Since the question of quality applies not only to production but in the first place to plays, some may ask: Why produce a new play of lesser quality when the same time could be spent in staging a Brechtian masterpiece? "New plays must be produced for discussion," declared Pintzka. "In the past the question of quality was used to get rid of plays. They'd say a play wasn't good enough, and the author would be asked to work on it to the point where the problem it dealt with was no longer current."

As Pintzka's remarks indicate, theater can be vital only if it is connected with the present. The Group Theatre felt the need to stage plays for "the pertinence of what they have to say," knowing "beforehand that some of the scripts chosen are by no means perfect." And every theater aiming for contemporary influence must make the same choice—a choice that also speeds the arrival of plays of higher quality by giving playwrights a chance to grow through production.

In a meeting on production plans up to 1980, Pintzka related, "The actors said, 'We must do more plays about our present time. It's very important for us to deal with contemporary conditions.'" This was Brecht's own outlook. "The actors decided, one play by Brecht, one on current times."

As RAINER KERNDL stressed, "non-antagonistic conflicts are real problems for us." But it would be difficult for Western actors to view one of these conflicts as a problem—a conflict that has reversed the biggest problem faced by actors in capitalist societies: "If we do nothing to change the situation, we'll have a shortage of actors by 1985," pointed out Ernst Schumacher. "We won't be able to satisfy the needs of the theater and the mass media." This situation is the result of complex contradictions.

On one hand socialism has produced masses of people who, as Kerndl put it, "really feel a great need for art." On the other hand this feeling for art doesn't necessarily lead to a desire to become a professional artist: Work in all areas is esteemed in socialism, and there are multiple avenues for fulfilling creative aspirations. In a socialist society young people learn that the arts play a special role in life, and to be an artist one must be seriously interested in carrying out this role. This means that the ranks of aspiring actors are not swelled, as they are in the West, by those who desperately view this profession as a passport for escape from obscurity into recognition—which arrives for so few.

A society that ended unemployment for actors can certainly find ways to increase the number of actors. In fact, steps have already been taken to solve this problem, and one result is a greater number of applicants for drama school. "In a socialist society cultural as well as scientific and technological processes need planning," noted Schumacher.

WHEN THE Group Theatre actors called for "an open recognition not only that the actors were an integral part of the organization but that they had every right to function systematically as such," they had probably never heard of "co-determination." Yet this is what they were demanding.

As early as 1920 the German workers' movement had put forth a demand for co-determination. But genuine co-determination—the participation of workers with management in decision making—can be realized only under socialism. As the Gorki Theater's *Chefdramaturg* Fritz Rödel put it, "The question is: How big a part should workers play in management decisions? This question plays a big role in our literature because it plays a big role in our lives."

Socialist society's answer to this question is that workers must play a bigger and bigger part in decision making. And this holds true for the theater as well as industry.

"It was about fifteen years ago that some theaters started to form artistic/economic councils," related Rainer Kerndl. "No one said they should. It happened because of the need to overcome the structure of the past—where orders went from the *Intendant* to the administration to the cast.

"The theater members felt a desire for more democracy, for more responsibility in play selection, quality of production and on a number of technical and economic questions. This council exists in all theaters and shares in determining how the theater will develop on big and small matters."

The members of the artistic/economic council are elected by the ensemble. The *Intendant,* however, is appointed by the state. The question may arise: Doesn't democracy, as a matter of principle, require that the *Intendant* also be elected by the ensemble?

"The question of democracy is not decided by whether an *Intendant* is elected or not. Every *Intendant* in the theater and every manager in a plant is bound to act according to the laws and philosophy of the working class, and to develop opportunities for democracy and co-determination at the work place," replied Eva Henniger, a member of the national executive of the Cultural Workers Union.

What is involved in leadership in a socialist society is the matter of democratic centralism. The centralism aspect is expressed in the appointment of the *Intendant.* "Here," noted Wolfgang Pintzka, "the leading role of the working class comes in. The *Intendanten* in the theaters and the managers in the plants are chosen by the whole state."

At the same time the democratic aspect is expressed in the ensemble's control over the appointment. While the *Intendant* is appointed by a state body—for instance, a city council—the appointment will be made only with the agreement of the ensemble. Further, the *Intendant* appointed to head a particular theater more and more frequently comes from that theater itself.

The underlying question, as Eva Henninger's remarks suggest, is: What kind of *Intendant* is required in a socialist theater? Not, in the first place, the kind required in a bourgeois theater.

"You can be sure I'd never be appointed as head of a theater in the FRG. My background would exclude that," said Ilse Rodenberg, who was an actress in the old German state. She became active in the revolutionary theater movement, and was a political prisoner during the Nazi era. After the founding of the GDR, she became first head of the Friendship Theater for children in Berlin, and is now vice-president of the International Association of Children's Theaters. "If I ever tried to put on a play here glorifying war or racism," she declared, "I'd quickly be recalled. There would be a revolt from the ensemble!"

By contrast, "If one or two left plays are produced in an FRG theater," noted Rainer Kerndl, "all of a sudden the leading people are chucked out and the municipal council has no more money for the theater."

The same contrast between socialist and bourgeois theaters applies to inner-theater matters. At the Scandinavian theater where Wolfgang Pintzka was a guest director, "The manager is an absolute administrator. He doesn't give a damn what the actors or technicians think. He can't act any differently because he depends on money from a bourgeois state.

"I think it's easier for us than for the Scandinavian boss, but sometimes it's also more complicated. Here the workers have the right to say what they think. We have contradictions between the people's opinions and the demands we must make as the leadership."

In the early days of GDR theater, there was a contradiction within the personalities of some *Intendanten* and directors whose social outlook was revolutionary but whose professional experience had come from the bourgeois theater. As a result, said Pintzka, "They would dictate, 'It's going to be done like this.' Those methods are no longer possible."

Today a theater can develop successfully only through the collaboration of leadership and ensemble. "It's the responsibility of the theater to develop democracy to such a degree that the initiative and suggestions of every member of the group are involved in the *Intendant*'s decisions," said Ruth Berghaus. At the same time democratic centralism includes the concept of individual responsibility. "The *Intendant* alone bears the responsibility for decisions so he can make them (although he can't make a decision against a person without the trade union's agreement). This is a contradiction and it keeps us constantly discussing."

Can this contradiction lead to a situation where the *Intendant* makes a decision against the majority's wishes? It can happen, replied Ilse Rodenberg. "An *Intendant* might make an unpopular decision. Then it's the *Intendant*'s responsibility to try to convince people. My experience is that with the proper arguments you can persuade three-quarters of the collective, but you can't always have complete agreement. In a collective there are people of different views and backgrounds. Sometimes what is most popular doesn't take the highest degree of understanding."

But what happens if the *Intendant* is unable to convince the collective that his or her decision is right? "There can be further discussion—a full meeting of all the theater's trade union members," replied Herbert Bischoff, head of the Cultural Workers Union.

After this reconsideration, the collective may recognize the *Intendant*'s view as correct. On the other hand, "If the *Intendant* sticks to a position that's proved wrong, he can be compelled to change. The union committee may ask for disciplinary action. If his position has major repercussions, he can be recalled. But," Bischoff stressed, "we prefer to correct things through discussion rather than administrative measures. Socialism is young and we try to reduce the area where mistakes occur."

Through the processes of democratic centralism, in other words, the *Intendant* has a right to make a decision, but the theater workers have a corresponding right to participate in and control that decision. However, artistic progress requires not only the existence of rights but an atmosphere in which agreement can be reached in a creative manner.

"There must be a relationship on political, moral and artistic questions between the *Intendant* and the ensemble," said Rainer Kerndl. "After a certain time you can tell whether an *Intendant* can create such an atmosphere." As for decision making itself, "in a socialist society an *Intendant*'s decision is not the lonely decision of King Lear. It's the result of a number of necessities."

And the starting point for decision making is the mutual desire of management and workers to carry out socialist goals in the theater. This feeling of mutuality is growing. "Never before did we have such an open and productive discussion between leadership and ensemble as when we discussed our plan until 1980 and beyond," said Wolfgang Pintzka. It wasn't always so.

"Fifteen or twenty years ago when there was a real struggle in the trade union in this theater, Helene Weigel would say to some idiots, 'What kind of attitude do you have that makes you think you always have to be against something instead of being together for something?' In our society," Pintzka concluded, "I notice such attitudes disappearing more and more."

14. Democracy's New Dimensions

The Group Theatre went out of existence because it could no longer cope with the problems that have been solved in GDR theaters. Now new problems must be solved in GDR theaters. And these problems will be solved because in the first place these theaters will not disappear. The existence of the socialist state guarantees the existence of the theaters.

Many theater problems can be solved within the theaters themselves. But many other problems cannot be overcome by the theater alone. The theater itself could not solve the old problem of unemployment, and the theater itself cannot solve socialism's reversal of this problem. New artistic, social and material questions will be solved in the way the old ones were solved: through the theater artists' collaboration with socialist society.

But such a collaboration is not the path pressed upon these artists by Western sources. The more the attitude of "being against something instead of being together for something" disappears in socialist countries, the more bourgeois ideologists strive to instigate it. And the "something" they urge artists and working people in general in socialist countries to be against is socialism.

Now, however, this advice is likely to be dispensed in more sophisticated forms than in the past, when people in socialist countries were told outright to reject their system. Today they are instructed to "improve" their system. "Real" socialism, they are told, is not what exists but something that can exist only if this, that or the other direction for "improvement" is carried out. Upon examination, all these instructions are found to have one thing in common: If followed, socialism would no longer exist.

At the same time, parallel instructions for "new and improved" socialism are given to those in Western countries who seek an alternative to capitalism. As is to be expected, this advice comes from "radical" as well as openly bourgeois sources.

Among those currently offering such advice is one who gained attention in the sixties as a radical playwright: Barbara Garson, author of the parody *MacBird!* In 1975 one of this country's biggest publishers issued her book, *All The Livelong Day.* In it she writes:

What we need is socialism with workers' control. As long as control over the means of production stays in the hands of owners, managers, or pharaohs, we will be forced to make goods that we don't necessarily need and to work in ways that are debilitating and humiliating.[1]

To state that in the U.S. we are "forced to make goods that we don't necessarily need and to work in ways that are debilitating and humiliating" may sound radical, but to say this is to admit nothing that masses of the people don't already know. What makes this statement perfectly respectable, however, is its unmistakable implication that things are no different in socialist countries because they don't have "socialism with workers' control," as defined by Barbara Garson. If "socialism with workers' control" is what we need, they must need it too (particularly since this is now a widely promoted form of "new and improved" socialism). Such turns out to be the case.

In an article first published in the FRG and later in the U.S. in *New German Critique,* Bernd Rabehl, an FRG writer, asserts that "socialist democracy" is a "catchphrase" in the GDR, while "worker control" is a "catchphrase" of "socialist opposition" in the West. Rabehl warns the GDR against socialist democracy, while urging that country to turn to "worker control":

If the socialist system wants to present its own development as a model for the revolutionary workers' movement in the West, the socialist economy must at least demonstrate initial forms of worker control.[2]

First one must note that no socialist country wants "to present its own development as a model for the revolutionary workers' movement in the West." The revolutionary movement in each country must work out its own course of development based on the principles of scientific socialism. As for the substance of Rabehl's recommendation, one would never know that the Soviet Union and other socialist countries have not only experienced "initial forms of worker control," but long ago passed through a *phase* of workers' control. (Socialist democracy and workers' control may be "catchphrases" to Rabehl, but they have specific meaning to scientific socialists.)

Workers' control, based on a concept first advanced by Lenin in 1905, was put into effect in Russia not long before the October 1917 Revolution. This was a period when the means of production were not yet in the hands of the people, and disruption from the exploiting class included everything from plundering the factories to burning them down. To suppress this resistance from the exploiters, the workers established control over production and distribution in the factories. In this period workers also began to learn to manage the factories. Workers' control, which Lenin regarded as a *transitional* step to socialism, was also in effect in the Eastern part of Germany immediately after World War II. Again it was used to control members of the old exploiting class and to suppress resistance from them.

When the working people become the owners of the means of production, they no longer exert control only in individual plants. Through their state they now have power, which includes many aspects besides control, over the total economy.

"In socialist countries the working class has power. The working class together with the other working people determines the state's role—but the working class is the leading force," stated Dr. Dietrich Gayko of the GDR's Institute of International Politics and Economy.

"The workers in one enterprise are not only the owners of that one plant but of all the others too. So they have the same right to influence the management of other plants as the one they work in. They can do this only through overall political representation."

BARBARA GARSON says, "What we need is socialism with workers' control." (This may sound very "revolutionary," but she doesn't say a word about the need for working people in the U.S. to exert maximum control over the corporate monopolists.) Yet whenever and wherever workers' control has been in effect, its purpose has been to establish control over exploiters.

When Bernd Rabehl identifies workers' control as a demand applicable both to the "socialist opposition in the West" and to the people in the GDR, he is saying that working people in socialist as well as capitalist countries face a class of exploiters (although Rabehl's article is not a warning against what exists in the West but against existing socialism). That this is also what's involved in Barbara Garson's concept of "socialism with workers' control" is made clear when she states:

If factories feel the same in the Soviet Union as in the United States one should not look first at modern technology. One should ask instead whether that too is an exploitative system in which a class of managers is using a class of workers for its own profit . . .[3]

If one claims that conditions under socialism are the same as conditions under capitalism, one creates as much misunderstanding about the situation in this country as in the socialist countries. To suggest that a "class of managers" is responsible for the "exploitative system" in the U.S. is to do a disservice to the struggle here by directing the people's attention away from their real enemy: the corporate monopoly class that owns the means of production and controls the state.

There is no such thing as a "class of managers." In both social systems managers are selected for their posts by the ruling class, and identify their interests with that class. The difference between the two systems arises from the difference between the two ruling classes, that is, the owners of the means of production.

In capitalism the means of production have corporate owners, and it's profitable for corporate owners to force people to work in "ways that are debilitating and humiliating." In socialism the working people own the means of production and it's in their interest to produce what they need under the best possible conditions.

Garson asserts that factories in socialism and capitalism "feel the same" because both are products of "exploitative systems." If a socialist plant did "feel the same" as a capitalist one, then the socialist as well as the capitalist system *would* be exploitative. But *does* it "feel the same" to work in a socialist as a capitalist factory?

Does it "feel the same" to work in a Soviet or GDR plant with a permanent contract, which you yourself may terminate—as it does to come into a U.S. plant in the morning and know you may be fired before the sun goes down? Does it "feel the same" if you fall ill in a socialist plant that has its own free clinic, complete with physicians, dentists, nurses and the latest medical equipment—as it does to fall sick in a U.S. plant with no medical services at all? Does it "feel the same" when you get hungry in a socialist plant that serves a variety of wholesome hot meals at low cost—as it does in a U.S. plant whose main culinary offerings come out of candy bar and Coke machines at high prices? Does it "feel the same" to work in a socialist plant with a house of culture offering theater, film, dancing and art groups, as well as a library—as it does to work in a U.S. plant where the only available "culture" blares out of radios on the lunch break?

In a U.S. plant, management's interest in a worker begins and ends with one thing: How much does that worker produce for corporate profit? In socialist plants, where production is not for profit but for people's needs, it's logical that management would be interested in the workers' needs as well as in production. "We have a term 'labor culture.' It means the conditions under which people work, materially and in a human sense. This is very important because workers are in the plant all day long—they don't consider themselves as part of a machine, but as individuals," said Hannelore Lerhmann, director of economics at the NARVA lighting equipment plant.

The trade unions share the same concern. "Clean air, good lighting, neatness, air conditioning where possible—all this comes under the heading of culture on the job," stated Herbert Bischoff. "The idea is to make people comfortable not only after working hours but on the job. But the aim is not only to make the workplace attractive, but to encourage workers to have good relations, rapport, to take a high level of responsibility, and to behave in an overall humanist way."

According to Barbara Garson, "If factories feel the same in the Soviet Union as in the United States one should not look first at modern technology." But again, if one wants to determine whether factories in socialism and capitalism "feel the same," one must not fail to look at "modern technology." In the U.S. and all capitalist countries, technology is the enemy of workers. Every worker knows that his or her job can be stolen by a machine—leaving the worker "free" to hit the unemployment lines. In socialism, workers welcome technological advance. It lightens work and means higher productivity—not for corporate profit but for higher material standards for all the people.

This in turn means increased leisure for the working people, more time to devote to a fuller and fuller life. It is advances in science and technology that will provide the material basis for the transition from socialism to communism.

BECAUSE WE don't have "socialism with workers' control" in the U.S., Barbara Garson asserts, we are "forced to make goods that we don't necessarily need." The implication of this statement is that the same holds true for workers in socialist countries because they don't have the Garson/Rabehl-type of "socialism with workers' control" either.

In reality if the socialist countries *did* try to operate in this way, they would soon find themselves "forced to make goods" they "don't necessarily need." Why this would happen can be gleaned from these remarks by Bernd Rabehl:

Democratic centralism in the economy can only mean that self-administration of workers in individual plants is governed by the needs of central social planning of production and distribution. Self-administration or worker control would mean that the labor forces of individual cooperating plants make the definitive decisions. Centralism in the economy has to originate in the plants themselves.[4]

One needn't be an economist to realize that it's impossible for "centralism in the economy" to originate from thousands of individual plants. Clearly, Rabehl counterposes his incredible version of "centralism" to democratic centralism because he opposes "central social planning"—and justifies his opposition by implying that "central social planning" contradicts the needs of "workers in individual plants." But is it planning through the process of democratic centralism or "socialism with workers' control" that contradicts the workers' needs?

"Let's look at practical life," replied Günter Simon, an editor of the GDR trade union newspaper *Tribune*. "The petroleum works in Schwedt, for example, was built from the means of society, or the state. Nearby there's a plant that makes children's wear. The petroleum workers could now make huge profits if they were to take advantage of the oil shortage." On the other hand, "the textile workers would produce at a loss. Their production is subsidized—given state financial support—so children's wear can be inexpensive for all parents. But if there were no central regulation, the petroleum workers would abound in wealth, the textile workers would get a bare minimum—and there wouldn't be the necessary children's clothing. If the group ownership Rabehl has in mind came about, anarchy would result. But we want socialism for all. And socialism doesn't mean group ownership but ownership by the entire society."

If GDR plants had what is variously called "group ownership," "workers' control" or "self-administration," the great advances made under socialism would soon be undermined. The state, for example, would no longer have the ability to guarantee an individual's right to work or to qualify for more advanced work. And only the state *can* guarantee these rights.

"If there were self-administration, no one would have the responsibility for employing a young person ready to start work. No individual enterprise can guarantee this right," commented Dr. Joachim Hoffmann of the Institute of International Politics and Economy. "If one plant doesn't need as many workers as it has trained, where would these young workers go? The same thing would apply to actors—no one theater can guarantee that actors will find work in their field. Bourgeois ideologists"—and those on the pseudo-left who echo them—"try to counterpose the interests of the workers and the interests of the socialist state. But the right to work, to qualify and many other rights are guaranteed only because the socialist state assumes the responsibility."

If individual enterprises decided—without state participation—on what should be produced, production would center around what each enterprise considered most profitable. The state would no longer be able to mobilize the people around social and economic goals that benefit *all* the people, and socialist relations would degenerate into anarchy.

"In socialism the working class produces as much as possible for itself, for the people as a whole," said Dr. Horst Noack, a department head at the Party College. "To claim that 'centralism in the economy' can 'originate in the plants themselves'—to say that thousands of plants can have their own 'centralism'—is to oppose unified management, unified planning, and to call for splintering the production forces. Lenin said that organization and unity are the greatest weapons the working class has. To speak of 'centralism' in each plant is to advocate splintering the working class—by creating competition among the workers themselves. To do this is to wind up quite openly with the demands made by the enemies of socialism."

To transfer property that belongs to the working class as a whole—socialist state property—to thousands of competing enterprises would erode the state power of the working class. This would lead toward the goal of the enemies of socialism: the kind of "group ownership" that exists in the U.S.—ownership by groups of corporate monopolists.

We in the U.S. experience what this means every day of our lives. And we got an especially bitter taste of it during the terrible winter of 1977, when the monopolists who control natural gas used their artificially created shortage of this product to crack what exists in the way of price regulation. Because of this "shortage," factories were closed and over two million workers were thrown out of jobs. Schoolchildren were sent out of cold schools into cold homes. Countless people got sick and some froze to death. "I hope we realize that we are in it together," was President Carter's message to the people—whom he advised to put on more warm clothes for wear indoors and to turn down the heat in their already freezing homes. (Landlords were only too happy to comply.) Carter also had another message—this one more openly on behalf of the monopolists: He called upon Congress to enact a law to decontrol the price of natural gas.

State power, in other words, is administered on behalf of the owners of the means of production. *How* it's administered depends on who owns the means of production.

"The state is the ruling instrument of the ruling class. This is true for the GDR and the USA," commented Michael Drechsler, who at twenty-six has been a member of Parliament in the GDR for a number of years. "The question is, who is the ruling class. Here it's the working class. And the material basis for democracy is the people's ownership of the means of production."

WORK IN each GDR enterprise, from plants to theaters, is based on fulfilling a plan. In the theater this plan, which revolves around the repertory, originates within each ensemble itself—since socialist artistic goals can be carried out in a great variety of ways. "You can see by looking at the tremendous variations in our theater that the repertory is determined in great part by each ensemble," noted Rainer Kerndl.

But each plant does not originate its plan by itself: To meet the people's material needs, each plant must play a specific role within a national production perspective.

"Planning isn't done in an isolated way—our plan is worked out in connection with the entire plan for the Republic," said Günter Stöcklein, Party Secretary at the VEB Hans Beimler* Locomotive Construction and Electro-Technical Works in Henningsdorf. "We are part of the whole, and we must look at things from the standpoint of the necessities of the national economy. Now, for instance, we have to decide whether we'll continue producing locomotives. Ten years ago we could overfulfill our target for locomotives—there was a great need for them. But that's no longer true.

"In a socialist way of producing," Stöcklein continued, "all the wealth goes back to the people. We have high goals to reach in order to guarantee better living conditions." By contrast with the U.S., "Prices and rents must not rise—while wages, salaries and pensions must. Who gets the surplus value is the difference between capitalism and socialism. What we call the plus product goes back to the people."

The plan, which includes measures in such areas as worker qualification, culture, sports and health, "is discussed with every worker in the plant—every worker participates," said Stöcklein. "With better results, at the end of the year every worker will get more. We can pay higher wages, there will be more possibilities for workers to qualify—and there'll be a bigger plant fund for better apartments, culture and sports. Of course, a certain part of the plus product will go to the state for measures in the Republic as a whole—new plants, new apartments, and for all phases of working and living conditions."

Although the plan for each enterprise is developed as part of the national plan, it's up to the workers to decide whether they will accept or revise the targets for their plant. They can also revise or reject other aspects of the plan, and add new prosposals.

"During the discussions, which last several weeks, there are many criticisms and suggestions from the workers," said Stöcklein. "There may be proposals for a new dining hall and more places in kindergartens. And there may be complaints about food, working conditions, production gaps—material that doesn't arrive on time. Suggestions and criticisms become part of the plan. Our aim isn't to put a golden water tap in every worker's kitchen but we develop better standards. And some plants, of course, develop better than others."

In practice, how far can criticism of the plan go? "Last year the plan

*Hans Beimler, a German Communist, was a leader of the Thälmann Battalion of the International Brigades during the war against fascism in Spain. He died in that struggle.

was rejected by the workers," replied Detlev Narr, a construction manager at the Hans Beimler plant. "The workers were absolutely right. It was up to the general manager to change the plan. Several weeks later he proposed a new plan, there was a new discussion, and the plan was confirmed. We can only carry out the plan with the workers' cooperation, not through pressure."

In carrying out the plan the starting point is the common objectives of workers and management.

"You must understand that we as workers and our management are both interested in fulfilling the plan," declared Dietmar Roessel, a twenty-two-year-old construction worker, as we talked at a housing construction site. "We have a housing shortage and we work with management to solve it."

Construction worker Herbert Pratch agreed: "Eventually we work for ourselves. It may sound surprising to the people in your country, but for us it's natural. What else can I say? If we don't fulfill the plan, we make less money. If we work overtime, we get extra pay—but we don't slow down to make overtime." Each brigade has its own plan as part of the whole, "and it takes very hard, very intensive work to fulfill it because the building time is short. But we try to overfulfill our plan—to build additional apartments for the people. And if other brigades lose time, we try to help them in a socialist manner." The brigade's plan doesn't only include construction targets.

"Part of our plan," said Dietmar Roessel, "is to visit cultural events—the cinema, the theater. We also take excursions and trips with members of our family—last year our brigade went to Prague. We'll go again. And we also plan for further training for our colleagues—three of our brigade members now want to specialize."

And the leader of this brigade, Frank Beithan, said: "How we work today is how we'll live tomorrow—this is an expression of ours. During the war Berlin was heavily destroyed, and new housing must still be built to satisfy the people's needs. As construction workers, we can see how fast residential complexes are built—and we see the same thing going on in other industries. This is to benefit all of the people. This is the only way we can raise living standards." He added: "We're a youth brigade—we all grew up in the GDR. I never think that socialism couldn't be my aim—socialist aims are so natural to me. I'm not a member of the Party, but I fully support our government's course."

WHEN IT comes to writing about the Soviet Union or other socialist countries in the bourgeois media, anything goes—so long as it's negative. In a *New York Times* article allegedly dealing with conditions in the Soviet Union, Christopher S. Wren states that "full employment means that it is often as hard to get promoted as to get laid off the job."[5]

Full employment, in other words, is bad for people. It keeps them from getting ahead in life. Still, how can you be promoted if you've been laid off? If Wren were to check with the workers on U.S. unemployment lines, he might be surprised to discover they're not holding out for promotion. They'd be more than willing to settle for jobs. In fact, skilled workers who are laid off are often forced to take jobs in an unskilled category—if they can get anything at all. Even executives who've been out of work for a while may take just about whatever kind of job they can get.

Actually, if you want to be promoted in the U.S., you should start out young—by being born the son of a white, affluent family who can give you whatever education you may want. But the way things are going these days, even that's no guarantee of promotion. If you want to make sure all doors will be open to you, you should be born a member of a corporate ruling-class family.

In a socialist society, one learns, all doors are also open to members of the ruling class: In the GDR 60 percent of all state posts are held by men and women who come from the working class. And 75 percent of the managers of enterprises are also recruited from the working class.

"In our whole society the development of young cadres is planned," said Alexandra Martin, group leader for cadre instruction at the Berlin Housing Construction Combinate, the enterprise that employs the building workers we spoke with. "In our combinate," she continued, "we have our own plan of development. Young cadres are trained to take over leading functions. Someone with the ability to manage will be prepared to become a section manager in the combinate."

Since education at all levels is free, ability to pay is no longer the criterion for deciding whether a person goes on to advanced studies. The new criterion is evaluation by one's peers. "If one of our colleagues wants to go to engineering college, then he must get an assessment from his brigade," pointed out Martin. "Only if the assessment is good can he be delegated for advanced study."

The opportunity to undertake advanced studies is by no means limited to young cadre. "I'm a brick layer by trade," said Siegfried Koenig. "I worked on a constructon site for five years and became a foreman. Then the director needed a scientific assistant and at the age of forty I studied to become one." Koenig is now a scientific cooperator of the production director at the Housing Construction Combinate. His on-the-job promotion within the same enterprise "was typical. With about 80 percent of our cadre this is the way it happens."

It happened that way with Benno Radtke too. In 1958 when he was a skilled construction worker, "I was asked to undertake further studies. I didn't rush to study—I felt I knew enough—but the Party said, 'If workers have power, they must use it.' When my colleagues delegated me, I recognized the necessity." Radtke (whose wife and three sons are construction workers) went to a technical university and became an economics enginer. He's now a senior foreman at the Housing Construction Combinate.

"The demands on managers grow every hour. We're accountable to our colleagues and it's difficult to satisfy them," stated Radtke. "As managers we have individual responsibility and we can give directions—it's not anarchy. We sometimes sympathize with our colleagues when we make difficult demands—we know from our own experience they're hard to fulfill. Some workers," he went on, "see only their own field. We must convince them to see the whole, and sometimes there are clashes, conflicts and contradictions. Working these out takes time, but this is necessary in order to advance."

"Clashes, conflicts and contradictions"? What kind?

ONE VIEW of the contradictions in the GDR's economy comes from Bernd Rabehl: "The inability of Western visitors to understand contradictory features of GDR society," he writes, "and the inability of GDR intellectuals to understand demands of socialist opposition in the West marks a loss of a sense of history and reality on both sides."[6] Does it?

When a proponent of "socialism with workers' control" speaks of "socialist opposition in the West," he is obviously referring to individuals such as himself whose "opposition" is directed against existing socialism.

But GDR intellectuals, who have a "sense of history and reality," understand this "opposition" very well. They also understand—and identify with—the genuine opposition (socialist or not) directed against exploiters in the West.

By contrast, Rabehl's view that exploitation exists in the GDR "marks a loss of a sense of history and reality"—since resistance from the old exploiting class in the Eastern part of Germany was smashed three decades ago, and the last remnants of exploitation abolished at the time the GDR was founded. If one refuses to recognize these facts, it's impossible to understand the "contradictory features of GDR society."

On the other hand, it's possible for Westerners to be genuinely confused by "contradictory features" of a socialist economy. For instance, workers organize trade unions in the U.S. to protect themselves against management, whose interests are in basic conflict with their own. If workers and management have the same goals in a socialist country, why do the workers need trade unions?

"There are always problems to solve," responded construction worker Karl Heinz Prust. "For example, there's the question of catering and facilities"—which can present greater difficulties at a construction site than in a plant. "When we started here there was no lavatory—we had quite a fight. And then there were the snacks—the sandwiches didn't have butter and the sausage was like a razor blade. We complained to the union and they took care of these problems. The union also organizes vacations, and takes care of people if they're sick. They're sent to the Baltic sea coast."

And Peter Kirsch, leader of a youth brigade at the Köpenick Radio Works, pointed out, "In the work process you have conflicts. There may be disputes between workers and management on the annual premium, or on problems in regard to the Labor Code. Every worker can get legal advice without charge from the trade union. And if a legal step needs to be taken, the worker gets free counsel."

There can also be problems on production. "If the targets are to be reached, we must have the construction prerequisites—the supply of materials," declared Brigade Leader Frank Beithan. "If we have to wait we can't do our own specific work.

"We keep a timetable diary," he continued, "which includes a record of all time not used productively. We interpret this together with management. But some combinate directors don't like this record, because through it we can very often show managers their mistakes. Sometimes it's a hard fight to convince them they didn't fulfil their duties. Very frequently the trade union has to put pressure on a manager."

There are innumerable ways of noting the differences in production relations in an exploitative society and a socialist one. For instance, in the U.S. a manager can fulfill his production quota only at the expense of the workers. It's his job, on behalf of the owners, to speed up the workers—while trying to cut back on wages and safety and health measures. In socialism everything produced is for the people, and to produce at the workers' expense would contradict the aim of production.

"Production targets must not be achieved at the expense of workers but through the role of science and technology—by improving the production processes and the scientific organization of labor," declared Charlotte Bombal, head of the Textile, Clothes and Leather Workers Union. The specifics of how this will be carried out are part of each plant's plan.

While this method of work is established in basic ways, it may not automatically be followed in all particulars: A manager may use the socialist aims of production to justify infractions of socialist rules of production. Thus the union's role is two-fold: It may have to put pressure on the manager to overcome production problems so the workers can fulfill the plan, while preventing the manager from attempting to fulfill the plan by putting pressure on the workers.

"Some managers want to solve technical problems before improving working and living conditions," said Charlotte Bombal. "And some managers will try to fulfill the plan with overtime at the expense of the workers' leisure. A basic question of the development of consciousness is that sometimes you must work overtime to fulfill the plan, because we don't have enough workers. But we make sure that such matters aren't handled without the trade union. If overtime is necessary, there must be a joint discussion with the workers. Management can't just tell them, 'You must work on Saturday.'"

"If a manager tries to fulfill the plan by taking measures at the expense of the workers' conditions," said Regina Zwanzig, newspaper editor at the Köpenick Radio Works, "the trade union must see that the manager sticks to the rules."

At the Housing Construction Combinate, Horst Lehmann, production director, agreed that the union must see to it that the manager "sticks to the rules." "The trade union," he said, "is decisive for raising production—for encouraging emulation in the broadest socialist sense. But in specific terms, the state manager is responsible for production. And without the trade union, some managers—even I myself—would sometimes not quite stick to the rules."

The workers' control over the manager applies to every phase of plant activity, starting with appointment of the manager. "All state managers are appointed by the working class—they are charged, so to speak, by the entire working class in the GDR," stated Lehmann. "But in practice it's the workers who do the appointing through their trade union, because no manager or director can be appointed without the union's approval." Proposals for a manager generally come from within the plant itself, but whether they do or not "it's the workers who say yes or no through their elected representatives."

In a capitalist society managers are responsible to the corporate owners of the means of production. In a socialist society managers are responsible to the new owners of the means of production: to the working people as a whole through their state on one hand, and on the other to the working people in the plants. For example, "The state manager is accountable to the trade union—which represents the interests of all working people—for all phases of working and living conditions," said trade union leader Dieter Neumann at the Housing Construction Combinate. "We cooperate with the manager in carrying out decisions, but we also control the manager's decisions. The manager can't carry out decisions without our consent. At any time we can have a manager's appointment canceled. But a state manager can't fire me—trade union leaders are elected representatives of the working people."

At the Köpenick Radio Works, Annetta Lechowicz, a twenty-two-year-old production worker and a member of the Party leadership in the plant, said: "The trade union represents our interests, the interests of the workers. If in our opinion a state manager isn't tolerable, we can have him replaced."

The working people's control over decisions affecting their lives runs through every phase of GDR life. "The rights of working people are defined by a whole system of laws and the Labor Code," pointed out Dr. Dietrich Gayko. "In a dispute between management and workers the trade union can intervene and defend workers at the plant level. If this fails, the matter can go to the next higher level—up to the presidium of the Free German Trade Unions. And the trade union can defend workers by criticism and even by legal means if necessary on the state level.

"But this system doesn't function by itself. The Party must consistently and energetically call upon the trade union leadership to use these rights. The Party's work," he pointed out, "isn't parallel to the work of management and the trade union. It's at the core of both."

But, again, control is only one aspect of socialist democracy: Workers' co-determination in decision making and control over decisions are two phases of a single process. In a plant, workers participate in decision making in, for example, general assemblies. And management must report back to the general assemblies on how these decisions have been carried out. The plants have permanent production councils whose members—production workers, technicians, engineers, economists and scientists—are elected by their fellow trade unionists. The council makes proposals and criticisms on all phases of production, and the manager's participation in council meetings, which is obligatory, must include reports on the action taken on council recommendations.

But again, co-determination and control don't stop at the plant level: Workers are elected representatives at all levels of government. And the FGTU (with 7.3 million members, the largest organization in the GDR) has its own group in Parliament. It initiates legislation on behalf of the working people, and exercises public control to make sure the measures are observed.

IN THE SAME article where Christopher Wren deplores the effect of full employment in the Soviet Union, he also states: "One Western economic specialist noted, 'If a worker lives in a system where he is always told what to do, why should he take the initiative?'"

Although the "Western economic specialist" would like us to believe this is the behavior of workers in socialist plants, he is really describing the behavior of workers in capitalist ones. As every U.S. worker knows, he or she is "always told what to do"—in fact, compelled to do it under threat of firing. U.S. workers must continually fight management—which tries to force them to "take the initiative" by working faster and faster to increase production. And if they should "take the initiative" by increasing production through technological improvements or better organization, they'd only do themselves or their co-workers out of a job.

In a socialist country workers have every reason to "take the initiative," since they personally and the entire society will benefit from it. But during the period of the transition to socialism, it may be difficult for some workers to understand this. In the early days of the GDR many people continued to act as they did under capitalism because they still thought in the old way. As Brecht wrote in 1953, "Large sections of our population still have a completely capitalist way of looking at things. This is true even of parts of the working class." But the corollary to this statement was that sizable sections of the working class were already beginning to develop a new "way of looking at things."

An event that had a powerful effect on changing workers' consciousness was the exemplary deed of a miner, Adolf Hennecke, who in 1948 tremendously overfulfilled his production norm by improving the work process. Other workers reacted with hostility and ridicule "because they were thinking in a bourgeois way—they believed more production would be at their expense," related Charlotte Bombal. "This was the level at the beginning."

But soon other workers began to perform exemplary deeds, and an activist movement—encouraged by the Party and the trade unions—grew into a broad current. This in turn developed into the emulation movement, where whole brigades vie with each other to fulfill and overfulfill production targets, and to achieve outstanding records in cultural, educational and overall human ways. Today there's also an innovators' movement, in which workers' proposals and inventions contribute to advancing the production process.

"The innovators' movement has become a massive one, with one out of every four workers participating," said Charlotte Bombal. "The workers wouldn't take such an active part in carrying out this policy if it didn't correspond to their interests. And outstanding workers also join brigades that are lagging behind—they lend their own experience so these brigades can achieve their targets."

If socialist plants did "feel the same" as capitalist ones, workers would continue to act the same. Instead they act in a new way—not because they are "told what to do" but because developing consciousness leads them to "take the initiative." And the trade union plays a special role in bringing about this understanding.

"As the class organization of the working class, the trade union has the task of winning all the working people in a plant to carry out socialist goals," pointed out Bombal. "We speak of the unity of our economic and social policy. This means that we as the trade union must do all we can to raise productivity by increasing the initiative of workers. This is the prerequisite for the continual improvement of living and working conditions."

And Frank Beithan said, "For us the fronts have changed. In the 1930s the German Thälmann Battalion fought against fascism in Spain. Today our construction brigade must work first. We wouldn't call ourselves heroes. We do the same work as workers all over the world. But the difference between capitalism and our socialist state is a vast one. Every day the Western news media tell us the FRG housing problem is solved. Many apartments have been built there, but almost 100,000 are empty. People can't afford to move into them. Our housing problems—we haven't quite solved them, but we have a grip on them. But they will be fully solved in the next years, and everyone will have a reasonable apartment. Three years ago," he added, "my wife and I got a new apartment. Life became better."

As socialism develops, workers become increasingly aware of the relationship between what they do and social and economic advance. It is within this context that their consciousness of themselves as the owners of the means of production grows.

"For everyone to immediately feel himself or herself as the owner of the means of production—it would be utopian to believe that's possible. That feeling can't be achieved through an act of law," commented Günter Simon. "This consciousness of ownership develops in our daily socialist life—for instance, through people's experiences with co-determination, and when they see how their work and the work of their colleagues influences living standards."

And Charlotte Bombal said, "You can see how the workers' awareness has developed in the many new initiatives occurring in the plants." But the workers' initiatives, she stressed, aren't limited to improving life only within their own country. "Workers here have the understanding to extend their help beyond our Republic. For example, they volunteer to work solidarity shifts—their pay goes for reconstruction in Vietnam and for liberation struggles in Africa, Chile and other parts of the world."

THE PROBLEMS theater workers face in capitalist society are solved by socialism only because socialism solves the problems *all* working people face in capitalism. And with the old problems solved—with everyone's right to education, work, medical care and cultural opportunities assured—socialism goes on to solve the new conflicts.

As socialism forges ahead, attacks from its enemies intensify—and take new forms. Suddenly anti-Marxists present themselves as defenders of Marxism, claiming that the socialist countries are failing to carry out Marx's ideas. One accusation made with particular frequency is that the socialist countries contradict Marx because they aren't the classless societies he envisioned (Bernd Rabehl is among those who make this allegation).

But Marx never visualized an instant leap from class-divided capitalism to classless communism. The great achievement of the socialist revolution is not that it abolishes all classes but that it abolishes all exploiting classes. Socialism—the first, the lower stage of communism—replaces the exploitative class power of corporate capital with the liberating class power of the working class in alliance with the farmers and all strata of the people.

At the same time, the classes in socialist society are not what these same classes were in the old society. Under socialism the formerly exploited classes take on new characteristics—an integral part of the development toward the disappearance of classes, toward the classless Communist society.

Already there are great harbingers of this future society: In the GDR now most intellectuals come from the working class. And workers now have ever-expanding intellectual and cultural interests. All this is reflected in the new relations among the people of the GDR—which are so natural to GDR people that they don't even think of them. Unless, that is, they happen to be in a Western country.

Telling of a Berliner Ensemble tour, actress Barbara Dittus said, "We were giving a guest performance in a big theater in the FRG, and we were in the canteen. At one table there were the actors of the higher category. The actors of the lower category wouldn't dare sit at the same table. For each category there was a table, and for the *Intendant* there was also a table. The technicians were sitting separately, and we sat with them. Someone from the FRG theater said, 'What if your *Intendant* should see this?'

"But with us there's no categorization. We all sit together. It's a natural thing."

15. "Not Against but With Each Other"

An April afternoon. Sunlight streams through big windows into a high-ceilinged room. About thirty men and women, some wearing white coats, are seated around two long tables. We are in a meat-packing plant in Berlin, where a discussion is in progress. The participants—working people at the plant—address their remarks to a bearded man sitting at a small head table.

YOUNG MAN: I'm not quite sure—but I don't think I agree with the way King Lear was acted. I imagined him a broken man who wouldn't become mad so soon but would show his inner emotions more. An old man, thrown out. At least I'd play him that way. At times I had to laugh. Still, I thought it was very good. Why did you interpret it like that?

WOMAN: I saw another production of *King Lear* some years ago. I liked the way yours was acted, but I was also disturbed by it. The actors were painted white. It was too primitive. It seemed like pantomime. I'm not sure if Shakespeare would have liked it or if he would have turned over in his grave. The whole stage design was also too primitive—I preferred the old way. The modern way makes it too difficult to think back.

SECOND YOUNG MAN: I also saw *The Tempest* at your theater and *Edward II* at the Berliner Ensemble. I must say, I like the contemporary plays better. My question: Why do we stage the classics so often when we have so many possibilities with plays about the present?

YOUNG WOMAN: *(Turns to the previous speaker)* We like plays about today, but we must know what came before. *(Turns toward the bearded man)* It was quite an interesting evening. But the masks disturbed me too—you can't see expressions. This discourages people who don't go to the theater often. They wondered, was it necessary? Those holes for the eyes—like open wounds. This created a certain distance. Too great a distance—especially since the painted masks weren't used by all the actors. It was artificially modern.

MAN: We like to buy out a performance of a play that people might not go to by themselves. We sold 500 tickets for *King Lear*. And even people that we consider barbarians when it comes to culture—who say "leave me alone about the theater"—they really enjoyed the evening.

THIRD YOUNG MAN: I was surprised at how big the audience was. And some of the acting I liked very much. The technique of the thunderstorm—it was wonderful visually. But it was distracting. The technique was too good, the rain was too real. And the performance—almost four hours—it was too long for the production workers who start very early in the morning.

(The bearded man—director Friedo Solter of the Deutsches Theater—begins to respond to the questions and comments.)

SOLTER: Shakespeare *is* long—another director did a five-hour production. If you cut out too much you take out what Shakespeare put in with so much effort and talent. We have a certain responsibility for authenticity. As to the masks, I must say your criticisms make me think. And when you say at times you had to laugh at Lear—sometimes we didn't know if we should laugh or feel sorry for him, so your reactions are right. As for the stage design, at first we were going to build a palace. Then we thought, how would Shakespeare do it? Be honest: Did you need a door? A window? A palace?

WOMAN: I missed it.

SOLTER: Shakespeare didn't need it.

YOUNG MAN: Why was the rain so natural?

SOLTER: The thunderstorm—we think we did it in an elegant way. It was an element of nature injected into art—it wasn't naturalism. The critic who said it was was wrong. We had to show how Lear is chucked out of society into nature. *(He turns to his conception of Lear)* Imagine you have three daughters and you want a nice end to your life. You give away power, give it away without understanding what power means. Our deepest aim was to destroy sympathy for this absolutist, autocratic king who never thought where power came from. He thought it came from God. If he says, "I'm not loved," one can only say, so what? He starts to think what love is only when his power is gone . . .

□ □ □

WE ARE in the crowded lobby of the Maxim Gorki Theater. We have just seen a dress rehearsal (to us, a preview) of a new play. The play is over but a large part of the audience isn't leaving. There's an atmosphere of eagerness, as people seat themselves on folding chairs and wait for the *Foyergespräch*—foyer discussion—to begin.

The play, *The Family Birnchen,* is about a family that runs an inn (a small number of enterprises, particularly in the service area, are still family-owned in the GDR; because of the labor shortage, it's helpful that these families want to run such marginal operations). The members of the Birnchen family and the people who come to their inn aren't particularly developed in a social sense. Their thoughts center around their own personal problems. Yet to a degree, the play reflects a clash between the old and the new: The characters deal with their problems in a society that offers them a perspective. (To us *The Family Birnchen* contains one ironic note: In plays from *Juno and The Paycock* to *Raisin in The Sun,* when a family expects to come into money it spells tragedy or near that. The Birnchen family wins a state lottery, but it has no great significance for them. In a socialist society, people simply have no big financial problems.)

Chefdramaturg Fritz Rödel arrives and the discussion begins.

MAN: The public will see many things in this play. People who went through such experiences will see one thing, others will see something else. What interests me is, how will our young people see it?

YOUNG MAN: I liked it very much—I'm sure the public will like it. But I wonder what conclusions the audience will draw. The workers' quarters of the past had many inns. There are still some inns left. But drinking is not the way out of problems. The author has tried to raise the level of his material—tried to give it a socialist level. But the play doesn't correspond to the needs of average workers.

OLDER WOMAN: What happens in this inn is exaggerated. But such inns used to exist and some still do. I've got nothing against corner inns, but in the old Germany, workers went to them. Jobless workers. They were miserable and they drank.

YOUNG WOMAN: Is the inn supposed to be real?

OLDER MAN: The inn is in the foreground but that's just an external accident. Human fates are shown but not nostalgically. Fates continue to be individual. But I'm afraid the critics will be negative because the public will talk about the inn, not what's happening to the people. What does the author want to say? Did he want to depict an inn or human beings?

RÖDEL: I can only say the play is the author's exact observation of people. In that sense the inn is purely accidental. What's interesting is that the people he observes are at the edge, not the center, of socialist development. But you can see that socialism has put its stamp even on the lives of these people.

SECOND YOUNG MAN: Our literature has been showing these sidelines for a long time. I want something moving—something that excites my whole evening in the theater!

THIRD YOUNG MAN: It's too bad if you have to worry about negative reactions after the play opens. If anyone has a negative opinion about it, they should speak up right now. I'm sorry if I sound too sharp—the play had certain moments. But it's a piece of life put in a corner. Take *Weather For Tomorrow*—that was a play on a certain level. I'm afraid this one is less important. So they win the lottery—so what? And the author's way of handling real problems is just too easy—too haphazard.

SECOND YOUNG WOMAN: I wouldn't put this play in the category of *Weather For Tomorrow*, but I think it's mostly positive for young people—they don't know this kind of atmosphere. And in some contemporary plays set at the workplace, personal problems are on the side. Here personal problems are at the center. I liked that.

THIRD YOUNG WOMAN: It's not a real inn. In my opinion the question is, is it a humane atmosphere? That depends on one's interpretation.

WE ARE in a small arena theater at the Volksbühne. The actors have taken their bows, the houselights go up. But the spectators remain in their seats.

We have just seen *The Award,* by the worker/playwright, Regina Weicker. The play concerns a brigade of women workers who learn they are to be awarded a title for outstanding achievement. The women are pleased at first, but their satisfaction is jarred when they read a letter from another brigade member, a very young woman who has spent two years in a reform institution. She states that the brigade doesn't deserve the title, but gives no reasons. The reasons come out in the play, which develops in a dual way: The women's lives and relationships are explored both in the plant and in their homes. Although the brigade members individually come to the conclusion that they don't deserve the title, they fail to say so—thus allowing their leader, Martha, to accept it as they stand by.

An actor walks on stage and opens the discussion.

ACTOR: Do you think the collective was right? Don't expect the answer from me. Would you give the award to this brigade, yes or no?

WOMAN: If I want to say a brigade doesn't deserve the award, I can't just write a letter. I must have the guts to go there and insist that I myself won't accept the award.

MAN: The play exaggerates. There can be very big problems in a brigade—but such a cool attitude toward a girl who came out of a reform institution—that's not typical.

ACTOR: That part may be an exaggeration—but we know from discussions we've had here and in the plants that this play is real.

SECOND WOMAN: Martha fulfilled her obligations in the work but not the main point—to make them a collective.

YOUNG WOMAN: Martha isn't the problem. The problem is the others who follow her without criticizing.

SECOND MAN: Martha says, "I'll accept the award." The others say nothing. Sometimes we don't speak up.

OLDER WOMAN: In the end the truth is most important. They should have said to Martha, "Let's think it over. It's better to refuse the award." It would have been better if she had learned the opinions of others.

SECOND OLDER WOMAN: They are supposed to be a socialist brigade—women who work, learn and live in a socialist way. But they finish work, they go home—they don't bother to see if anyone is lonely at Christmas or Easter. Naturally everyone has personal problems—but they don't understand what a socialist brigade is. It's not simple to build a brigade—in the beginning it was almost too hard for us. It's a hard struggle to carry through to the point where you're a socialist brigade.

ACTOR: What does it mean to the brigade members when they fight for a title?

THIRD WOMAN: When you fight together for the title of best brigade, a certain common thing develops—you come together and the people change by coming together. You're together at the work place, you also see each other outside—the feeling of a collective is developed in this fight. In a certain way you feel with your colleagues—and you feel with them outside the work place too.

FOURTH WOMAN: Political attitudes develop. In the beginning we said Communists aren't born—when you fight for the title, your socialist awareness, your consciousness grows. Your requirements become higher.

THE ATMOSPHERE is charged with excitement at the Maxim Gorki Theater. The curtain has just come down to ringing applause. Now people are coming into the lobby. They are heading for the area where the *Foyergespräch* will take place.

We have just seen *Protocol Of A Meeting,* a Soviet play. Where *The Award* centers around the relationships between brigade members and their leader, *Protocol Of A Meeting* is concerned with the relationship between a brigade of construction workers and the management of their enterprise.

The skeleton of this complex play: The organization has over-fulfilled its plan—which means a bonus for the workers. But Potapov, a brigade leader, has come to inform management, the trade union and the Party leadership that his brigade is refusing its share of the bonus. Why? The original plan for construction was reduced. Had it been fulfilled—and, Potapov maintains, it could have been fulfilled—the workers would have earned much more. This was the starting point, but now much more is involved: The workers consider the money offered them not a bonus but a bribe. To lower the figures on the plan was cheating the socialist state. Delays weren't due to missing materials but bad organization. What we want, declares Potapov, is not just for ourselves. We want the organization to change. Management must acknowledge its errors and correct them.

The manager, directors, engineers are outraged, furious at Potapov's accusation. They demand proof—which is forthcoming from a woman economist. Management seems to have no alternative to accepting responsibility. Then word comes: Potapov's brigade has decided to accept the bonus. Potapov leaves, filled with discouragement. Manager, directors, engineers—filled with relief—get ready to go home. The Party Secretary stops them. Why did the workers decide to take the bonus? he asks. Money, money, they reply. No, counters the Party Secretary. The workers changed their vote because they felt their protest was useless, that management would ignore them. If they can't trust us, he declares, they may as well take the money. He calls for a vote on the workers' criticism of management. Outrage, anger. The vote is taken. The manager casts the deciding vote—in favor of the workers' resolution. Both the manager and Party Secretary come to the conclusion that they must resign their posts.

Two of the actors from *Protocol Of A Meeting* arrive for the *Foyergespräch*. A man from the audience rises and begins speaking.

MAN: Especially for young people this play is important. It shows that you have to question a matter once in a while—not just say yes. It's good how the experienced worker works with his young brigade.

YOUNG WOMAN: As I came down the stairs at the end I thought, the management of our plant should also come here. They would have to look in the mirror and act as is expected of us as socialists.

YOUNG MAN: I also found many parallels to my own work. And I too thought our leadership should come here.

SECOND MAN: I think not only the leadership but the workers should come here—they should see their own responsibility. I'll say that at my plant. I think the workers should come here and we could discuss it. They are thinking of their power. They should know more about their own power. As for myself, I want to come often—not just once.

SECOND YOUNG MAN: I thought to myself, how do our directors react to criticism? I just couldn't conceive of such a reaction in our plant as in this play. A manager in such a rage about criticism from the workers? When I think of my plant, I think what happens in the play is exaggerated.

WOMAN: Usually when I go to the theater I think afterwards—was it entertaining, what did it give to me? Here you don't think about such questions. You think about the problems—that's what I find so positive about the staging. You feel personally spoken to about the problems and you're provoked to think: How would I act in such a conflict?

SECOND MAN: Are our people as advanced as this Potapov and his brigade? I probably would not return a bonus. We have a long way ahead of us.

SECOND WOMAN: I felt quite ashamed because I couldn't act like Potapov.

ACTOR: When the youth from a construction brigade were here, they started talking and shouting when Potapov was speaking—they shouted out the name of a brigade leader who's well known in Berlin.

SECOND YOUNG WOMAN: You do the best for your plant. Everybody wants their own plant to be the best.

THIRD MAN: The manager is not shown as a negative character. Everybody's profile includes good and strong sides but also weak ones. It's not as hard to be honest and open in the area of production as in the area of leadership. One has to learn to get at problems objectively. This play should be recommended to all leaders.

THIRD WOMAN: The most detailed questions of daily life are taken up in this play. A constant struggle goes on—but in our system it's not a struggle against each other but with each other. There are differences among people building socialism, even among Communists. They don't always agree with each other, but it's not against each other but with each other. It might have been correct if the brigade had insisted that instead of quitting, the manager stay and learn from experience.

FOURTH MAN: In all the years he's been a manager he hasn't shown any understanding of how to lead in the work. If a manager created disorganization in a collective, he has no place there. This manager displays himself as an educated guy because he has a shelf full of books. But does he ever go to the construction site? Does he ever talk to a worker like Potapov who has really read Lenin and is wise from his experiences of life? I think you can say to this manager, you haven't lived up to your position. It's not un-socialist to demand that he be removed. He may be a very good man, but some heads are too small for a big hat.

ACTOR: To me it's not so important whether the manager goes or if the leadership is guilty. To me the decisive thing is that as a member of a brigade I have my own responsibility—independent of the leadership's responsibility. This attitude that we experience daily in our own deeds—taking the most comfortable way and neglecting what's necessary. While we worked as a collective on this play, we were constantly confronted with the question, are we being honest with ourselves?

FOURTH WOMAN: What's interesting isn't the question of rejecting the bonus—but the artistic presentation of the social relationships. The play reveals problems we have to overcome to keep advancing.

SECOND ACTOR: As long as there's still money, people will fight to get it. That's the starting point. But a new quality develops in this brigade when they say what we want is not just for ourselves. What this brigade is involved in is a struggle for the whole class.

To DISCUSS a play with those who produce it is a normal part of GDR cultural life. For the working people at the meat-packing plant it was nothing out of the ordinary to exchange views on the staging of *King Lear* with its director. To us it was amazing. Could anyone imagine such a thing happening in a U.S. factory? But when enterprises are owned by the people, a plant becomes a human place—and for workers to have access to culture becomes a human right. In socialist society, as we could plainly see, the concept of human rights acquires altogether new dimensions.

In the U.S. we have not yet won the elementary human right to a job. In socialist countries this right is taken for granted and as a result the people's "requirements become higher": To be creative in one's work, to have rewarding human relations in the workplace becomes a human right and opportunity.

For centuries people have had to put up with whatever comes their way in daily life. But in a socialist society (as *Protocol Of A Meeting* in particular shows), the people—through socialist democracy—have the human right to exert control over their day-to-day life, with an increasing effect on the total society. To bring this about involves a complex struggle, but for people building socialism the struggle is "not against each other but with each other."

From hearing GDR people express themselves in dozens of situations and settings, we ourselves could see the emergence of two indivisible characteristics: concern for the whole class, for the whole people—together with a new attitude toward work, because only through work can all the people's human right to live well materially and culturally be attained.

As Brigade Leader Frank Beithan said, "For us the fronts have changed. In the 1930s the German Thälmann Brigade fought against fascism in Spain. Today our construction brigade must work first." Young people have a big role to play in socialist construction, and carrying it out takes socialist understanding.

"Brecht wrote, 'The hardships of the mountains are behind us/ Before us lie the hardships of the plains.' But young people are so full of energy they feel they would love the hardships of the mountains," commented Wolfgang Reuter of the Free German Youth's Department of Culture. "In a world of transition from capitalism to socialism, the struggles in their most obvious form take place in capitalist societies—where the enemies are right opposite you. And many of our heroes, like Thälmann,* really proved themselves. Many young people ask, 'Where's the bull I can fight?'

"To be a revolutionary in building socialism may not be surrounded by so much glory. It can be difficult to explain to young people the characteristics needed in this struggle—patience, discipline, a high quality of work. These are the ways in which you declare yourself for the socialist system. And to be for the socialist system is the characteristic of a revolutionary today."

*Ernst Thälmann, the leader of the Communist Party of Germany, was murdered by the Nazis shortly before the liberation of Germany.

In the GDR, as in other socialist countries, the central construction goal is new housing. The aim is a high one: a separate, complete apartment for each family. This is such a vast program that one out of every four GDR students goes into the building trades. "Our program for housing really enthuses young people—because by 1990 the housing problem will be solved for everyone," said Heinz Schuldt of the FGY national leadership. (One can easily imagine the enthusiasm of U.S. youth if this approach were applied in our own country: Young people by the millions would come off the unemployment lines, off the street corners—to become part of a great program for realizing everyone's human right to a decent place to live.)

In socialist countries the working people not only build the apartments, but they also decide who will live in them. "You must understand, our society decides things for itself," said Günter Simon of the *Tribune*. "In this part of the city the municipal administration has a committee on apartments. The committee has some employees—but they don't work alone. They work with a committee of volunteers.

"My son Axel," he continued, "wants to leave our family apartment and get married. He's a building worker but he must go to the housing committee and make his demand there. But it's complicated because we don't yet have enough apartments to meet demands—and everyone who comes to the committee has a reason for demanding one. The committee members will ask Axel about his situation. They know about conditions all over and they'll have their say democratically. They must think hard and make responsible decisions—which will still bring headaches because they can't be right for everyone."

In Potsdam where thousands of new apartments are being built, "public discussions were held in all residential neighborhoods," said Mayor Brunhilde Hanke. "The people decide exactly who gets the apartments, whose needs are greatest. In this system of public discussion, the people exercise initiative and control.

"To exercise real democracry," she noted, "isn't easy for people. One must overcome egoism and feel responsible for the whole society. Before the public discussions, there were people who demanded apartments for themselves. Afterwards they became more modest, more realistic. They saw there were others whose needs were greater."

Besides allotting apartments after they're built, GDR citizens decide *what* will be built. "We've just had two general meetings of our citizens to discuss a new concept for building," said Mayor Hanke. "Several hours were spent on protection of the ecology, then on the direction of the streets and the angle for placing the buildings. Some very outspoken people wanted a center for youth instead of one of the apartment buildings. If housing construction serves only the people and is not for profit, the people can say that instead of an apartment building they prefer a social center. Such a procedure is possible only if the territory belongs to the people. The people's representatives—who are not full-time in this capacity but are themselves working people—will take all views into consideration and correct the plan accordingly. Through socialist democracy the people can shape their own living conditions."

As these remarks suggest, each city has its own plan developed from the outset with the people's participation. Commenting on this point, Berlin City Councillor Hannelore Mensch said, "Democracy doesn't start in parliament but in plant meetings with the working people. The people's representatives go to the plants and discuss the plan in the brigades, with the trade union representatives, in general meetings. Forty-six thousand, six hundred suggestions were made for our last plan," which included building and remodeling of tens of thousands of apartments, plus building more nurseries and kindergartens.

A broad popular movement, the National Front—composed of the GDR's five political parties and the mass organizations—draws citizens into electoral and community activities. Horst Noack of the Party College, president of the National Front committee in his area for twelve years, said, "Fifteen citizens work on the executive of this group in our borough of Berlin. Six are Socialist Unity Party members, three are members of the Christian Democratic, Liberal Democratic and National Democratic Parties, and six belong to no party. During these twelve years we've never spoken about specific points of our parties' policies. The basis for the National Front is that all parties and organizations have socialist goals. Our discussion is around our work—what we can do in our borough to develop socialism." Of the alliance between Communists and Christians, Noack remarked, "The social teachings of Christians, the needs of the working class—all this corresponds with socialist goals. We do as Heine said—we leave heaven to the sparrows and angels and don't quarrel about it."

To further socialist development in all areas and at all levels, the people's criticisms are of basic importance. As the theater discussions reveal, socialist art helps stimulate people to carry out this vital aspect of their role. In such a play as *Protocol Of A Meeting* "shortcomings and faults are uncovered with relentless candor from a socialist-communist point of view," states Albert Hetterle who directed the Gorki production of this work. "Such criticism induces the audience to think in a productive way, a fact proved by many performances and discussions in the theater's lobby."[1]

In a socialist country people have unprecedented opportunities to make their criticisms known and felt, whether in a plant, a theater, or a public forum.

"Our work," pointed out Mayor Hanke, "is under constant criticism from our citizens. I'm criticized by the Potsdam citizens—but within the framework of socialism. Our people have no interest in criticizing our social system. The alternative is capitalism—with its unemployment. Four hundred fifty thousand young people in the Federal Republic of Germany are leaving school without the opportunity for getting jobs or acquiring skills. One million in the FRG are unemployed. When our young people meet youth from the West and hear about their life without perspective, they're convinced anew that for human beings life must hold both perspective and security. And," she emphasized, "through socialist democracy people can shape their own living conditions"—which is most certainly a human right.

In the U.S. it's ever more difficult for us to exert any effect on our living conditions, with the people's hard-won gains increasingly falling victim to corporate aggression. In New York, for instance, the banks are more and more blatantly shaping (misshaping would be more accurate) our living conditions. In early 1977 the banks demanded that the city set up a Budget Review Board with, as *The New York Times* described it, "sweeping powers of prior approval over virtually every city fiscal procedure." The banks accompanied this demand with orders for the city to cut back even further on its already woefully inadequate transportation services. And although there weren't enough hospital beds for the people, there were too many for the banks. Both state and city officials sprang into action to comply with their wishes.

And right at the top of the banks' scrap heap list was what was left of the city's affirmative action programs for Blacks, Puerto Ricans, Asian-Americans, and for women. "A group of rich white bankers who are not elected are dictating to the city how it should conduct not only its fiscal operation, but also its policies and practices regarding the employment of non-white minorities and women," declared Herbert Hill, then labor director of the NAACP.[2]

In the GDR and other socialist countries masses of people are drawn into decision-making processes. In the U.S., as the assault against human rights and human needs is intensified, the corporate monopolists more and more brazenly reveal that they are the ones holding decision-making power.

IN SOCIALISM, the lower stage of communism, distribution is based on a high principle: "From each according to his ability, to each according to his contribution." In the Communist stage, distribution is based on an even higher principle: "From each according to his ability, to each according to his need." However, during the socialist stage the transition to the higher principle is underway.

In the socialist stage in addition to their individual income, people receive the benefit of public funds. But these funds represent something more than a supplement to personal income—since they are distributed according to need. Take housing. The principle of the Communist stage can't be fully applied here because, for one thing, there still isn't enough modern housing for all. Yet the progression toward the new stage is apparent: Apartments go to those who need them most. Rents are minimal because public funds are used to subsidize housing, with individual subsidies available to families who require them. Or take municipal transportation. Fares are so low that they presage the Communist stage. (Payment on subways, buses, elevated trains and street cars is on the honor system.)

For all people to live well is a revolutionary goal. "Marx said that socialism will produce a person rich in needs and demands. We want people's lives to be as good as possible—and in the coming years still more will be possible," said Ursula Hafranke, *Für Dich* Deputy Editor. "The point is to create a good life for the masses, not only for a few. That's why we think through what can be improved at a particular time—the most important thing now is apartments. In order for everyone to have as much as they need under communism, the society must be richer than it is today. Production must develop and there must be further development of people."

In realizing the revolutionary aim of good material conditions for all the people, socialist society distinguishes between consumption (goods that make life easier and pleasanter) and "consumerism" (the investing of material objects with subjective qualities: status, power, etc.)—which is inculcated in a profit-motivated economy. "We have no consumer manipulation—there are only the TV commercials that come in from the West, where demands are artificially regulated for profit," commented *Für Dich* Editor Liselotte Thoms-Heinrich. "We don't say we have no people who think in consumer categories—with some, there's still such thinking. But through education and culture we've built counter-weights against this."

From the nursery on, socialist education aims to develop human beings with well defined personalities, a responsible feeling toward others and a new attitude toward work. "Starting from the nursery the children learn to live in a community," said kindergarten/nursery principal Erica Strube. "From the beginning they learn to solve tasks—for instance, each child carries out responsibilities for the benefit of the whole group. As the children develop mentally, physically, and morally, their tasks also develop. And while the children are educated to live in a collective, the personality of each grows." As the children's feeling of responsibility toward their immediate group develops, they simultaneously learn to care for people far beyond it.

"Our children feel friendship for all the peoples of the world. That's a basic principle of our society," stated Erica Strube. "A small child is emotionally quite approachable, and our children begin to learn about international solidarity and friendship according to what they can understand. Through toys and literature they learn about children of other nations. Our children are never confronted with the idea that any people could be different in the sense of being inferior."

As we spoke, small girls and boys, beautifully dressed in brightly colored wool jersey outfits, played around us. Some, wearing plastic "hard hats," were engaged in construction. Others were doctors and nurses in a make-believe clinic. Still others were serving "lunch" to Black dolls and white dolls seated around a little table. "They learn to love all people," said Erica Strube.

The kindergarten's halls were decorated with big posters of Black, brown, yellow, and white children holding a dove of peace. Windows were covered with tempera paintings of construction workers, health workers, mail carriers and other working people.

"Our children are educated to love and respect working people," commented Strube. "We show the younger children the work done by caretakers, cleaners and other workers in the school. And almost all our schools have a sponsoring plant—the children visit the plant and the workers visit the children. The children themselves develop a desire to do work, and to contribute through their activity to shaping the life of the school. They're also educated toward an esthetic outlook—to have everything around them clean, neat and beautiful. And at the same time they learn that they themselves must do something toward this. Everything," she stressed, "is not directed narrowly to one goal. What you do to help children love work—everything you do—has an effect on their entire development."

All children receive a ten-year education that includes mathematics, natural sciences and polytechnical instruction, together with a broad cultural orientation encompassing social sciences, literature and art. All students learn at least one foreign language (most learn two) and engage in sports. As an essential part of their polytechnical education, students receive training right in the plants.

"In 1958 we began to send hundreds of thousands of children into the plants for training," related Marianne Lange, head of the Department of Culture and Education at the Party College. "At first it was very difficult"—because the workers teaching the children had received their own training in capitalist-owned factories: "For a time some children were given jobs others didn't want to do. It was an educational process on both sides."

Now the students carry out responsible tasks under the guidance of concerned as well as capable instructors. "The educational goal," said Lange, "is what Lenin taught us: to overcome the gap between school and life. We bring the students right into production—they learn to have esteem for the working class and for work as such. We link mathematics, chemistry and physics with practical questions. We aren't educating young people for a single mechanical function. We are creating the basis for very diversified personalities who can function in many situations—who will regard themselves as masters of their futures."

After the basic ten-year education, advanced training for vocations and professions is available through a variety of avenues. All levels of education through the doctorate degree are free. Instead of paying tuition, students receive state stipends.

Since cultural development is an integral part of education, cultural activities are available to young people in and outside of school. This is true of every area of the GDR.

NEUBRANDENBURG WAS part of an area in the old Germany where the big landowners said, "There's one ox in front of the plow and another behind it." This section was so barren of culture that during the post-war reconstruction a special appeal was made to artists to move there. Today this area has its own artists of all disciplines. The center of town is dominated by a tall slender structure, known as "the finger of knowledge." This is the House of Culture and Education. We visited it one night while a meeting of a writers' circle was in progress.

"Her poetry is very bold and ironic," said the group's leader, Otto Teuscher, as he introduced us to a young economics student. "And he writes very modern, very intellectual poems—but also very emotional ones," said Teuscher nodding toward a young engineer. The group, which ranged in age from fifteen to forty-seven, also included a machinist, a teacher of sports, a dentist and a number of other students. That night a special question was under discussion: how to introduce these writers to a public.

"If anyone has chickens, they can show the baby chickens—but how to introduce writers, that's another question," said a young man named Arman Goldenbaum, a volunteer worker with the House of Culture. Telling of a new café that had opened in town, he said, "I thought we could present there some of the work done in this house—because it's difficult to exhibit the work of writers."

Teuscher, a free lance writer and theater critic, agreed. "Many of the things we've written would be good for this purpose—easy to understand, quite humorous. Some of the older people who come to this café aren't as well acquainted with literature as the young people."

"One of the writers could speak—someone who can speak well. Not someone who writes well but can't explain why he writes," added Goldenbaum. "You'd find a new public there."

The writers weren't so sure.

"If they come for a social evening, they may be disappointed if they're offered poetry instead," warned a student.

"It will be difficult to choose things that really interest them," cautioned another.

"I saw something like this once and it didn't work," asserted the engineer. "If only young people were going to be there, it would be very good. But it's hard to give readings for a mixed public."

But Teuscher was concerned with the public as well as the writers. "Some people aren't acquainted with literature. We must find little hooks for them to bite."

Later that evening Arman Goldenbaum walked with us to the door, where he stopped and told us about himself: thirty-one years old, an electrician, Jewish. "My father was killed in a concentration camp. When I was a year old, my mother was going to drown herself. She was saved by Polish soldiers. Life is good for my mother in the Republic, but she can't forget. As for myself," he said, "I have a daughter, two years old. She's named Fania—after Angela Davis' sister."

Shortly after our return from Neubrandenburg to Berlin we attended another cultural evening featuring young people: opening night for *Valentin and Valentina* at the Cable Workers Theater. It was a great success. Afterwards, there was the traditional party for the cast. Amid congratulations to actors and director, champagne toasts and delicacies, there were speeches.

"I'm not a man of the arts but this is a special occasion for me," said the general director of the cable plant. "It's important to show that theory and practice agree in our country. The working class has many talents, and with the liberation from capitalism it's necessary to develop them fully. We saw an excellent performance tonight that probably impressed many people deeply. I myself am very much impressed and as the representative of our state, I promise we'll do everything to develop the Cable Workers Theater collective."

The next speaker was an eighteen-year-old apprentice carpenter in the building trades, Axel Gärtner, who played Valentin. "I'd been thinking for some time that I'd like to act," he began. "When I came to the workers' theater a year and a half ago, I saw my chance. At first I had many illusions. I thought I could handle the part without difficulty. I didn't know the work involved. It was very hard, a very difficult time. I'd come here and then I'd get up at five in the morning. You tire yourself terribly as a carpenter and twice I almost left the cast. But tonight after it was over I felt like crying when I heard the applause and I knew it was all right. Last week at the final rehearsal I had a few minutes to myself and I thought of this year and a half. I can say without feeling ashamed because it's not empty words—this collective is my second home."

A few days later we visited the Hans Beimler plant, where a young trade union leader, Rainer Hinz, also spoke of a feeling of collectivity—and how difficult it had been to achieve. "After the end of the war, people were in such a state—whatever sense of collectivity they might once have had had been destroyed by fascism. The whole cultural level was destroyed. We had to overcome the egoism that had been created. People had to learn to help each other and to become active in a collective in a voluntary way—not the forced 'collectivity' of Hitler's army. This was a process and it's still continuing—the building of a developed socialist society isn't yet completed.

"Ideologists in the West say we should raise prices for the theater and for sports events. They say education shouldn't be free. Instead we should give people cheaper cars. These influences come in from the FRG. But through active cultural work—our socialist idea of culture—we've made great steps forward. And we could never have done it without the help of the Soviet Union. The inverse way of development lies two kilometers to the West," he said—pointing toward the boundary of the plant, which forms the frontier with the West.

THE CRUCIAL test of a people's feeling of collectivity, of concern for the whole, is whether that people expresses this concern toward other peoples.

"Improving living standards is a major task for us—but we don't interpret that in a narrow way," said Charlotte Bombal of the Textile, Clothes and Leather Workers Union. "The stronger we are as a socialist state, the greater the chance for insuring peace, for living in security. For three decades there's been peace in Europe—and that's only been possible because of the socialist states' policy of detente and peaceful coexistence and the leading role of the Soviet Union."

The socialist community's success, together with the world peace forces, in preventing World War III has made it possible for socialist construction to forge ahead. At the same time the socialist countries' internal progress is the basis for their ever-greater support to anti-colonial national liberation struggles and developing nations.

In the U.S. those who support liberation struggles clash with U.S. government policy. Since in the GDR there is no clash of interest between the people and their state, the people support the liberation struggles—those great battles for human rights—through their government and through their own personal actions.

In the GDR in the early seventies this story traveled far and wide: A very small boy is lost. A policeman sees his plight, picks him up and asks: "What's your name?" "I don't know," says the child. "What's your mother's name?" "I don't know." "What's your father's name?" "I don't know." "Are there any relatives whose names you do know?" "I don't know." "Is there *anyone's* name you know?" "Yes," replies the little boy. "Angela Davis."

In the GDR millions took part in a "one rose for Angela" campaign: Red roses, painted and pasted on postcards, were sent to Angela Davis in prison. Millions of signatures were collected and sent to the U.S. Senate. "Free Angela Davis" posters went up everywhere throughout the Republic. From plants to theaters to apartment houses protest actions were organized. On Angela Davis' twenty-seventh birthday, celebrations were held, including an enormous one at Berlin's House of Young Talent. "When news came that Angela Davis' release had been won, everyone felt, 'My signature, my rose counted,'" said Kurt Krüger, general secretary of the Solidarity Committee of the GDR. After this victory Angela Davis came to the GDR. Flanked by a GDR group playing guitars and singing, "Angela is free! Angela is free!" she was greeted by mammoth crowds.

One afternoon at the children's Friendship Theater we learned how close to the literal truth is the story of the little lost boy. During intermission we asked members of the grade school audience if they knew about Angela Davis. Child after child said that she or he had painted a "red rose for Angela," and many asked that their greetings be brought back to her.

Solidarity posters—on the African liberation struggles, Chilean political prisoners and many others—can be seen on GDR plant walls, school walls, in apartment halls, inside apartments. (*Für Dich* carries a different, detachable solidarity poster in every issue.) Within the solidarity struggles artists play their own special role.

A GDR author devotes himself to writing books for young people on the African liberation struggles. A GDR composer has dedicated an opera to the South African anti-apartheid fight. Since 1973 more than a dozen GDR films have been made on themes of support to the anti-fascist struggles in Chile. "And at the moment GDR artists are making a film on women of Mozambique," said Edda Eisenhardt, who heads the African Section of the Solidarity Committee. "It will be called *The Unknown Mother,* and will show how the mother and the whole family took part in the liberation struggle." Each year an international festival of documentary films is held in Leipzig. An annual International Festival of Political Song is held in Berlin. Artists participate in solidarity events in the plants as well as the theaters. Huge solidarity concerts have been held in plants, such as one in a chemical enterprise attended by 30,000 workers.

In April 1976 some of the most prominent GDR artists participated in a memorial concert for Paul Robeson. Shortly before leaving the GDR we had attended Robeson's funeral, and in Berlin we went to the memorial. Both funeral and memorial were attended by people of all ages, and both began with Robeson's voice singing "We Are Climbing Jacob's Ladder." At both funeral and memorial Robeson was hailed for his dedication to peace, liberation and socialism. The memorial ended when a group of Free German Youth came from audience to stage to sing "John Brown's Body."

During the Vietnam War Hanoi's symphony hall was bombed and all instruments destroyed. GDR musicians sent the Vietnamese musicians a complete set of instruments, including a grand piano. Radio Hanoi was bombed. GDR television and radio workers contributed to rebuilding it. TV studios in Hanoi were bombed. A shipload of equipment sailed from the GDR to Hanoi. Ships and planes stowed with food and medicine have gone from the GDR to Angola. The day we visited the Solidarity Committee a plane was leaving Berlin with eighteen tons of food, medicine and clothing for Mozambique and Guinea-Bissau. The day we visited the Cultural Workers Union, "News came from Spain that a well-known director, Antonio Barden, has been arrested again because he wanted to establish a union of theater workers," related Gabrielle Mylius, who is in charge of international relations for the union. "Our first steps were to send the news to all the socialist countries and wires of protest for his release."

Many men and women from "third world" countries come to the GDR to learn skills and professions for use in developing their own lands. The GDR also provides a refuge for victims of class and national liberation struggles. In the Berlin airport we saw wounded African freedom fighters arriving for medical treatment. And in Rostock we met Anibal Reyna and Patricio Bunster, two of the many Chilean artists now living and working in that city.

"We want to defend the values the junta has tried to destroy and we are doing this with our German comrades," said Anibal Reyna. Reyna, a Socialist, is a noted Chilean actor, president of the Chilean actors union and an officer of the International Federation of Actors.

"When we arrived in Rostock," he continued, "we got all the necessary material assistance—work corresponding to our artistic backgrounds, as well as apartments. We are all doing the same work we did in Chile. With the cooperation of our German comrades, we carry on our traditions, we work for solidarity—and prepare for the cultural work we will do when we go back." Reyna and Bunster are part of Aparcoa and Teatro Lautaro, two ensembles of Chilean artists that form distinct entities within the Volkstheater Rostock.

Bunster, a distinguished choreographer and a Communist, said, "Living here we feel the marvelous solidarity of the socialist countries every day. Not only do we feel the solidarity that is given to all of us to live and to work. We feel the problem of Chile—this danger which is a danger not only for Latin America—is in the heart and mind of everyone with great clarity."

That the Chilean and other liberation struggles are in the "heart and mind of everyone with great clarity" is demonstrated in the GDR in myriad ways. One notable gauge of the consciousness of the working class as a whole, of the working people in general, is to be seen in GDR trade union membership books. These books not only have a place for dues stamps but solidarity stamps. The brigades' annual plan also includes a solidarity pledge, redeemed through the solidarity shifts and other initiatives.

When we were out at the building site talking with the members of a construction brigade, we asked these "hard hats" if they'd taken part in the fight to free Angela Davis. "We fought for Angela Davis," replied young Dietmar Roessel. "But what about the Rosenbergs? Will the sons succeed in getting the papers from the FBI? Will the case be reopened? What will you do to see that it never happens again?"

AMONG THE countries of the socialist community, international solidarity has achieved a qualitatively new dimension.

One aspect of this is mutual economic planning, where competition is replaced by cooperation: Through agreements, one socialist country produces certain equipment or materials for use by all the countries of the socialist community. This is accompanied by cooperation on scientific and technological development.

"No one country can do everything. The division of labor among members of the socialist community—the fact that we cooperate according to a plan—is an advantage of the socialist system," pointed out Detlev Narr at the Hans Beimler plant. Accompanying the growth of economic ties is the development of closer and closer cultural ties, whose significance can be appreciated only if one remembers the past.

"Millions of people in the socialist countries lived through an era when Germany played a terrible role toward its neighbors," said Narr. "But as economic integration grows, cultural links and the people themselves become closer. There are not only letters but human, personal meetings. Our partners in the other socialist countries see we're not responsible for the mistakes of our fathers.

"When we go to the Soviet Union for a scientific conference," he continued, "we not only talk in the plants—we also go to concerts and the theater together. We learn the culture of the other country. In the Soviet Union we visit towns that were completely destroyed in World War II—you can still see that. Then we discuss the past. To learn from the past is to build a better future."

Exchanges of many types—involving workers, children's vacations, scientific conferences, etc.—take place on a big scale among the socialist nations. In the textile industry, for example, "Ten workers from a garment plant in Leipzig will leave to work for a while in a garment plant in Kiev, while ten workers from the Kiev plant will come to Leipzig," related Charlotte Bombal. "With Poland we're organizing an exchange of apprentices. And with Bulgaria we'll hold a competition for the best apprentices in the textile industry in our Republic and in theirs. With this contact, which is widespread, friendship between workers is developed and strengthened."

One of the most dramatic examples of cooperation among the socialist countries is the building of the Friendship Pipeline. "I volunteered for this because of its vast importance—it's the most important venture of my life up to now," said Gisela Kanus during her vacation in Berlin. "This is a youth project—taking part in it is an expression of the co-determination of youth.

"We're working now in the Ukraine, this area where Germans did such terrible things. That's why it's so impressive for us to see how we're accepted by the people—so warmly, without reservations. We can speak of friendship and mutual assistance but it's best expressed in personal relations. When we say we feel at home there, it's no exaggeration. We work as fast as possible but it will be hard to say goodby."

The friendship felt by the people in what was once the Eastern part of Germany for the Soviet Union is one of history's most striking reversals. "Our Constitution says the GDR will always and forever be linked in friendship with the Soviet Union. There's no plant, school or institution without a branch of our organization," said Herbert

Grünstein, head of the German-Soviet Friendship League. The organization has over four million members.

"Friendship with the Soviet Union is the concern of our whole people," added Gerhard Römer, the league's press officer. From an opposite standpoint it's equally the concern of those who control the FRG. "We carry on our work under the ideological fire of an enemy that employs a terrific anti-Soviet hate campaign on TV and radio."

This is a campaign with twin themes.

> The German darkness
> Descends over my spirit
> It darkens overpowering in my song
> It comes because I see my Germany
> So deeply torn

What has descended over this poet's spirit is, unfortunately, the influence of those who aim to restore "one Germany." In fact, these lines from "The German Darkness Descends" by Wolf Biermann aptly express the sentiments of the FRG reactionaries whose campaign for "one Germany united" is intertwined with and indivisible from their anti-Soviet campaign.

Ironically, those corporate monopolists who lament "my Germany/ So deeply torn" are the ones responsible for its division. They imposed this separation to prevent establishment of "one Germany" along peaceful, democratic lines. Supported by the U.S. and the other Western powers, they sabotaged the Potsdam agreement to demilitarize and democratize the Western part of Germany—the agreement carried out in the Eastern area with the support of the Soviet Union. (Although Biermann would like us to believe he is an adherent of socialism, those really committed to socialism rejoice that reaction was prevented from reimposing exploitation over the whole territory of the former German state.)

Unable to "roll back" social advance in the Eastern area, Hitler's corporate supporters—with the assistance of the U.S. and its allies—established a new state, the Federal Republic of Germany, on two-thirds of the old German territory, while continuing to occupy two-thirds of Berlin as a military outpost.

After Germany had been "deeply torn"—"one German nation" was, in fact, the first casualty of imperialism's cold war—only one option was left to the working class and its allies in the Eastern area: the formation of their own state to protect their democratic gains.

"The founding of the two German states," said GDR Cultural Ambassador Dr. Kurt Merkel, speaking with us at the Foreign Ministry, "is the consequence of a long historical development," with two aspects: the struggle of the working class and its allies on one hand, and "the founding of the German Reich by Bismarck with blood and iron" on the other. "If we regard the GDR as the only state inheriting the democratic line of development—unfortunately, it's true. I'd like it much better if the other state would also continue this line."

"In the founding of the GDR," commented Rudolf Kranbold, second secretary at the Foreign Ministry, "another of Marx's ideas is realized. In every capitalist state there are two 'nations,' one rich and the other poor. Our proletariat created the wealth but others possessed it. Today the working class possesses the material and cultural goods in the socialist state." In its relations with the FRG, continued Kranbold, the GDR "pursues a policy of peaceful coexistence," as it does with other capitalist states. "These are the only relations possible," he stressed, "between an imperialist German state and a socialist one."

Integral to peaceful coexistence is the principle of non-interference in the internal affairs of other states—a principle continually violated by the FRG, including through its campaign for "one Germany."

"In their drive for 'one Germany united,'" said Horst Noack at the Party College, "the FRG reactionaries say, 'We're all Germans, all in one boat.' This is an ideology that is supposedly classless but is really bourgeois. When they say, 'We're all Germans, all brothers and sisters,' they're trying to stimulate an emotional orgy. That's what makes it so dangerous—this attempt to convert national sentiments into national chauvinism."

Through its economic, social and cultural development the GDR has become an advanced socialist nation. The differences between England and the U.S.—born over two hundred years ago in a revolution against English colonial rule—are minor as compared to the fundamental distinctions that have emerged between the FRG and the GDR in only three decades. There must be peaceful coexistence between the FRG and GDR, and between all capitalist and socialist nations—but the idea of "one Germany" is chauvinist fiction, because "convergence" or "merger" between the socialist GDR and the capitalist FRG is an impossibility.

When those responsible for a Germany "deeply torn" turned around and demanded "one Germany united," the inconsistency in their behavior could be explained only by the continuity of their class aims. These class aims are most directly expressed inside the FRG, where the "nation" of the rich carries on its anti-working class, anti-democratic strategy against the "nation" of the poor.

But these same class aims are also expressed beyond the FRG's borders, with grave international implications. They are pursued through the neo-fascist, militarist "one Germany" propaganda that creates an atmosphere for violations of treaties regarding the GDR's sovereign borders, as well as West Berlin's special status. It is the FRG's denial of the GDR's existence as a sovereign socialist nation that provides the rationale for its failure to respect GDR borders. (To be reminded of how dangerous this is, one need only recall the behavior of the former German state toward the borders of other nations.) At the same time the chauvinist "one German nation" myth also offers the rationale for the FRG, together with its NATO allies, to carry on the arms race against the "Soviet threat" in the East.

From the GDR's founding in 1949 until 1961 the border between West Berlin and the GDR was uncontrolled. "Before we put an end to uncontrolled crossings of our Berlin frontier," said Herbert Grünstein, who was then GDR Secretary of State, "they sabotaged, burned and mined inside our borders. They introduced a different currency— arbitrarily determining the rate of exchange: one of their marks against five of ours. There was a terrific black market." During this period thousands worked in West Berlin while living in the GDR. They made no contribution to the GDR economy, yet they not only had the advantage of the exchange rate on currency but also the benefits of non-inflated GDR prices, minimal rents and free medical services.

A vast traffic engaged in counterrevolutionary, black market and smuggling activity moved from West Berlin streets—occupied by the combined military presence of the U.S. and its imperialist allies—in and out of the GDR. West Berlin not only became an enclave of FRG reaction and neo-Nazism extending into the very center of the GDR. It also became the global center for conspiracies—directed by the CIA, the Pentagon and NATO—against the entire socialist community. By August 1961 this pattern of counterrevolutionary activity moving back and forth over the border had reached crisis proportions: The FRG and West Berlin reactionaries were now trying to draw their NATO partners into armed intervention against the GDR. (The U.S. had only recently demonstrated anew its willingness to participate in such ventures: It was in April 1961 that the U.S.-organized invasion of Cuba had been stopped by the Cuban people at the Bay of Pigs.)

The provocations against the GDR had become such a danger to peace in Europe that even among some in high places in the U.S. there was grave concern. "I don't understand why the East Germans don't close their border because I think they have every right to do it," declared Senator William Fullbright, then Chairman of the Senate Foreign Relations Committee. This was reported in *The New York Times* on August 11, 1961.

But the GDR, together with the Soviet Union and the socialist community, had already decided to take this step. From the third of August to the fifth the Warsaw Pact countries had met, declared their readiness to "take all measures to reach agreement with the Western powers on a peaceful settlement with the two German states," and had resolved to "reliably bar the way to subversive activity against the countries of the socialist community."

During the night of August 13 the People's Police of the GDR together with the voluntary workers' militia built border installations to end uncontrolled entrance into the GDR's capital. "We built the wall in Berlin—the anti-fascist resistance wall. I took part in this, I helped to build it. I watched everything and I wrote about it," playwright Helmut Baierl told us.

The Western mass media have also written about the wall standing at the GDR's border. To them it is, of course, not an anti-fascist resistance wall but "The Wall," "The Berlin Wall"—a symbol of evil intrinsic to the GDR's social system. Yet this wall is not an evil but a protection against it.

There is, however, a wall symbolizing evil—but the corporate-owned media say nothing about it. This is the wall erected by U.S. imperialism on Cuban territory: the electrified steel wall—seventeen miles long, interspersed with armed turrets—surrounding Guantanamo, occupied by the U.S. as a military base.

The Guantanamo wall was built by reaction to keep the people out, while "The Berlin Wall" was built by the people to keep reaction out. The anti-fascist resistance wall is a symbol of the solidarity of the Soviet Union and the other socialist countries with the GDR. The wall at the GDR's border is the way the socialist community said *No pasaran!* to counterrevolution. In 1961 at the anti-fascist resistance wall, the U.S. and its NATO allies suffered a second "Bay of Pigs" defeat—while the people won a second victory: the saving of peace in Europe.

THE BOURGEOIS media that so frequently inveigh against "The Wall" seldom give us a glimpse of what goes on to the West of it. However, in May 1975—on the thirtieth anniversary of the liberation from fascism—a particularly revealing glimpse was offered by a story in the *Los Angeles Times*. Describing the way the FRG rulers marked the occasion, the *Times* reported:

The current leaders of West Germany sat solemnly in the old Castle Church in Bonn while President Walter Scheel gave what one diplomat termed "a very honest and very eloquent address."

"We remember this day with pain," Scheel said, "because it marked the end of Germany as it had been known . . ." May 8, he said, was "the day of capitulation."

In the other German state, the story went on to say, the occasion was marked in quite a different way:

Not far away as the jets fly, the leaders of East Germany watched in Berlin while 40,000 German and Soviet Communist youth stood with torches to welcome from Moscow the arrival of a battle flag that had accompanied the Red Army 30 years before.

As the official East German Communist newspaper, Neues Deutschland, put it: "We may count ourselves among the victors of history."[3]

The victors of history after World War II were all the peoples of the world—including the masses in the FRG who are told by their leaders that the day of liberation was "the day of capitulation."

In the GDR the victory over fascism is recognized as "the decisive thing that enabled us to create a nation of a new character," stated Kurt Merkel. "But for the FRG monopolists the thirtieth anniversary represented nothing but a huge defeat. They are quite right. For them it was a huge defeat." Unreconciled to this defeat, they strive continually to restore the losses from it.

In an address to the FRG cabinet on the occasion of the thirtieth anniversary, Chancellor Helmut Schmidt said, "We have learned our lesson from the past." It would be more accurate to say that FRG reaction has learned how to bring the past into the present.

We are frequently reminded of this fact by events in the FRG and West Berlin: by the pardoning of Nazi war criminals; by the rallies honoring Nazi "war heroes"; by demonstrations commemorating "special occasions" in Nazi history; by reports of men armed with machine guns gathered around a bust of Hitler; by the alarm of the small Jewish community at the "increased nostalgia for the glory days of fascism and heightened neo-Nazi activity"[4]—a nostalgia built up by the massive publication of books "humanizing" Nazi leaders and obscuring the German monopolists' responsibility for the rise of fascism.

"We have learned the lessons of the past," said Schmidt—as his government carried on police-state inquisitions against thousands of anti-militarist advocates of social change, consigning them to the category of *Berufsverbot*—job forbidden. The victims of *Berufsverbot* join the huge number of other FRG citizens for whom jobs are not forbidden but simply unavailable. At the same time millions of foreign-born workers are told, "The rule is that German workers have preference for the jobs that are available." Added to this chauvinism faced by all the foreign-born workers is the multi-dimensional racism confronting those with dark skin. "Hundreds of thousands" of the children of Turkish workers in a "crumbling" West Berlin ghetto "are headed toward a grim future." The "symptoms of this stricken neighborhood sound like those that created New York's slums . . ."[5] And this same racism continually assaults the Black GI's stationed in West Berlin and the FRG for the alleged purpose of "defending human rights."

The forces responsible for these conditions are those "patriots" who campaign for "one Germany." Their patriotism was aptly described by Aristotle Onassis who once said, "My favorite country is one that grants immunity from taxes, trade restrictions and unreasonable regulations."

It's getting harder and harder to find such countries—a reality reactionaries refuse to accept. What they want is "immunity" to move the world backward until it meets the specifications of the multi-national corporations. And the FRG reactionaries have a special desire to move back to the days of "My Germany." What's behind the "one German nation" myth isn't patriotism but capitalism's innate, aggressive drive for expansion. And the virulence of the FRG's anti-Communist, anti-Soviet propaganda can be traced to the fact that the Soviet Union, the GDR and the whole socialist community block FRG reaction from moving eastward. The FRG uses the same propaganda to escalate its militarization program—part of an overall NATO armaments buildup against the socialist countries. This intensifying militarization also assists the FRG in its rivalry with fellow imperialists, while synchronizing with the strategy of U.S. and West European neo-colonialism in Africa and elsewhere in the "third world."

In its "third world" policies the FRG continues in new forms the colonialist traditions of Germany's first Imperial Commissioner of Southwest Africa (Namibia), who was the father of Nazi leader Hermann Göring. This is among the reasons why the FRG is the principal ally of the U.S. and apartheid-fascist South Africa.

By contrast, the intrinsically non-expansionist, non-aggressive socialist system brought a break in what was once the Eastern part of Germany with the "blood and iron" expansionism of the old German state. From this break the GDR went on to active partnership with the Soviet Union and the socialist community, which forms a worldwide bulwark against imperialism. In the "third world," for example, the socialist community's support to liberation struggles is an increasingly important factor in blocking neo-colonialism.

In carrying out its policies for peace and in support of national liberation, the socialist community comes into conflict with the policies of the U.S., the FRG and their partners. To conceal what's involved in this clash, the imperialists and their allies raise the cry of "Soviet threat" in every situation. But to conform to their particular requirements in the Mideast, these forces also level the charge of anti-Semitism against the socialist countries.

In the Mideast, imperialism's partners include both the Zionist rulers and reactionary Arab rulers (such as those in Egypt and Saudi Arabia), who act with the U.S. against the African liberation movements. Both the Israeli ruling class and Arab reactionaries are more and more overtly allied with the South African apartheid fascists and world imperialism against the liberation movements in South Africa, Zimbabwe (Rhodesia), Namibia and elsewhere. The pursuit by reactionary Israelis and reactionary Arabs of their own class aims simultaneously brings them into a clash with each other and with the interests of the people of their respective countries.

Yet the main reactionary force in the Mideast is not a resident of that area. It's U.S. imperialism. Zionist occupation of Arab lands requires U.S. support, as do the anti-Israeli policies of reactionary Arabs. U.S. imperialism's support to both Zionists and reactionary Arabs is not a contradiction, because imperialism supports *all* enemies of the people's national and democratic rights.

Those forces who charge the socialist community with anti-Semitism try to give credence to their claims by making it appear that to be a Zionist is synonymous with being a Jew, and therefore to be anti-Zionist is to be anti-Semitic. But Zionism is no more synonymous with the interests of the masses of Jews in Israel or anywhere else than white supremacy is in the interests of white masses in the U.S. or anywhere else. Zionism is a reactionary nationalist ideology that denies class divisions among Jews, thus serving as a screen for the pursuit by Israel's exploiting class of its own interests in partnership with U.S. imperialism. This exploiting class permits Israeli Jews certain privileges forbidden to Israeli Arabs. This is as divisive to the working people in Israel as white supremacy is to the working people in the U.S. At the same time Zionism makes it difficult for Israeli Jews to see that the struggle against the Zionist ruling class's expansionist aims is in the interests of peace and Israel's security.

Far from being antithetic ideologies, Zionism and anti-Semitism both spring from the concept of superior and inferior peoples. Because of this, Zionism also has similarities with white supremacy, "one German nation" neo-aryanism, apartheid racism and the anti-Jewish focus of Arab reactionaries. (We are well aware of the intense pressure on Jews not to dissent against Zionism. But it's particularly up to those who are Jewish, as we are, to speak out against a reactionary ideology particularly addressed to Jews.)

Since the foreign policies of the capitalist FRG and the socialist GDR are consistent with their respective domestic policies, the FRG engenders anti-Semitism and supports Zionism while the GDR does the opposite.

"For Germans the Jewish question is a very special one. The crimes committed were so terrible that even my generation is confronted by them," said Kurt Merkel, who is in his thirties. "The most important thing is to guarantee that this can never happen again. No one can honestly deny that we've created such a situation in the GDR. And in our international relations, we must live up to this same responsibility. As a German state, we have a duty to the victims of fascism—the millions of Jewish, Soviet, Polish and other victims."

This responsibility is fulfilled by the GDR in its struggle, together with the Soviet Union and the socialist community, for detente, peaceful coexistence and in support of all peoples struggling for their liberation and human rights.

THE CONTRADICTION between the U.S. government's "human rights" stance and the reality of its actions confronts the peoples of Asia, Africa and Latin America every day of their lives. At home we too are confronted with the same grim contradiction between rhetoric and reality. We see it in the way pseudo-crises are constantly created while real ones are consistently ignored.

One such example occurred when the oil monopolists maneuvered an "energy shortage." Jimmy Carter obligingly escalated this into an "energy crisis." He then called upon the people to conserve energy through a program of further hardships—which he promoted as a "moral equivalent of war."

Shortly before this occasion Carter had offered a particularly revealing glimpse of his concept of morality. Asked at a press conference whether he felt "any moral obligation to help rebuild" Vietnam, Carter replied, "I don't feel that we ought to apologize or castigate ourselves or to assume the status of culpability."[6] (Speaking now from the White House was the man who as Governor of Georgia had brought the people of that state "Lt. Calley Day," in honor of the mass murderer of My Lai.)

Only an individual with such an idea of morality could talk of a "moral equivalent of war." That there is no "moral equivalent of war" was verified in what Carter presented as one: His demand that the people conserve energy came as the government continued to add billions to the war budget—which squanders more human and natural resources on weapons, missiles, military planes, ships and submarines than could be saved by any conservation program conceivable. Although Carter speaks of "conserving energy," he intensified the *real* energy crisis: capitalism's waste of the human energy of millions by denial of that most basic human right, the right to work.

There is no "moral equivalent of war." But there are moral *alterna-*

tives to war. For us the immediate moral alternative is the fight for peace, jobs, equality and against racism—a struggle that conflicts with the interests of the oil and other monopolists Carter represents.

In 1913 Lenin wrote:

People have always been the foolish victims of deception and self-deception in politics, and they always will be until they have learnt to seek out the *interests* of some class or other behind all moral, religious, political and social phrases, declarations and promises.[7]

The Russian workers understood what Lenin meant, and led the struggle to liberate their country from a ruling class that tried to hide its real interests behind moral-sounding phrases, as it forced the people to go to war. The Russian working class found a moral alternative to war in its struggle for peace: The first decree of Soviet power in 1917 was the Decree of Peace for ending World War I. From there the Russian workers and their allies went on to build socialism, the moral alternative to capitalism, the system engendering war and oppression.

Speaking of the first country to bring socialism to the world, the premier of the first country to bring socialism to the Americas stated, "Humanity will ever be thankful to the Soviet Union for what it has done not only for a better future for the people but also to defend the people's right to life and security, the most human of all rights.

"The most important of these [tasks], and the one most highly valued by all the peoples," declared Fidel Castro, "consists in the noble and important task of preserving peace and delivering humanity from the threat of nuclear war."[8]

"HUMAN RIGHTS is a central concern of my Administration," wrote President Carter[9] in a heavily-publicized answer to a heavily-publicized letter from "dissident" Andrei Sakharov. Carter assured Sakharov that he would use his "good offices" to "shape a world responsive to human aspirations."

For more and more U.S. citizens the contradiction between "human rights" rhetoric and inhuman reality at home was becoming harder and harder to take.

"I think the world will die laughing [at any government] policy that talks about human rights if it does not contain the solution to the anguish, misery and humiliation that the American Indian has suffered over the past 400 years," declared Marlon Brando.[10] If President Carter had any comment, he chose to keep it secret.

In Wilmington, North Carolina, nine Black men and one white woman were sentenced by an all-white jury to a total of 282 years in prison. "North Carolina ranks first in the country in the number of prisons in proportion to population. There are 72 of them, and they hold 12,000 inmates. Not a single inmate is officially listed as a political prisoner, but the crime of many, just as in the case of the Wilmington 10, was only to seek equality," wrote James Baldwin in a letter[11] urging Carter to use his "good offices" to free the Wilmington 10. Still Carter expressed no interest in using his "good offices" on behalf of the Wilmington 10's "human aspirations."

From his prison cell, Reverend Ben Chavis, one of the Wilmington 10, also wrote to Carter. "Will you not speak out for us?" he asked. "Will you not use your good offices to bring about our release?"[12] President Carter did not reply.

But at a press conference a few months later he was reminded by a reporter that many forces have "implored you for your intervention on behalf" of the Wilmington 10. "What comments do you have?"[13]

President Carter took time out from his intervention in the internal affairs of socialist states to say that he could not intervene in the internal affairs of the states of this country.

As Carter once again confirmed, there is no contradiction between this government's actions at home and abroad. When the President *does* use his "good offices," it's on behalf of those whose views conform to U.S. policies. And the extent to which the views of the "dissidents" harmonize with those of the U.S. government is more than coincidental.

In fact, the views that go into socialist countries via such sources as U.S. government-funded Radio Free Europe and Radio Liberty are the same ones that come out via the "dissidents"—who have "ties to the West, financial resources and good public relations techniques," as one syndicated columnist admitted.[14] The "dissidents"—Solzhenitsyn, Sakharov, Bukovsky, etc.—"warn" U.S. leaders against the very policies these leaders are already sabotaging, detente and peaceful coexistence. The "dissidents" call for U.S. intervention in the socialist countries, although from Vietnam to Chile to Angola the world has experienced what U.S. intervention means.

In "Bukovsky's Own Story,"[15] an article appearing shortly before Carter greeted him at the White House, Bukovsky stated that he had wanted to organize an armed overthrow of the Soviet government but found this "impracticable." "Replacement of the present system," he declared, will not come about "so long as the West accepts the rule that it may not 'interfere in the internal affairs of the Soviet Union'"—a rule Western governments have violated ever since the October Revolution.

When Bukovsky arrived in Switzerland, his first Western stop, he announced, "I would love to exchange Brezhnev for Pinochet." Bukovsky would, in other words, "love to exchange" socialism for fascism. Bukovsky revealed the thinking of his backers, who would go to any lengths to preserve the only "human right" they care about.

As Fidel Castro points out, "The leaders of the imperialist countries are now talking with amazing hypocrisy about human rights. Clearly, they are first and foremost worried about the bourgeois 'right' to exploit humans.

"There is nothing more inhuman in the history of humanity than the capitalist and imperialist system . . . Those of us who have visited Africa and have seen the scars of colonialism, capitalism, imperialism and racism, well understand what 'human rights' the imperialists are defending," stated Castro,[16] who had just returned from a trip to African countries.

Fidel Castro is First Secretary of the Communist Party of Cuba. Henry Winston is National Chairman of the Communist Party of the United States. "Human rights," noted Winston during a talk with us, "are not an abstraction. What are 'human rights' that involve the 'right' to act against the will of the people struggling to free themselves from oppression? One must ask whether human rights are on the side of U.S. imperialism and its CIA assassins, or on the side of those fighting to save humanity from nuclear war.

"Those who talk about 'dissidents'—in reality they're talking about, at most, hundreds of individuals. And again one must ask, what kind of 'dissidents' are they? What are they dissenting against? They're in dissent against the hundreds of millions of people in the socialist system who have moved away from capitalism because of its inhumanity. They are 'dissidents' against the national liberation movements—which include tens of millions of Africans, Asians and Latin Americans. They're in dissent from humanity as a whole—from all the people of the world who want to prevent nuclear war." There are, pointed out Winston who is Black, dissidents of another kind. "Africans, Asians and Latin Americans are dissidents against imperialism. And what about the people in our country? Could 30 million

Blacks or any of the oppressed minorities be described as satisfied and happy? Or could the white workers who are part of the army of unemployed be described in such terms? Tens of millions of people in the U.S. are dissidents against unemployment, inflation, poverty and racism—and more and more of them are moving into dissent against the system itself."

The reason that people moving in a revolutionary direction number in the billions while anti-socialist "dissidents" number in the hundreds, pointed out Winston, is because "the imperialists can't find a real base today for counterrevolution among the people of any country. That's why they have to export counterrevolution. But revolution isn't exported. When the 'third world' peoples struggle for their national liberation, the imperialists call it 'Soviet expansionism.' But what's expanding is the struggles of the people. The people themselves are doing the struggling, supported by the Soviet Union and the socialist countries, as well as the people in every country who are in dissent against oppression and exploitation."

THE PEOPLE move toward the future. "Dissidents" long for the past. Solzhenitsyn yearns for Czarist Russia, Wolf Biermann for "my Germany"—evoking nostalgic images of what was a racist aryan past.

Concluding his lament for "my Germany/So deeply torn," written while he was in the GDR, Biermann avows "twice the sorrow" because "I find myself in the better half." Since in poem after poem he reveals his antagonism for "the better half," this sentiment cannot be taken seriously—although in expressing it, he seriously hopes to be taken for a revolutionary. How deeply embedded is his anti-revolutionary course can be seen in his very attempt to prove the opposite. "Better half"? A state where the working class and its allies are in power and a state where monopoly is in power could never be two parts of one whole. And this was demonstrated once again by the way the FRG rulers, who are moving in an increasingly militaristic, anti-socialist direction, have welcomed Biermann's attacks upon the GDR.

Revolutionary poets identify with the people. Biermann celebrates his aversion to them: "*I, I, I/* Am full of hate," he writes in another poem. For whom? "The collective." Why? "The collective has become isolated from me."

For a response to this poem Biermann must count once again on nostalgia, on evoking certain images that may linger in a reader's mind—images of poets isolated through the ages from an indifferent mass; images of rebellious poets such as Villon, or Shelley who wrote, "Poets are the unacknowledged legislators of the world." Are they?

To take this romantic idea literally is to grant immunity to poets because they are poets. To accept such concepts, that appear today in far less romantic forms, is to believe artists exist beyond class ties. If one does this, one forgets that a poet can be a racist, an anti-Semite, a fascist sympathizer, as was Ezra Pound. On the other hand, Bertolt Brecht and Pablo Neruda were also poets. The people do acknowledge their true representatives after all.

Biermann's scorn for the people, his affinity for the artist as isolated entity, may evoke other images too. Of, perhaps, Thoreau's lone individual who "hears a different drummer." But was this individual who did not "keep up pace with his companions" really alone? Thoreau himself did not "keep up pace" with the powerful citizens of Concord when he refused to pay taxes in protest against slavery and was jailed. But he was not alone. He was keeping up pace with the Black slaves struggling to be free, with the Abolitionists, with history itself. Many artists and intellectuals of the time did the same. But some stepped to other sounds.

It was an actor, John Wilkes Booth, who assassinated Lincoln. He heard the voices of the former slaveowners, proclaiming their "right" to regain what they had lost. The "dissidents" in socialist countries have also fallen into step with those who never stop trying to regain what they have lost. And those who try to recapture lost possessions make this attempt sound like a crusade for freedom—as did the former slaveowners.

When the slaves won their freedom, the slaveowners lost the freedom to hold men and women as chattel. With the socialist revolution, the capitalist class loses the freedom to exploit women and men—as well as the freedom to try to restore this "right." Because this old freedom doesn't exist in socialist countries, there is a new freedom. It starts at birth: In a socialist country, people are born with an equal chance.

In the U.S. there's an expression, "born to lose." It's never applied to a Rockefeller, a DuPont or a Ford—only to workers, to oppressed people. But the multi-racial, multi-national working class and its allies are born to win. Actors, playwrights, poets and all intellectuals who realize this are bound for the future.

A GRAY, RAW afternoon on a late winter day. We walk through the gate and are greeted by a gaunt handsome man with white hair. After you see the place, he says, we'll talk. Now we're alone with a guide. After we see the place? We have seen it. This one or some other one. We've seen the pictures, haven't we? This time the medium is reality. This was roll call square, the guide says. They had to line up here. Every day. Stood here for hours while their names were called out. In heat, cold, rain, snow. Once they stood in bitter cold for twenty hours. A prisoner had escaped. The guide points to a building. That was Tower A. The SS Command Post. Every inch of the camp was in firing range of the eighteen SS watchtowers. And the camp was surrounded by electrically-charged barbed wire. Eighty-eight barracks stood around roll call square. Some are still there. Now we go in and out of barracks. In and out of underground cells. In and out of isolation cells. Now we enter a white-tiled room. This was the pathological department, the guide explains, where SS doctors conducted studies on previously healthy patients. Now we're at Station Z. Station Z. Entire transports of people were murdered here. By gas, bullets, ovens, hanging, guillotine. We walk on. Those barracks over there were the sick rooms, the guide tells us. And that was Barracks 58. That's where prisoners accused of resistance were taken. And Barracks 37, 38 and 39 were over there. That's where Jews and Poles were brought. Now a memorial stands there, the Museum of the Resistance and Suffering of the Jewish People. We go inside, and from there to the Camp Museum. We look at records showing how the SS rented out the prisoners to monopolists, armaments-makers Farben, Krupp, Thyssen. The SS made about 50 million marks a month from this. The neatly-kept records show it all. Down to the value of the gold fillings extracted from the prisoners' teeth after their deaths. Germans, Hungarians, French and English were among those brought here. Eighteen thousand Soviet prisoners of war were murdered here. We walk into an area honoring these prisoners of all nations. From there we move into a room where the story of the anti-fascist struggle is told in stainglass murals, sculpture, poetry. And in this same room we see the story as it is told in the prisoners's own art, their last letters.

Now we have seen what was Sachsenhausen Concentration Camp. The guide walks with us to Tower A, where the white-haired man waits for us. His name is Werner Staake. As he leads us inside and up a flight of stairs, he tells us that 100,000 died in Sachsenhausen. In spring 1945,

30,000 prisoners were forced to leave the camp for a death march to the sea. That destination was never reached: The march was overtaken and the prisoners were liberated by the advancing Red Army.

Werner Staake opens a door and we pass into a room. During the years I was a prisoner in Sachsenhausen, he says, this was the office of the SS Commandant. Now it's my office. Werner Staake is the Commander of Sachsenhausen National Memorial.

Thousands of visitors come here now. And each year in the GDR the passage of young people into adulthood is marked by Youth Week. It's a week of celebration but during it the young adults visit this national memorial. And here they deepen their determination to build socialism and defend peace.

Our thoughts jump now to Brecht and Mother Courage. Mother Courage, who went through years and years of war without learning anything. Mother Courage didn't learn, but Brecht hoped other people would.

The German people were led into militarization, a massive arms buildup, fascism and war to defend themselves, they were told, against a "Soviet threat."

Now in the U.S. we are being led deeper and deeper into militarization and a greater and greater arms buildup to defend ourselves, we are told, against a "Soviet threat."

The threat comes from those who tell us this.

Mother Courage didn't learn. But others did. We can too.

Notes

1. Double Image

1. *The New York Times,* October 6, 1975.
2. *Variety,* May 17, 1975.
3. *The New York Times,* April 3, 1975.
4. Ibid.
5. Ibid.
6. *The New York Times,* May 18, 1975.
7. "'Black' Shows for White Viewers," by Eugenia Collier. *Freedomways,* Vol. 14, Number 3, 1974. Emphasis in the original.
8. *The New York Times,* April 19, 1977.
9. "The Black Film—'Supernigger' As Folk Hero," by Loyle Hairston. *Freedomways,* Vol. 14, Number 3, 1974.
10. *The New York Times,* December 8, 1974.
11. "The Way It Was: Professional Theater Employment, 1973–74 Season," by Alan Hewitt. Prepared for Actors' Equity Association. February 1975.
12. *New York* magazine, September 1, 1975.
13. *New York Post,* August 19, 1975.
14. *The New York Times,* September 7, 1975.
15. *The Season,* by William Goldman. Harcourt, Brace, Jovanovich, New York, 1970, pp. 217–18. Emphasis in the original.
16. Quoted in *Enter Joseph Papp,* by Stuart W. Little, Coward McCann and Geoghegan, Inc., New York, 1974, p. 119.

2. Theater: Microcosm of a Society

1. "How 'All Over Town' Got On Boards," by Mel Gussow. *The New York Times,* January 2, 1975.
2. Ibid.
3. Ibid.
4. *The New York Times,* February 27, 1975.
5. *Enter Joseph Papp,* p. 271.
6. Ibid.
7. Ibid., p. 272.
8. Ibid., p. 273.
9. Ibid.
10. *The Season,* p. 215.
11. *The New York Times,* September 28, 1975.

3. "We Are the State"

1. *Los Angeles Times,* June 19, 1975.
2. *Los Angeles Times,* May 25, 1975.
3. *The New York Times,* July 13, 1975.
4. "A Playwright's Invention Named Papp," by Mel Gussow. *The New York Times Magazine,* November 9, 1975.
5. "What's New? Old Shows," by Mel Gussow. *The New York Times,* May 9, 1976.
6. *The New York Times,* December 29, 1974.
7. "What's New? Old Shows."
8. "A Playwright's Invention Named Papp."
9. "Journeyman Years With Brecht," by Erwin Strittmatter, in *Brecht As They Knew Him,* International Publishers, New York, 1974, p. 160.

4. Conflicts On Stage and Off

1. *Plays and Players,* February 1975.
2. Ibid.
3. Ibid.
4. Ibid. Emphasis in the original.
5. *Theatre in the German Democratic Republic,* No. 7, December 1974.
6. Ibid.
7. *The Christian Century,* April 25, 1973.
8. Ibid.
9. Ibid.
10. *Plays and Players.* March 1973.
11. Ibid., February 1973.
12. *The Christian Century,* April 25, 1973.
13. Ibid.
14. *Theatre in the German Democratic Republic,* No. 7, December 1974.

5. U. S. Strategy To Assimilate Protest

1. *Revolution As Theatre,* by Robert Brustein. Liveright, New York, 1971, pp. 6-7.
2. Ibid., p. 7.
3. Ibid.
4. Ibid., p. 8.
5. Ibid., p. 10.
6. *Guerilla Street Theater,* edited by Henry Lesnick. Bard Books/Avon Books, New York, 1973, p. 38.

7. Ibid., p. 288.
8. *A Time To Die*, by Tom Wicker, Quadrangle-NYT Book Co., New York, 1975, p. 256.
9. *Guerilla Street Theater*, p. 21.
10. Ibid.
11. Ibid.
12. Ibid., pp. 24-25.
13. *The Impossible Theater*, by Herbert Blau. The Macmillan Company, New York, 1964, pp. 63-64.
14. Ibid., p. 62.
15. Ibid.
16. Ibid.
17. Ibid., p. 65.
18. Ibid., p. 172.
19. Ibid., p. 116.
20. Ibid., p. 134.
21. *New York Post*, February 7, 1976.
22. "A Playwright's Invention Named Papp."
23. *The Fervent Years: The Story of the Group Theatre and the Thirties*, by Harold Clurman. Alfred A. Knopf, Inc.. Copyright © 1945, 1957, 1973 by Harold Clurman, p. 264.

6. From Antagonism to Advocacy

1. "The Dialectics of Legitimation: Brecht in the GDR," by David Bathrick. *New German Critique*, Number 2, Spring 1974.
2. "The Brecht-Lukács Debate," by Werner Mittenzwei. Appears in *Preserve and Create*, translated and edited by Gaylord C. LeRoy and Ursula Beitz. Humanities Press, New York, 1973, p. 199.
3. "Practical Comments on the Expressionism Debate," *Werkausgabe*, Suhrkamp Verlag, Frankfurt-am-Main, 1967, Vol. 19, p. 296.
4. "On Formalism And New Forms," *Werkausgabe*, Suhrkamp Verlag, Frankfurt-am-Main, 1967. Vol. 19, p. 527.
5. "Notes on Realistic Writing," *Werkausgabe*, 1967, Vol. 19, p. 361.
6. "The Brecht-Lukács Debate," in *Preserve and Create*, p. 210. Emphasis added.
7. *Deutsche Zentral-Zeitung*, Moscow, May 16, 1935.
8. "Socialist Realism in the Theater," *Werkausgabe*, Vol. 16, pp. 935-36.
9. Ibid., p. 361.
10. *Women Under Socialism*, by Susanne Statkowa. Panorama DDR, Berlin, 1974, p. 44.

7. Stronger Than the Night

1. Quoted in *The Movies, Mr. Griffith & Me*, by Lillian Gish and Ann Pinchot, Prentice-Hall, Inc., Englewood Cliffs, N.J., 1969, pp. 161-62.
2. Ibid., p. 163.
3. *Toms, Coons, Mulattoes, Mammies & Bucks*, by Donald Bogle. Bantam Books, Inc., New York, 1974, pp. 14-15.
4. Ibid., p. 19.
5. *The New York Times*, October 14, 1975.
6. "A Comeback for Leni Riefenstahl?" by Ulrich Gregor. *Film Comment*, Winter 1965, p. 9.

7. "Jackboot Cinema," by Helmut Blobner and Herbert Holba. *Films and Filming*, Vol. VIII, No. 3, London, 1962.
8. Ibid.
9. *Theater und Film im Dritten Reich*, by Josef Wulf. Guttersloh: Sigbert Mohn Verlag, 1964, pp. 9-10. Quoted in *Film In The Third Reich*, by David Stewart Hull. University of California Press, Berkeley and Los Angeles, 1969, p. 170.
10. Quoted in *Brecht As They Knew Him*, p. 195.
11. *Cue*, August 21, 1948.
12. *Tiefernste Mahnung zur Wachsamkeit*, October 17, 1946.
13. Klaus Wischnewski, *Deutsche Film-kunst*, No. 6, 1954.
14. "Kulturpolitik und Akademie der Künste," *Neues Deutschland*, August 12, 1953.
15. *The Afro-American*, July 22-26, 1975.
16. Ibid., July 29-August 2, 1975.
17. Ibid.
18. Ibid., July 22-26, 1975.
19. Ibid., August 12-16, 1975.

8. The Other Side of Advocacy (I)

1. *The Season*, p. 102.
2. *New York Post*, September 24, 1975.
3. Quotes appeared in ads running in *The New York Times, New York Post* and *Daily News*, August 1975.
4. *The New York Times*, August 25, 1975.
5. *Les Blancs: The Collected Last Plays of Lorraine Hansberry*, edited by Robert Nemiroff. Introduction by Julius Lester. Random House, Inc., New York, 1973, p. 209.
6. Ibid.
7. "An Author's Reflections: Willy Loman, Walter Younger, and He Who Must Live," by Lorraine Hansberry. Appears in *The Village Voice Reader*, Doubleday & Co., Inc., Garden City, N.Y., 1962, p. 194.
8. *Les Blancs*, pp. 181-82. Emphasis in the original.
9. Ibid., p. 173.
10. Quoted in *Les Blancs*, p. 173.
11. Ibid., p. 174.
12. Ibid., p. 175.
13. Ibid.
14. *The New York Times*, November 16, 1970.
15. Ibid.
16. *The New York Times*, February 18, 1974.
17. Ibid.
18. *The New York Times*, November 5, 1975.
19. *Variety*, November 5, 1975.
20. *The New York Times*, October 19, 1975.
21. *Travesties*, by Tom Stoppard. Grove Press, Inc., New York, 1975, pp. 76-77.
22. *The New York Times*, November 28, 1975.
23. Ibid.
24. Ibid.
25. Ibid.
26. Ibid.
27. Ibid.

9. The Other Side of Advocacy (II)

1. Appears in *Sinn und Form,* No. 5/6, 1954, Potsdam.
2. "Can the Present-Day World Be Reproduced by Means of Theater?" Published in *Sonntag,* Berlin, May 8, 1955.
3. *Daily World,* October 13, 1976.

10. Brecht in Two Worlds

1. *The Impossible Theater,* p. 62.
2. Ibid., p. 118.
3. Ibid., p. 160.
4. Ibid., p. 198.
5. Ibid., p. 193.
6. "Formal Problems Arising From the Theater's New Content," *Theaterarbeit,* Dresdener Verlag, Dresden, p. 253.
7. Ibid.
8. *The Impossible Theater,* p. 109.
9. Ibid., p. 98.
10. "Notes on Brecht's Work in 1926," by Elisabeth Hauptmann. Appears in *Brecht As They Knew Him,* p. 53.
11. *The Impossible Theater,* p. 193.
12. "General Your Tank Is A Powerful Vehicle," by Bertolt Brecht. Appears in *Bertolt Brecht Poems, 1913–1956,* edited by John Willett and Ralph Manheim, with the cooperation of Erich Fried. Eyre Methuen Publishers Ltd., London.
13. *The Impossible Theater,* p. 91.
14. *Seven Plays by Bertolt Brecht,* edited and with an introduction by Eric Bentley. Grove Press, Inc., New York, 1961, p. xxxvii.
15. *The Theatre of Revolt,* by Robert Brustein. An Atlantic Monthly Press Book, Little, Brown & Co., Boston, 1964, p. 278.
16. *Brecht: The Man And His Work,* by Martin Esslin. First published in 1959 under the title *Brecht: a choice of evils.* The Norton Library. W.W. Norton & Co., Inc. New York, 1974. Quotation appears on cover.
17. "Brecht at Seventy," by Martin Esslin. *The Drama Review,* Fall 1967.
18. "Hollywood." Appears in *Bertolt Brecht Poems, 1913–1956.*
19. *Brecht: The Man And His Work,* p. 73.
20. *The Kindness of Strangers,* by Salka Viertel. Holt, Rinehart & Winston, New York, 1969, p. 284.
21. Ibid.
22. Ibid., p. 258.
23. Ibid.
24. Ibid.
25. Ibid., p. 285.
26. *Brecht: The Man And His Work,* p. 205.
27. Ibid.
28. Ibid.
29. Ibid., p. 68.
30. Ibid., p. 180.
31. Quoted in *Brechts Weg zum epischen Theater,* Werner Hecht. Henschelverlag, Berlin, 1963, p. 154.
32. *Brecht: The Man And His Work,* p. 186.
33. "Formal Problems Arising From the Theater's New Content."
34. Ibid.
35. *Brecht: The Man And His Work,* p. 188.

36. *Neues Deutschland,* June 21, 1953.
37. *Brecht: The Man And His Work,* p. 68.
38. *Bertolt Brecht: His Life, His Art And His Times,* by Frederic Ewen. The Citadel Press, New York, p. 456.
39. "Not What Was Meant," *Bertolt Brecht Poems: 1913-1956.*
40. Reported by Erwin Leiser in *Brecht: Gespräche auf der Probe,* p. 43. Appears in *Bertolt Brecht: His Life, His Art and His Times,* p. 458.
41. *Brecht: The Man And His Work,* p. x.
42. "Models," *Theaterarbeit,* p. 285.
43. "Das Theater am Bertolt-Brecht-Platz," *Sonntag,* July 18, 1977.
44. Ibid.
45. Ibid.
46. Ibid.
47. *The New York Times,* January 11, 1976.
48. *Tynan Right and Left,* by Kenneth Tynan. Longmans, 1967, London, p. 416.
49. *The New York Times,* January 11, 1976.
50. Ibid.
51. *The New York Times,* March 14, 1976.
52. *Plays and Players,* January 1976.
53. *The New York Times,* January 11, 1976.

11. Women: USA/GDR (I)

1. Monitored on *The Young And The Restless,* CBS-TV, October 22, 1976.
2. "The Female Facade: Fierce, Fragile and Fading," by Jane Trahey. Appears in *Woman In The Year 2000,* edited by Maggie Tripp. Arbor House, New York, 1974, p. 27. Emphasis in the original.
3. "Sex Role Stereotyping in Prime Time Television," a United Methodist Women's Television Monitoring Project.
4. Quoted in *It Changed My Life,* by Betty Friedan. Random House, New York, 1976, p. 54.
5. "There Isn't Anything Wishy-Washy About Soaps," by Beth Gutcheon. *Ms.* magazine, August 1974.
6. "The Media Image of Black Women," by Jean Carey Bond. *Freedomways,* Vol. 15, No. 1, 1975.
7. Ibid.
8. "Bad Times On The 'Good Times' Set," by Louie Robinson. *Ebony,* September 1975.
9. Ibid.
10. Ibid.
11. Ibid.
12. *The Mary Hartman Story,* by Daniel Lockwood. Bolder Books, New York, 1976, p. 88. Emphasis in the original.
13. *From Reverence to Rape,* by Molly Haskell. Penguin Books, Ltd., Middlesex, England, pp. 327-28. First published by Holt, Rinehart & Winston, Inc., New York, 1974.
14. *New York Post,* June 12, 1976.
15. *From Reverence to Rape,* p. 363.
16. Ibid., pp. 327-28.
17. *New York Womensweek,* September 13, 1976.
18. *From Reverence To Rape,* p. 31.
19. Ibid., p. 370.
20. Ibid., p. 329.

21. Appears in *The New York Times,* June 2, 1974.
22. *From Reverence To Rape,* p. 329.
23. Ibid., p. 28.
24. Appears in *Woman In The Year 2000.*
25. Ibid., p. 39.
26. Ibid.
27. *The Feminine Mystique,* by Betty Friedan. Dell Publishing Co., Inc., New York, 1974, pp. 188–89. First published by W.W. Norton & Company, Inc., New York, 1963.
28. Ibid., p. 11.
29. Ibid., p. 21.
30. *The Second Sex,* by Simone de Beauvoir. Vintage Books. Division of Random House, New York, p. 335. First published in the U.S. by Alfred A. Knopf, Inc., 1953.
31. Ibid., pp. xxxiii–xxxiv.
32. Ibid., p. 798.
33. Ibid., pp. 810–11.
34. Ibid., p. xxii.
35. Ibid., p. 807.
36. *Sexual Politics,* by Kate Millett. Doubleday & Company, Inc., New York, 1971.
37. Ibid., p. 46.
38. Ibid., p. 62.
39. Ibid.
40. Ibid., p. 92.
41. *The Female Eunuch,* by Germaine Greer. McGraw Hill, New York, 1971.
42. Ibid., p. 350.
43. Ibid.
44. Ibid., p. 318.
45. *Against Our Will: Men, Women and Rape,* by Susan Brownmiller. Simon and Schuster, New York, 1975, p. 15. Emphasis in the original.
46. Ibid., p. 114.
47. Ibid., p. 252.
48. *Journal of A Georgian Plantation,* by Frances Anne Kemble. First published in 1863. Republished by Alfred A. Knopf, London and New York, 1961, p. 39.

12. Women: USA/GDR (II)

1. *It Changed My Life,* p. 365.
2. "Epilogue" to *The Feminine Mystique,* pp. 378–79. Originally appeared in *The New York Times Magazine,* 1973.
3. *It Changed My Life,* p. 384.
4. *Los Angeles Times,* November 11, 1976.
5. *The New York Times,* September 9, 1976.
6. *It Changed My Life,* p. 364.
7. *The New York Times,* January 23, 1976.
8. *Does Socialism Liberate Women?* by Hilda Scott. Beacon Press, Boston, 1974, pp. 213–14.
9. *The Emancipation of Women,* V.I. Lenin, International Publishers, New York, 1966, p. 81.
10. Quoted in *Women in Socialist Society,* by Marlis Allendorf. International Publishers Co., Inc., New York, 1976, p. 97.
11. *Does Socialism Liberate Women?* p. 215.
12. *Los Angeles Times,* December 31, 1976.

13. New York *Daily News*, October 16, 1976.
14. *Los Angeles Times*, December 8, 1976.
15. *The New York Times*, July 14, 1977.
16. *Women in Socialist Society*, p. 126.
17. Ibid., pp. 135-37.
18. Ibid., p. 187.
19. *Equal Rights for Women in the German Democratic Republic*, by Dr. Herta Kuhrig. GDR Committee for Human Rights, Berlin, 1973, pp. 29-30.
20. *Daily World*, November 28, 1975.
21. *Los Angeles Times*, December 25, 1976.
22. *Women in Socialist Society*, p. 194.
23. Ibid., p. 158.
24. "The Woman Question," by Eleanor Marx and Edward Aveling, 1886. Appears in *Green Mountain Quarterly*, No. 2, February 1976.
25. *A Room of One's Own,* by Virginia Woolf, Harvest/ HBJ Book, Harcourt, Brace, Jovanovich, Inc., New York and London. Copyright 1929, Harcourt, Brace and World, Inc. Copyright 1957, Leonard Woolf, p. 48.
26. Ibid.
27. Ibid.
28. Ibid., p. 50.
29. Ibid.
30. Ibid.
31. Ibid.
32. *Does Socialism Liberate Women?* p. x.
33. Ibid., p. 210.
34. Ibid.
35. *The Emancipation of Women*, p. 81.
36. *It Changed My Life*, p. 379.
37. *The New York Times*, July 13, 1977.

13. "Not Life Printed on Dollar Bills"

1. *The Fervent Years*, p. 106.
2. Ibid., p. 138.
3. Ibid., p. 139.
4. Ibid., pp. 113-14.
5. Ibid., pp. 182-83.
6. Ibid., p. 197.
7. Ibid.
8. Ibid., p. 264.
9. Ibid., p. 265.

14. Democracy's New Dimensions

1. *All The Livelong Day*, by Barbara Garson. Doubleday & Co., Garden City, New York, 1975, p. 219.
2. "A Trip to the GDR," by Bernd Rabehl. Appears in *New German Critique*, Vol. 1, Number 2, Spring 1974.
3. *All The Livelong Day*, p. 212.
4. "A Trip to the GDR."
5. *The New York Times*, January 30, 1977.
6. "A Trip to the GDR."

15. "Not Against but With Each Other"

1. Appears in *A Matter For Our Comment*, Panorama DDR.
2. New York *Daily News*. January 28, 1977.
3. *Los Angeles Times*, May 10, 1975.
4. *Los Angeles Times*, November 16, 1976.
5. *The New York Times*, March 4, 1977.
6. *The New York Times*, March 25, 1977.
7. *Lenin: Collected Works*, Volume 19, p. 28. Progress Publishers, Moscow, 1968. Emphasis in the original.
8. *Daily World*, April 7, 1977.
9. *The New York Times*, February 18, 1977.
10. New York *Daily News*, March 16, 1977.
11. *The New York Times*, March 3, 1977.
12. *The New York Times*, March 18, 1977.
13. *The New York Times*, June 14, 1977.
14. Joseph Kraft, *New York Post*, February 26, 1977.
15. *British Sunday Times*, January 9, 1977.
16. *Daily World*, April 7, 1977.

Index